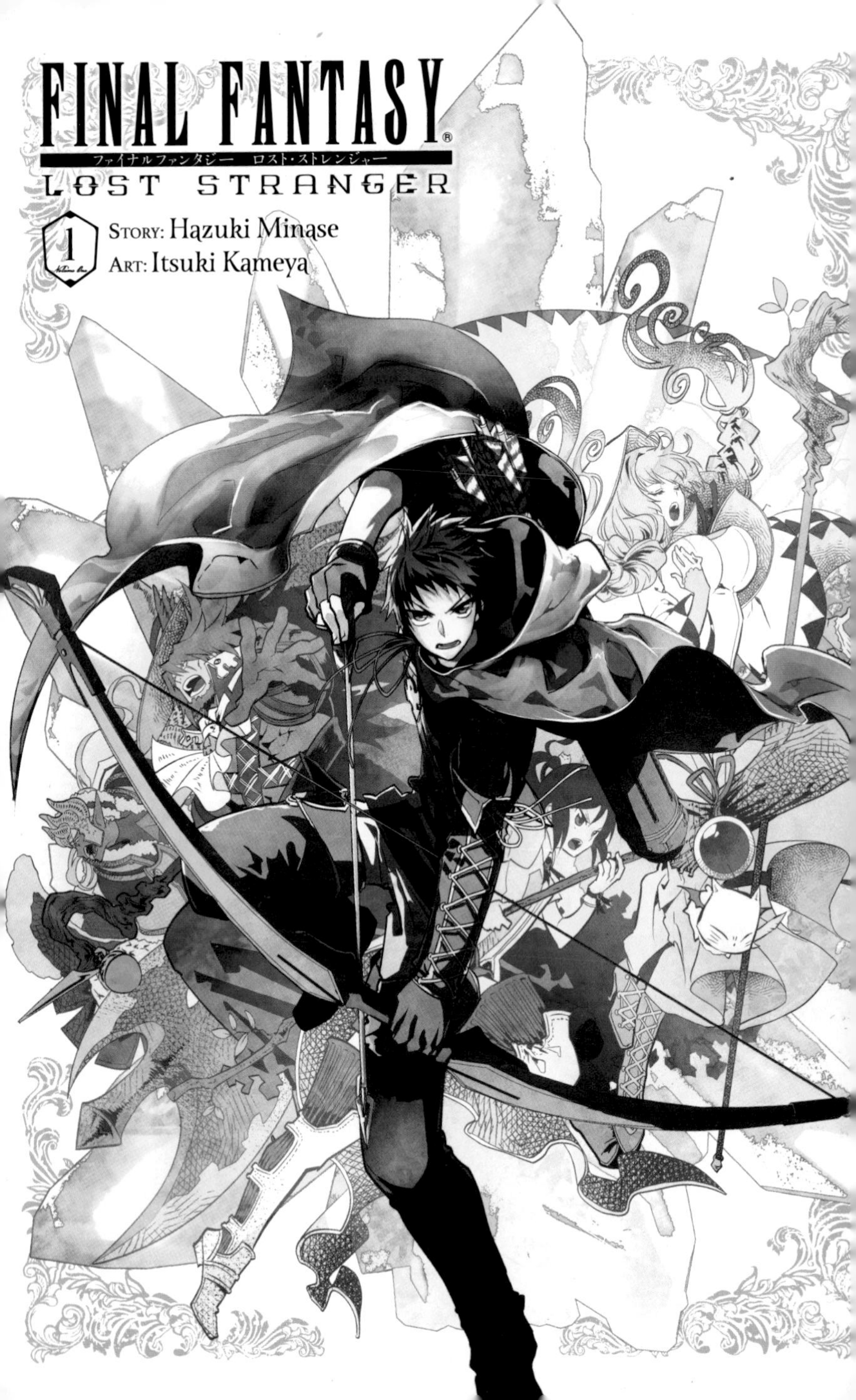
FINAL FANTASY®
ファイナルファンタジー　ロスト・ストレンジャー
LOST STRANGER
1
STORY: Hazuki Minase
ART: Itsuki Kameya

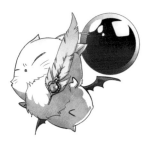

Contents

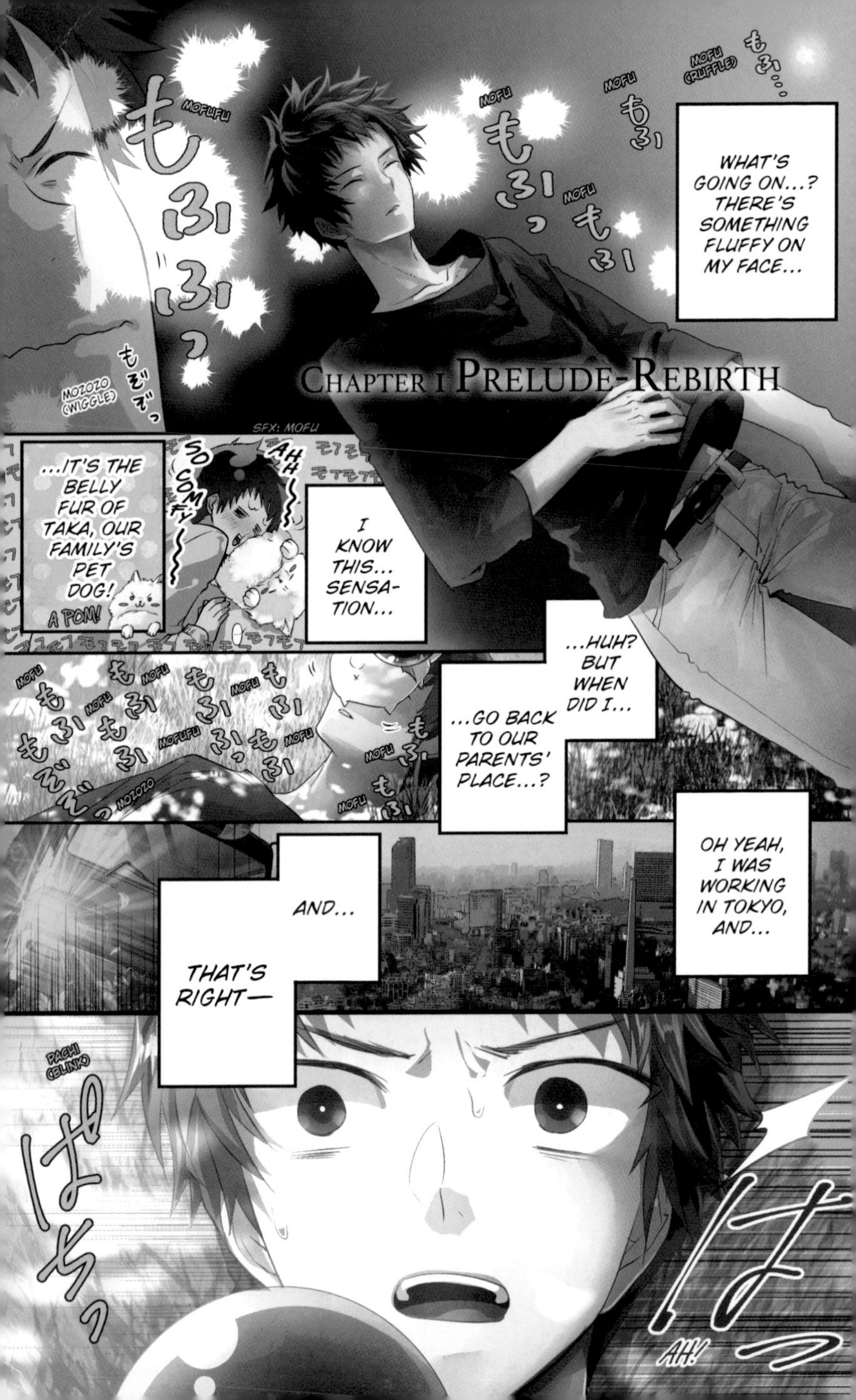
MOFU (RUFFLE)
MOFU
MOFU
MOFU
MOFUFU
WHAT'S GOING ON...? THERE'S SOMETHING FLUFFY ON MY FACE...
Chapter 1 Prelude-Rebirth
MOZOZO (WIGGLE)
SFX: MOFU
I KNOW THIS... SENSATION...
AHH~~
SO COMFY~~
...IT'S THE BELLY FUR OF TAKA, OUR FAMILY'S PET DOG!
A POM!
...HUH? BUT WHEN DID I...
...GO BACK TO OUR PARENTS' PLACE...?
MOFU
MOFU
MOFU
MOFUFU
MOFU
MOFU
MOFU
MOZOZO
OH YEAH, I WAS WORKING IN TOKYO, AND...
AND...
THAT'S RIGHT—
AH!
PACHI (BLINK)

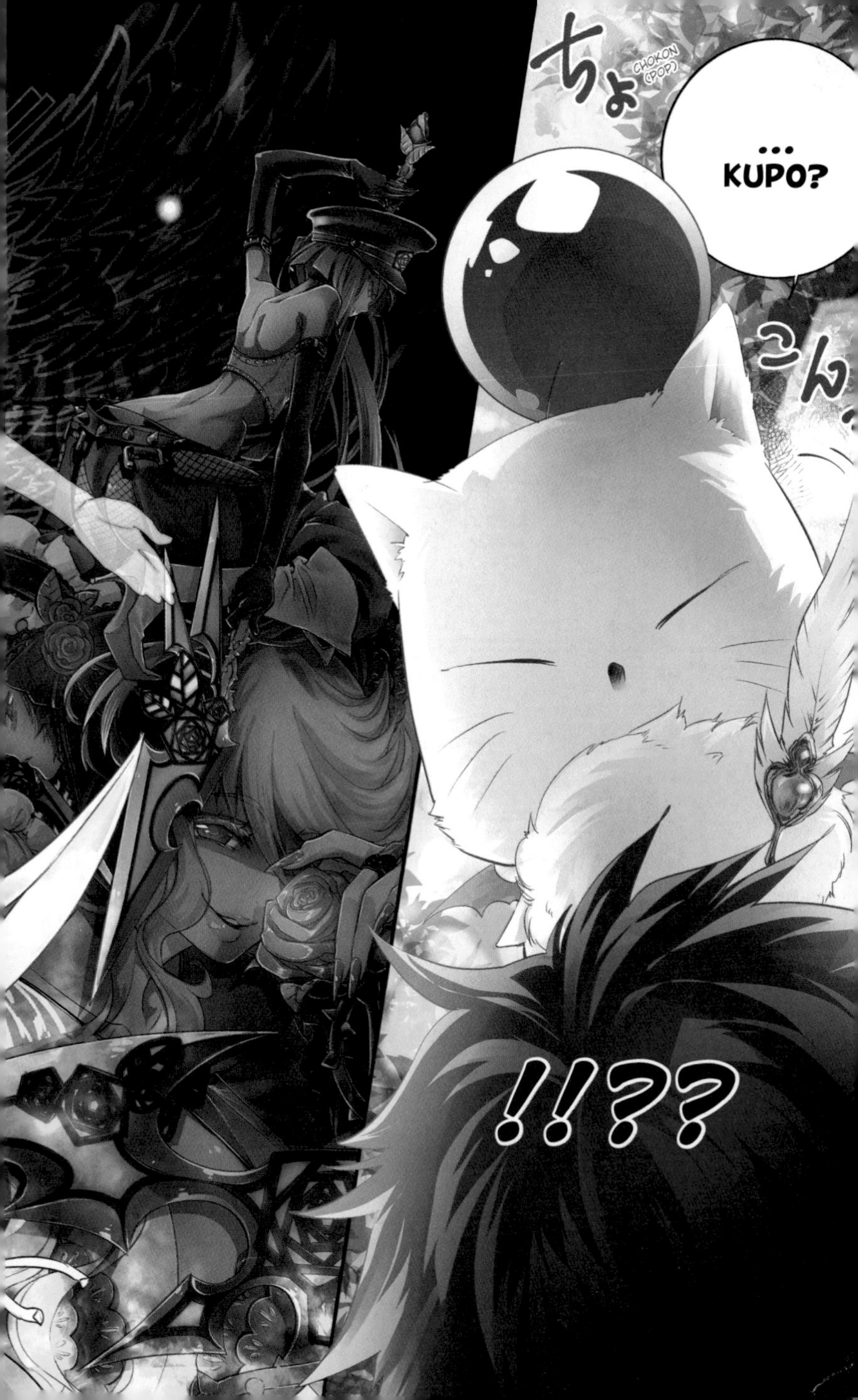

ちょ
CHOKON (POP)
... KUPO?
こん
!!??

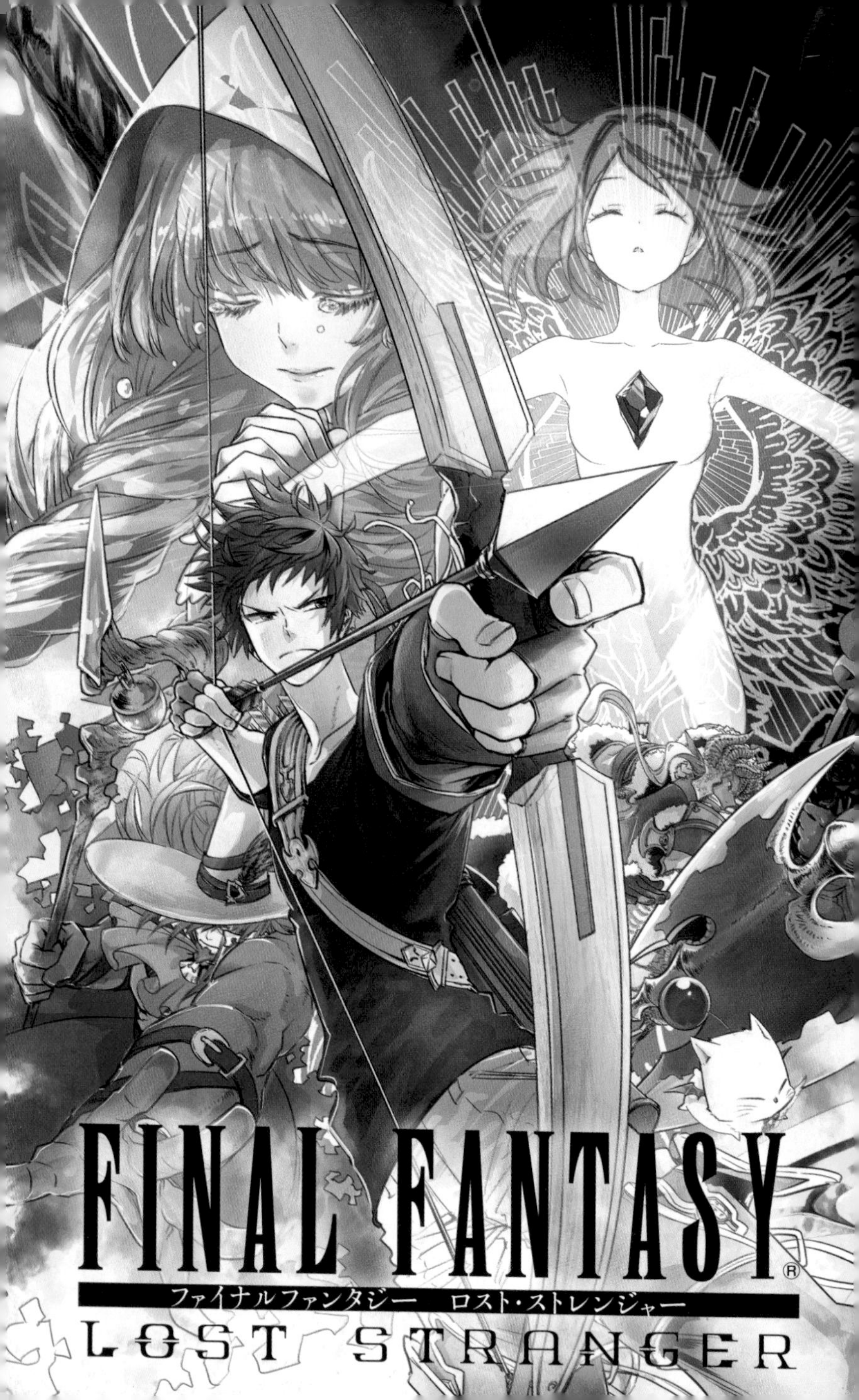
FINAL FANTASY®
ファイナルファンタジー　ロスト・ストレンジャー
LOST STRANGER

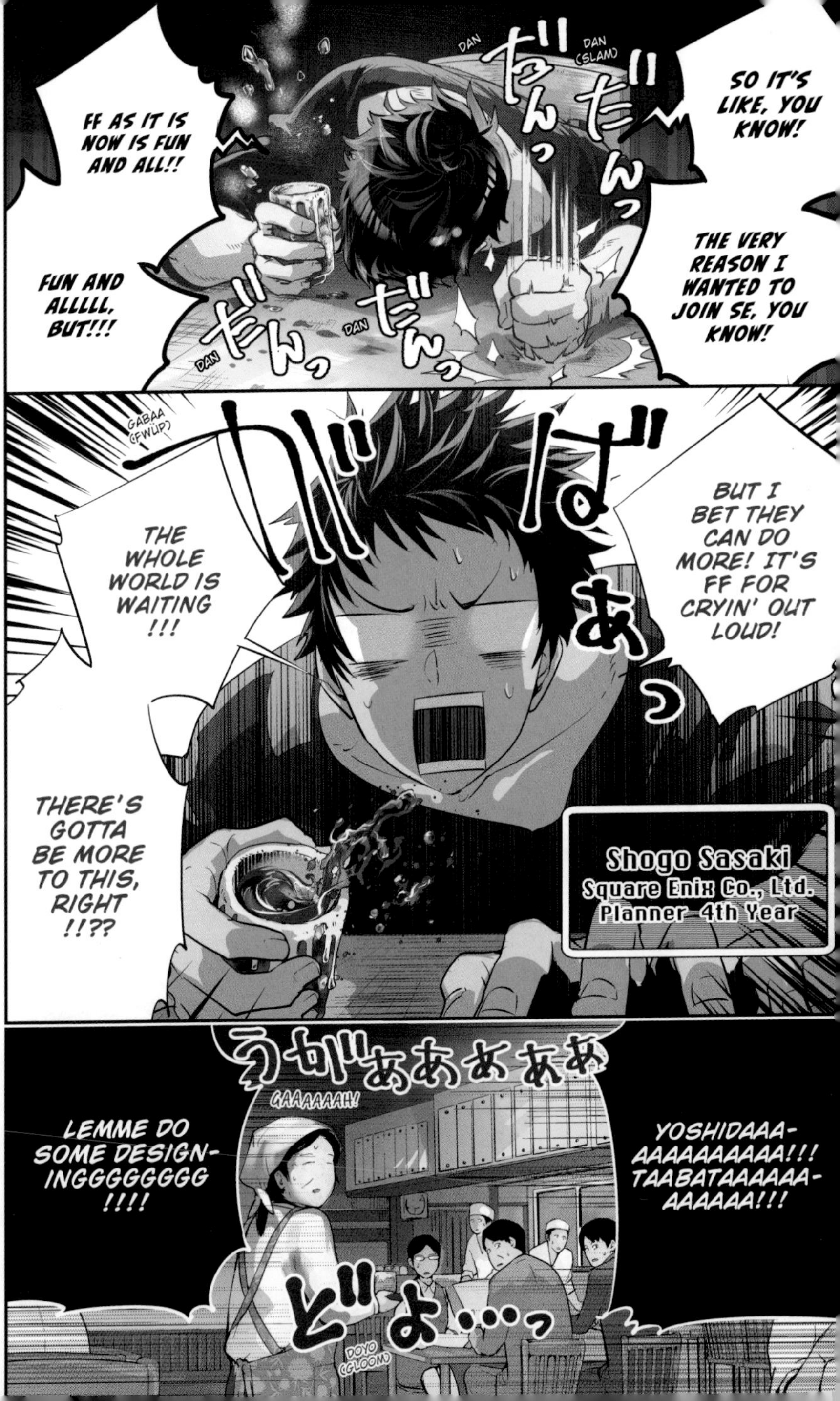
DAN DAN (SLAM)
SO IT'S LIKE, YOU KNOW!
THE VERY REASON I WANTED TO JOIN SE, YOU KNOW!
FF AS IT IS NOW IS FUN AND ALL!!
FUN AND ALLLLL, BUT!!!
DAN DAN
GABAA (FWUP)
BUT I BET THEY CAN DO MORE! IT'S FF FOR CRYIN' OUT LOUD!
THE WHOLE WORLD IS WAITING!!!
THERE'S GOTTA BE MORE TO THIS, RIGHT!!??
Shogo Sasaki
Square Enix Co., Ltd.
Planner 4th Year
GAAAAAAH!
YOSHIDAAA-AAAAAAAAAA!!! TAABATAAAAAA-AAAAAA!!!
LEMME DO SOME DESIGN-INGGGGGGG!!!!
DOYO (GLOOM)

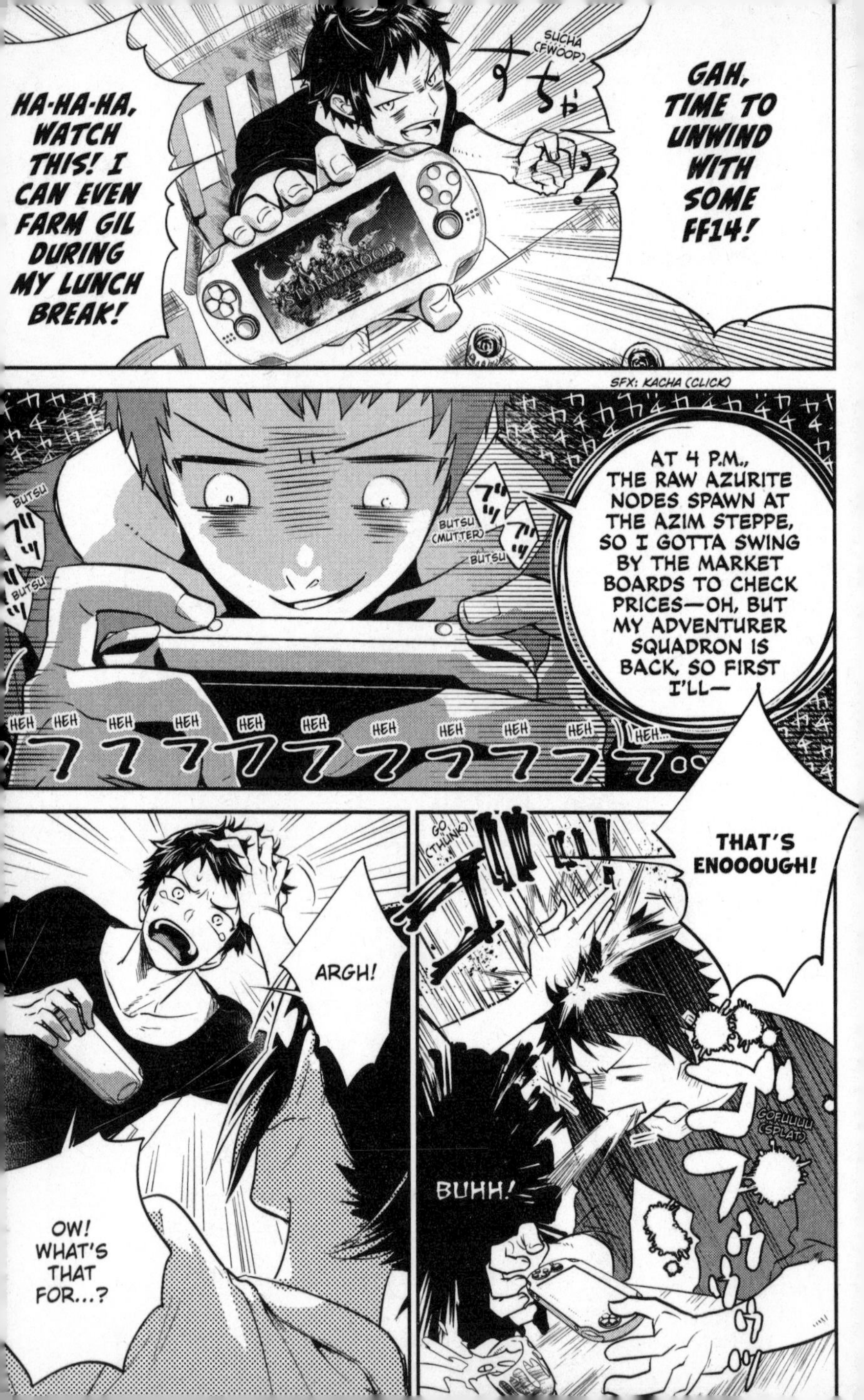
GAH, TIME TO UNWIND WITH SOME FF14!
SUCHA (FWOOP)
HA-HA-HA, WATCH THIS! I CAN EVEN FARM GIL DURING MY LUNCH BREAK!
STORMBLOOD
SFX: KACHA (CLICK)
AT 4 P.M., THE RAW AZURITE NODES SPAWN AT THE AZIM STEPPE, SO I GOTTA SWING BY THE MARKET BOARDS TO CHECK PRICES—OH, BUT MY ADVENTURER SQUADRON IS BACK, SO FIRST I'LL—
BUTSU (MUTTER)
BUTSU
BUTSU
BUTSU
HEH HEH HEH HEH HEH HEH HEH HEH HEH HEH HEH...
THAT'S ENOOOUGH!
GO (THUNK)
GOFUUUU (SPLAT)
BUHH!
ARGH!
OW! WHAT'S THAT FOR...?

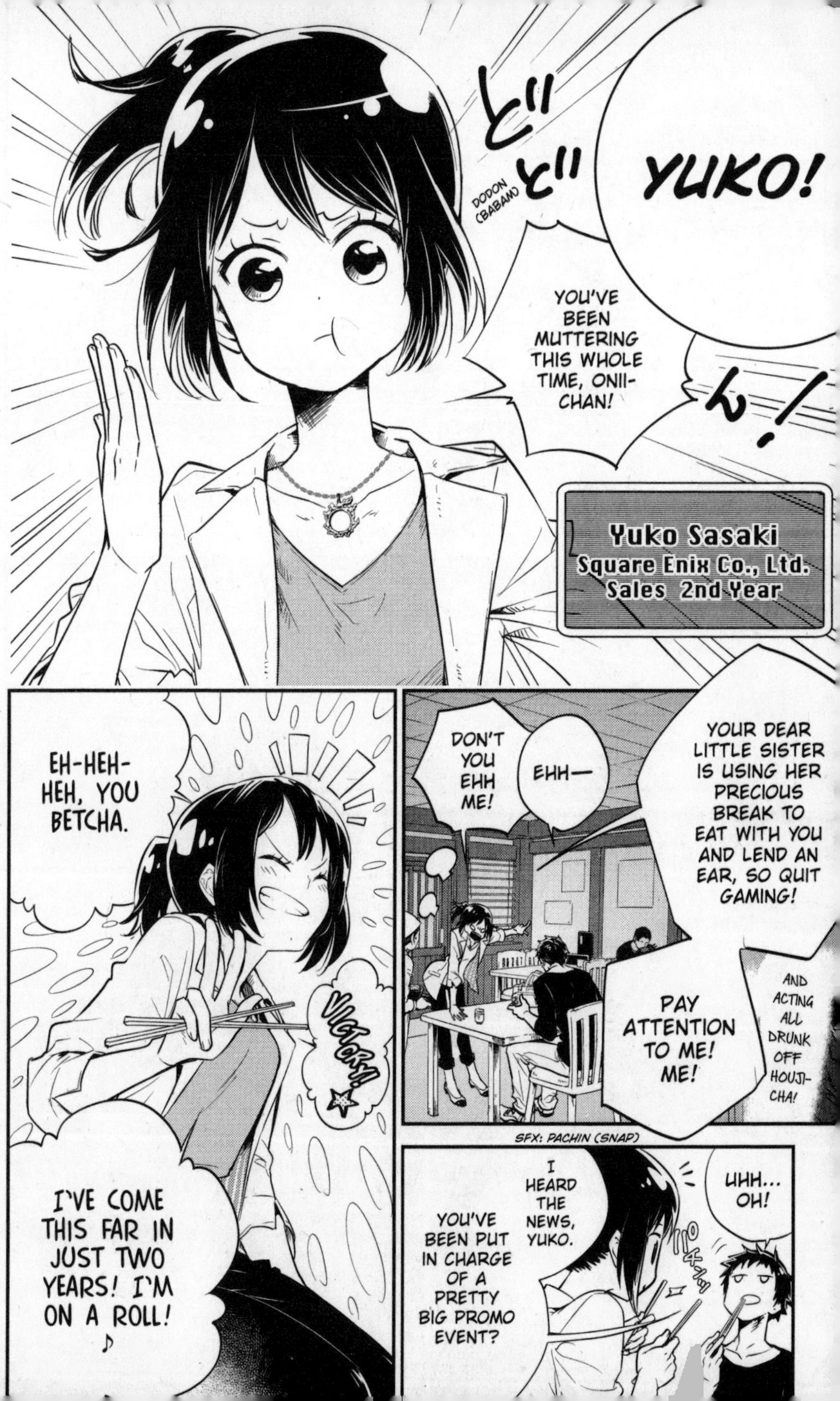
YUKO!
ん!
どど
DODON (BABAM)
YOU'VE BEEN MUTTERING THIS WHOLE TIME, ONII-CHAN!
Yuko Sasaki
Square Enix Co., Ltd.
Sales 2nd Year
YOUR DEAR LITTLE SISTER IS USING HER PRECIOUS BREAK TO EAT WITH YOU AND LEND AN EAR, SO QUIT GAMING!
EHH—
DON'T YOU EHH ME!
AND ACTING ALL DRUNK OFF HOUJI-CHA!
PAY ATTENTION TO ME! ME!
SFX: PACHIN (SNAP)
UHH... OH!
I HEARD THE NEWS, YUKO.
YOU'VE BEEN PUT IN CHARGE OF A PRETTY BIG PROMO EVENT?
EH-HEH-HEH, YOU BETCHA.
VICTORY!
I'VE COME THIS FAR IN JUST TWO YEARS! I'M ON A ROLL! ♪

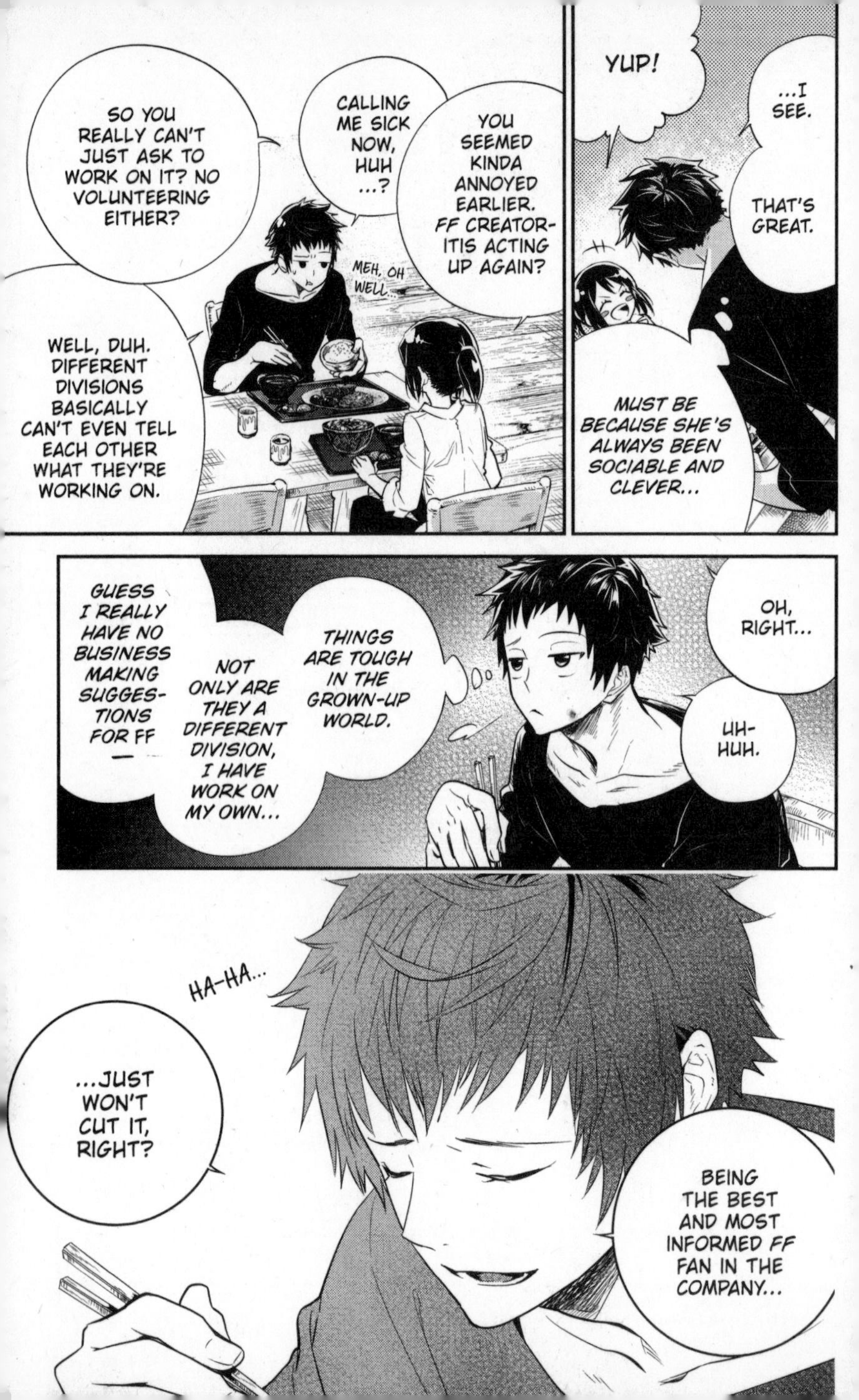
YUP!
...I SEE.
THAT'S GREAT.
MUST BE BECAUSE SHE'S ALWAYS BEEN SOCIABLE AND CLEVER...
YOU SEEMED KINDA ANNOYED EARLIER. FF CREATOR-ITIS ACTING UP AGAIN?
CALLING ME SICK NOW, HUH ...?
SO YOU REALLY CAN'T JUST ASK TO WORK ON IT? NO VOLUNTEERING EITHER?
MEH, OH WELL...
WELL, DUH. DIFFERENT DIVISIONS BASICALLY CAN'T EVEN TELL EACH OTHER WHAT THEY'RE WORKING ON.
OH, RIGHT...
UH-HUH.
THINGS ARE TOUGH IN THE GROWN-UP WORLD.
NOT ONLY ARE THEY A DIFFERENT DIVISION, I HAVE WORK ON MY OWN...
GUESS I REALLY HAVE NO BUSINESS MAKING SUGGES-TIONS FOR FF —
BEING THE BEST AND MOST INFORMED FF FAN IN THE COMPANY...
HA-HA...
...JUST WON'T CUT IT, RIGHT?

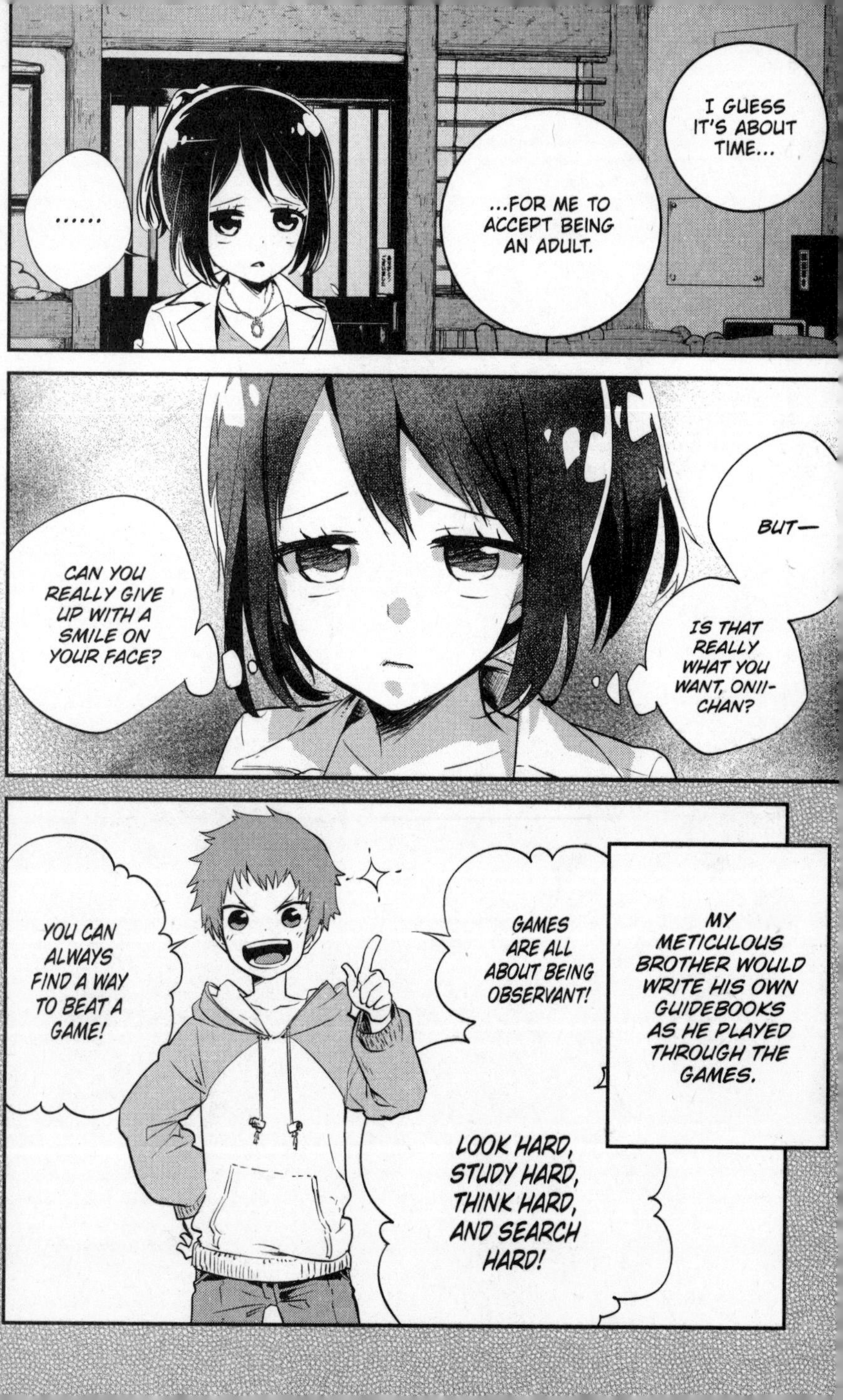

I GUESS IT'S ABOUT TIME...
...FOR ME TO ACCEPT BEING AN ADULT.
......
BUT—
IS THAT REALLY WHAT YOU WANT, ONII-CHAN?
CAN YOU REALLY GIVE UP WITH A SMILE ON YOUR FACE?
MY METICULOUS BROTHER WOULD WRITE HIS OWN GUIDEBOOKS AS HE PLAYED THROUGH THE GAMES.
GAMES ARE ALL ABOUT BEING OBSERVANT!
LOOK HARD, STUDY HARD, THINK HARD, AND SEARCH HARD!
YOU CAN ALWAYS FIND A WAY TO BEAT A GAME!

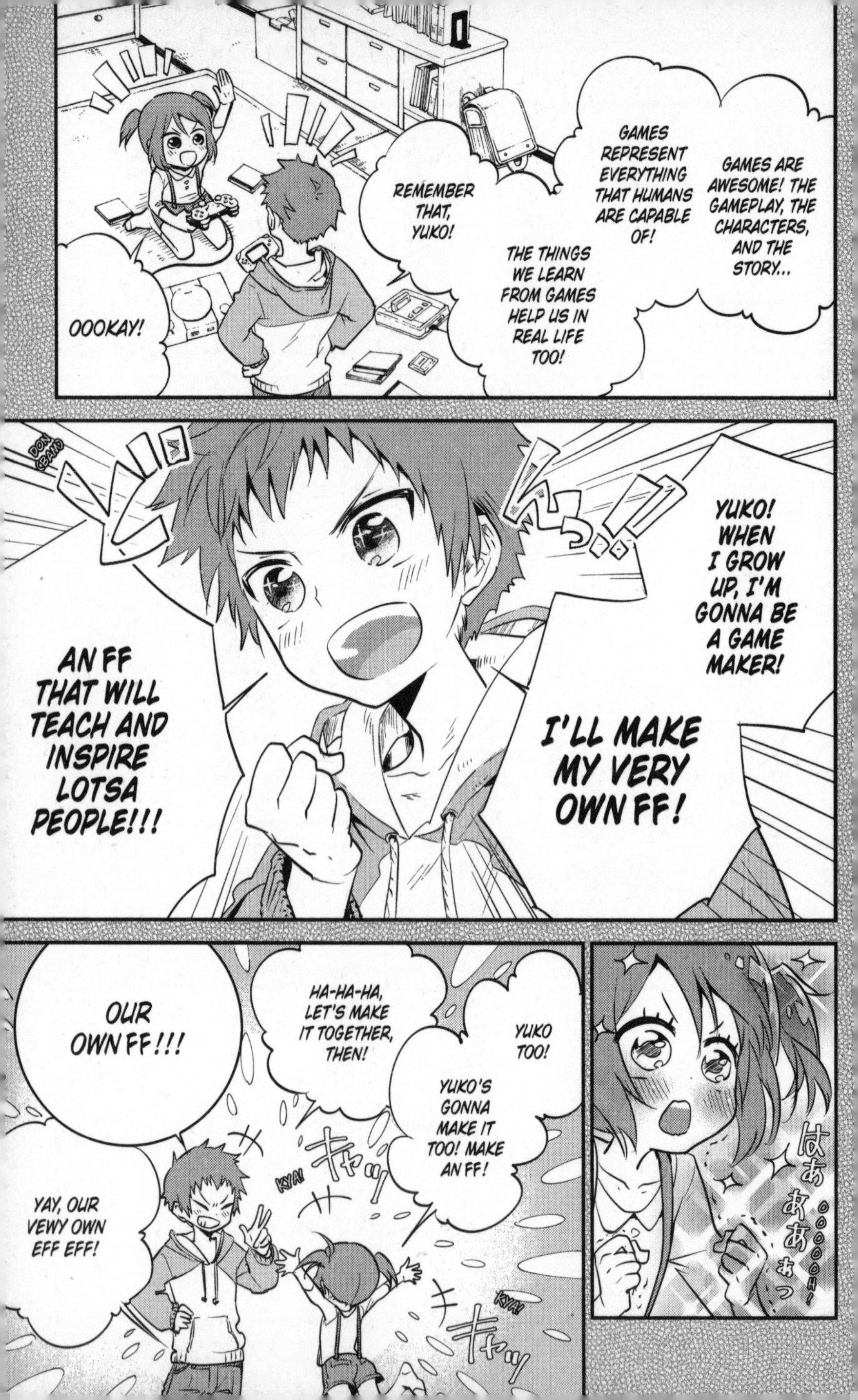
GAMES ARE AWESOME! THE GAMEPLAY, THE CHARACTERS, AND THE STORY...
GAMES REPRESENT EVERYTHING THAT HUMANS ARE CAPABLE OF!
THE THINGS WE LEARN FROM GAMES HELP US IN REAL LIFE TOO!
REMEMBER THAT, YUKO!
OOOKAY!
YUKO! WHEN I GROW UP, I'M GONNA BE A GAME MAKER!
I'LL MAKE MY VERY OWN FF!
AN FF THAT WILL TEACH AND INSPIRE LOTSA PEOPLE!!!
DON (BAM)
はああああっ
OOOOOH!
YUKO TOO!
HA-HA-HA, LET'S MAKE IT TOGETHER, THEN!
OUR OWN FF!!!
YUKO'S GONNA MAKE IT TOO! MAKE AN FF!
キャッ
KYA!
YAY, OUR VEWY OWN EFF EFF!
キャッ
KYA!

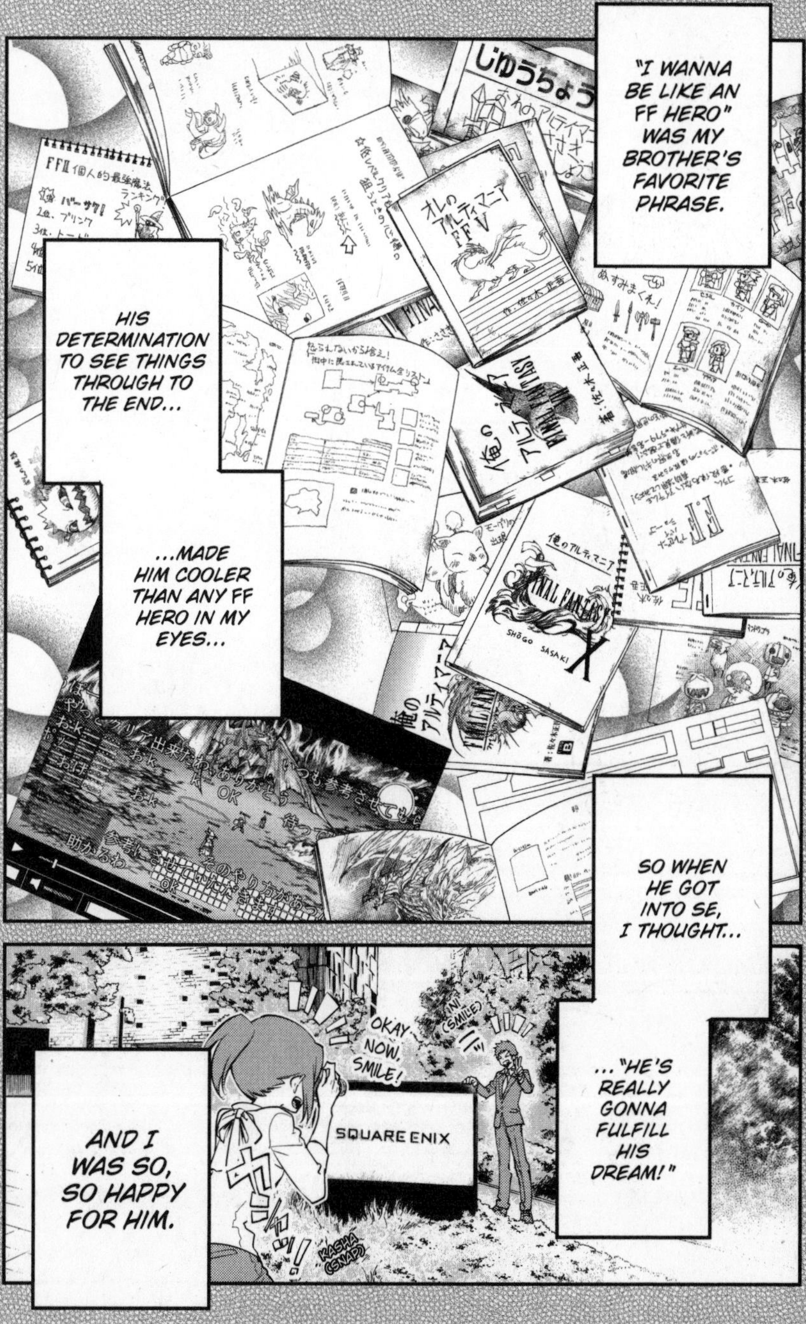
"I WANNA BE LIKE AN FF HERO" WAS MY BROTHER'S FAVORITE PHRASE.
HIS DETERMINATION TO SEE THINGS THROUGH TO THE END...
...MADE HIM COOLER THAN ANY FF HERO IN MY EYES...
SHŌGO SASAKI
SO WHEN HE GOT INTO SE, I THOUGHT...
..."HE'S REALLY GONNA FULFILL HIS DREAM!"
NI (SMILE)
OKAY NOW, SMILE!
SQUARE ENIX
KASHA (SNAP)
AND I WAS SO, SO HAPPY FOR HIM.

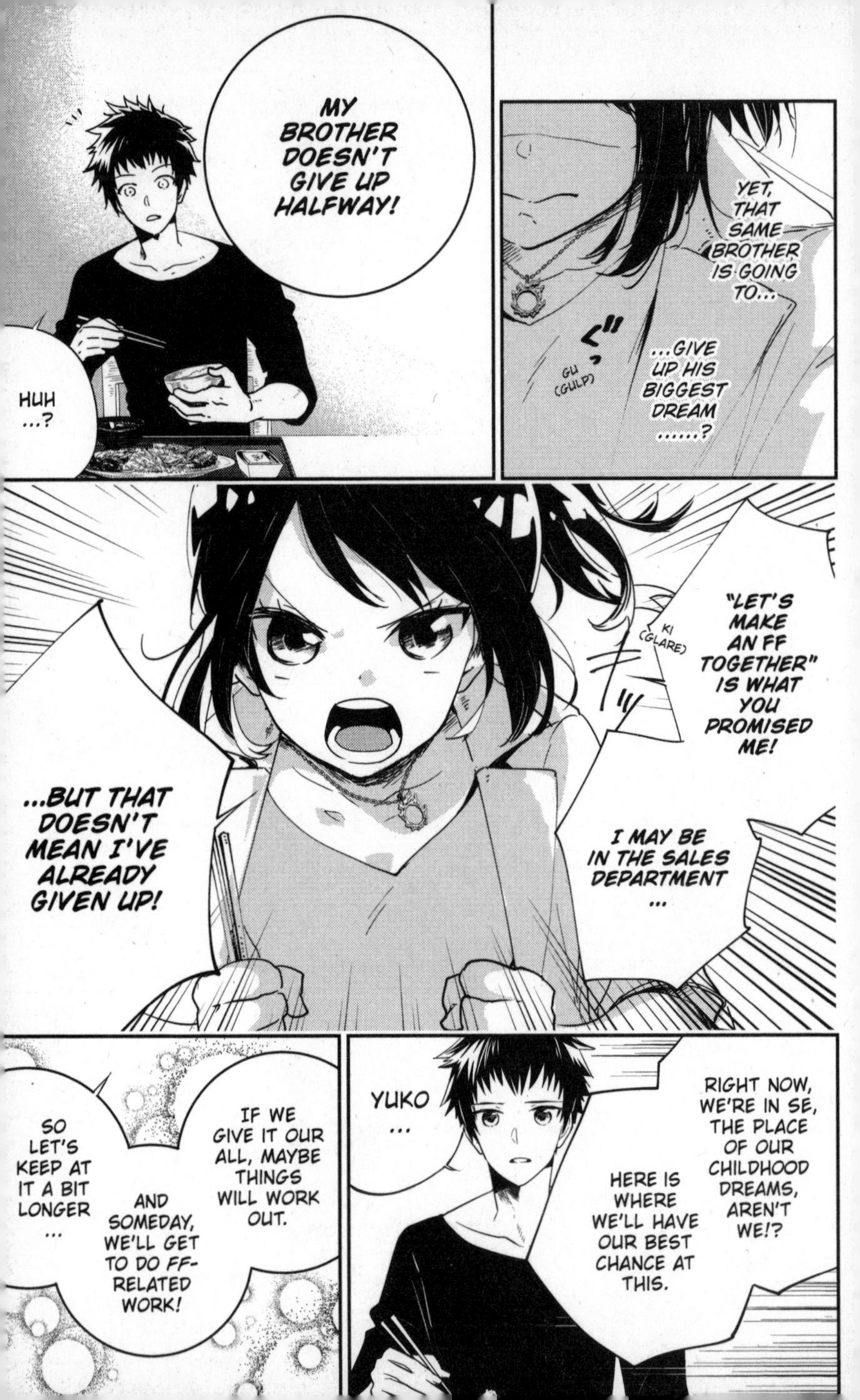
YET, THAT SAME BROTHER IS GOING TO...
GU (GULP)
...GIVE UP HIS BIGGEST DREAM ......?
MY BROTHER DOESN'T GIVE UP HALFWAY!
HUH ...?
KI (GLARE)
"LET'S MAKE AN FF TOGETHER" IS WHAT YOU PROMISED ME!
I MAY BE IN THE SALES DEPARTMENT ...
...BUT THAT DOESN'T MEAN I'VE ALREADY GIVEN UP!
RIGHT NOW, WE'RE IN SE, THE PLACE OF OUR CHILDHOOD DREAMS, AREN'T WE!?
HERE IS WHERE WE'LL HAVE OUR BEST CHANCE AT THIS.
YUKO ...
IF WE GIVE IT OUR ALL, MAYBE THINGS WILL WORK OUT.
AND SOMEDAY, WE'LL GET TO DO FF-RELATED WORK!
SO LET'S KEEP AT IT A BIT LONGER ...

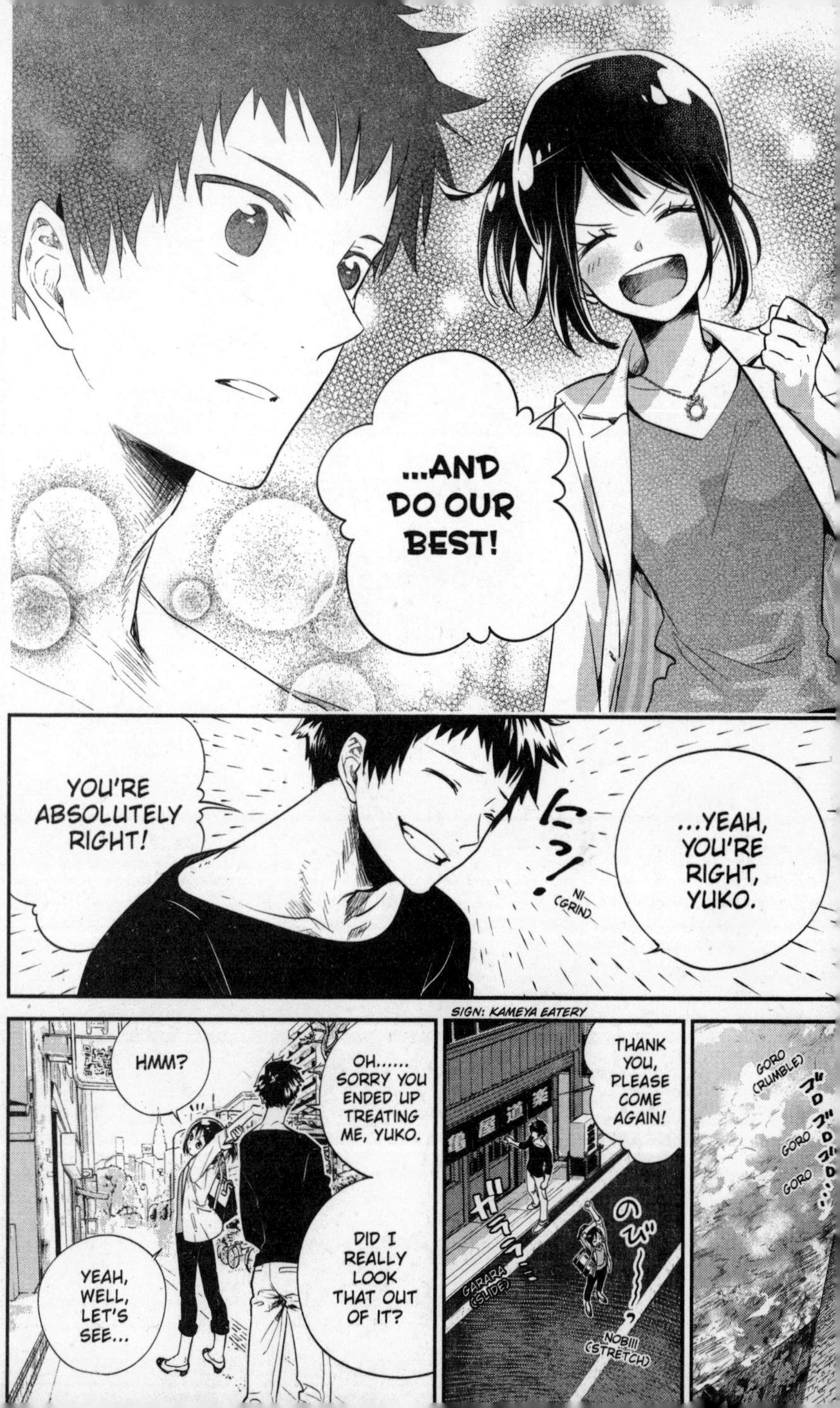

...AND DO OUR BEST!
...YEAH, YOU'RE RIGHT, YUKO.
にっ!
NI (GRIN)
YOU'RE ABSOLUTELY RIGHT!
SIGN: KAMEYA EATERY
GORO (RUMBLE)
GORO
GORO
THANK YOU, PLEASE COME AGAIN!
GARARA (SLIDE)
のび~~
NOBIII (STRETCH)
OH...... SORRY YOU ENDED UP TREATING ME, YUKO.
HMM?
DID I REALLY LOOK THAT OUT OF IT?
YEAH, WELL, LET'S SEE...

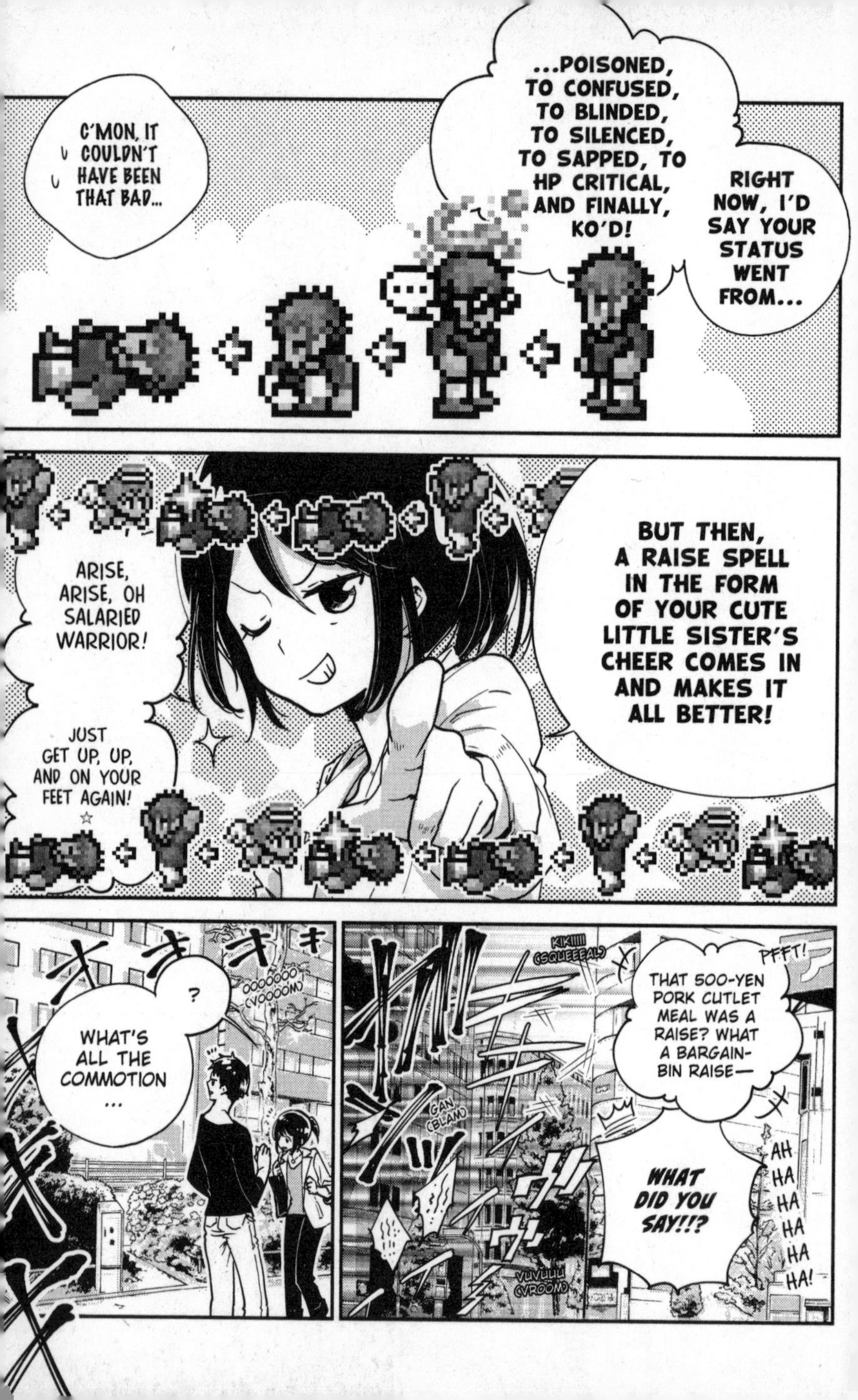
RIGHT NOW, I'D SAY YOUR STATUS WENT FROM...
...POISONED, TO CONFUSED, TO BLINDED, TO SILENCED, TO SAPPED, TO HP CRITICAL, AND FINALLY, KO'D!
C'MON, IT COULDN'T HAVE BEEN THAT BAD...
BUT THEN, A RAISE SPELL IN THE FORM OF YOUR CUTE LITTLE SISTER'S CHEER COMES IN AND MAKES IT ALL BETTER!
ARISE, ARISE, OH SALARIED WARRIOR!
JUST GET UP, UP, AND ON YOUR FEET AGAIN! ☆
PFFT!
THAT 500-YEN PORK CUTLET MEAL WAS A RAISE? WHAT A BARGAIN-BIN RAISE—
KIKIIIII (SQUEEEAL)
GAN (BLAM)
WHAT DID YOU SAY!!?
AH HA HA HA HA HA!
VUVUUUU (VROOM)
?
WHAT'S ALL THE COMMOTION ...
OOOOOOO (VOOOOM)

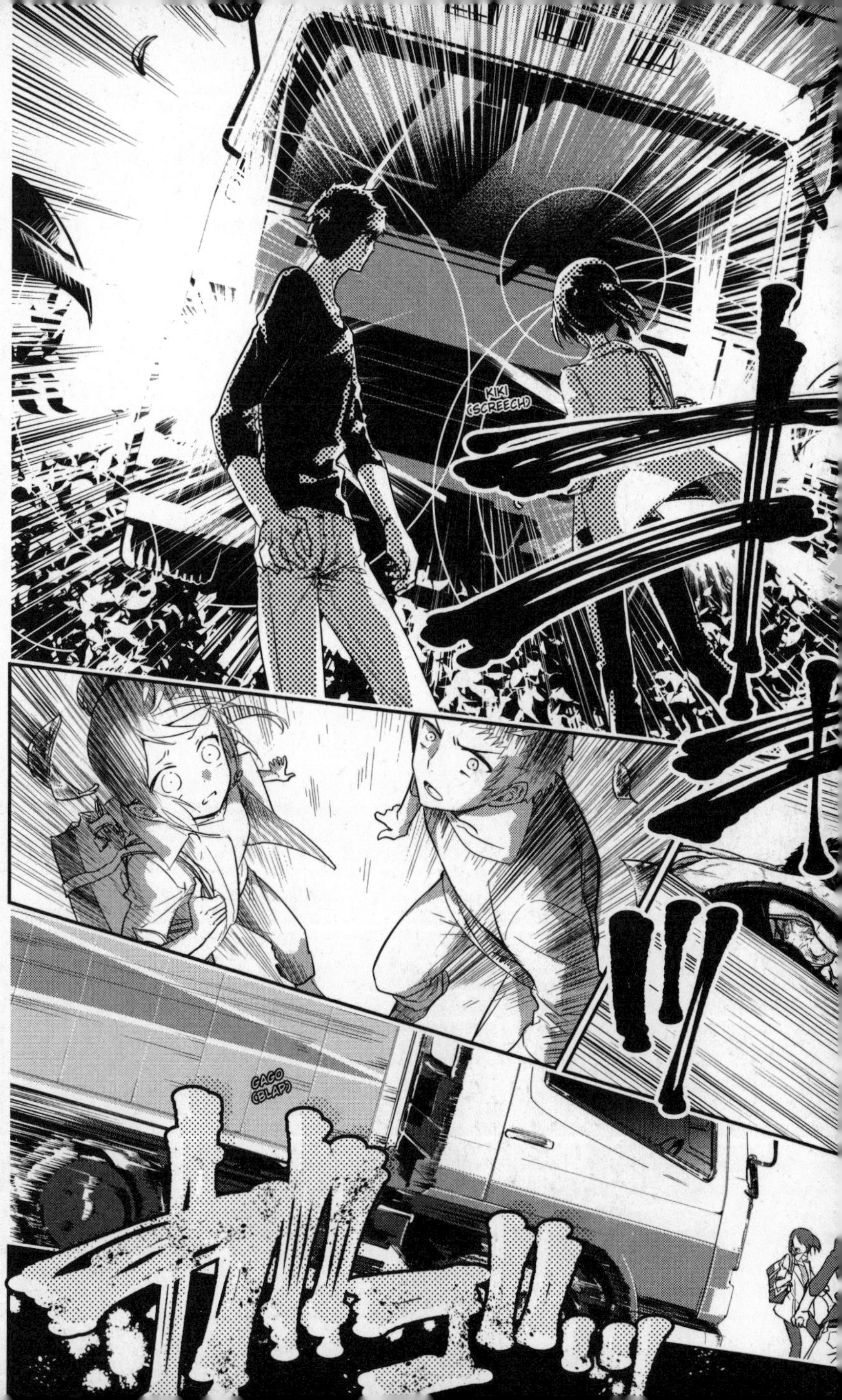
KIKI (SCREECH)
GAGO (BLAP)

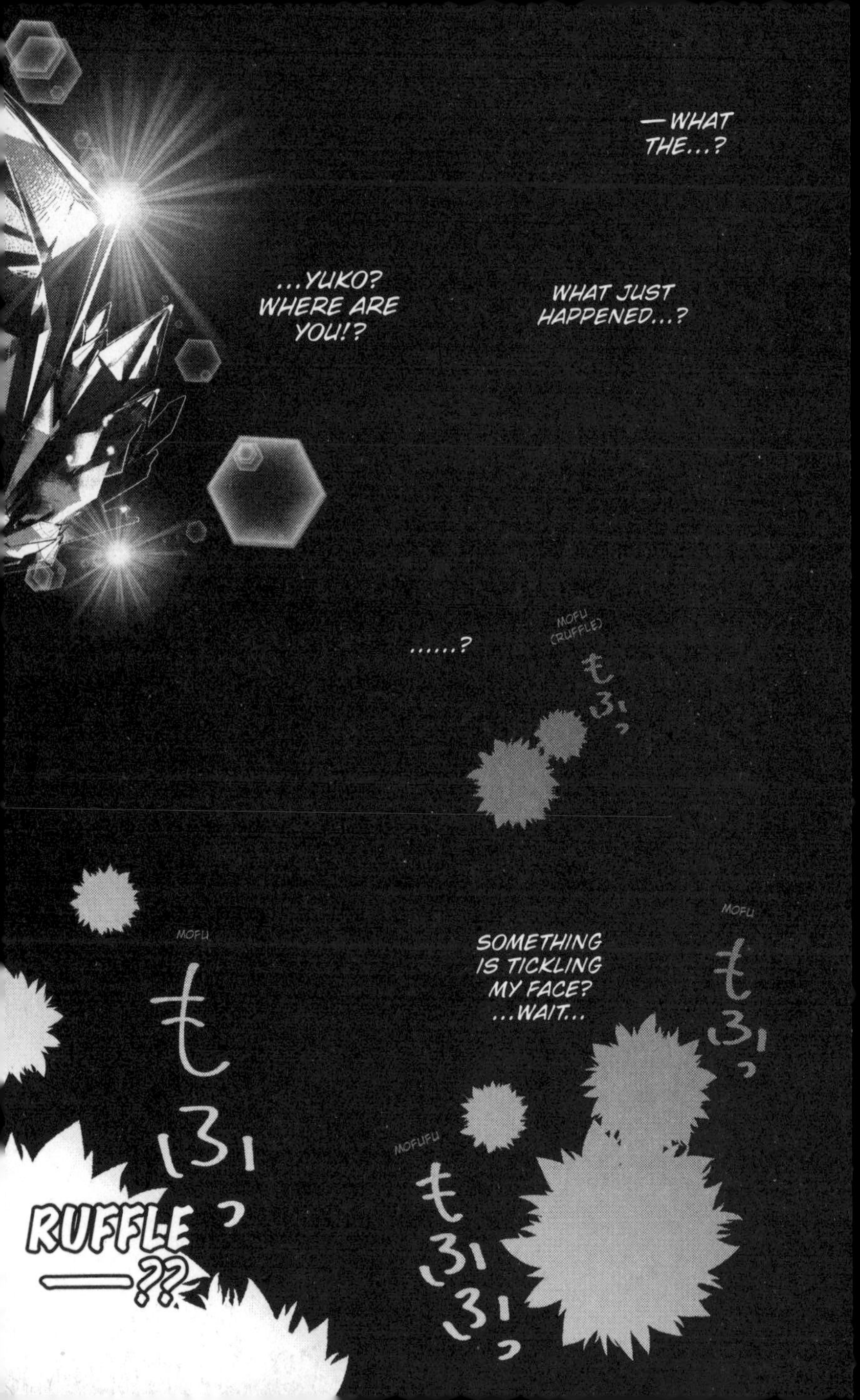
—WHAT THE...?
WHAT JUST HAPPENED...?
...YUKO? WHERE ARE YOU!?
MOFU (RUFFLE)
もふっ
......?
MOFU
もふっ
SOMETHING IS TICKLING MY FACE? ...WAIT...
MOFUFU
もふふっ
MOFU
もふっ
RUFFLE —??

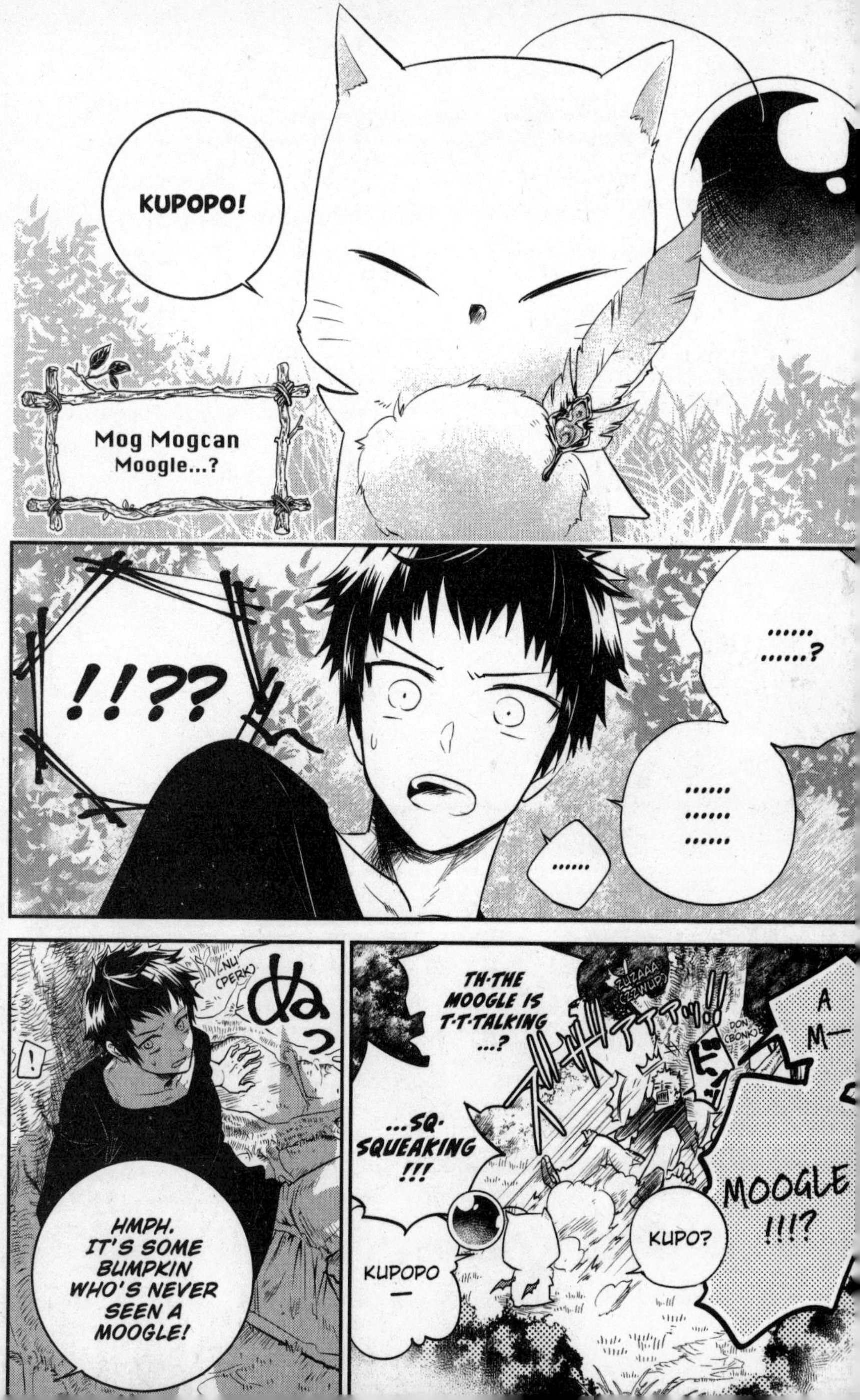
KUPOPO!
Mog Mogcan Moogle...?
......
......?
......
......
......
......
!!??
A M—
MOOGLE !!!?
DON (BONK)
TH-THE MOOGLE IS T-T-TALKING ...?
...SQ-SQUEAKING !!!
KUPO?
KUPOPO —
NU (PERK)
!
HMPH. IT'S SOME BUMPKIN WHO'S NEVER SEEN A MOOGLE!

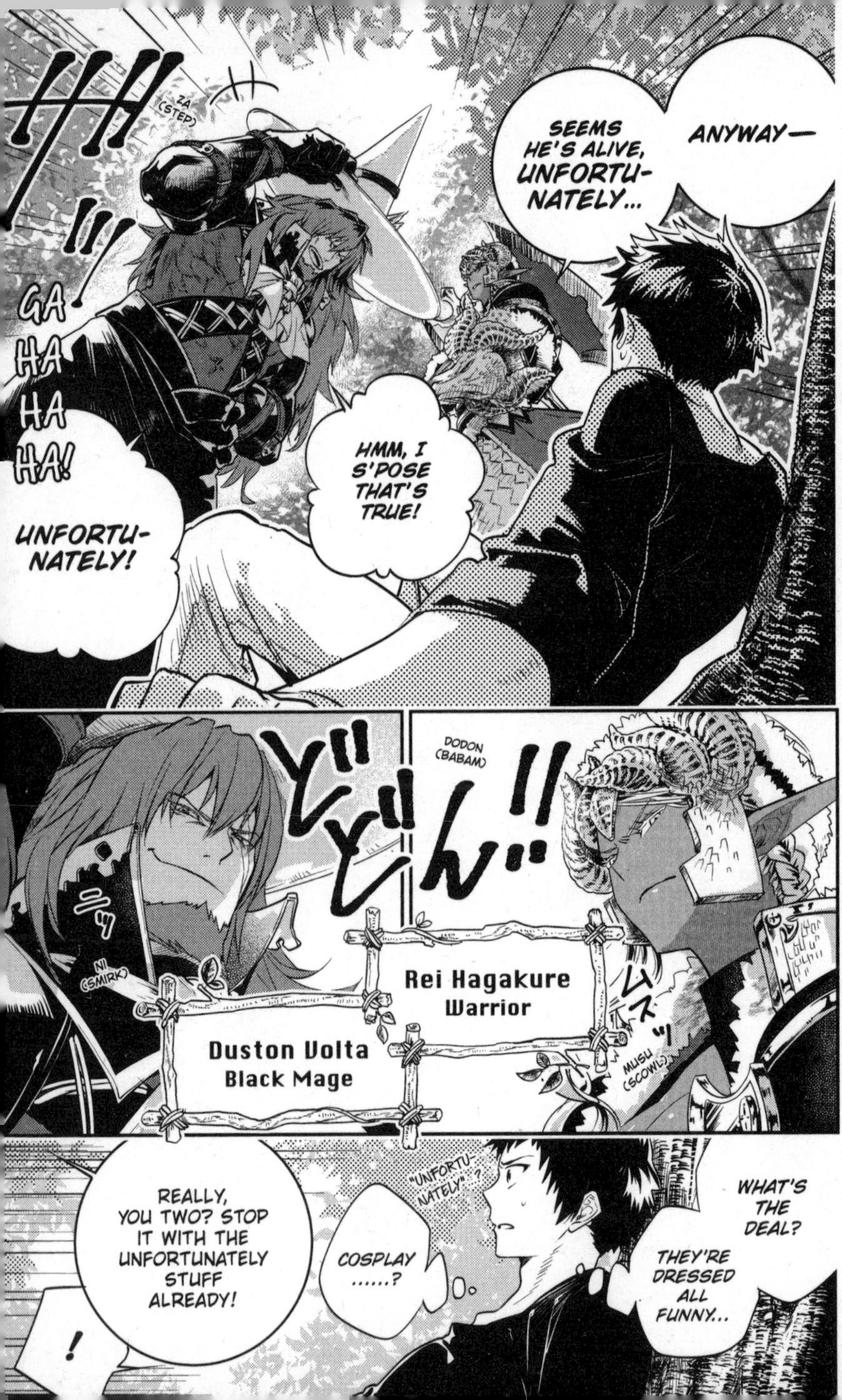
ANYWAY—
SEEMS HE'S ALIVE, UNFORTUNATELY...
ZA (STEP)
HMM, I S'POSE THAT'S TRUE!
GA HA HA HA!
UNFORTUNATELY!
DODON (BABAM)
Rei Hagakure
Warrior
ムスッ
MUSU (SCOWL)
ニッ
NI (SMIRK)
Duston Volta
Black Mage
WHAT'S THE DEAL?
THEY'RE DRESSED ALL FUNNY...
"UNFORTUNATELY"?
COSPLAY ......?
REALLY, YOU TWO? STOP IT WITH THE UNFORTUNATELY STUFF ALREADY!
!

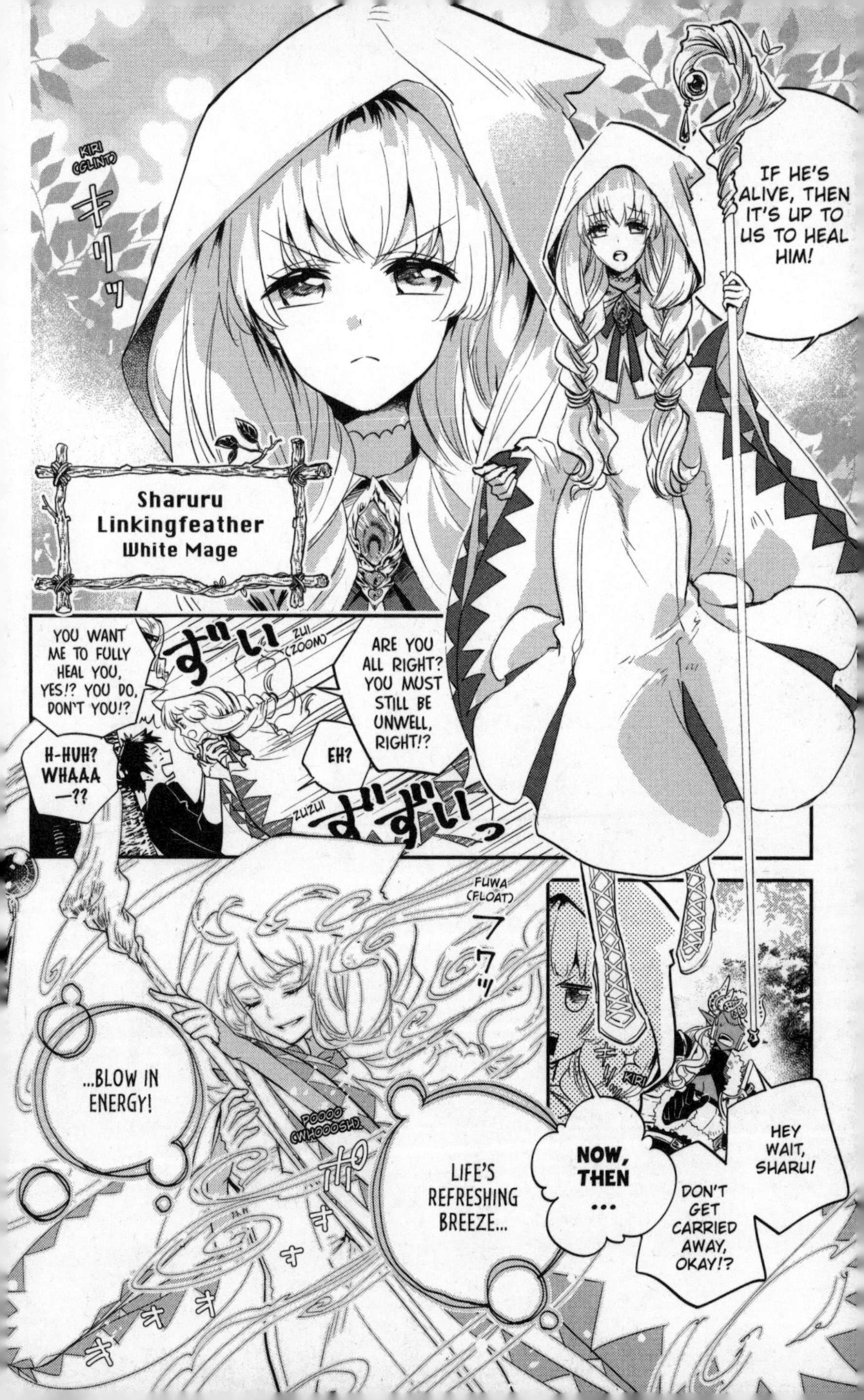
IF HE'S ALIVE, THEN IT'S UP TO US TO HEAL HIM!
KIRI (GLINT)
キリッ
Sharuru Linkingfeather
White Mage
ARE YOU ALL RIGHT? YOU MUST STILL BE UNWELL, RIGHT!?
ZUI (ZOOM)
ずいい
YOU WANT ME TO FULLY HEAL YOU, YES!? YOU DO, DON'T YOU!?
EH?
H-HUH? WHAAA—??
ZUZUI
ずずいっ
HEY WAIT, SHARU!
DON'T GET CARRIED AWAY, OKAY!?
KIRI
FUWA (FLOAT)
フワッ
NOW, THEN...
LIFE'S REFRESHING BREEZE...
...BLOW IN ENERGY!
POOOO (WHOOOSH)

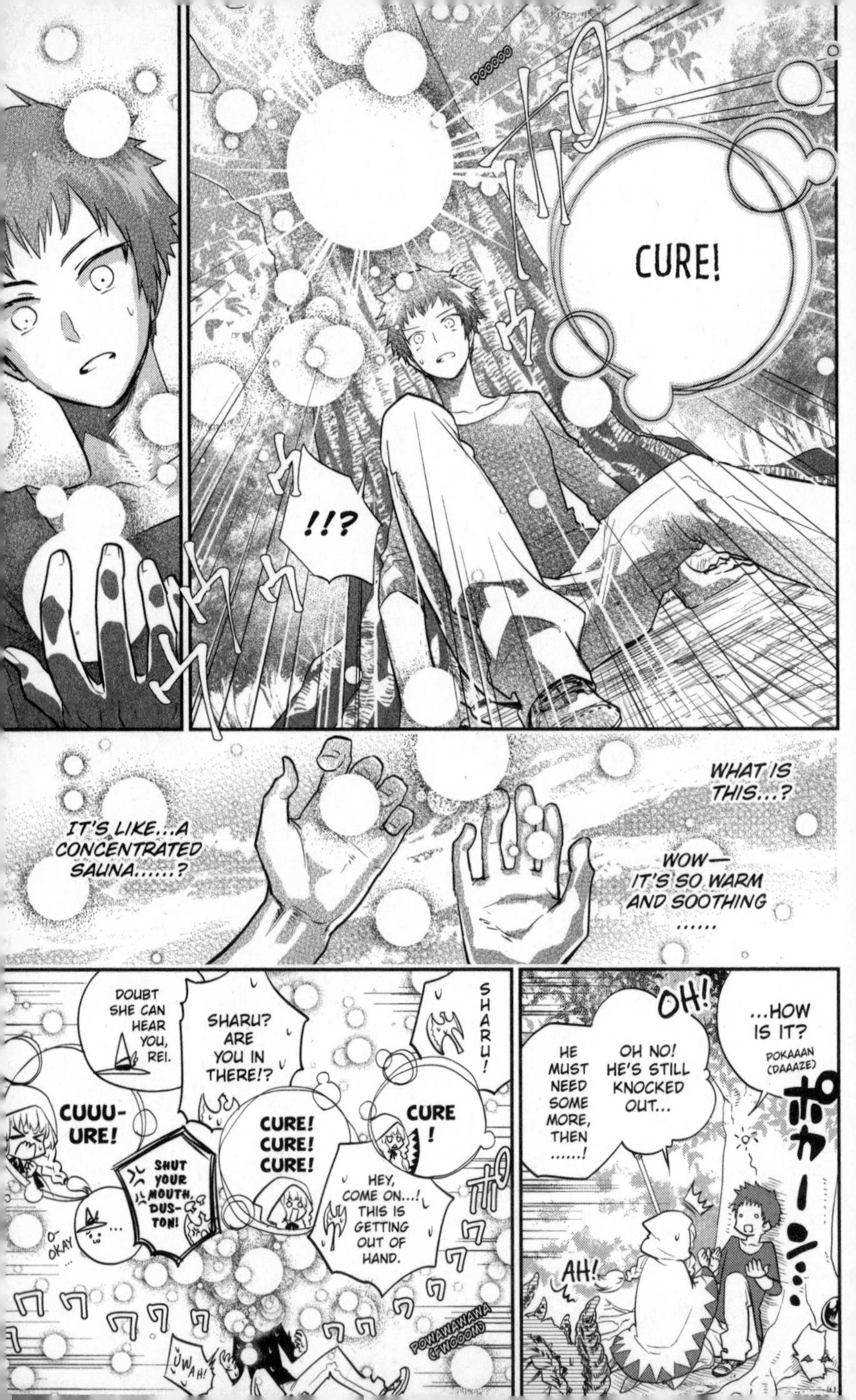
POOOOO
CURE!
!!?
WHAT IS THIS...?
WOW— IT'S SO WARM AND SOOTHING......
IT'S LIKE...A CONCENTRATED SAUNA......?
...HOW IS IT?
POKAAAN (DAAAZE)
OH!
OH NO! HE'S STILL KNOCKED OUT...
HE MUST NEED SOME MORE, THEN......!
AH!
SHARU!
SHARU? ARE YOU IN THERE!?
DOUBT SHE CAN HEAR YOU, REI.
CURE!
CURE! CURE! CURE!
CUUU-URE!
HEY, COME ON...! THIS IS GETTING OUT OF HAND.
SHUT YOUR MOUTH, DUS-TON!
...
O-OKAY...
POWANAWANA (FWOOOM)
UWAH!

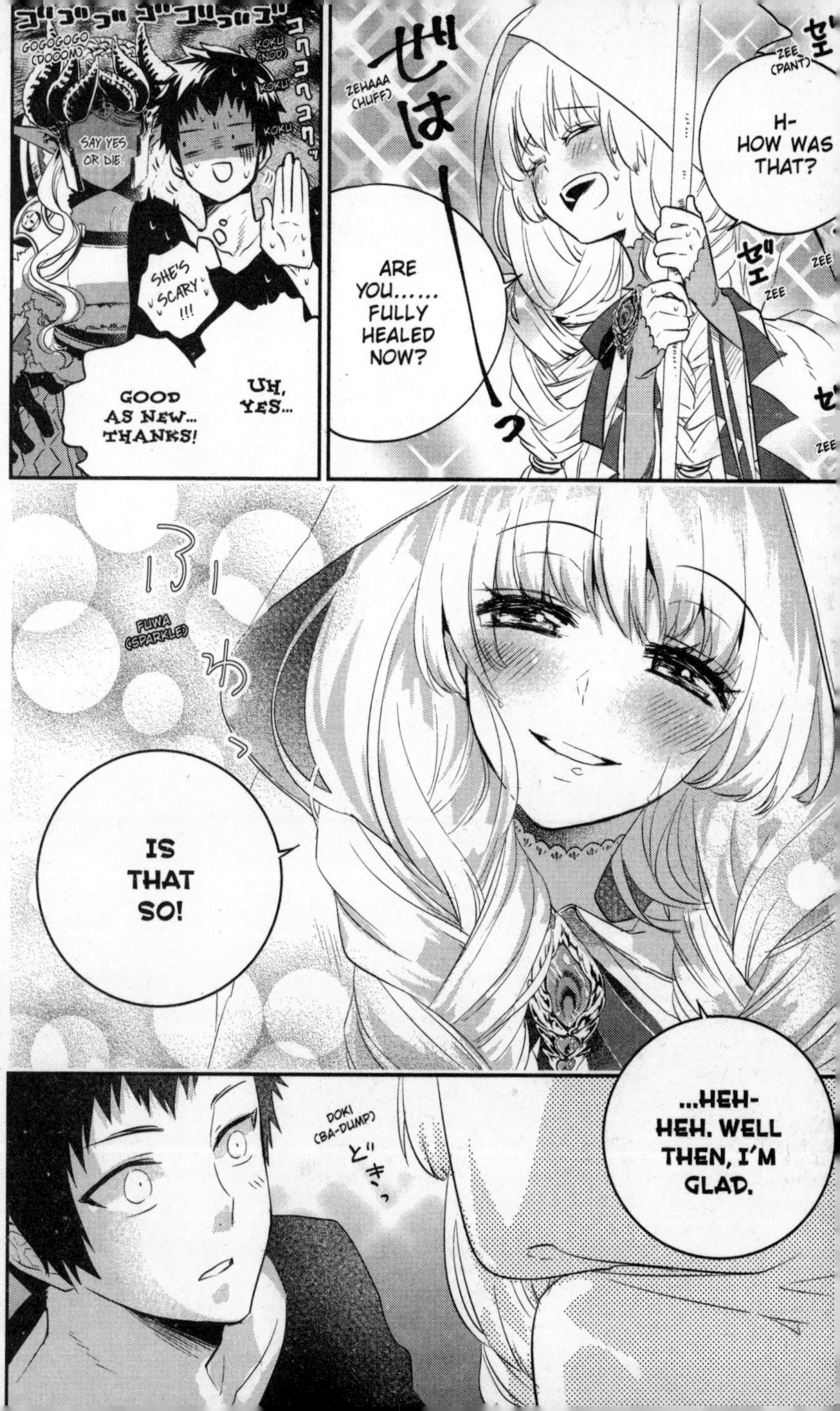
ZEE (PANT)
H- HOW WAS THAT?
ZEHAAA (HUFF)
ZEE
ZEE
ARE YOU...... FULLY HEALED NOW?
ZEE
KOKU (NOD)
KOKU
KOKU
GOGOGOGO (DOOOM)
SAY YES OR DIE.
SHE'S SCARY !!!
UH, YES...
GOOD AS NEW... THANKS!
FUWA (SPARKLE)
IS THAT SO!
...HEH-HEH. WELL THEN, I'M GLAD.
DOKI (BA-DUMP)

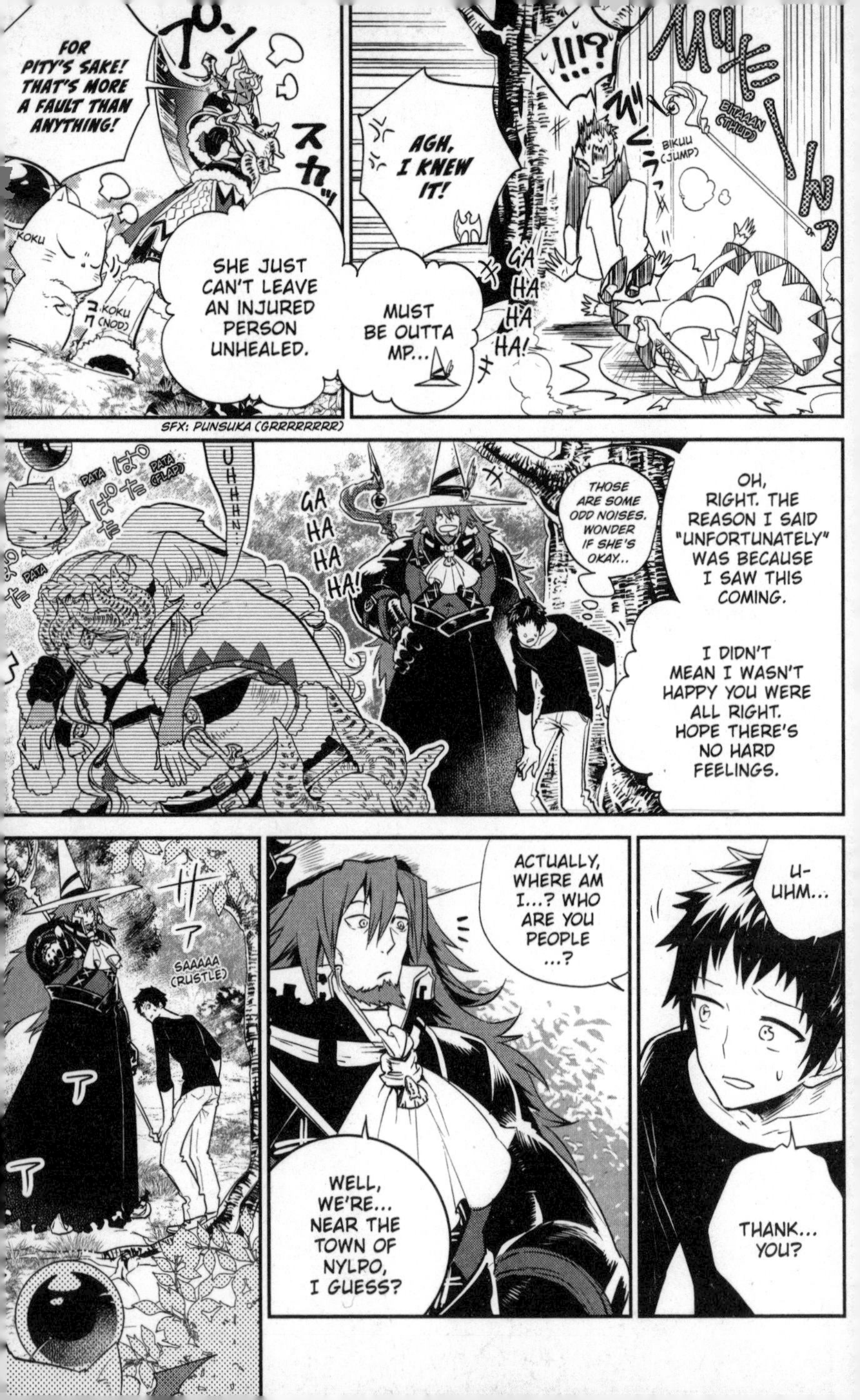

!!!?
BITAAAN (THUD)
BIKUU (JUMP)
AGH, I KNEW IT!
GA HA HA HA!
MUST BE OUTTA MP...
FOR PITY'S SAKE! THAT'S MORE A FAULT THAN ANYTHING!
KOKU
SHE JUST CAN'T LEAVE AN INJURED PERSON UNHEALED.
KOKU (NOD)
SFX: PUNSUKA (GRRRRRRRR)
OH, RIGHT. THE REASON I SAID "UNFORTUNATELY" WAS BECAUSE I SAW THIS COMING.
I DIDN'T MEAN I WASN'T HAPPY YOU WERE ALL RIGHT. HOPE THERE'S NO HARD FEELINGS.
THOSE ARE SOME ODD NOISES. WONDER IF SHE'S OKAY...
GA HA HA HA!
UHHHN...
PATA (FLAP)
PATA
PATA
U-UHM...
THANK... YOU?
ACTUALLY, WHERE AM I...? WHO ARE YOU PEOPLE ...?
WELL, WE'RE... NEAR THE TOWN OF NYLPO, I GUESS?
SAAAAA (RUSTLE)

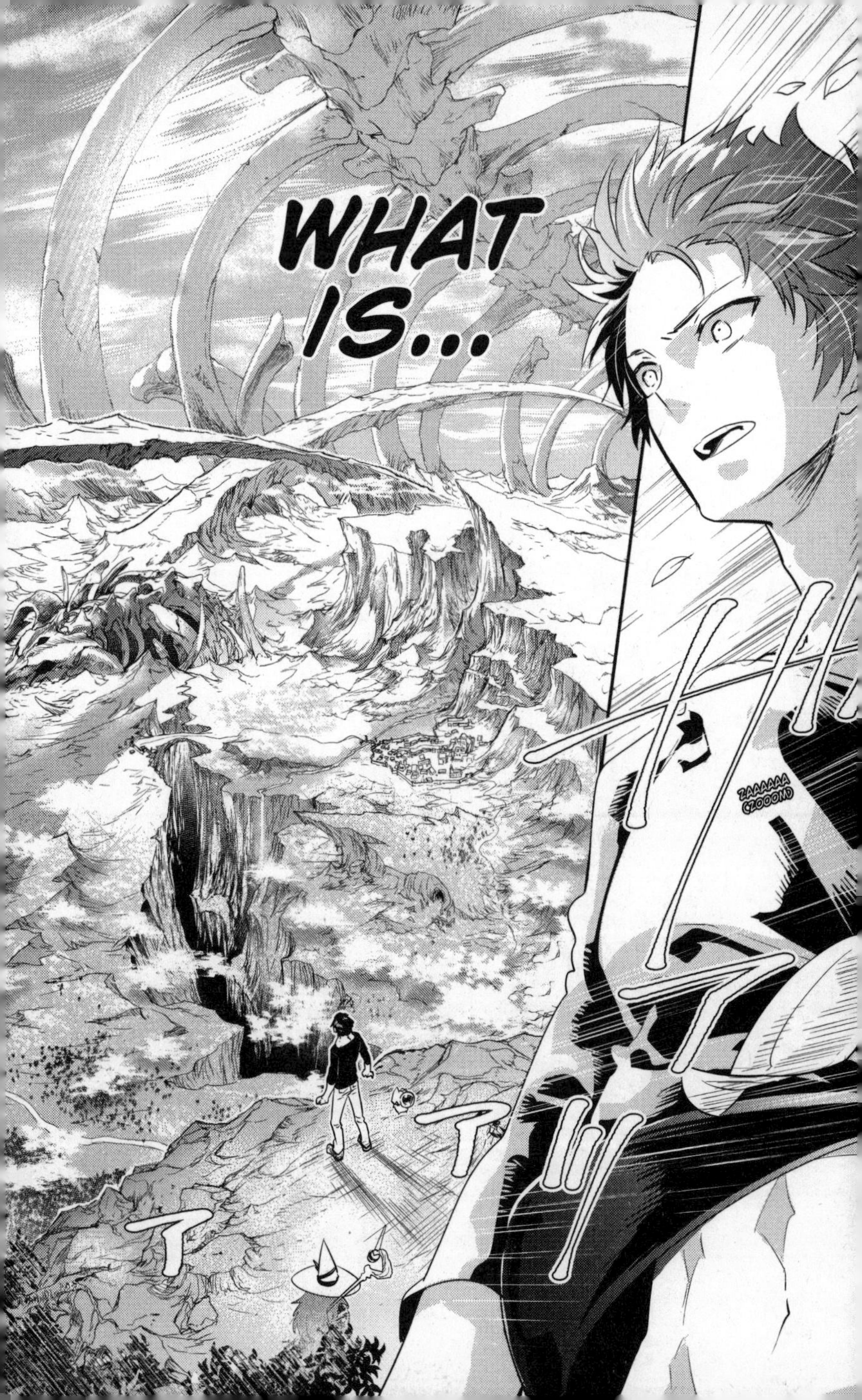
WHAT IS...
ZAAAAAA (ZOOOM)

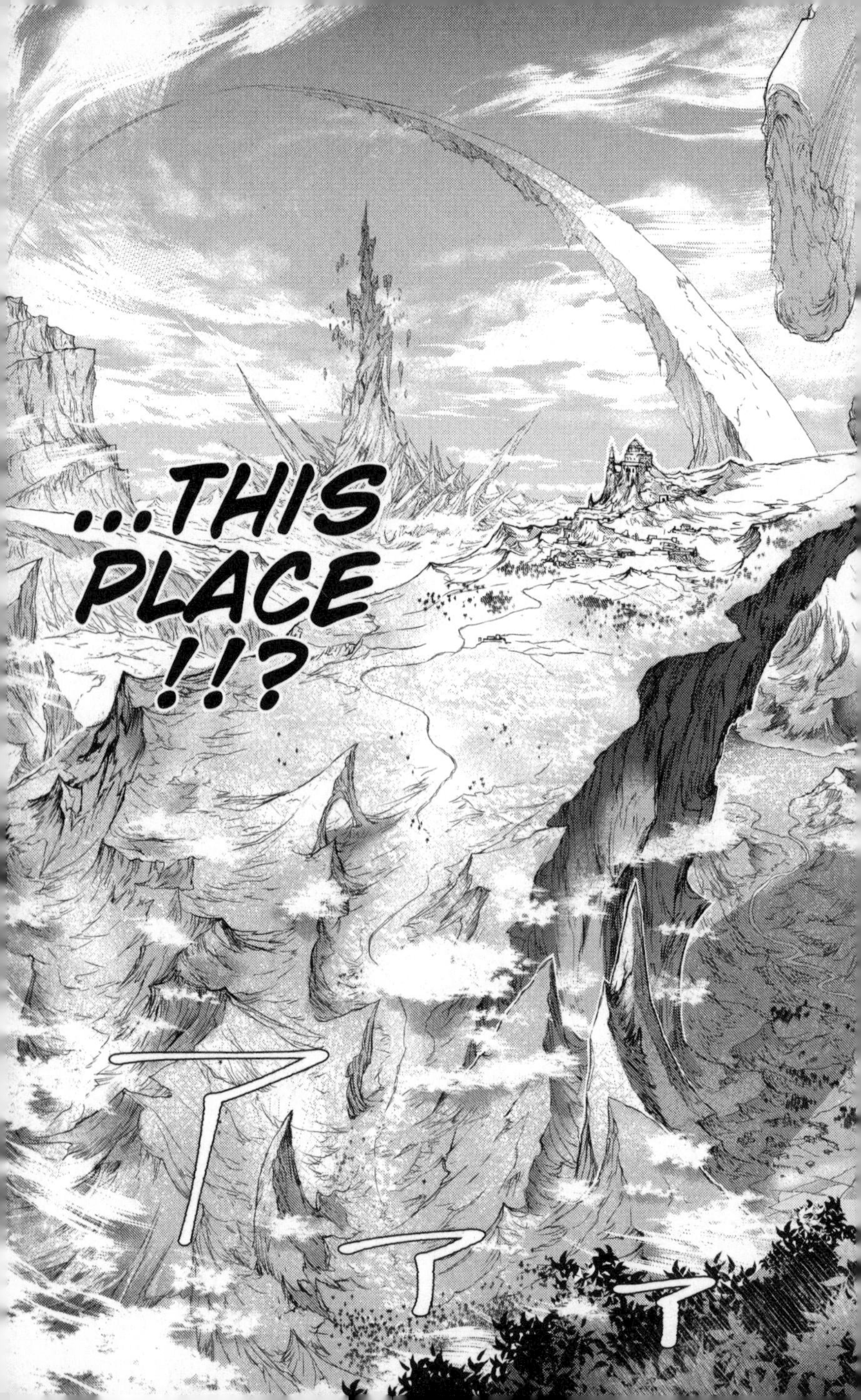
...THIS PLACE!!?

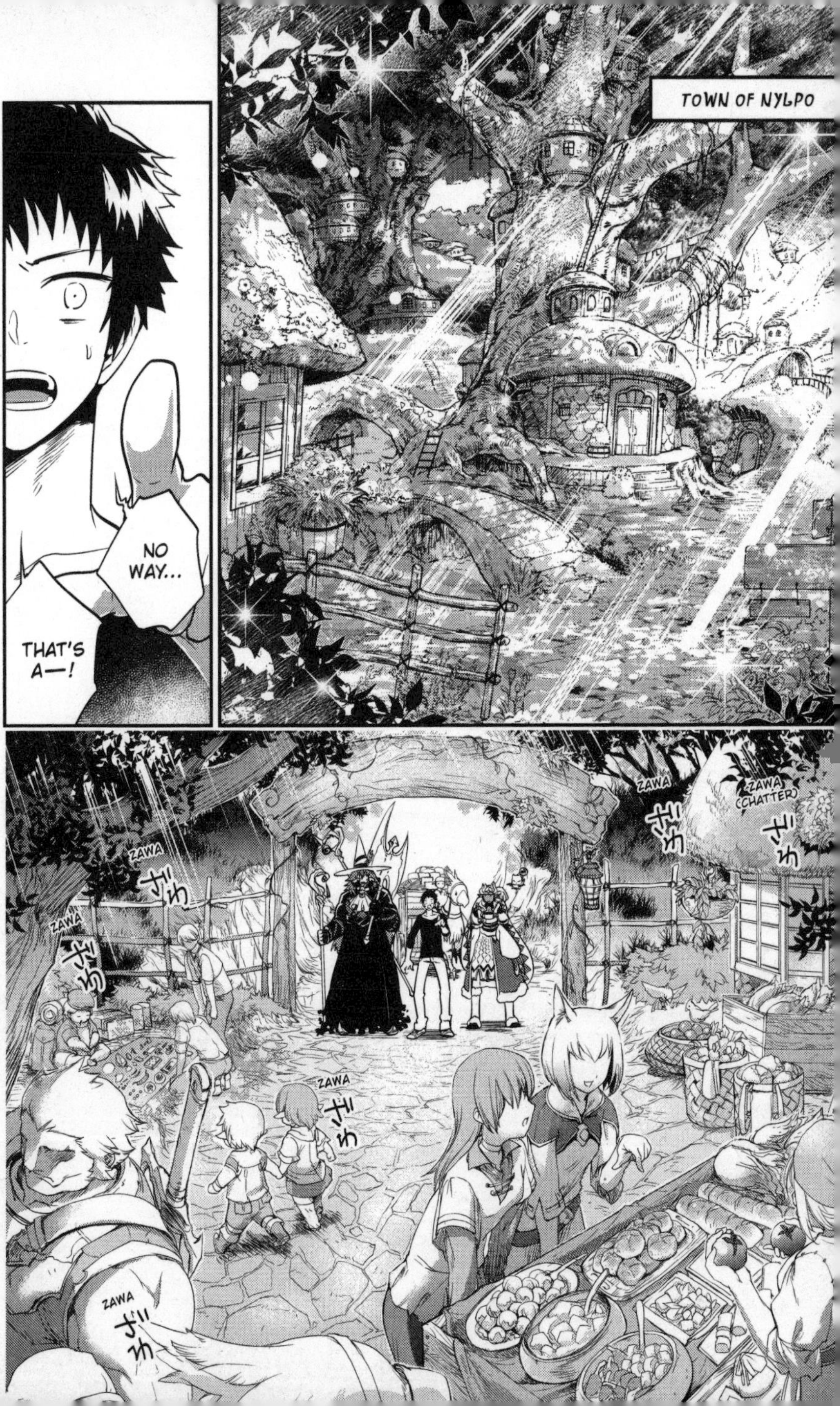
TOWN OF NYLPO
NO WAY...
THAT'S A—!
ZAWA
ざわ
ZAWA (CHATTER)
ざわ
ZAWA
ざわ
ZAWA
ざわ
ZAWA
ざわ
ZAWA
ざわ

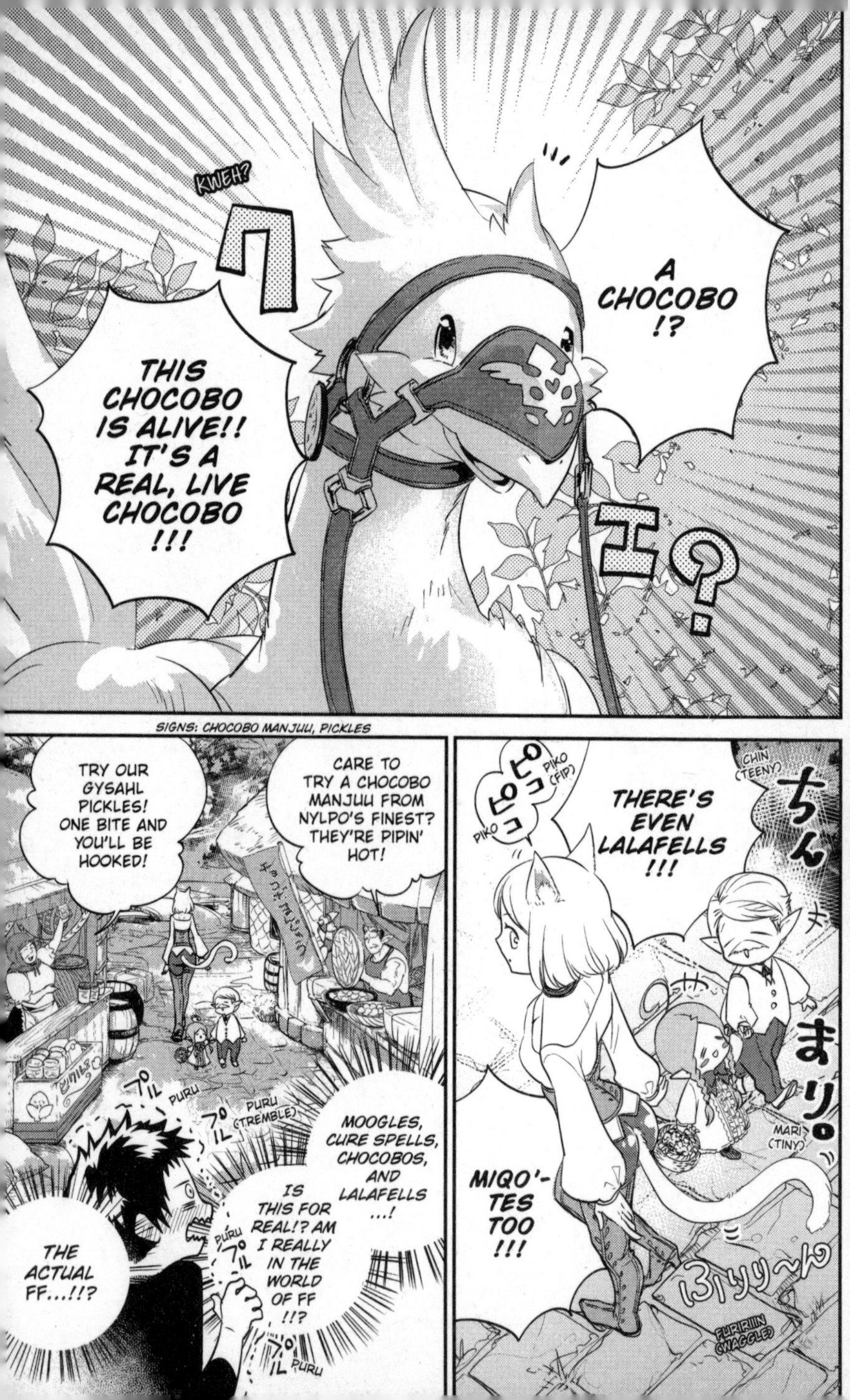
A CHOCOBO !?
KWEH?
クエ?
THIS CHOCOBO IS ALIVE!! IT'S A REAL, LIVE CHOCOBO !!!
SIGNS: CHOCOBO MANJUU, PICKLES
ピコピコ
PIKO PIKO (FIP)
ちん
CHIN (TEENY)
THERE'S EVEN LALAFELLS !!!
まり
MARI (TINY)
MIQO'-TES TOO !!!
ふりり〜ん
FURIRIIN (WAGGLE)
CARE TO TRY A CHOCOBO MANJUU FROM NYLPO'S FINEST? THEY'RE PIPIN' HOT!
TRY OUR GYSAHL PICKLES! ONE BITE AND YOU'LL BE HOOKED!
プル PURU
プル PURU (TREMBLE)
MOOGLES, CURE SPELLS, CHOCOBOS, AND LALAFELLS ...!
IS THIS FOR REAL!? AM I REALLY IN THE WORLD OF FF !!?
プル PURU
THE ACTUAL FF...!!?
プル PURU

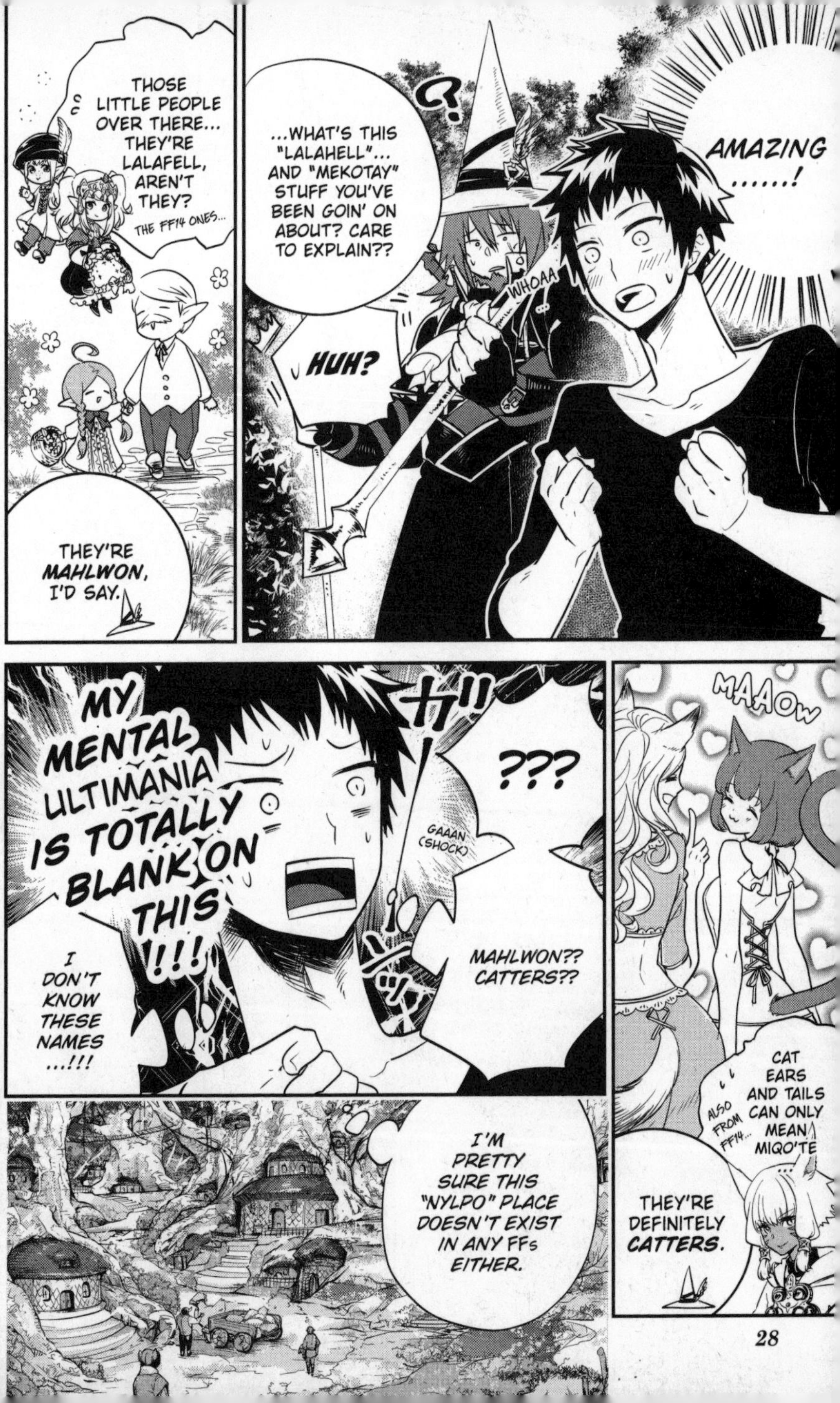
AMAZING ......!
WHOAA
...WHAT'S THIS "LALAHELL"... AND "MEKOTAY" STUFF YOU'VE BEEN GOIN' ON ABOUT? CARE TO EXPLAIN??
HUH?
THOSE LITTLE PEOPLE OVER THERE... THEY'RE LALAFELL, AREN'T THEY?
THE FF14 ONES...
THEY'RE MAHLWON, I'D SAY.
MAAOW
CAT EARS AND TAILS CAN ONLY MEAN MIQO'TE...
ALSO FROM FF14...
THEY'RE DEFINITELY CATTERS.
???
GAAAN (SHOCK)
MY MENTAL ULTIMANIA IS TOTALLY BLANK ON THIS!!!
MAHLWON?? CATTERS??
I DON'T KNOW THESE NAMES ...!!!
I'M PRETTY SURE THIS "NYLPO" PLACE DOESN'T EXIST IN ANY FFs EITHER.

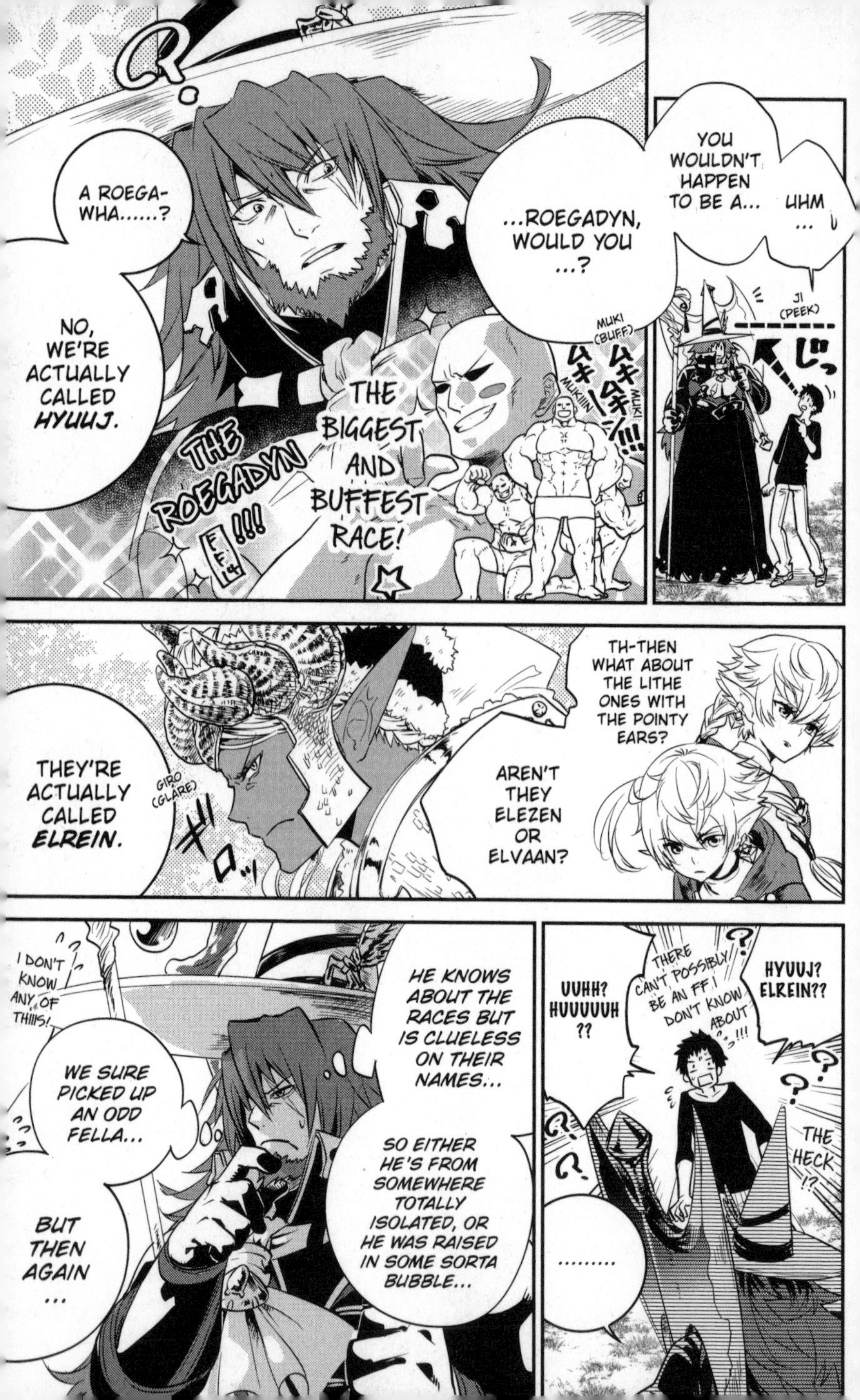
UHM ...
YOU WOULDN'T HAPPEN TO BE A...
...ROEGADYN, WOULD YOU ...?
JI (PEEK)
じっ
A ROEGA-WHA......?
NO, WE'RE ACTUALLY CALLED HYUUJ.
THE ROEGADYN!!!
FFI4
THE BIGGEST AND BUFFEST RACE!
MUKI (BUFF)
ムキ ムキ ムキーン!!!
TH-THEN WHAT ABOUT THE LITHE ONES WITH THE POINTY EARS?
AREN'T THEY ELEZEN OR ELVAAN?
GIRO (GLARE)
ギロッ
THEY'RE ACTUALLY CALLED ELREIN.
HYUUJ? ELREIN??
THERE CAN'T POSSIBLY BE AN FF I DON'T KNOW ABOUT!!!
UUHH? HUUUUUH ??
THE HECK!?
....
HE KNOWS ABOUT THE RACES BUT IS CLUELESS ON THEIR NAMES...
SO EITHER HE'S FROM SOMEWHERE TOTALLY ISOLATED, OR HE WAS RAISED IN SOME SORTA BUBBLE...
I DON'T KNOW ANY OF THIIIS!
WE SURE PICKED UP AN ODD FELLA...
BUT THEN AGAIN ...

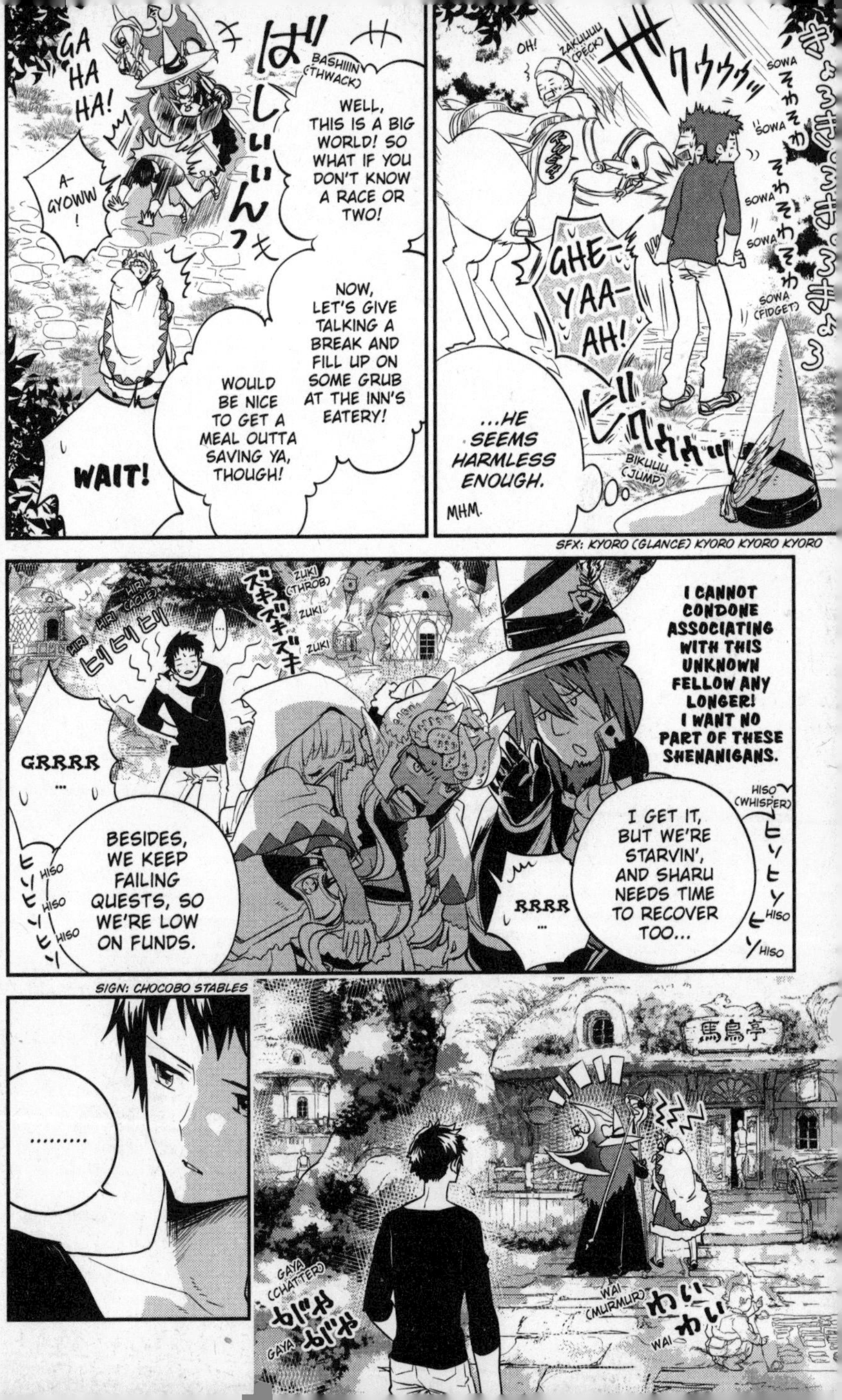
SOWA
SOWA
SOWA
SOWA
SOWA (FIDGET)
ZAKUUUU (PECK)
OH!
GHE-YAA-AH!
BIKUUU (JUMP)
...HE SEEMS HARMLESS ENOUGH.
MHM.
SFX: KYORO (GLANCE) KYORO KYORO KYORO
BASHIIIN (THWACK)
WELL, THIS IS A BIG WORLD! SO WHAT IF YOU DON'T KNOW A RACE OR TWO!
GA HA HA!
NOW, LET'S GIVE TALKING A BREAK AND FILL UP ON SOME GRUB AT THE INN'S EATERY!
WOULD BE NICE TO GET A MEAL OUTTA SAVING YA, THOUGH!
A-GYOWW!
WAIT!
I CANNOT CONDONE ASSOCIATING WITH THIS UNKNOWN FELLOW ANY LONGER! I WANT NO PART OF THESE SHENANIGANS.
HISO (WHISPER)
I GET IT, BUT WE'RE STARVIN', AND SHARU NEEDS TIME TO RECOVER TOO...
HISO
HISO
RRRR...
ZUKI (THROB)
ZUKI
ZUKI
HIRI (ACHE)
HIRI
HIRI
...
GRRRR...
BESIDES, WE KEEP FAILING QUESTS, SO WE'RE LOW ON FUNDS.
HISO
HISO
HISO
SIGN: CHOCOBO STABLES
馬鳥亭
GAYA (CHATTER)
GAYA
WAI (MURMUR)
WAI
....

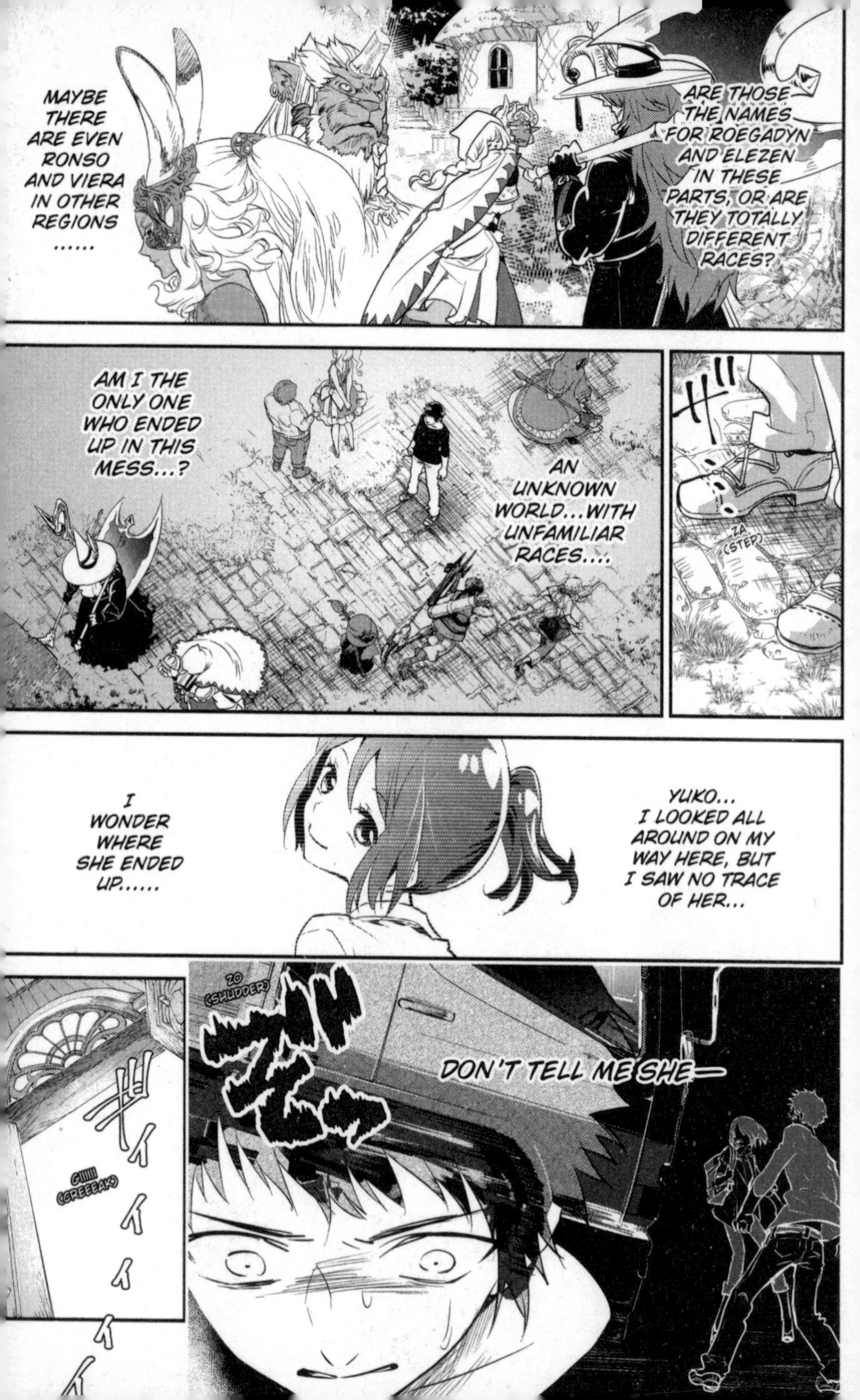
ARE THOSE THE NAMES FOR ROEGADYN AND ELEZEN IN THESE PARTS, OR ARE THEY TOTALLY DIFFERENT RACES?
MAYBE THERE ARE EVEN RONSO AND VIERA IN OTHER REGIONS......
ZA (STEP)
AN UNKNOWN WORLD...WITH UNFAMILIAR RACES....
AM I THE ONLY ONE WHO ENDED UP IN THIS MESS...?
YUKO... I LOOKED ALL AROUND ON MY WAY HERE, BUT I SAW NO TRACE OF HER...
I WONDER WHERE SHE ENDED UP......
ZO (SHUDDER)
DON'T TELL ME SHE—
GIIIII (CREEEAK)

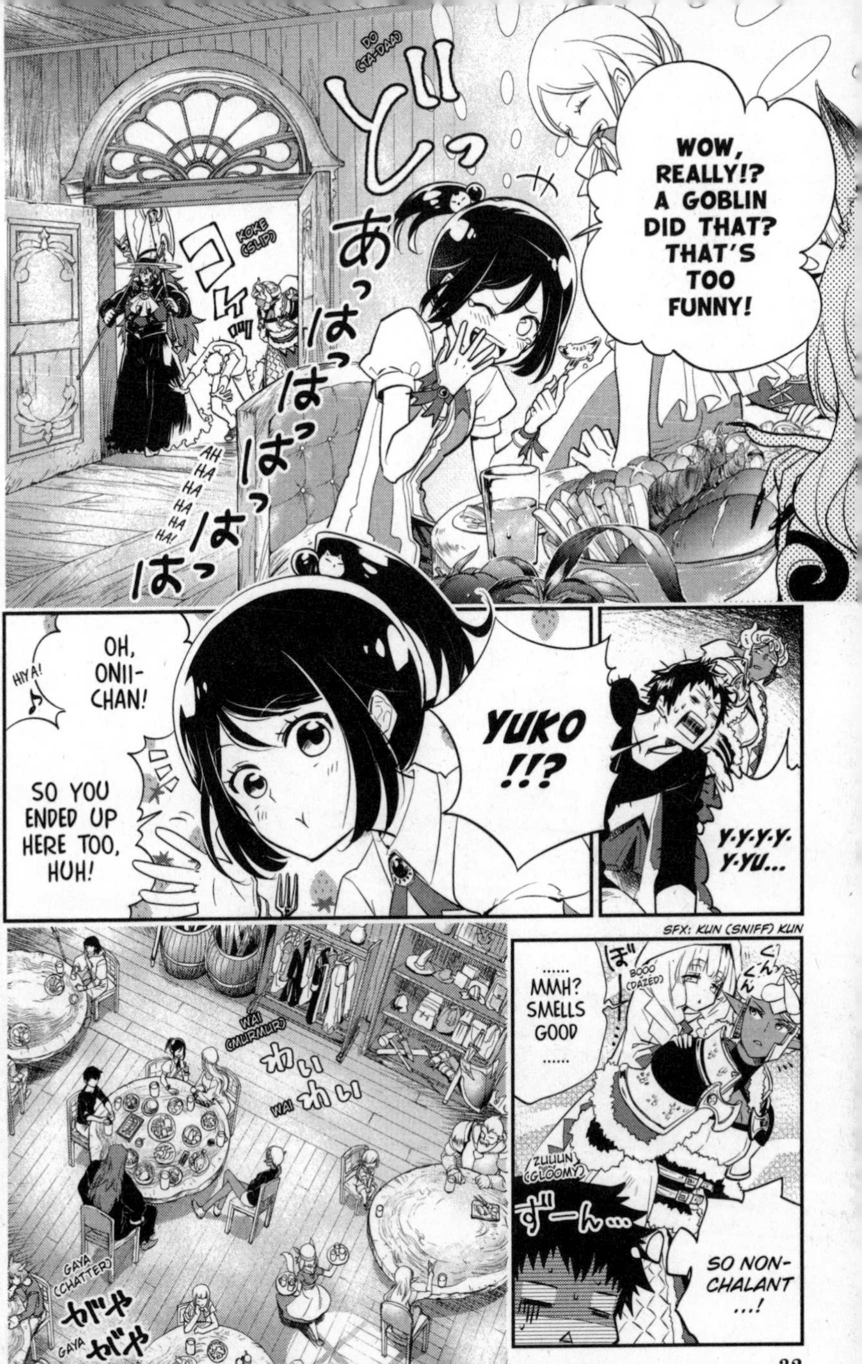
WOW, REALLY!? A GOBLIN DID THAT? THAT'S TOO FUNNY!
AH HA HA HA HA HA!
DO (TA-DAA)
KOKE (SLIP)
Y-Y-Y-Y-Y-YU...
YUKO!!?
OH, ONII-CHAN!
HIYA! ♪
SO YOU ENDED UP HERE TOO, HUH!
SFX: KUN (SNIFF) KUN
BOOO (DAZED)
......MMH? SMELLS GOOD ......
ZUUUN (GLOOMY)
SO NON-CHALANT ...!
WAI (MURMUR) WAI
GAYA (CHATTER) GAYA

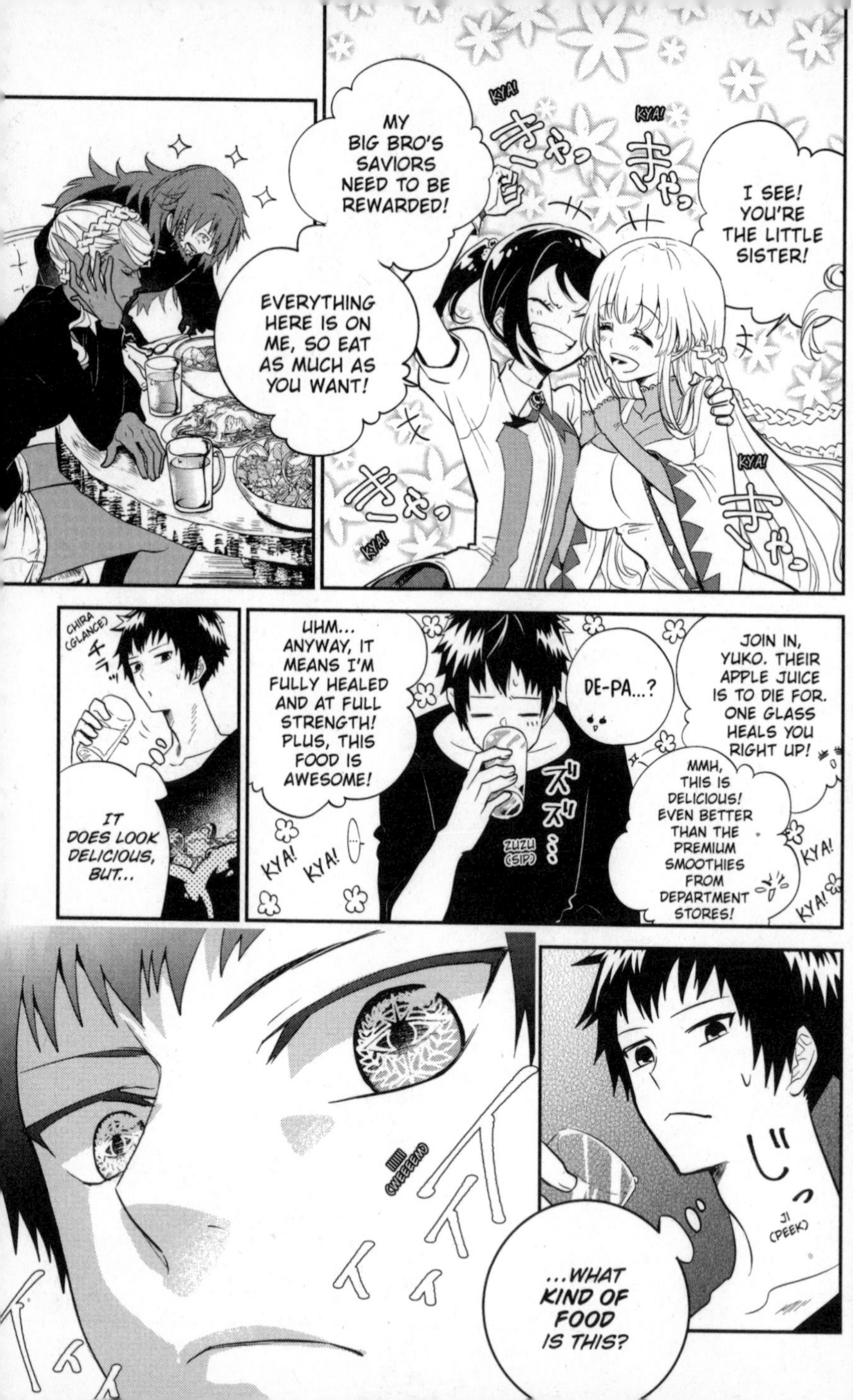
I SEE! YOU'RE THE LITTLE SISTER!
KYA!
KYA!
KYA!
MY BIG BRO'S SAVIORS NEED TO BE REWARDED!
EVERYTHING HERE IS ON ME, SO EAT AS MUCH AS YOU WANT!
KYA!
JOIN IN, YUKO. THEIR APPLE JUICE IS TO DIE FOR. ONE GLASS HEALS YOU RIGHT UP!
DE-PA...?
MMH, THIS IS DELICIOUS! EVEN BETTER THAN THE PREMIUM SMOOTHIES FROM DEPARTMENT STORES!
KYA!
KYA!
UHM... ANYWAY, IT MEANS I'M FULLY HEALED AND AT FULL STRENGTH! PLUS, THIS FOOD IS AWESOME!
ZUZU (SIP)
...
KYA!
KYA!
CHIRA (GLANCE)
IT DOES LOOK DELICIOUS, BUT...
JI (PEEK)
...WHAT KIND OF FOOD IS THIS?
IIIIII (WEEEEEN)

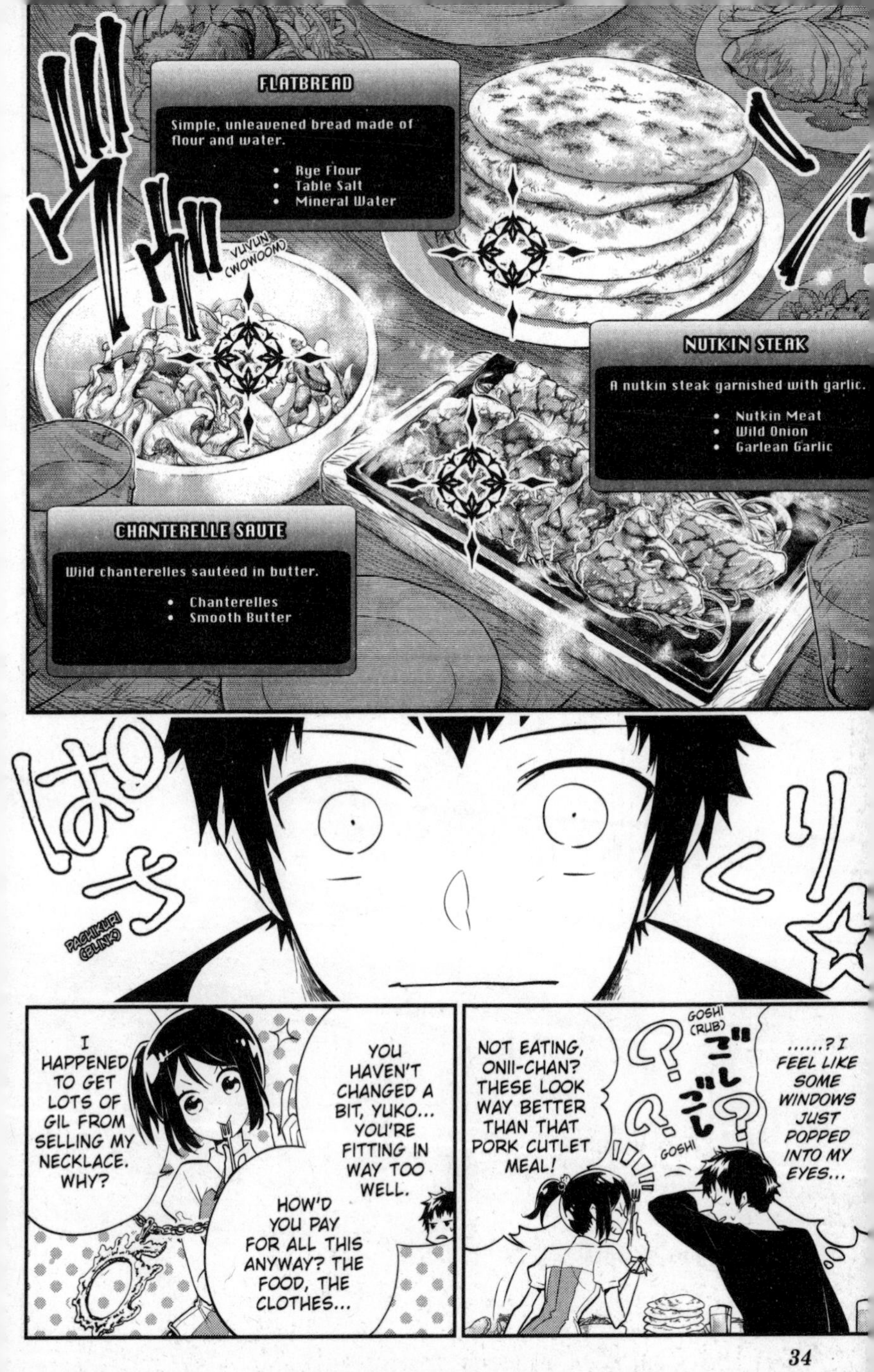
FLATBREAD
Simple, unleavened bread made of flour and water.
• Rye Flour
• Table Salt
• Mineral Water
VUVUN (WOWOOM)
NUTKIN STEAK
A nutkin steak garnished with garlic.
• Nutkin Meat
• Wild Onion
• Garlean Garlic
CHANTERELLE SAUTE
Wild chanterelles sautéed in butter.
• Chanterelles
• Smooth Butter
PACHIKURI (BLINK)
......?I FEEL LIKE SOME WINDOWS JUST POPPED INTO MY EYES...
GOSHI (RUB)
NOT EATING, ONII-CHAN? THESE LOOK WAY BETTER THAN THAT PORK CUTLET MEAL!
GOSHI
YOU HAVEN'T CHANGED A BIT, YUKO... YOU'RE FITTING IN WAY TOO WELL.
HOW'D YOU PAY FOR ALL THIS ANYWAY? THE FOOD, THE CLOTHES...
I HAPPENED TO GET LOTS OF GIL FROM SELLING MY NECKLACE. WHY?

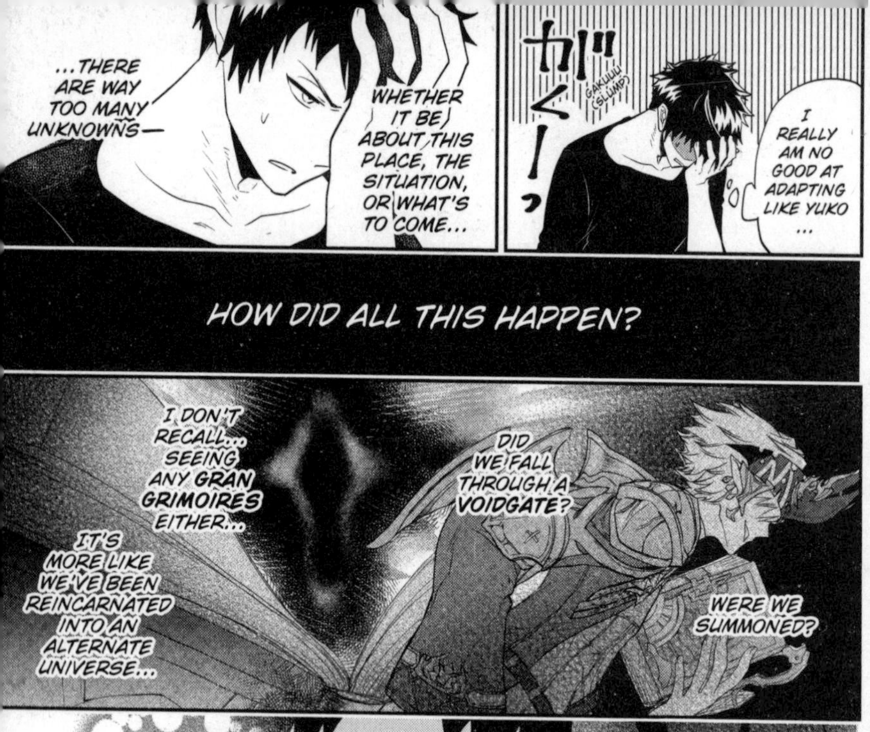
GAKUUU (SLUMP)
I REALLY AM NO GOOD AT ADAPTING LIKE YUKO ...
WHETHER IT BE ABOUT THIS PLACE, THE SITUATION, OR WHAT'S TO COME...
...THERE ARE WAY TOO MANY UNKNOWNS—
HOW DID ALL THIS HAPPEN?
WERE WE SUMMONED?
DID WE FALL THROUGH A VOIDGATE?
I DON'T RECALL... SEEING ANY GRAN GRIMOIRES EITHER...
IT'S MORE LIKE WE'VE BEEN REINCARNATED INTO AN ALTERNATE UNIVERSE...
...REINCARNATED?
WHAT IF...
...WE REALLY DID DIE THERE?
THEN OUR AMBITIONS... OUR DREAMS... OUR PROMISE...
LET'S MAKE IT TOGETHER!
ARE THEY NO LONGER ATTAINABLE?

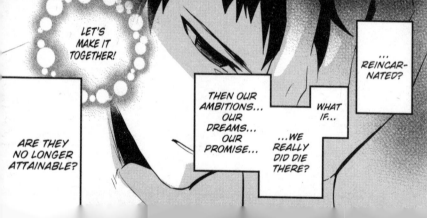

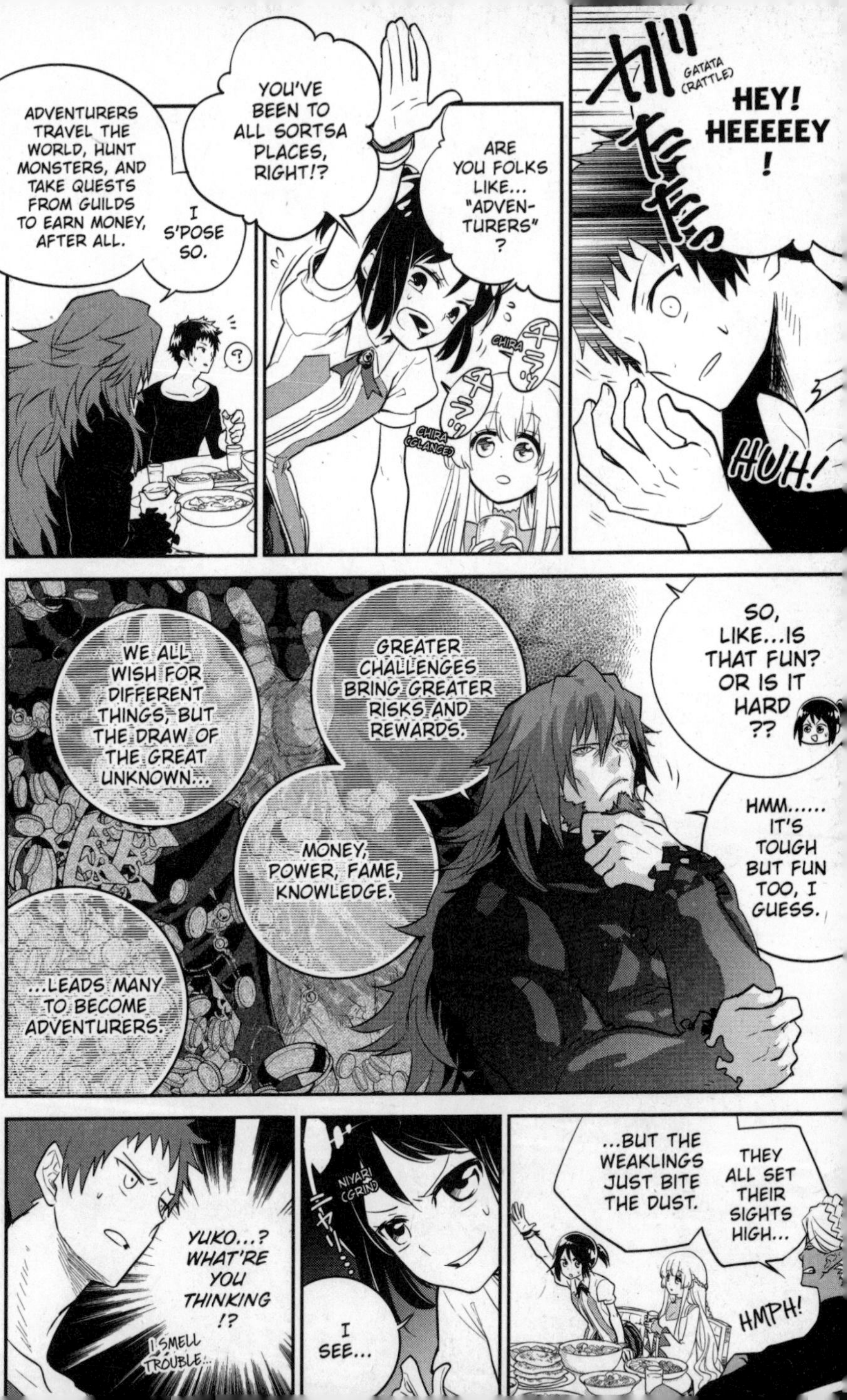
GATATA (RATTLE)
HEY! HEEEEEY!
HUH!
ARE YOU FOLKS LIKE... "ADVENTURERS"?
YOU'VE BEEN TO ALL SORTSA PLACES, RIGHT!?
CHIRA
CHIRA (GLANCE)
I S'POSE SO.
ADVENTURERS TRAVEL THE WORLD, HUNT MONSTERS, AND TAKE QUESTS FROM GUILDS TO EARN MONEY, AFTER ALL.
?
SO, LIKE...IS THAT FUN? OR IS IT HARD??
HMM...... IT'S TOUGH BUT FUN TOO, I GUESS.
GREATER CHALLENGES BRING GREATER RISKS AND REWARDS.
MONEY, POWER, FAME, KNOWLEDGE.
WE ALL WISH FOR DIFFERENT THINGS, BUT THE DRAW OF THE GREAT UNKNOWN...
...LEADS MANY TO BECOME ADVENTURERS.
THEY ALL SET THEIR SIGHTS HIGH...
...BUT THE WEAKLINGS JUST BITE THE DUST.
HMPH!
NIYARI (GRIN)
I SEE...
YUKO...? WHAT'RE YOU THINKING!?
I SMELL TROUBLE...

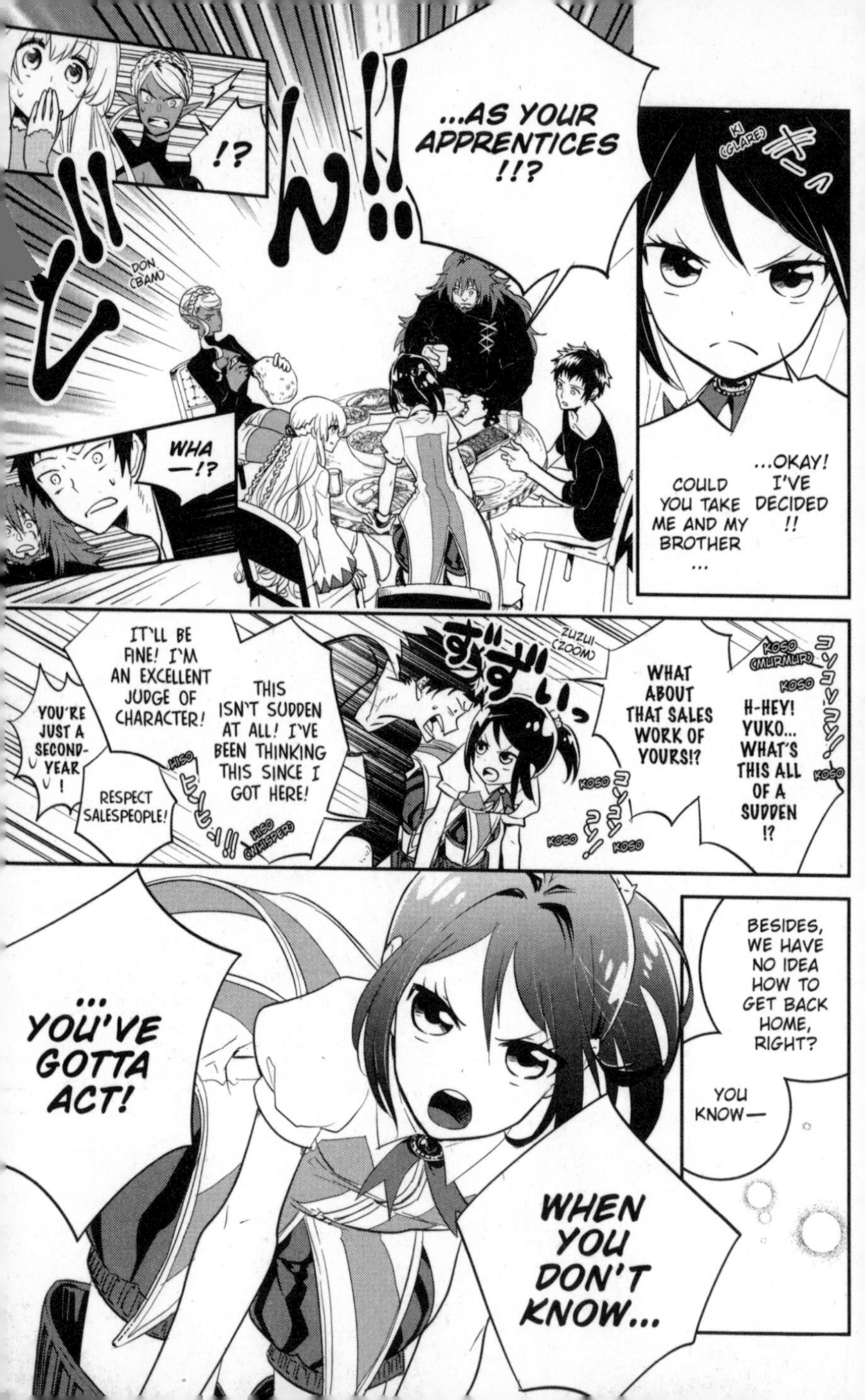

KI (GLARE)
...OKAY! I'VE DECIDED!!
COULD YOU TAKE ME AND MY BROTHER ...
...AS YOUR APPRENTICES!!?
DON (BAM)
!?
WHA—!?
KOSO (MURMUR)
H-HEY! YUKO... WHAT'S THIS ALL OF A SUDDEN!?
KOSO KOSO KOSO
WHAT ABOUT THAT SALES WORK OF YOURS!?
KOSO KOSO KOSO
ZUZUI (ZOOM)
THIS ISN'T SUDDEN AT ALL! I'VE BEEN THINKING THIS SINCE I GOT HERE!
IT'LL BE FINE! I'M AN EXCELLENT JUDGE OF CHARACTER!
HISO (WHISPER)
HISO
RESPECT SALESPEOPLE!
YOU'RE JUST A SECOND-YEAR!
BESIDES, WE HAVE NO IDEA HOW TO GET BACK HOME, RIGHT?
YOU KNOW—
WHEN YOU DON'T KNOW...
...YOU'VE GOTTA ACT!

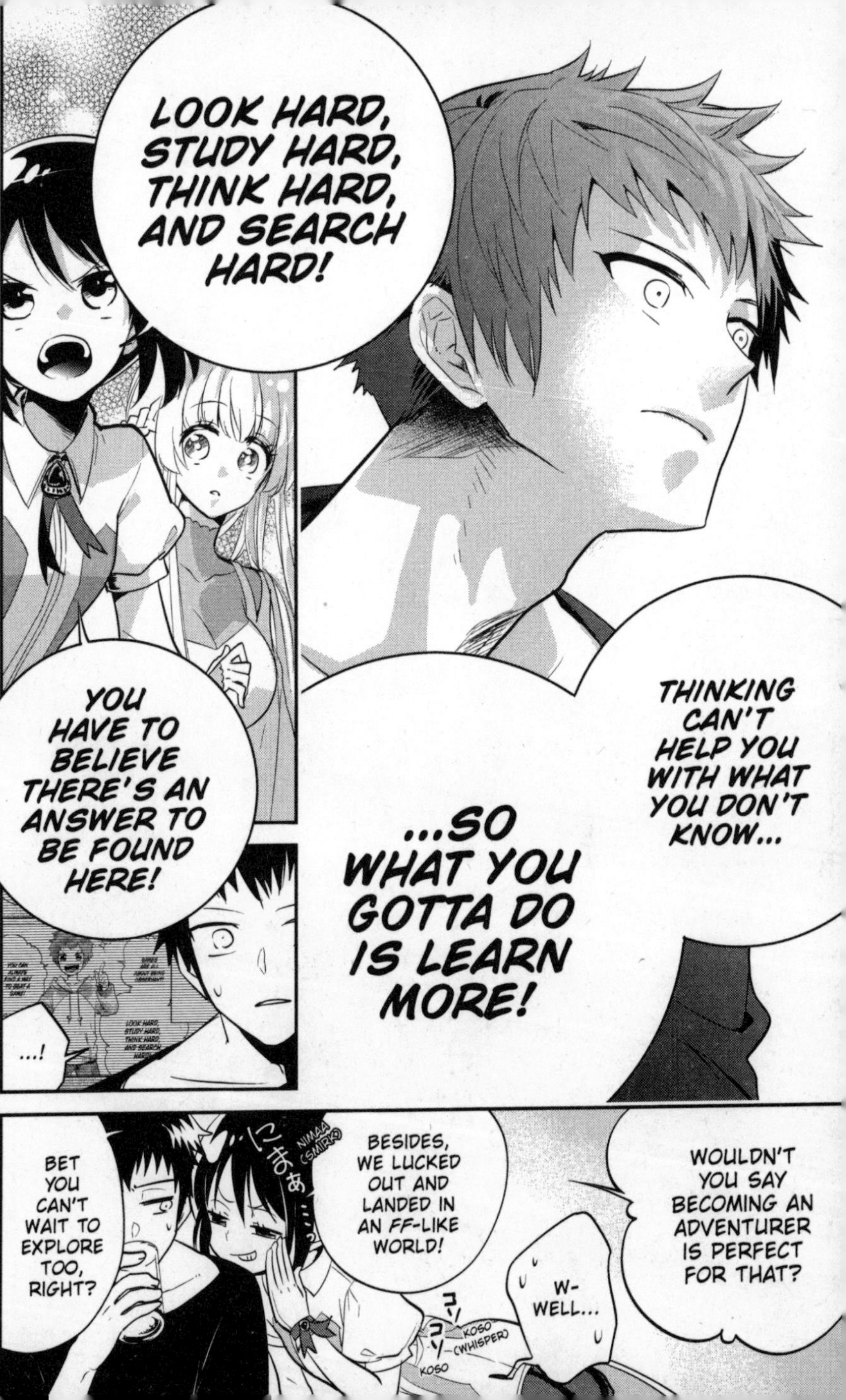
THINKING CAN'T HELP YOU WITH WHAT YOU DON'T KNOW...
...SO WHAT YOU GOTTA DO IS LEARN MORE!
LOOK HARD, STUDY HARD, THINK HARD, AND SEARCH HARD!
YOU HAVE TO BELIEVE THERE'S AN ANSWER TO BE FOUND HERE!
...!
WOULDN'T YOU SAY BECOMING AN ADVENTURER IS PERFECT FOR THAT?
W-WELL...
BESIDES, WE LUCKED OUT AND LANDED IN AN FF-LIKE WORLD!
コソ KOSO
コソ KOSO (WHISPER)
にまぁ NIMAA (SMIRK)
BET YOU CAN'T WAIT TO EXPLORE TOO, RIGHT?

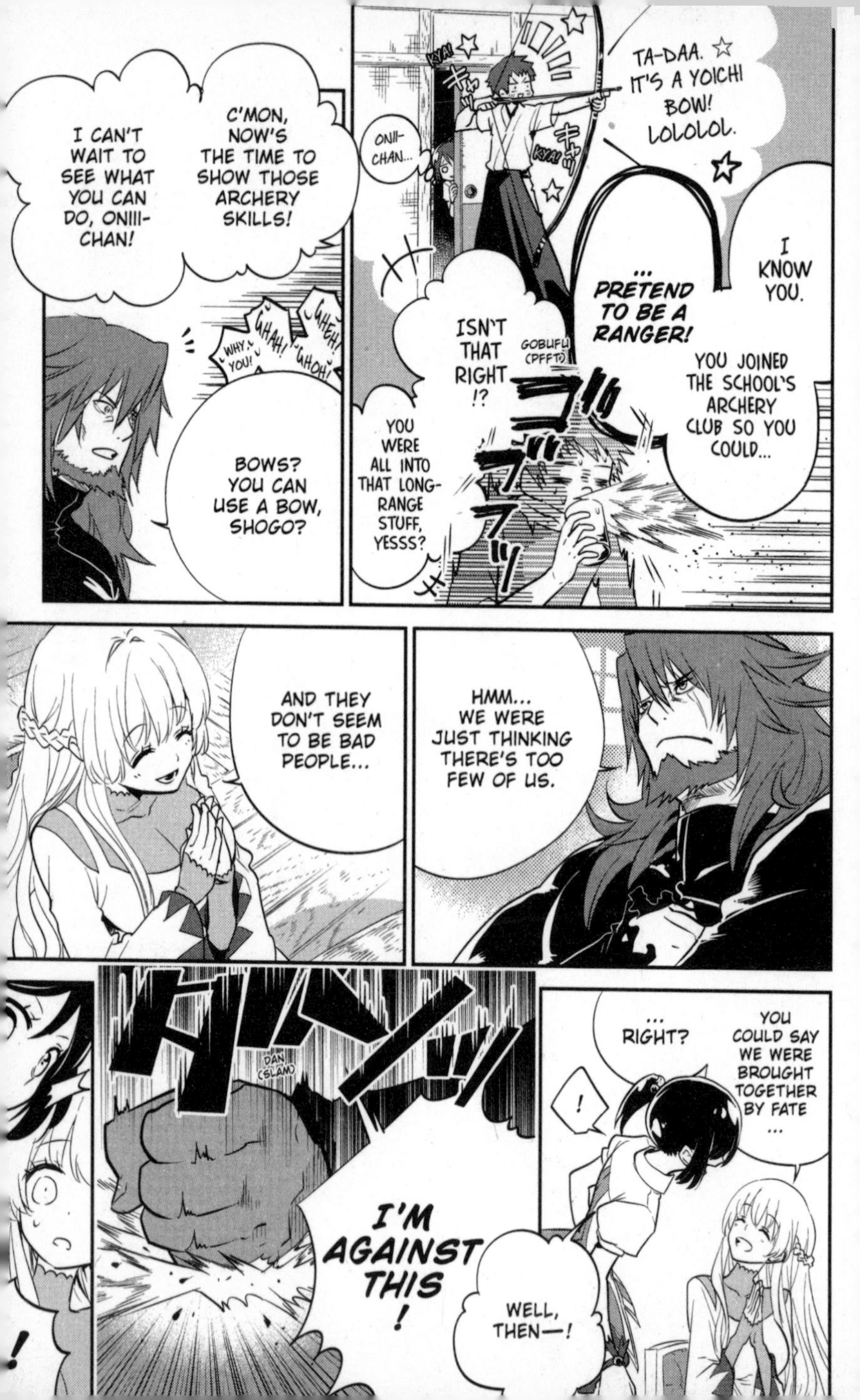
I KNOW YOU.
YOU JOINED THE SCHOOL'S ARCHERY CLUB SO YOU COULD...
...PRETEND TO BE A RANGER!
TA-DAA. ☆ IT'S A YOICHI BOW! LOLOLOL.
KYA!
KYA!
ONII-CHAN...
GOBUFU (PFFT)
ISN'T THAT RIGHT!?
YOU WERE ALL INTO THAT LONG-RANGE STUFF, YESSS?
C'MON, NOW'S THE TIME TO SHOW THOSE ARCHERY SKILLS!
I CAN'T WAIT TO SEE WHAT YOU CAN DO, ONIII-CHAN!
GHEH!
GHAH!
GHOH!
WHY, YOU!
BOWS? YOU CAN USE A BOW, SHOGO?
HMM... WE WERE JUST THINKING THERE'S TOO FEW OF US.
AND THEY DON'T SEEM TO BE BAD PEOPLE...
YOU COULD SAY WE WERE BROUGHT TOGETHER BY FATE...
...RIGHT?
!
WELL, THEN—!
DAN (SLAM)
I'M AGAINST THIS!
!

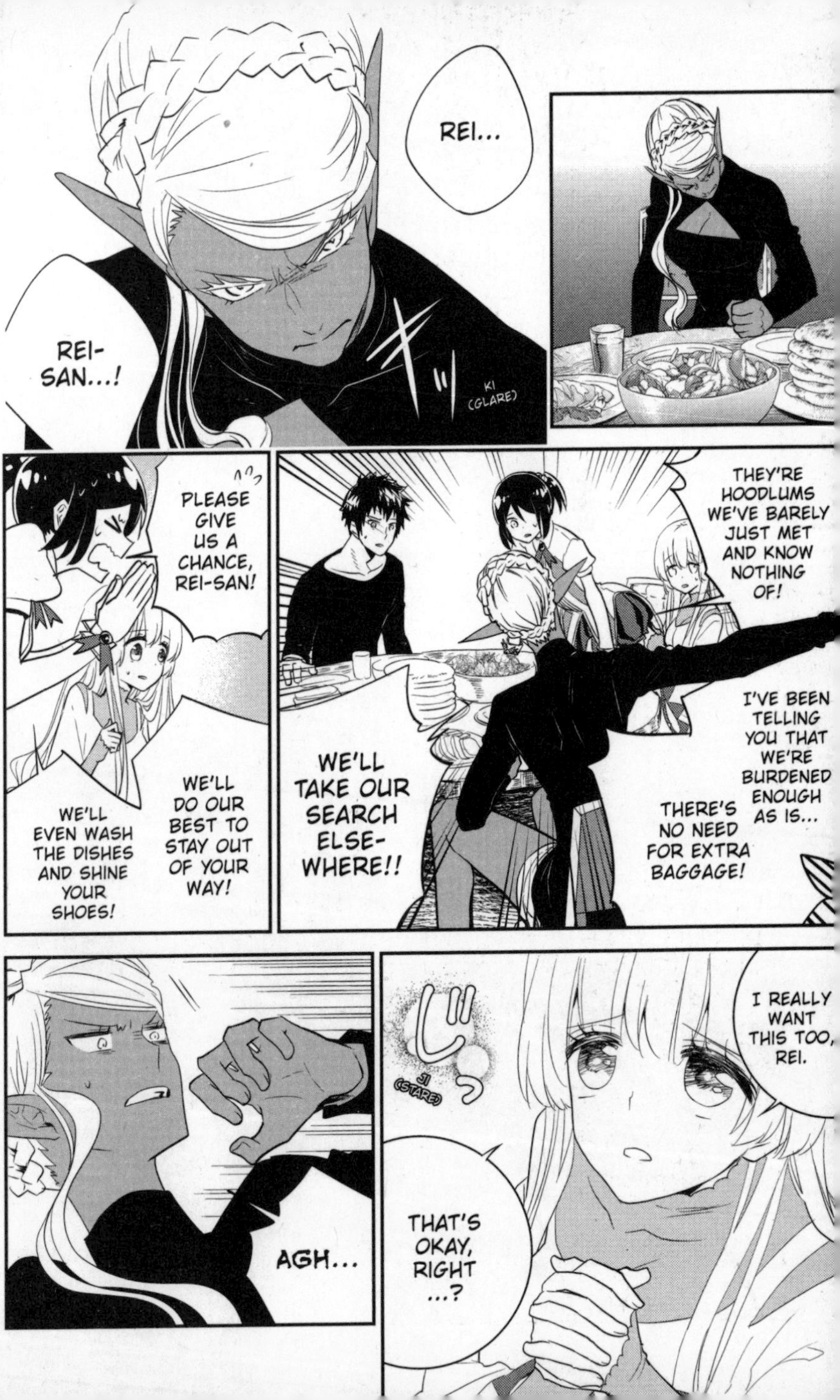
REI...
REI-SAN...!
KI (GLARE)
THEY'RE HOODLUMS WE'VE BARELY JUST MET AND KNOW NOTHING OF!
I'VE BEEN TELLING YOU THAT WE'RE BURDENED ENOUGH AS IS...
THERE'S NO NEED FOR EXTRA BAGGAGE!
WE'LL TAKE OUR SEARCH ELSE-WHERE!!
PLEASE GIVE US A CHANCE, REI-SAN!
WE'LL DO OUR BEST TO STAY OUT OF YOUR WAY!
WE'LL EVEN WASH THE DISHES AND SHINE YOUR SHOES!
I REALLY WANT THIS TOO, REI.
JI (STARE)
THAT'S OKAY, RIGHT ...?
AGH...

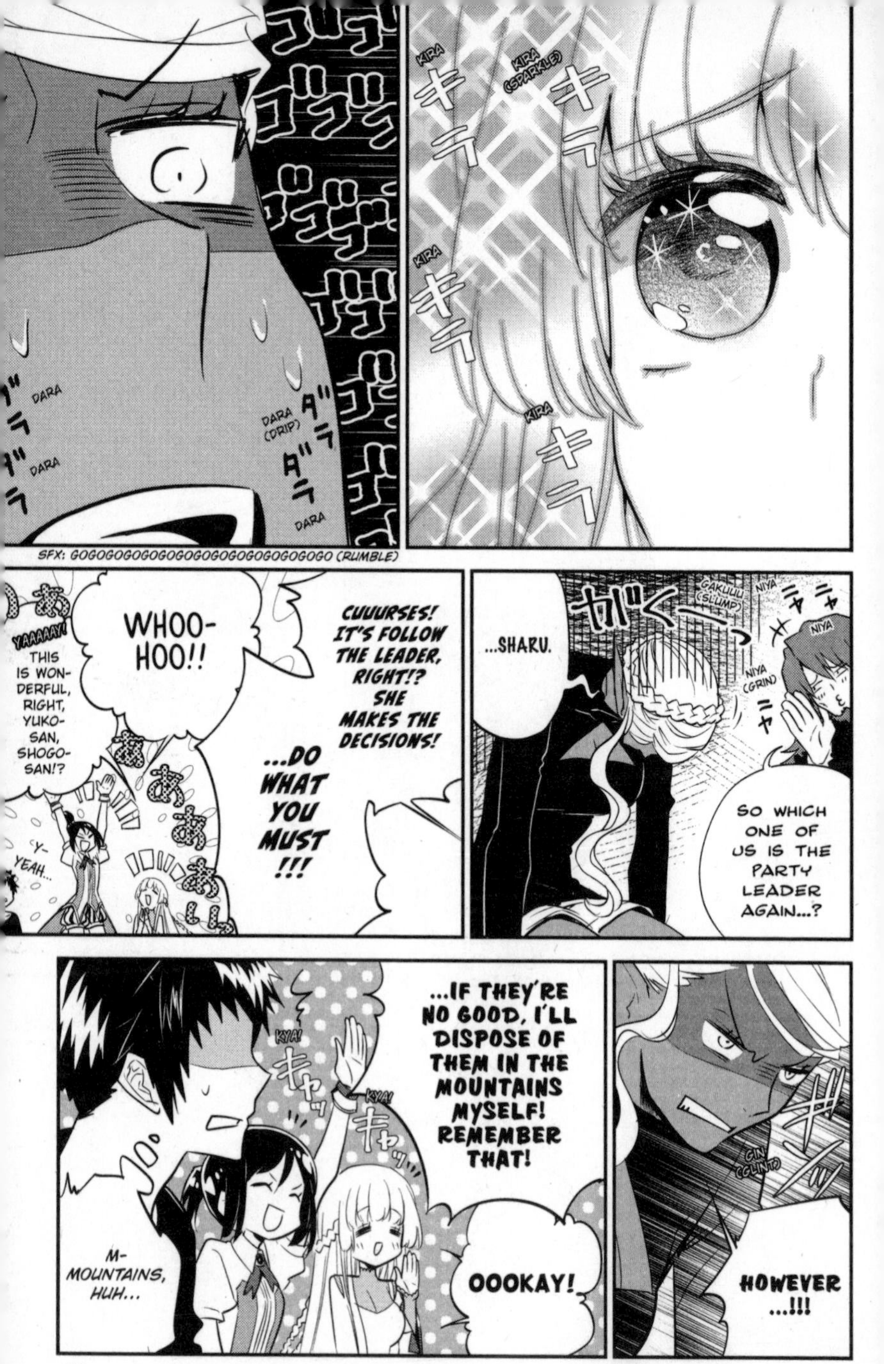
KIRA
KIRA (SPARKLE)
KIRA
KIRA
DARA (DRIP)
DARA
DARA
DARA
SFX: GOGOGOGOGOGOGOGOGOGOGOGOGOGOGO (RUMBLE)
NIYA
NIYA
NIYA (GRIN)
GAKUUU (SLUMP)
...SHARU.
SO WHICH ONE OF US IS THE PARTY LEADER AGAIN...?
CUUURSES! IT'S FOLLOW THE LEADER, RIGHT!? SHE MAKES THE DECISIONS!
...DO WHAT YOU MUST!!!
WHOO-HOO!!
YAAAAAY! THIS IS WONDERFUL, RIGHT, YUKO-SAN, SHOGO-SAN!?
Y-YEAH...
GIN (GLINT)
HOWEVER ...!!!
...IF THEY'RE NO GOOD, I'LL DISPOSE OF THEM IN THE MOUNTAINS MYSELF! REMEMBER THAT!
KYA!
KYA!
OOOKAY!
M-MOUNTAINS, HUH...

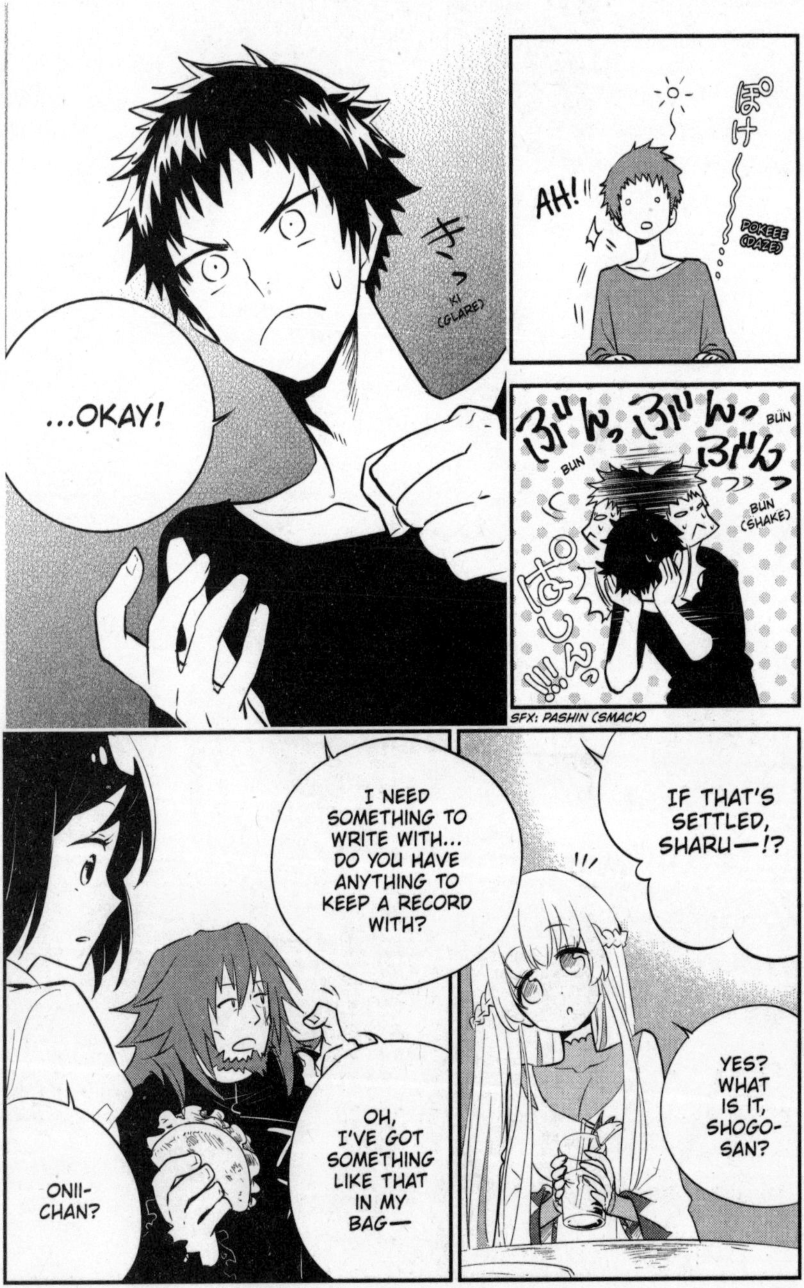
ぽけ〜〜
POKEEE (DAZE)
AH!!
ぶんっぶんっぶんっ
BUN
BUN
BUN (SHAKE)
ぱしんっ!!!
SFX: PASHIN (SMACK)
きっ
KI (GLARE)
...OKAY!
IF THAT'S SETTLED, SHARU—!?
!!!
YES? WHAT IS IT, SHOGO-SAN?
I NEED SOMETHING TO WRITE WITH... DO YOU HAVE ANYTHING TO KEEP A RECORD WITH?
OH, I'VE GOT SOMETHING LIKE THAT IN MY BAG—
ONII-CHAN?

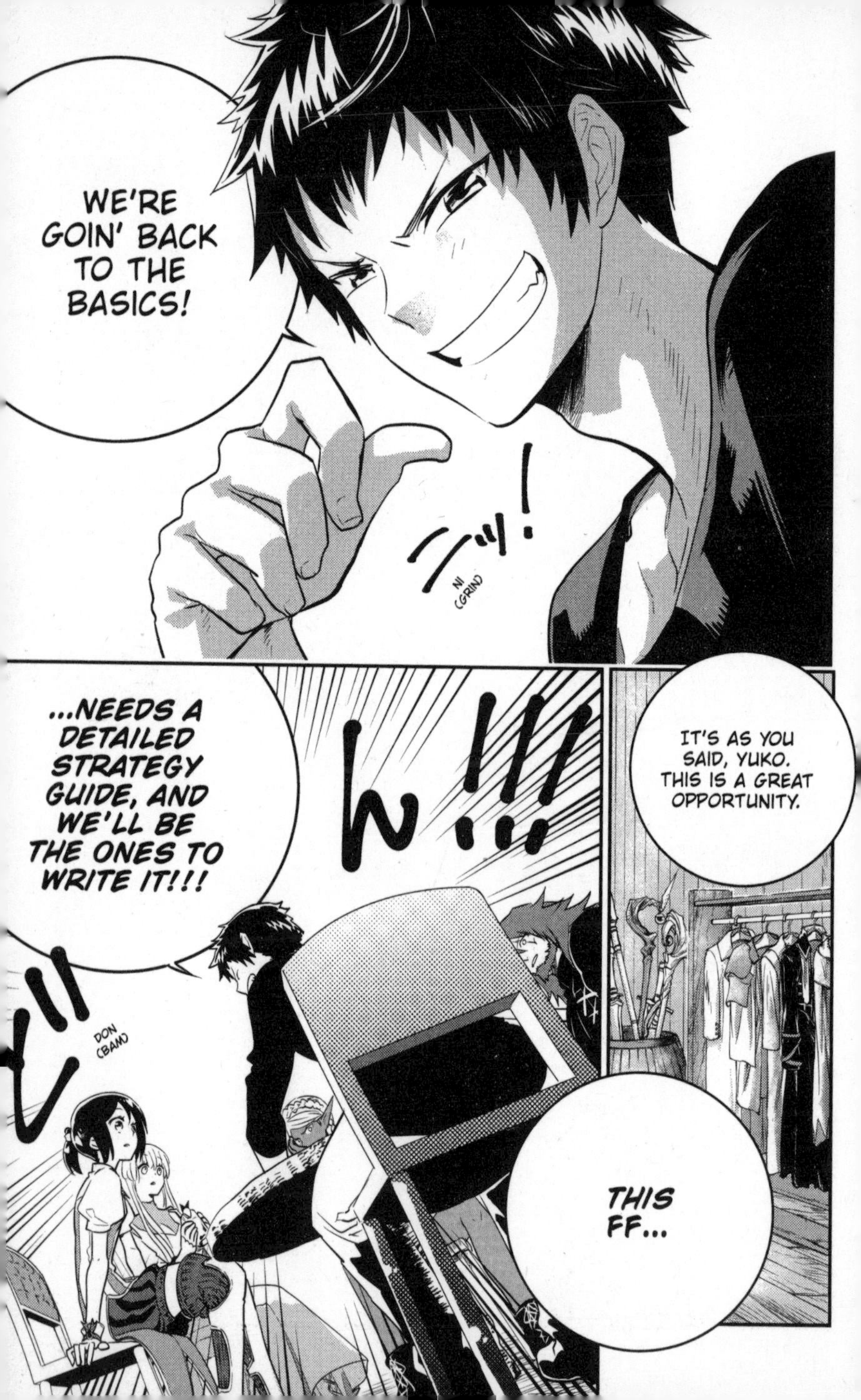
WE'RE GOIN' BACK TO THE BASICS!
NI (GRIND)
IT'S AS YOU SAID, YUKO. THIS IS A GREAT OPPORTUNITY.
THIS FF...
...NEEDS A DETAILED STRATEGY GUIDE, AND WE'LL BE THE ONES TO WRITE IT!!!
DON (BAM)

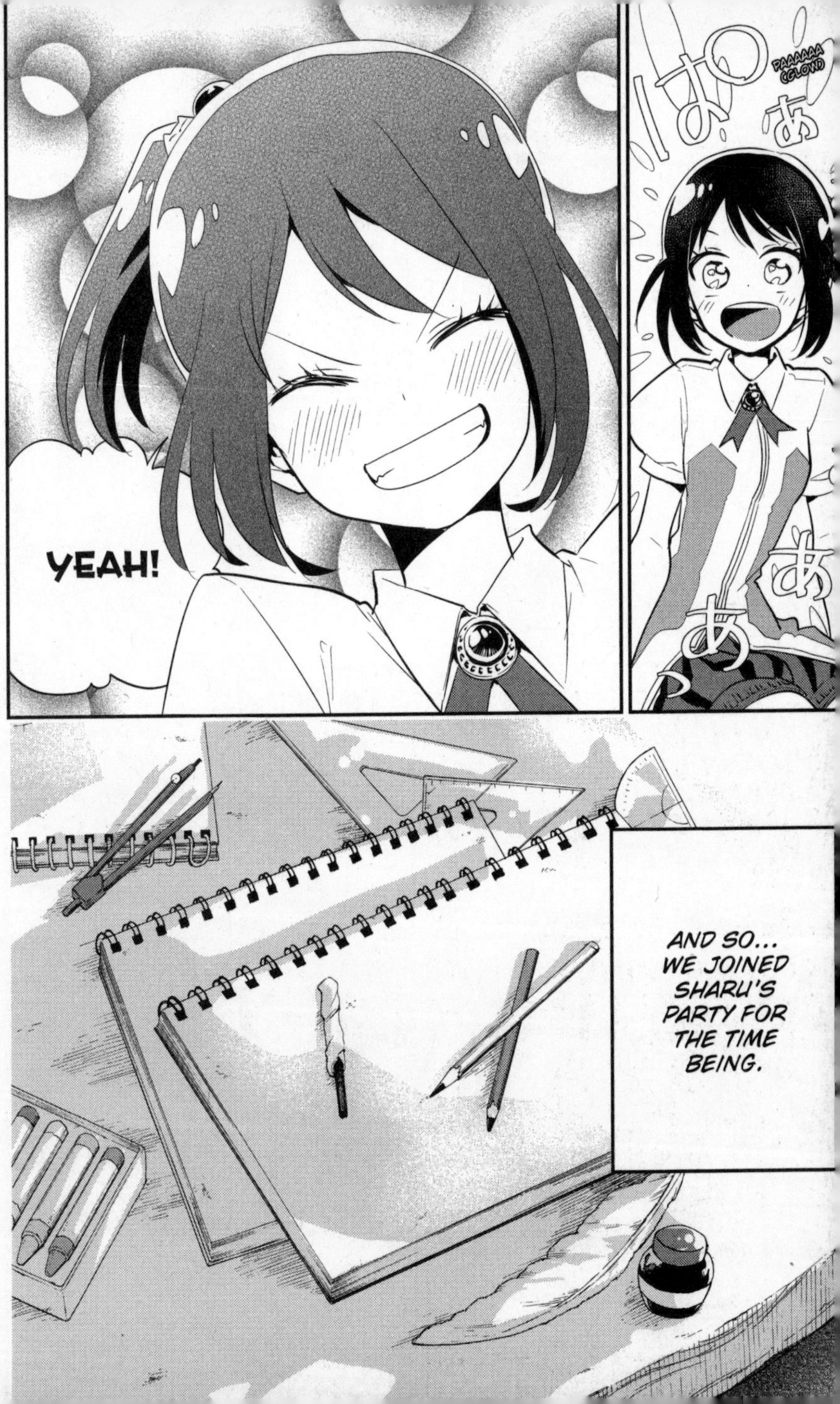
PAAAAAA (GLOW)
YEAH!
AND SO... WE JOINED SHARU'S PARTY FOR THE TIME BEING.

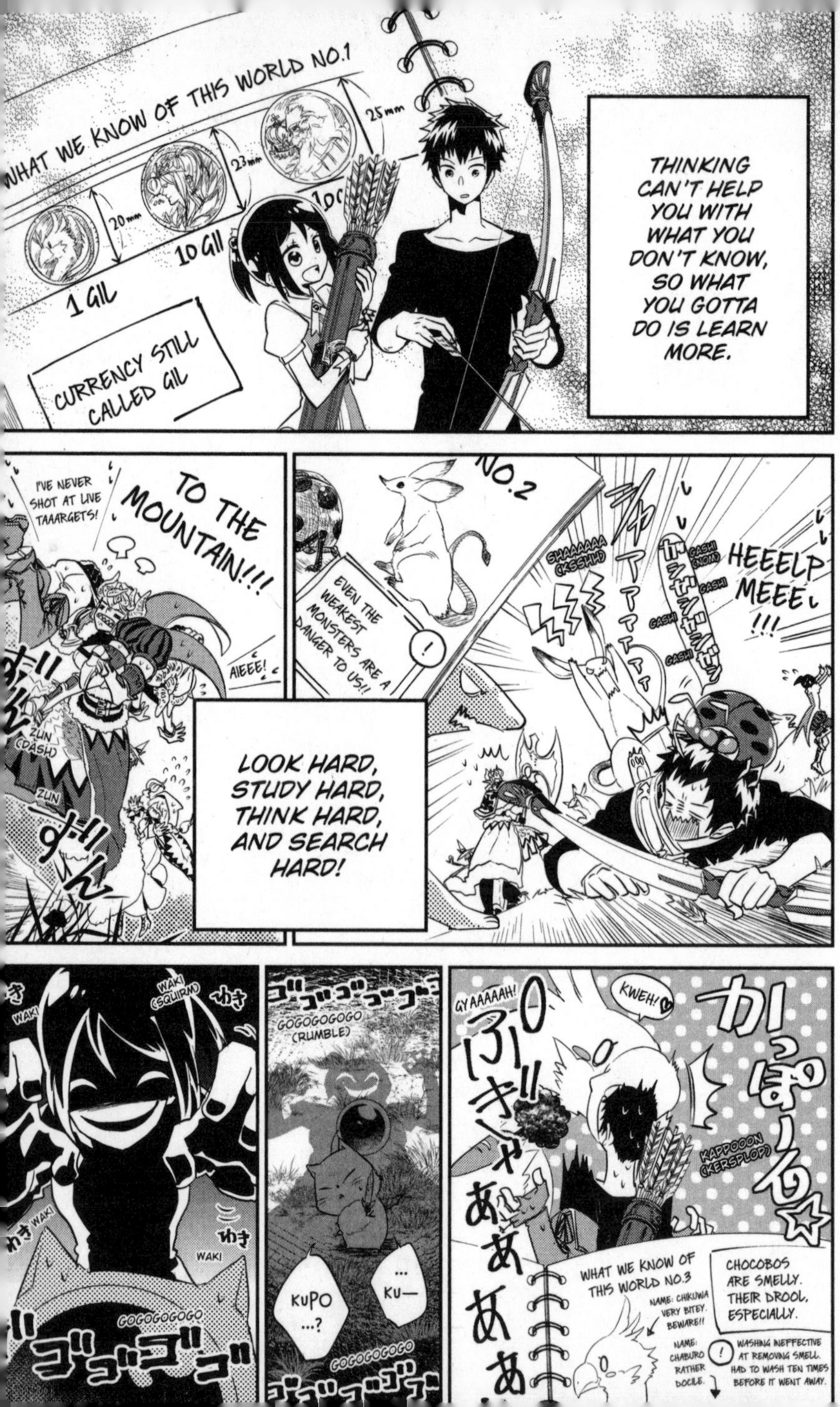
THINKING CAN'T HELP YOU WITH WHAT YOU DON'T KNOW, SO WHAT YOU GOTTA DO IS LEARN MORE.
WHAT WE KNOW OF THIS WORLD NO.1
25mm
23mm
20mm
10 GIL
1 GIL
CURRENCY STILL CALLED GIL
NO.2
HEEELP MEEE!!!
GASHI (NOM)
GASHI
GASHI
GASHI
SHAAAAAA (KSSHHH)
EVEN THE WEAKEST MONSTERS ARE A DANGER TO US!!
!
LOOK HARD, STUDY HARD, THINK HARD, AND SEARCH HARD!
TO THE MOUNTAIN!!!
I'VE NEVER SHOT AT LIVE TAAARGETS!
AIEEE!
ZUN (DASH)
ZUN
KWEH!♡
GYAAAAAH!
KAPPOOON (KERSPLOP)
CHOCOBOS ARE SMELLY. THEIR DROOL, ESPECIALLY.
WHAT WE KNOW OF THIS WORLD NO.3
NAME: CHIKUWA VERY BITEY. BEWARE!!
NAME: CHABURO RATHER DOCILE.
WASHING INEFFECTIVE AT REMOVING SMELL. HAD TO WASH TEN TIMES BEFORE IT WENT AWAY.
GOGOGOGOGO (RUMBLE)
...KU—
KUPO...?
GOGOGOGOGO
WAKI (SQUIRM)
WAKI
WAKI
WAKI
GOGOGOGOGO

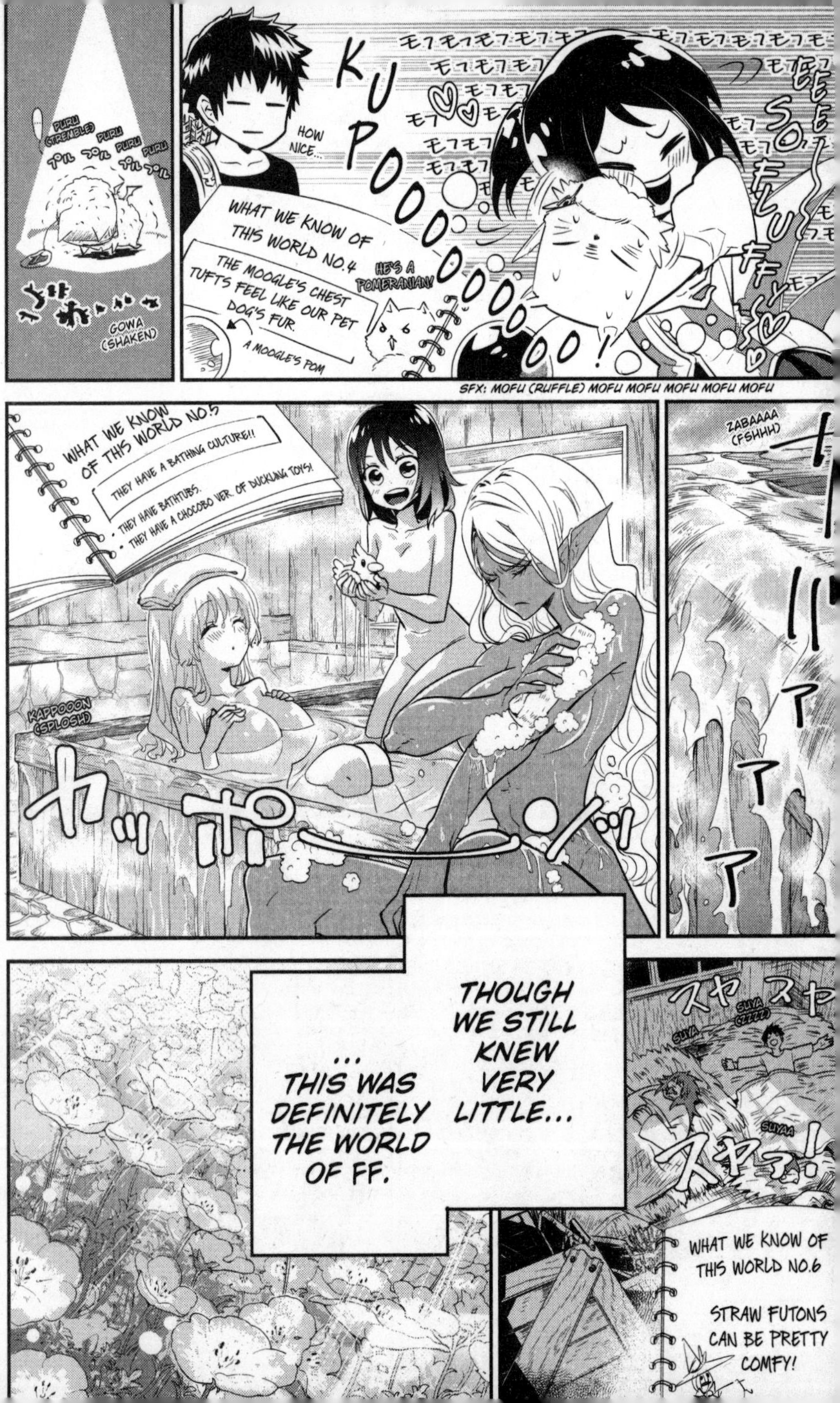
KUPOOOOOOOOOOOO!
SO FLUFFY~!
HOW NICE...
WHAT WE KNOW OF THIS WORLD NO.4
THE MOOGLE'S CHEST TUFTS FEEL LIKE OUR PET DOG'S FUR.
HE'S A POMERANIAN!
A MOOGLE'S POM
PURU (TREMBLE) PURU PURU PURU
GOWA (SHAKEN)
SFX: MOFU (RUFFLE) MOFU MOFU MOFU MOFU MOFU
ZABAAAA (FSHHH)
WHAT WE KNOW OF THIS WORLD NO.5
THEY HAVE A BATHING CULTURE!!
• THEY HAVE BATHTUBS.
• THEY HAVE A CHOCOBO VER. OF DUCKLING TOYS!
KAPPOOON (SPLOSH)
SUYA (ZZZZ) SUYA SUYAA
WHAT WE KNOW OF THIS WORLD NO.6
STRAW FUTONS CAN BE PRETTY COMFY!
THOUGH WE STILL KNEW VERY LITTLE...
...THIS WAS DEFINITELY THE WORLD OF FF.

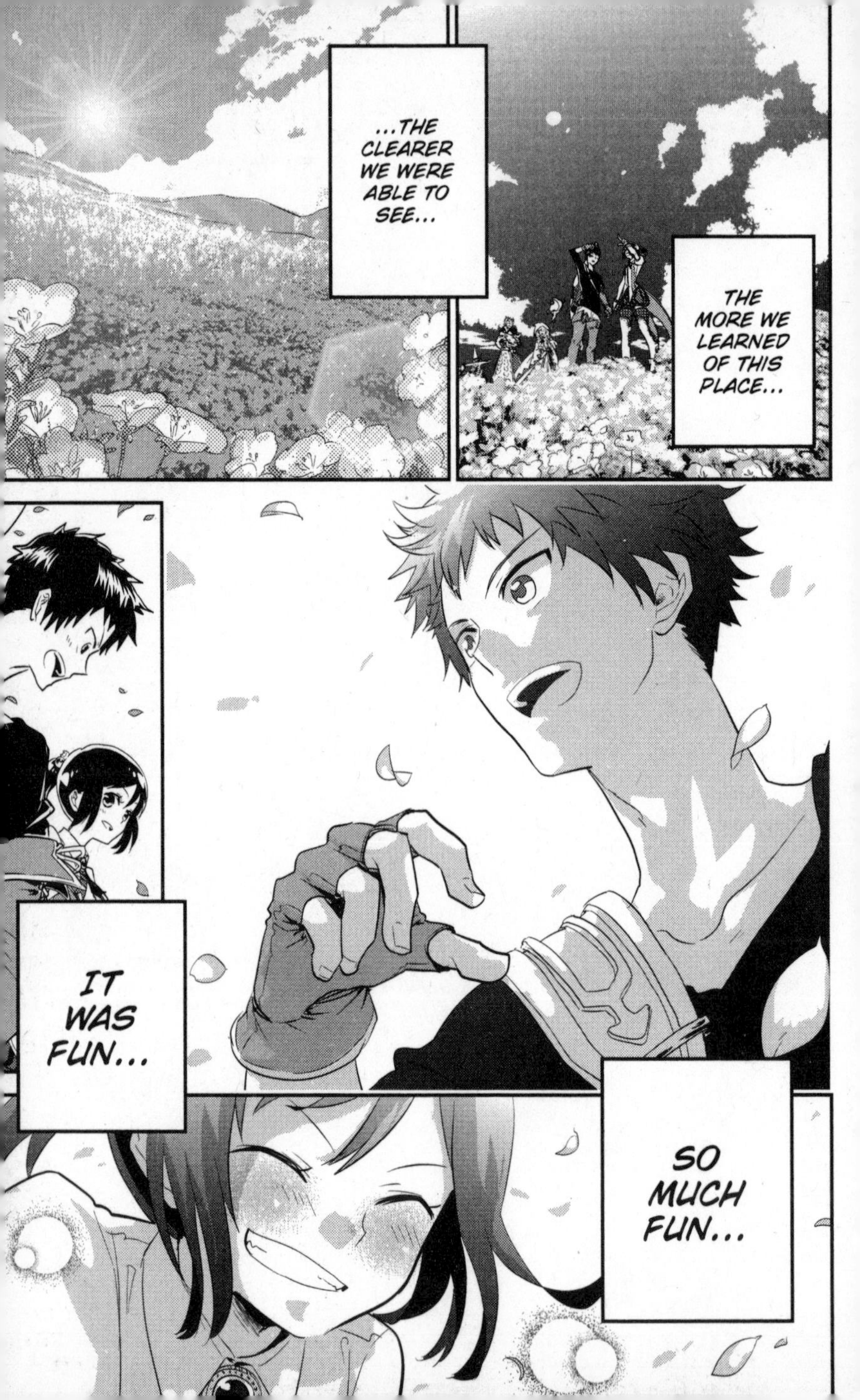
THE MORE WE LEARNED OF THIS PLACE...
...THE CLEARER WE WERE ABLE TO SEE...
IT WAS FUN...
SO MUCH FUN...

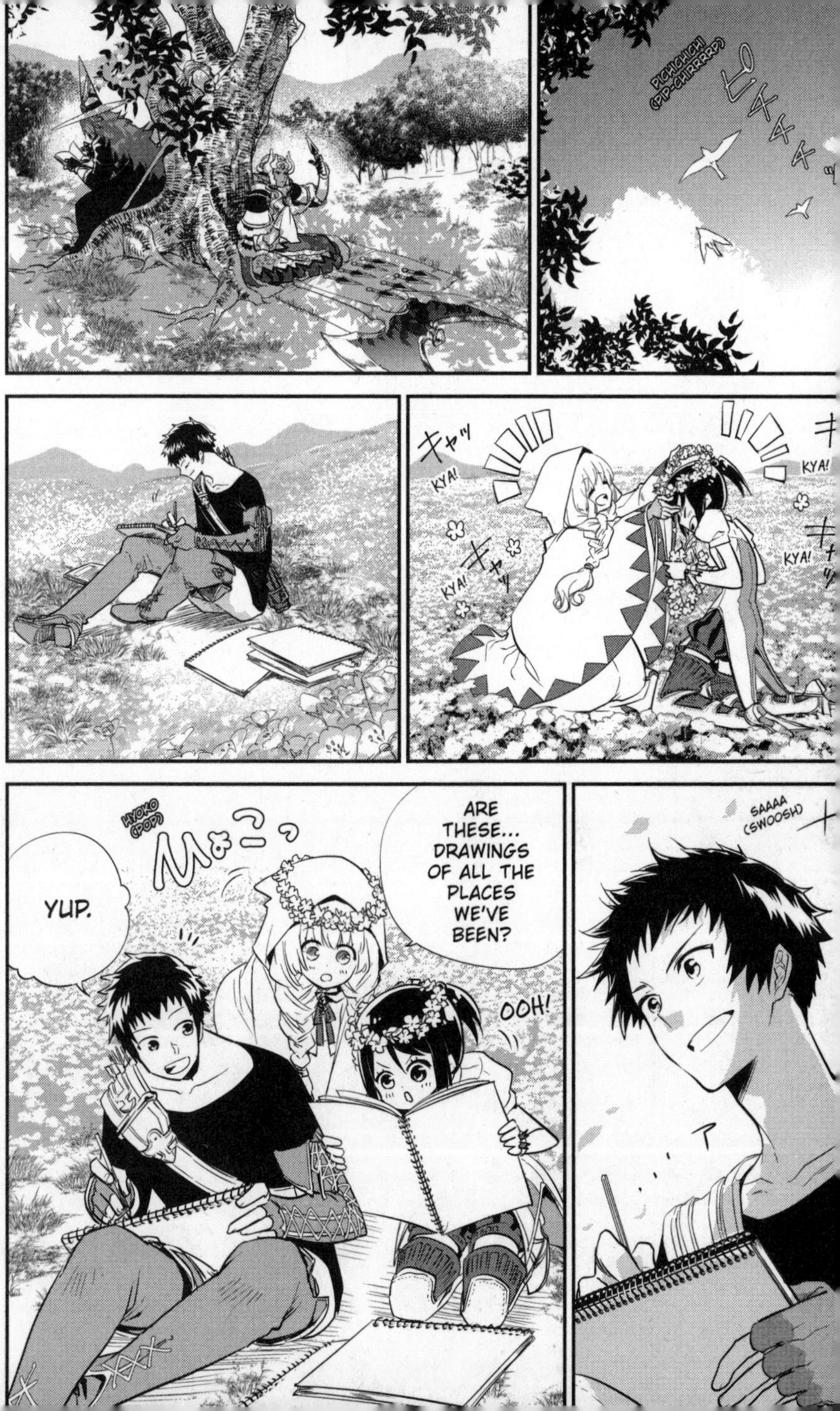
PICHICHICHI (PIP-CHIRRRRP)
KYA!
KYA!
KYA!
KYA!
SAAAA (SWOOSH)
ARE THESE... DRAWINGS OF ALL THE PLACES WE'VE BEEN?
HYOKO (POP)
YUP.
OOH!

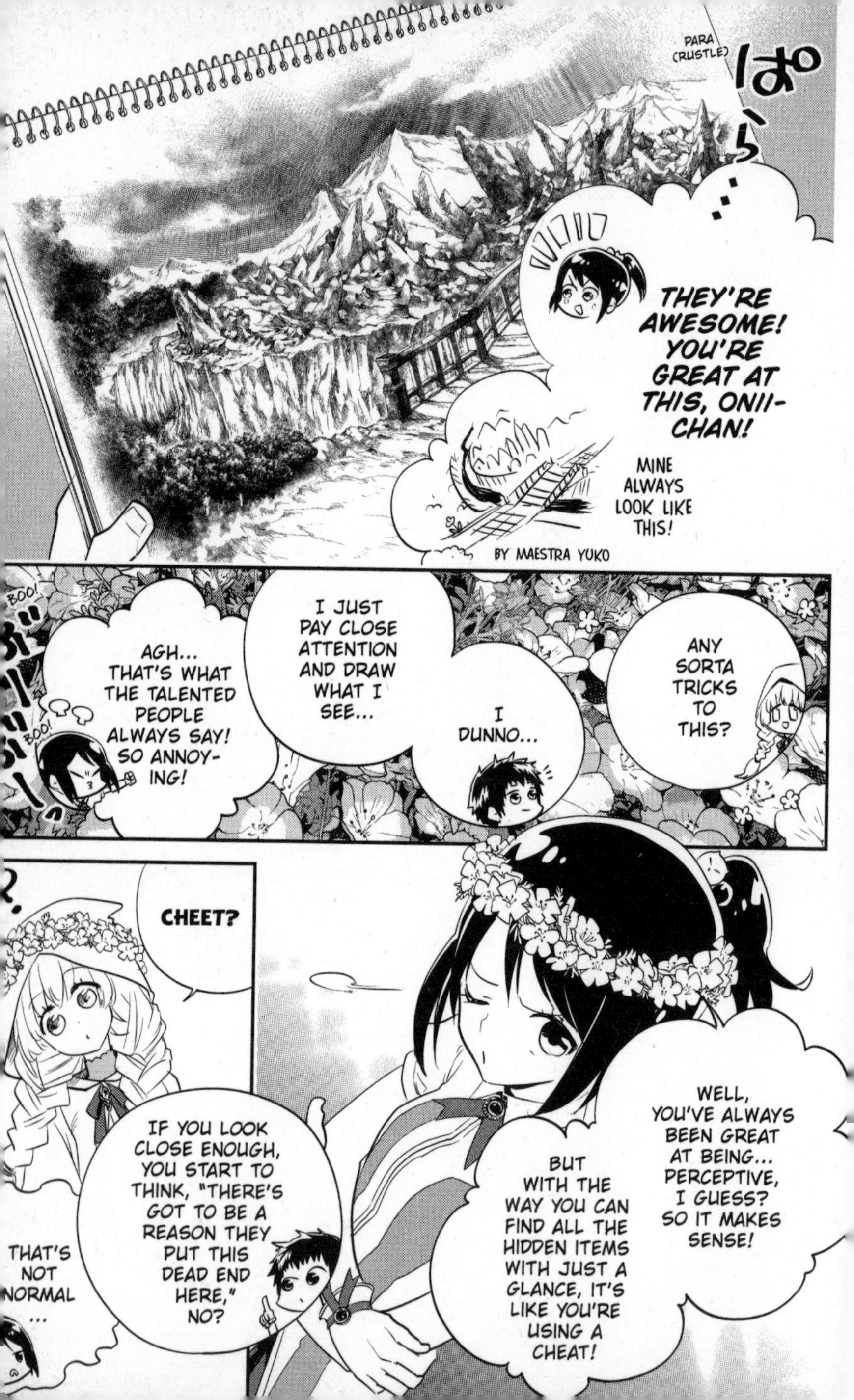
PARA (RUSTLE)
THEY'RE AWESOME! YOU'RE GREAT AT THIS, ONII-CHAN!
MINE ALWAYS LOOK LIKE THIS!
BY MAESTRA YUKO
ANY SORTA TRICKS TO THIS?
I DUNNO...
I JUST PAY CLOSE ATTENTION AND DRAW WHAT I SEE...
AGH... THAT'S WHAT THE TALENTED PEOPLE ALWAYS SAY! SO ANNOYING!
BOO!
BOO!
WELL, YOU'VE ALWAYS BEEN GREAT AT BEING... PERCEPTIVE, I GUESS? SO IT MAKES SENSE!
BUT WITH THE WAY YOU CAN FIND ALL THE HIDDEN ITEMS WITH JUST A GLANCE, IT'S LIKE YOU'RE USING A CHEAT!
CHEET?
IF YOU LOOK CLOSE ENOUGH, YOU START TO THINK, "THERE'S GOT TO BE A REASON THEY PUT THIS DEAD END HERE," NO?
THAT'S NOT NORMAL...

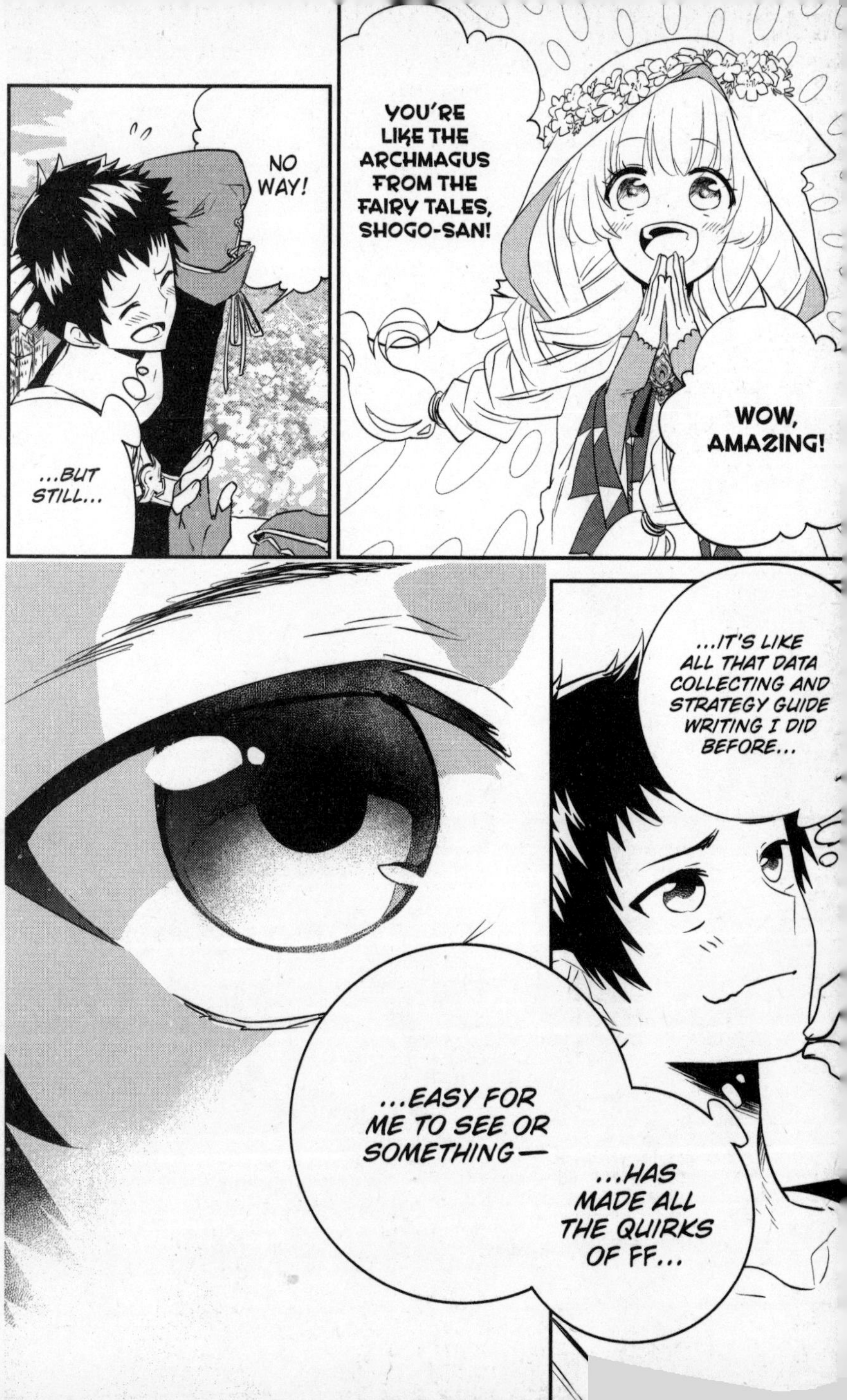
WOW, AMAZING!
YOU'RE LIKE THE ARCHMAGUS FROM THE FAIRY TALES, SHOGO-SAN!
NO WAY!
...BUT STILL...
...IT'S LIKE ALL THAT DATA COLLECTING AND STRATEGY GUIDE WRITING I DID BEFORE...
...HAS MADE ALL THE QUIRKS OF FF...
...EASY FOR ME TO SEE OR SOMETHING—

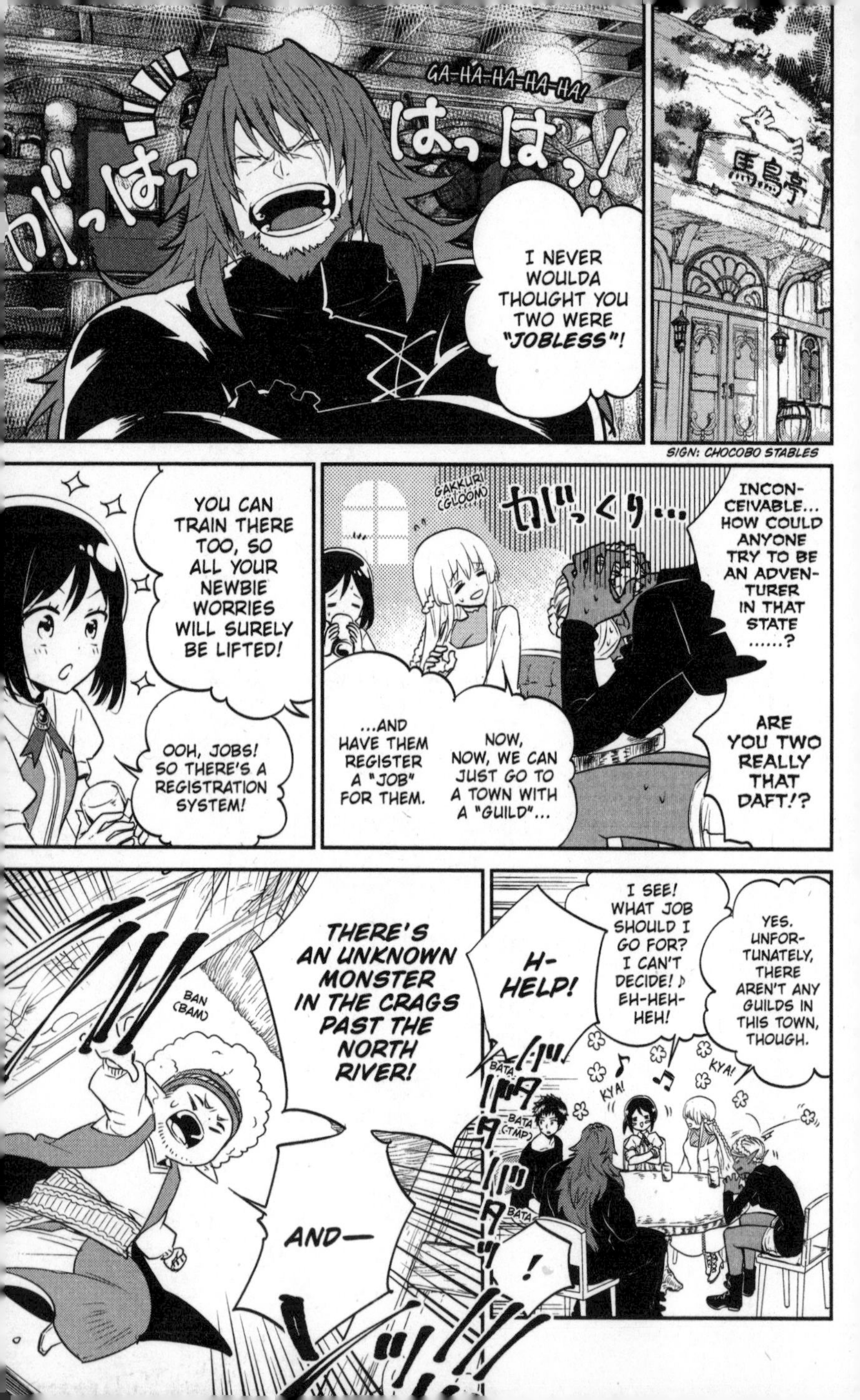
馬鳥亭
SIGN: CHOCOBO STABLES
GA-HA-HA-HA-HA!
がっはっはっはっ!
I NEVER WOULDA THOUGHT YOU TWO WERE "JOBLESS"!
INCONCEIVABLE... HOW COULD ANYONE TRY TO BE AN ADVENTURER IN THAT STATE ......?
ARE YOU TWO REALLY THAT DAFT!?
GAKKURI (GLOOM)
ガっくり...
NOW, NOW, WE CAN JUST GO TO A TOWN WITH A "GUILD"...
...AND HAVE THEM REGISTER A "JOB" FOR THEM.
YOU CAN TRAIN THERE TOO, SO ALL YOUR NEWBIE WORRIES WILL SURELY BE LIFTED!
OOH, JOBS! SO THERE'S A REGISTRATION SYSTEM!
YES. UNFORTUNATELY, THERE AREN'T ANY GUILDS IN THIS TOWN, THOUGH.
I SEE! WHAT JOB SHOULD I GO FOR? I CAN'T DECIDE! ♪ EH-HEH-HEH!
KYA!
KYA!
H-HELP!
BATA
BATA (TMP)
BATA
!
THERE'S AN UNKNOWN MONSTER IN THE CRAGS PAST THE NORTH RIVER!
AND—
BAN (BAM)

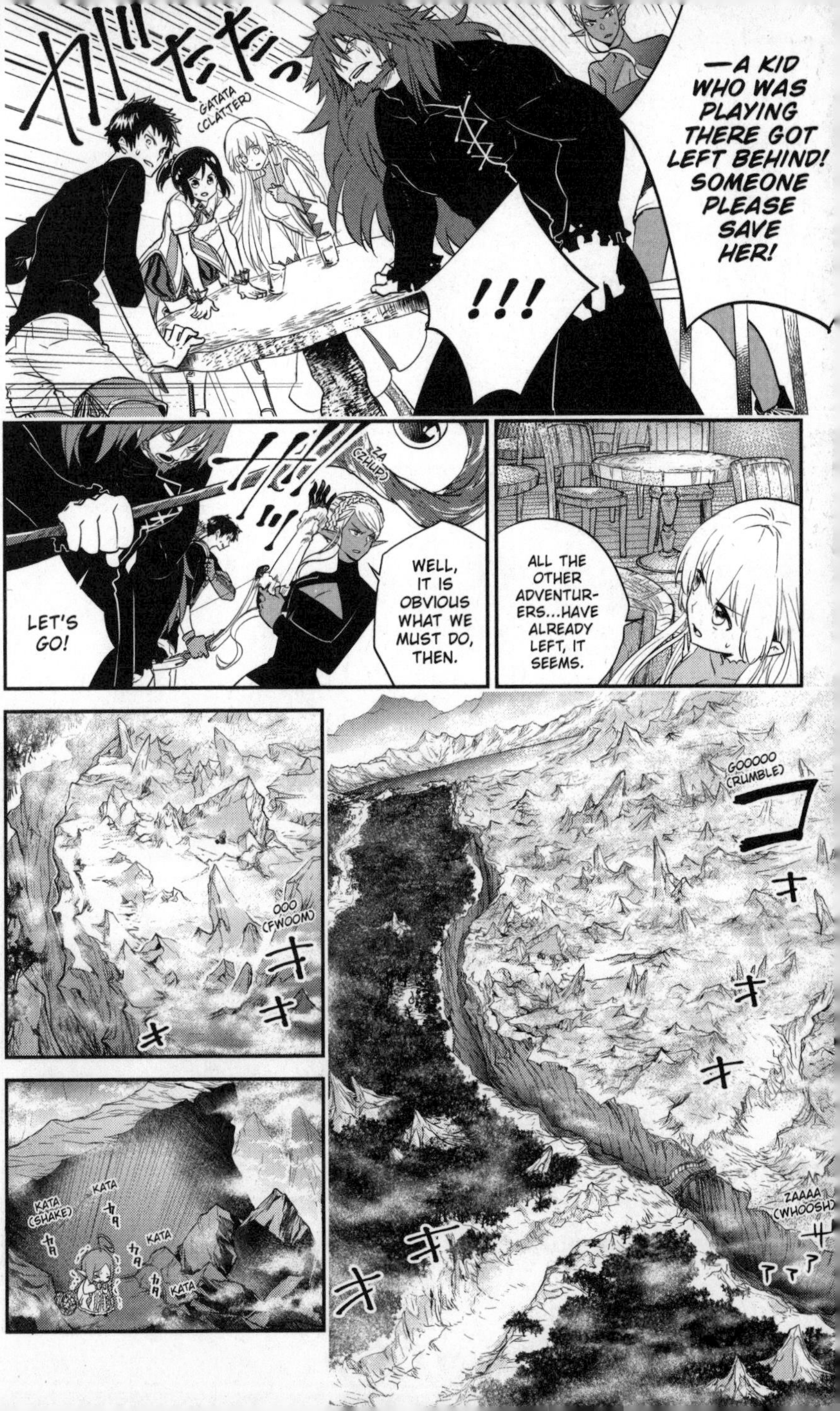
—A KID WHO WAS PLAYING THERE GOT LEFT BEHIND! SOMEONE PLEASE SAVE HER!
GATATA (CLATTER)
!!!
ALL THE OTHER ADVENTURERS...HAVE ALREADY LEFT, IT SEEMS.
ZA (ZHUP)
WELL, IT IS OBVIOUS WHAT WE MUST DO, THEN.
LET'S GO!
GOOOOO (RUMBLE)
ZAAAA (WHOOSH)
OOO (FWOOM)
KATA
KATA (SHAKE)
KATA
KATA

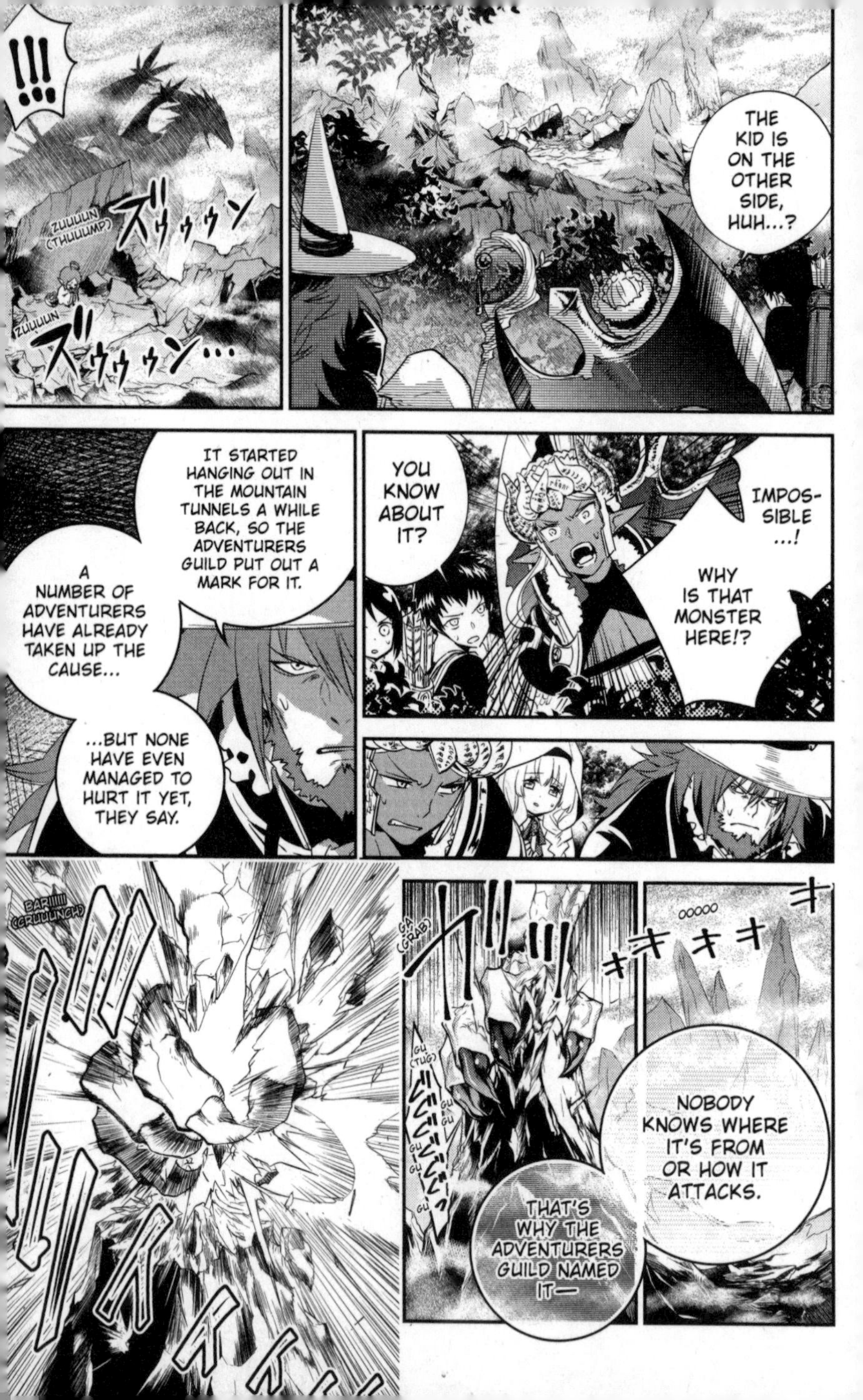
THE KID IS ON THE OTHER SIDE, HUH...?
!!!
ZUUUUN (THUUUMP)
ズゥゥゥン
ZUUUUN
ズゥゥゥン…
IMPOSSIBLE...!
WHY IS THAT MONSTER HERE!?
YOU KNOW ABOUT IT?
IT STARTED HANGING OUT IN THE MOUNTAIN TUNNELS A WHILE BACK, SO THE ADVENTURERS GUILD PUT OUT A MARK FOR IT.
A NUMBER OF ADVENTURERS HAVE ALREADY TAKEN UP THE CAUSE...
...BUT NONE HAVE EVEN MANAGED TO HURT IT YET, THEY SAY.
OOOOO
NOBODY KNOWS WHERE IT'S FROM OR HOW IT ATTACKS.
GA (GRAB)
GU (TUG)
GU
GU
GU
GU
THAT'S WHY THE ADVENTURERS GUILD NAMED IT—
BARIIIII (CRUUUNCH)

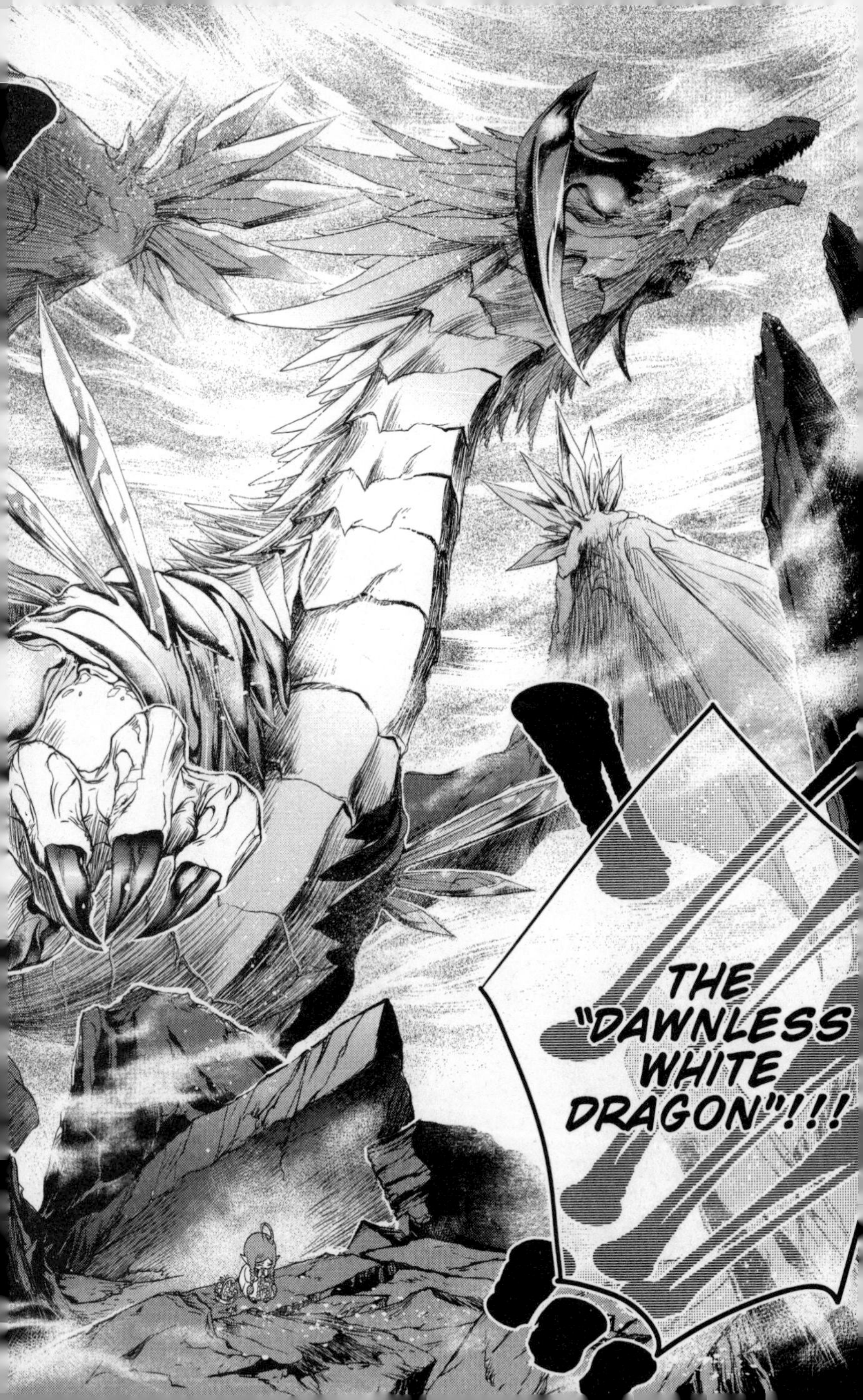
THE "DAWNLESS WHITE DRAGON"!!!

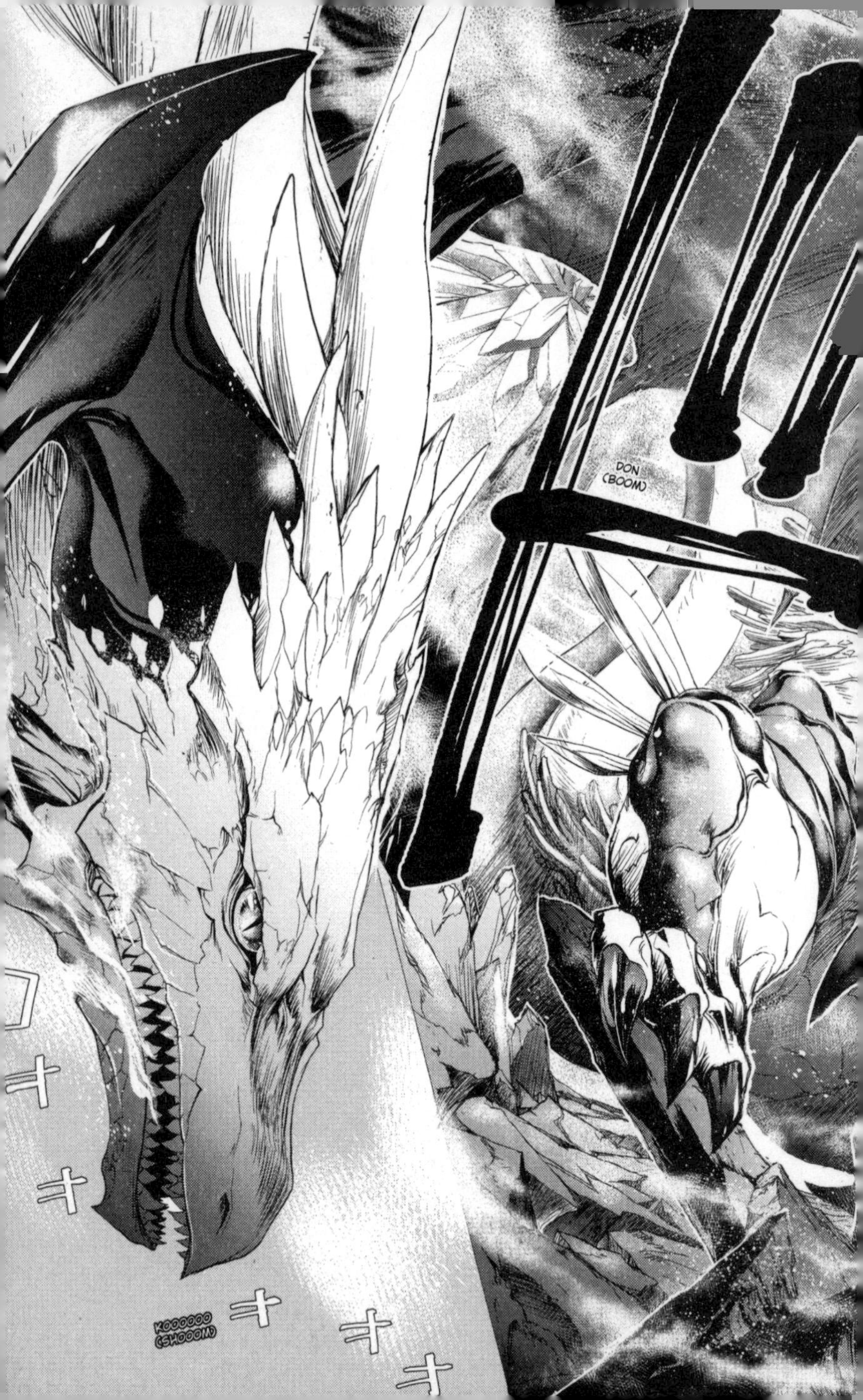
DON (BOOM)
KOOOOOO (SHOOOM)

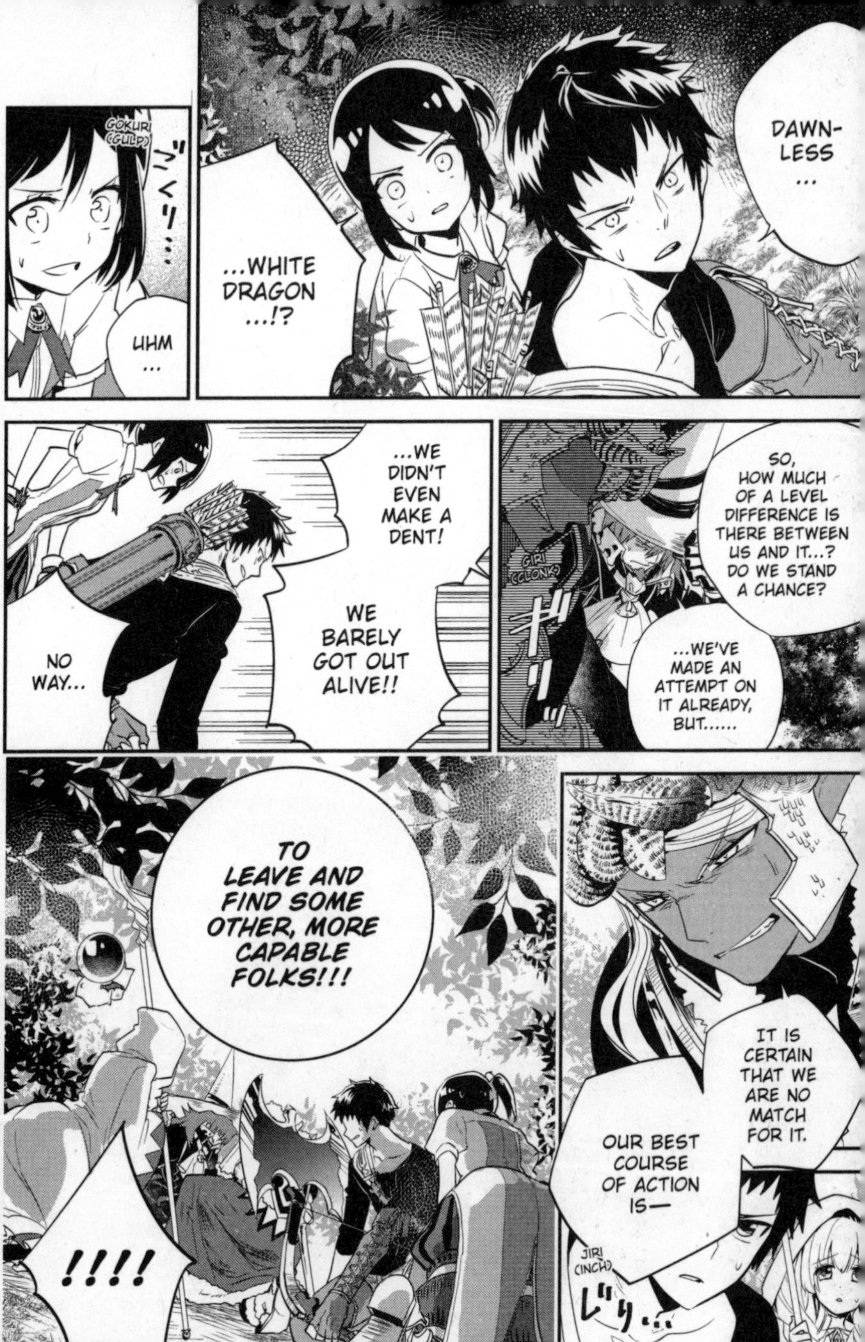
DAWN-LESS …
…WHITE DRAGON …!?
GOKURI (GULP)
ゴクリ…
UHM …
SO, HOW MUCH OF A LEVEL DIFFERENCE IS THERE BETWEEN US AND IT…? DO WE STAND A CHANCE?
GIRI (CLONK)
ギリ
…WE'VE MADE AN ATTEMPT ON IT ALREADY, BUT……
…WE DIDN'T EVEN MAKE A DENT!
WE BARELY GOT OUT ALIVE!!
NO WAY…
IT IS CERTAIN THAT WE ARE NO MATCH FOR IT.
OUR BEST COURSE OF ACTION IS—
JIRI (CINCH)
ジリ…
TO LEAVE AND FIND SOME OTHER, MORE CAPABLE FOLKS!!!
!!!!

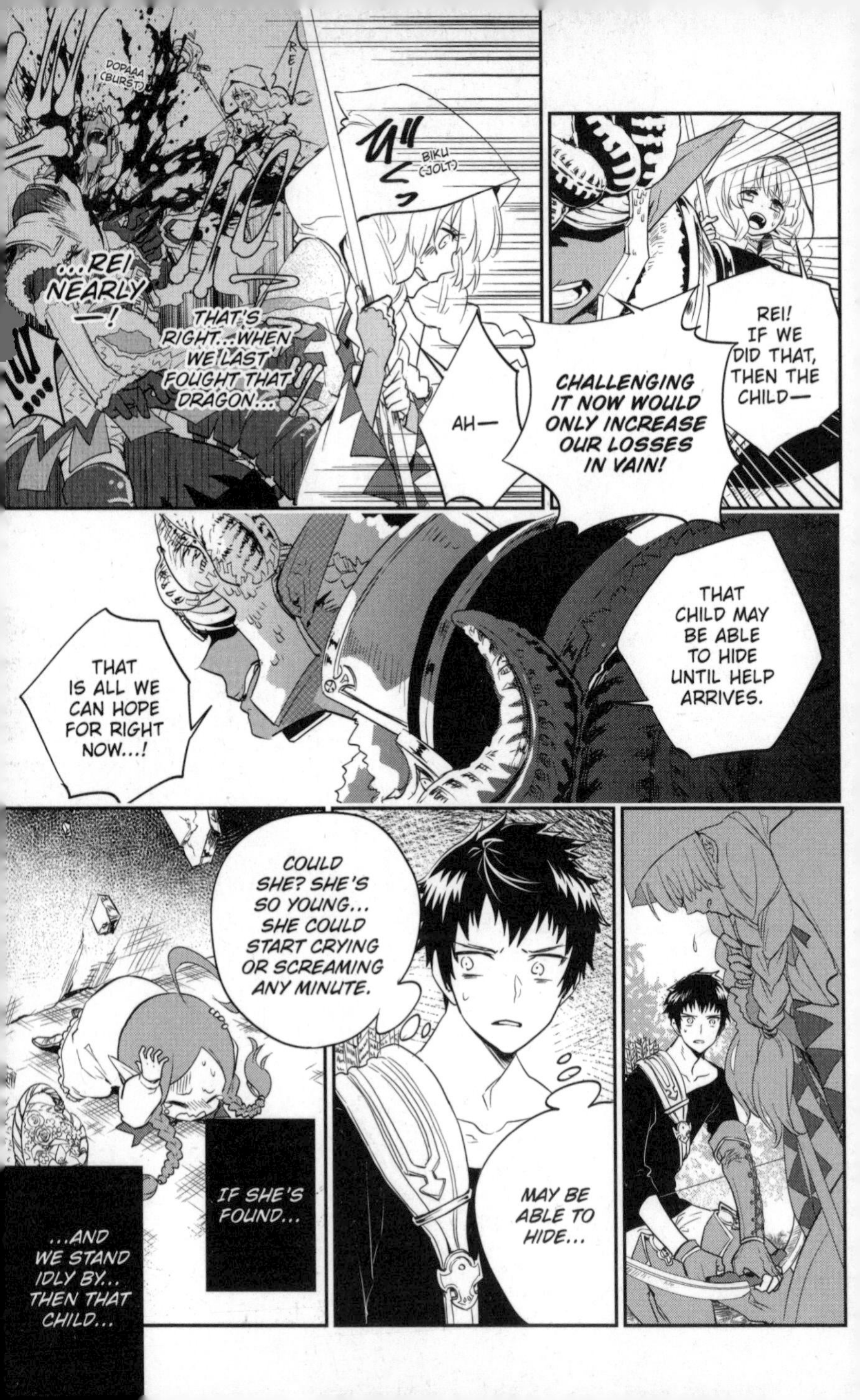
REI! IF WE DID THAT, THEN THE CHILD—
CHALLENGING IT NOW WOULD ONLY INCREASE OUR LOSSES IN VAIN!
AH—
BIKU (-JOLT-)
THAT'S RIGHT... WHEN WE LAST FOUGHT THAT DRAGON...
REI!
DOPAAA (BURST)
...REI NEARLY—!
THAT CHILD MAY BE ABLE TO HIDE UNTIL HELP ARRIVES.
THAT IS ALL WE CAN HOPE FOR RIGHT NOW...!
MAY BE ABLE TO HIDE...
COULD SHE? SHE'S SO YOUNG... SHE COULD START CRYING OR SCREAMING ANY MINUTE.
IF SHE'S FOUND...
...AND WE STAND IDLY BY... THEN THAT CHILD...

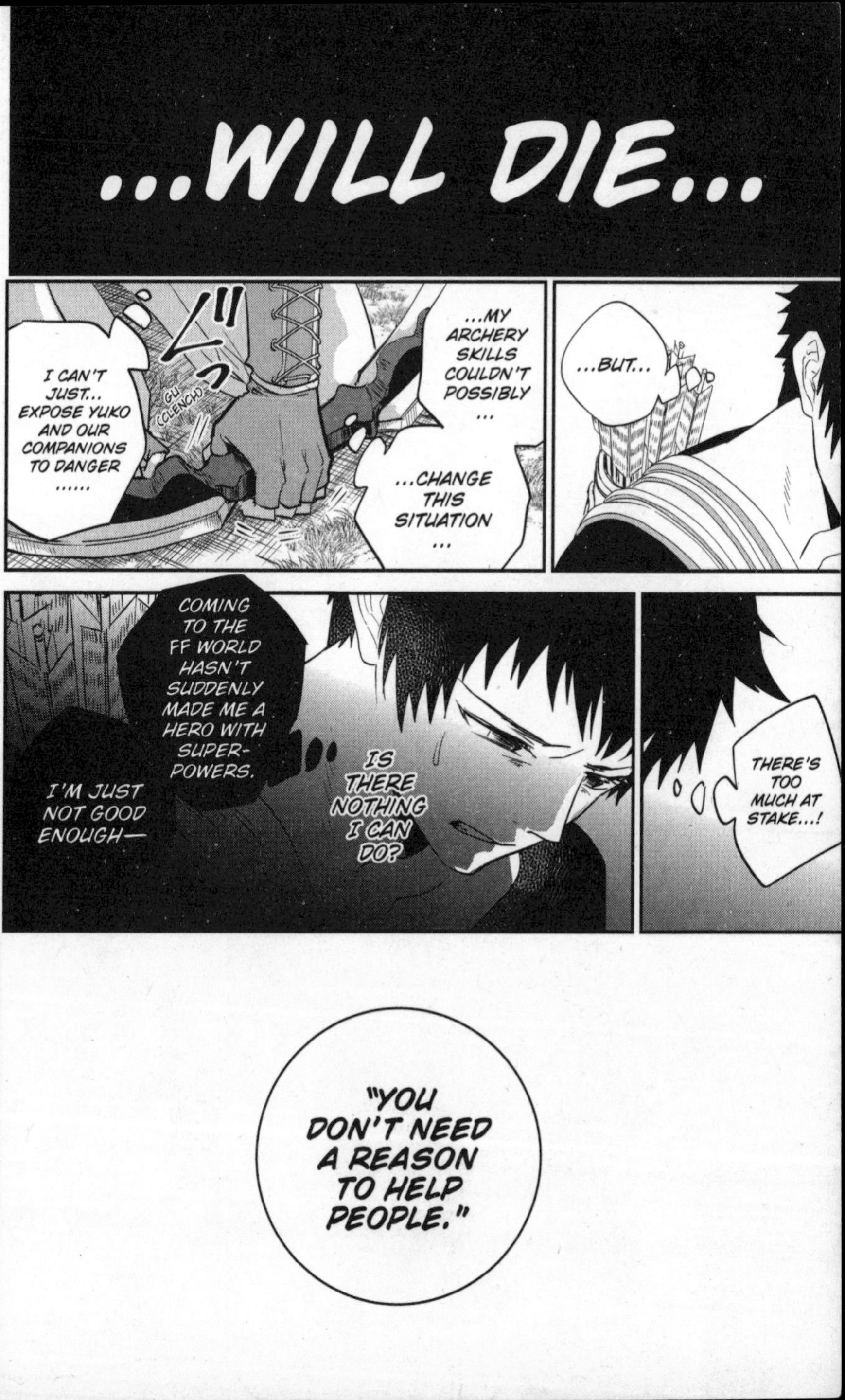
...WILL DIE...
...BUT...
...MY ARCHERY SKILLS COULDN'T POSSIBLY ...
...CHANGE THIS SITUATION ...
GU (CLENCH)
I CAN'T JUST... EXPOSE YUKO AND OUR COMPANIONS TO DANGER ......
THERE'S TOO MUCH AT STAKE...!
COMING TO THE FF WORLD HASN'T SUDDENLY MADE ME A HERO WITH SUPER-POWERS.
IS THERE NOTHING I CAN DO?
I'M JUST NOT GOOD ENOUGH—
"YOU DON'T NEED A REASON TO HELP PEOPLE."

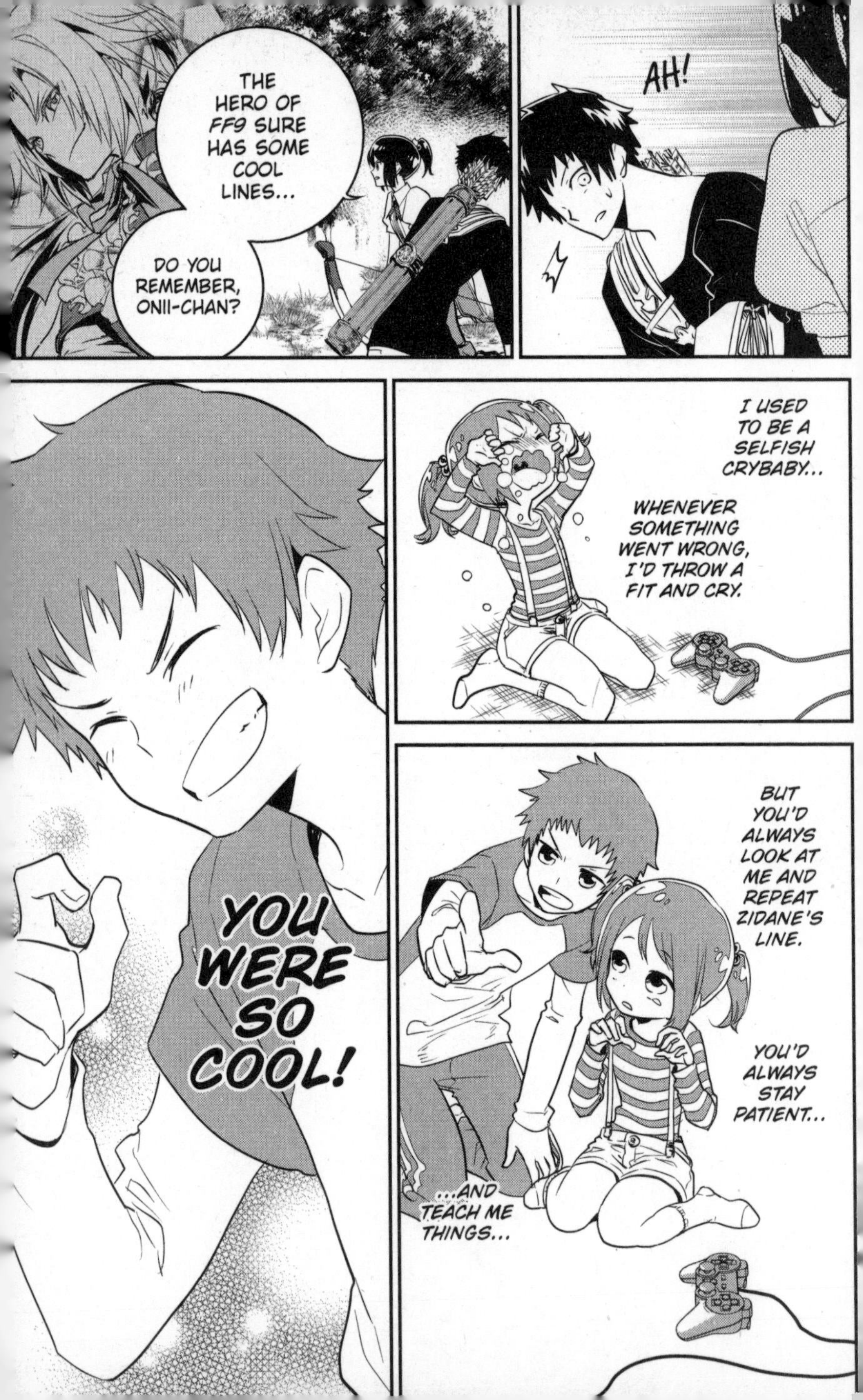
AH!
THE HERO OF FF9 SURE HAS SOME COOL LINES...
DO YOU REMEMBER, ONII-CHAN?
I USED TO BE A SELFISH CRYBABY...
WHENEVER SOMETHING WENT WRONG, I'D THROW A FIT AND CRY.
BUT YOU'D ALWAYS LOOK AT ME AND REPEAT ZIDANE'S LINE.
YOU'D ALWAYS STAY PATIENT...
...AND TEACH ME THINGS...
YOU WERE SO COOL!

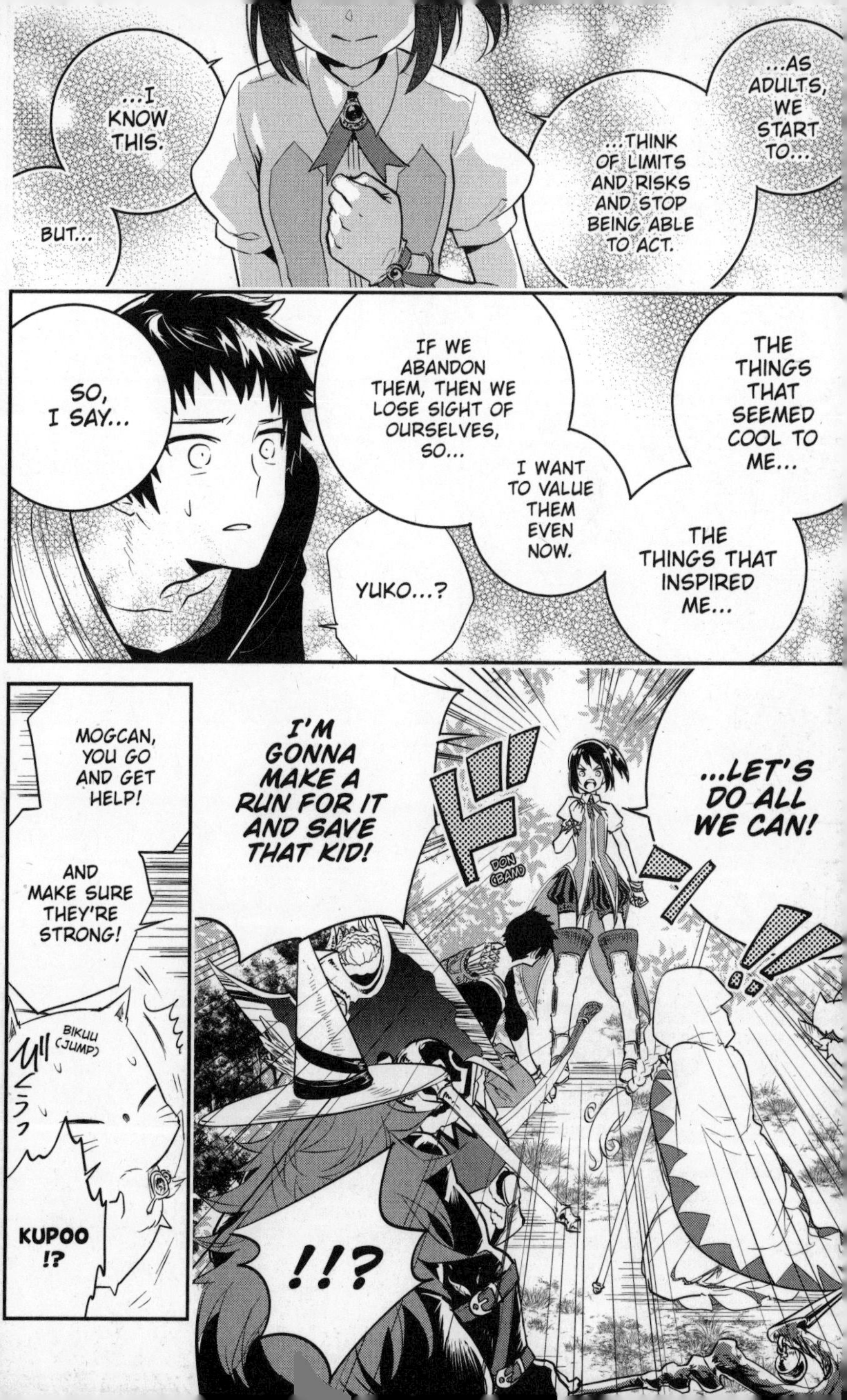
...AS ADULTS, WE START TO...
...THINK OF LIMITS AND RISKS AND STOP BEING ABLE TO ACT.
...I KNOW THIS.
BUT...
THE THINGS THAT SEEMED COOL TO ME...
THE THINGS THAT INSPIRED ME...
IF WE ABANDON THEM, THEN WE LOSE SIGHT OF OURSELVES, SO...
I WANT TO VALUE THEM EVEN NOW.
SO, I SAY...
YUKO...?
...LET'S DO ALL WE CAN!
!!
DON (BAM)
I'M GONNA MAKE A RUN FOR IT AND SAVE THAT KID!
!!?
MOGCAN, YOU GO AND GET HELP!
AND MAKE SURE THEY'RE STRONG!
BIKUU (JUMP)
KUPOO !?

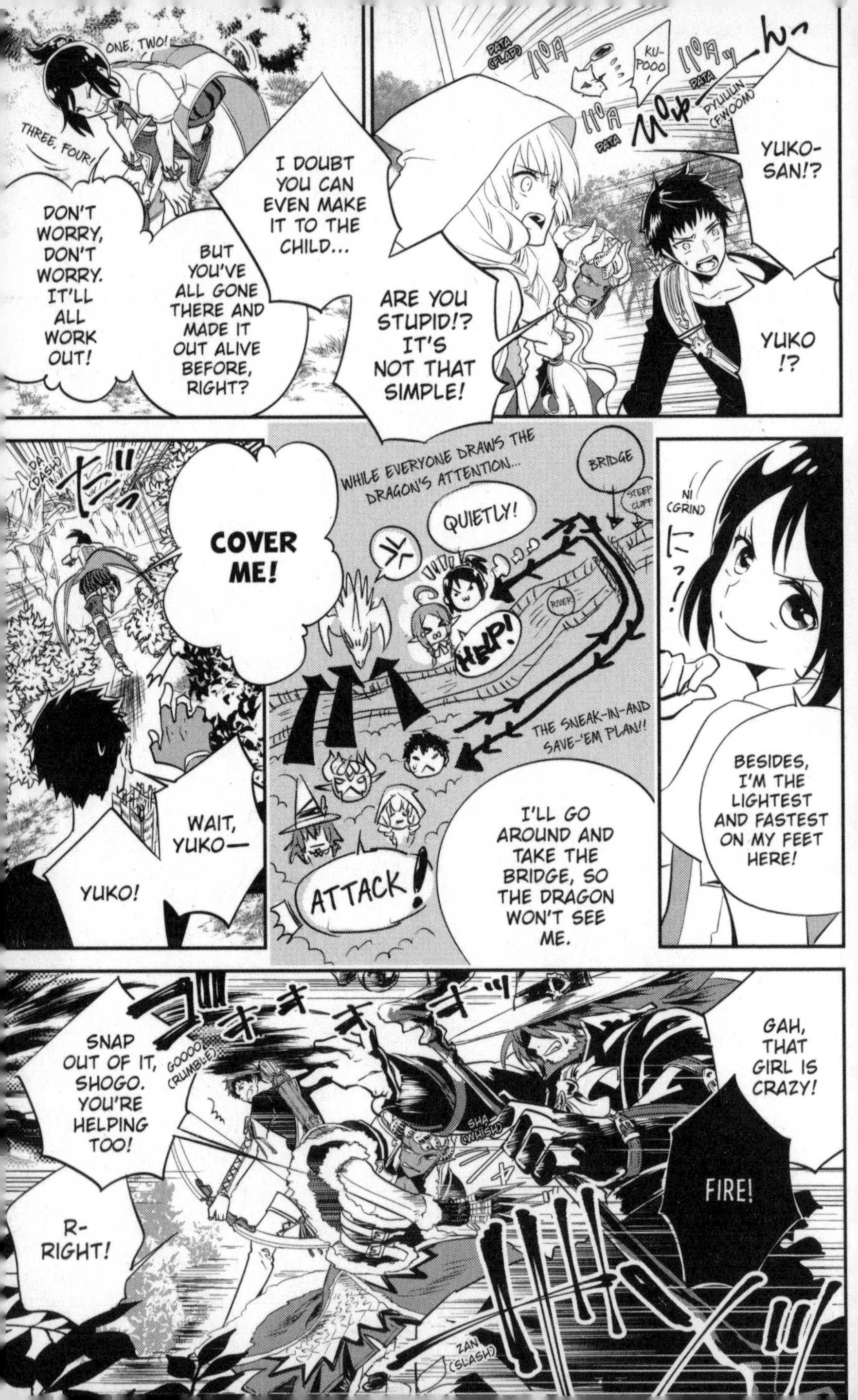
PATA (FLAP)
PATA
PATA
KU-POOO!
PYULLLIN (FWOOM)
YUKO-SAN!?
YUKO!?
ARE YOU STUPID!? IT'S NOT THAT SIMPLE!
I DOUBT YOU CAN EVEN MAKE IT TO THE CHILD...
ONE, TWO!
THREE, FOUR!
BUT YOU'VE ALL GONE THERE AND MADE IT OUT ALIVE BEFORE, RIGHT?
DON'T WORRY, DON'T WORRY. IT'LL ALL WORK OUT!
NI (GRIN)
BESIDES, I'M THE LIGHTEST AND FASTEST ON MY FEET HERE!
I'LL GO AROUND AND TAKE THE BRIDGE, SO THE DRAGON WON'T SEE ME.
WHILE EVERYONE DRAWS THE DRAGON'S ATTENTION...
BRIDGE
STEEP CLIFF
QUIETLY!
RIVER
HELP!
THE SNEAK-IN-AND SAVE-'EM PLAN!!
ATTACK!
COVER ME!
DA (DASH)
WAIT, YUKO—
YUKO!
GAH, THAT GIRL IS CRAZY!
FIRE!
SHA (WHISH)
GOOOO (RUMBLE)
SNAP OUT OF IT, SHOGO. YOU'RE HELPING TOO!
R-RIGHT!
ZAN (SLASH)

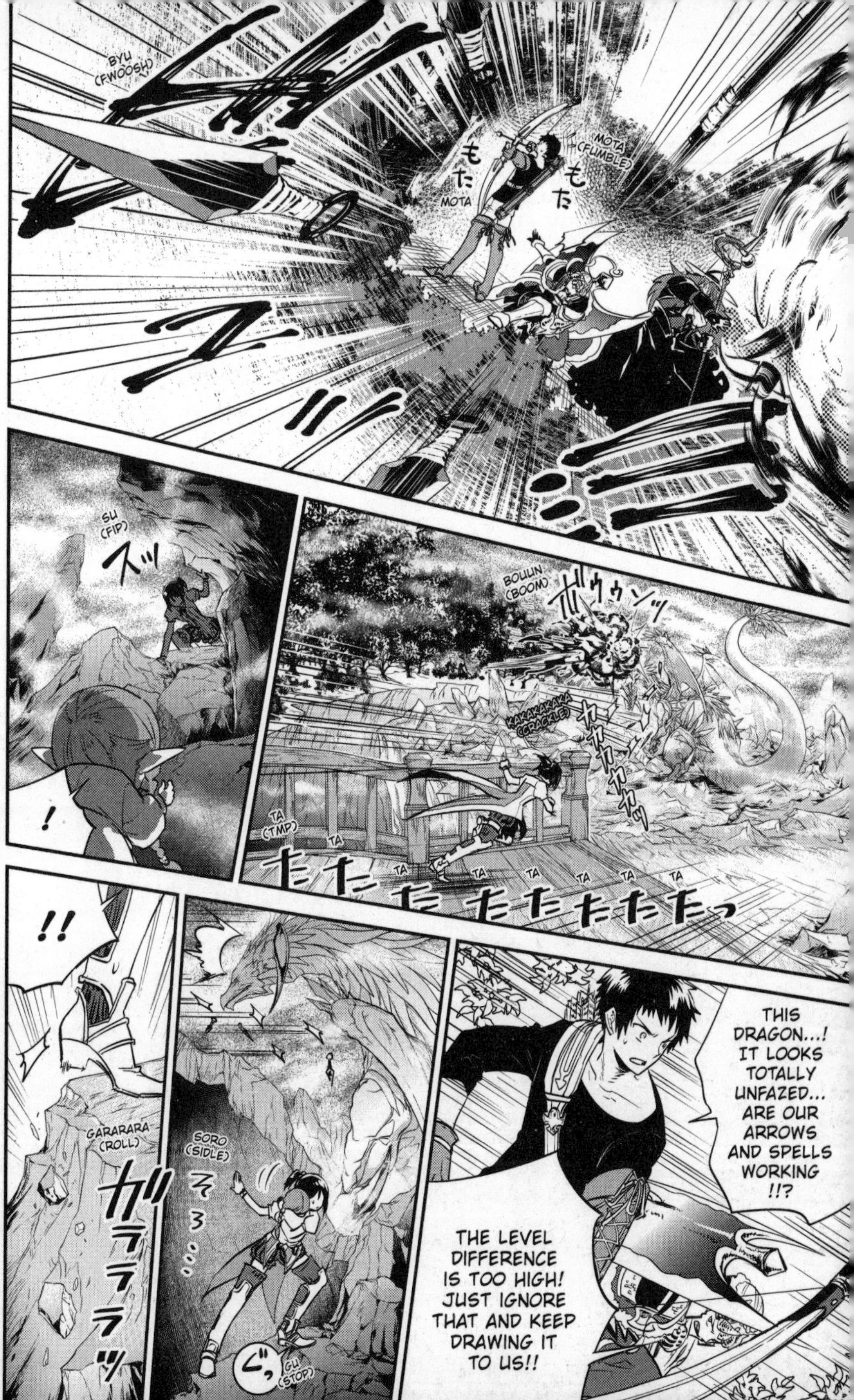
MOTA (FUMBLE)
もた
もた
MOTA
BYU (FWOOSH)
BOUUN (BOOM)
ボウゥンッ
KAKAKAKAKA (CRACKLE)
カカカカカッ
TA (TMP) TA TA TA TA TA TA TA
たたたたたたたたっ
SU (FIP)
スッ
!
THIS DRAGON...! IT LOOKS TOTALLY UNFAZED... ARE OUR ARROWS AND SPELLS WORKING!!?
THE LEVEL DIFFERENCE IS TOO HIGH! JUST IGNORE THAT AND KEEP DRAWING IT TO US!!
SORO (SIDLE)
そろ...
GU (STOP)
ぐっ
!!
GARARARA (ROLL)
ガラララッ

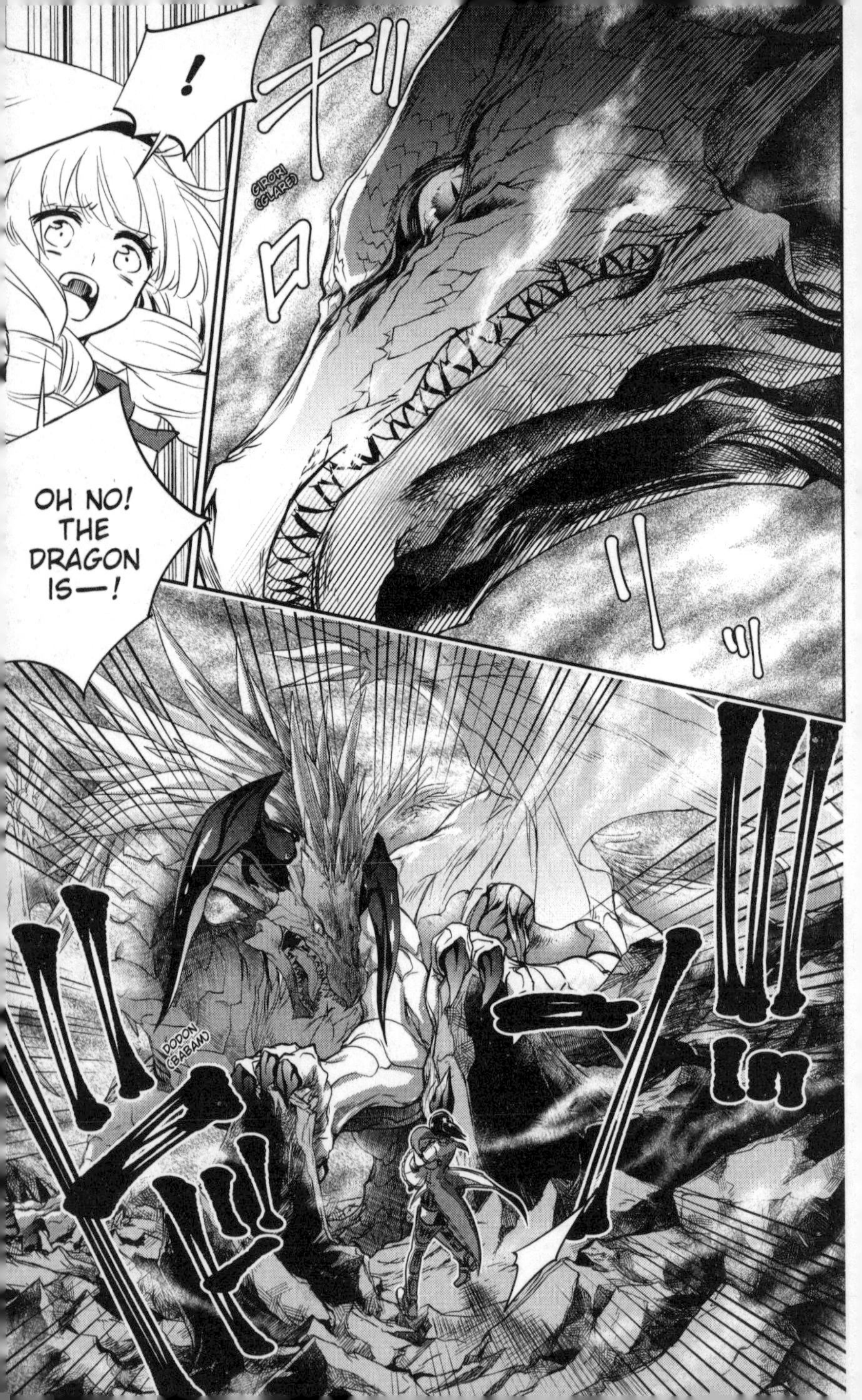
GIRORI (GLARE)
!
OH NO! THE DRAGON IS—!
DODON (BABAM)

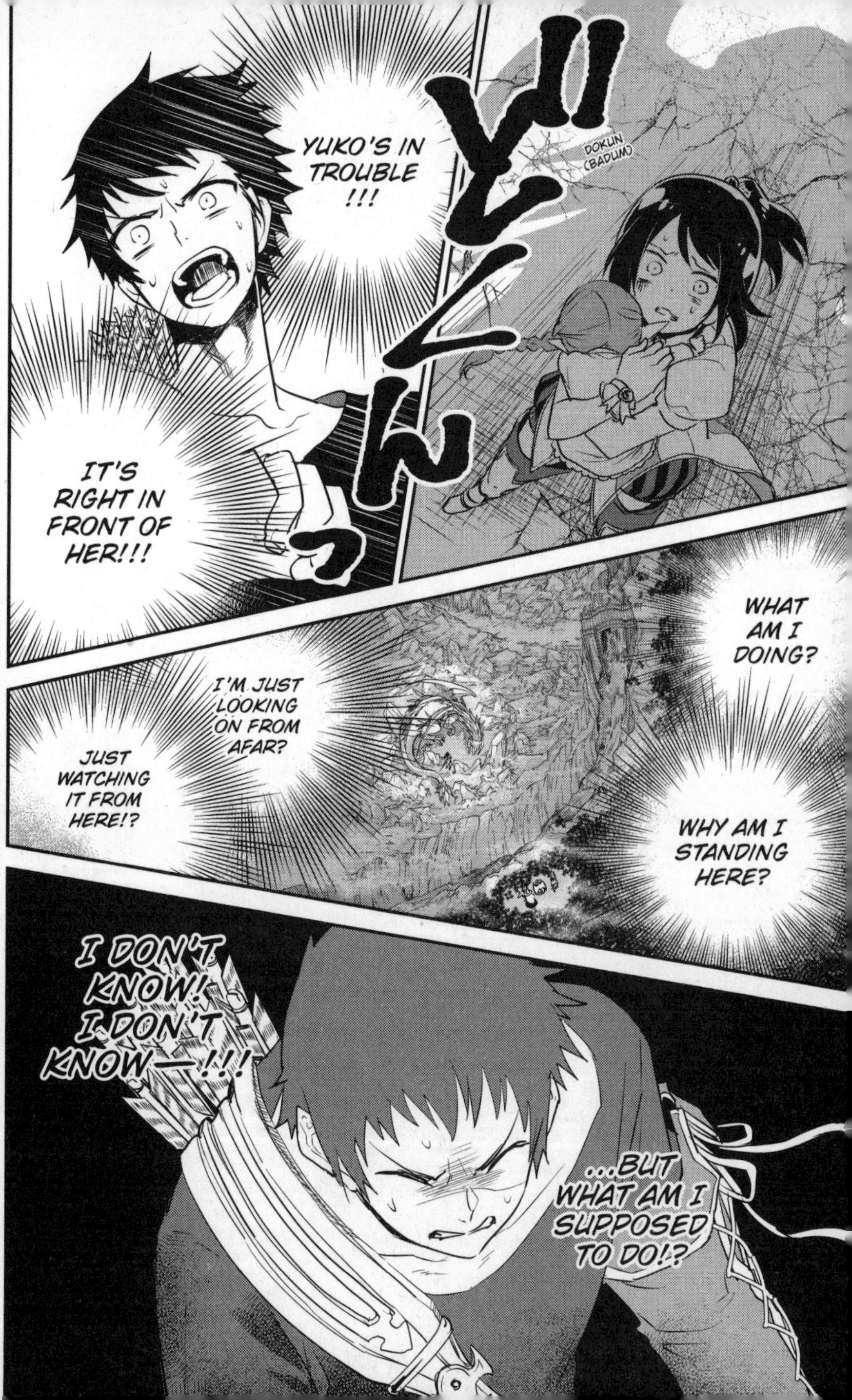
DOKUN (BADUM)
YUKO'S IN TROUBLE!!!
IT'S RIGHT IN FRONT OF HER!!!
WHAT AM I DOING?
WHY AM I STANDING HERE?
I'M JUST LOOKING ON FROM AFAR?
JUST WATCHING IT FROM HERE!?
I DON'T KNOW! I DON'T KNOW—!!!
...BUT WHAT AM I SUPPOSED TO DO!?

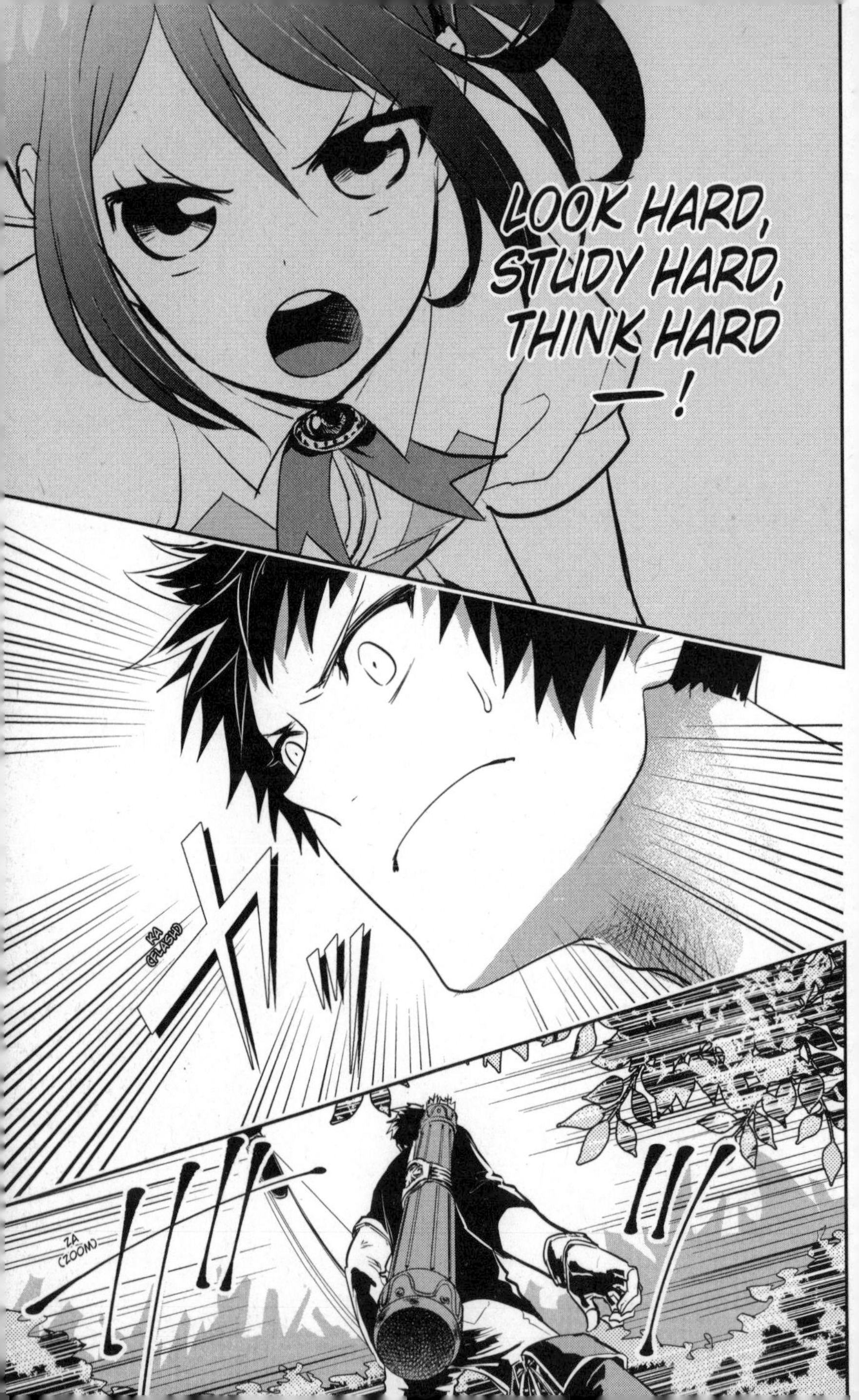
LOOK HARD, STUDY HARD, THINK HARD —!
KA (FLASH)
ZA (ZOOM)

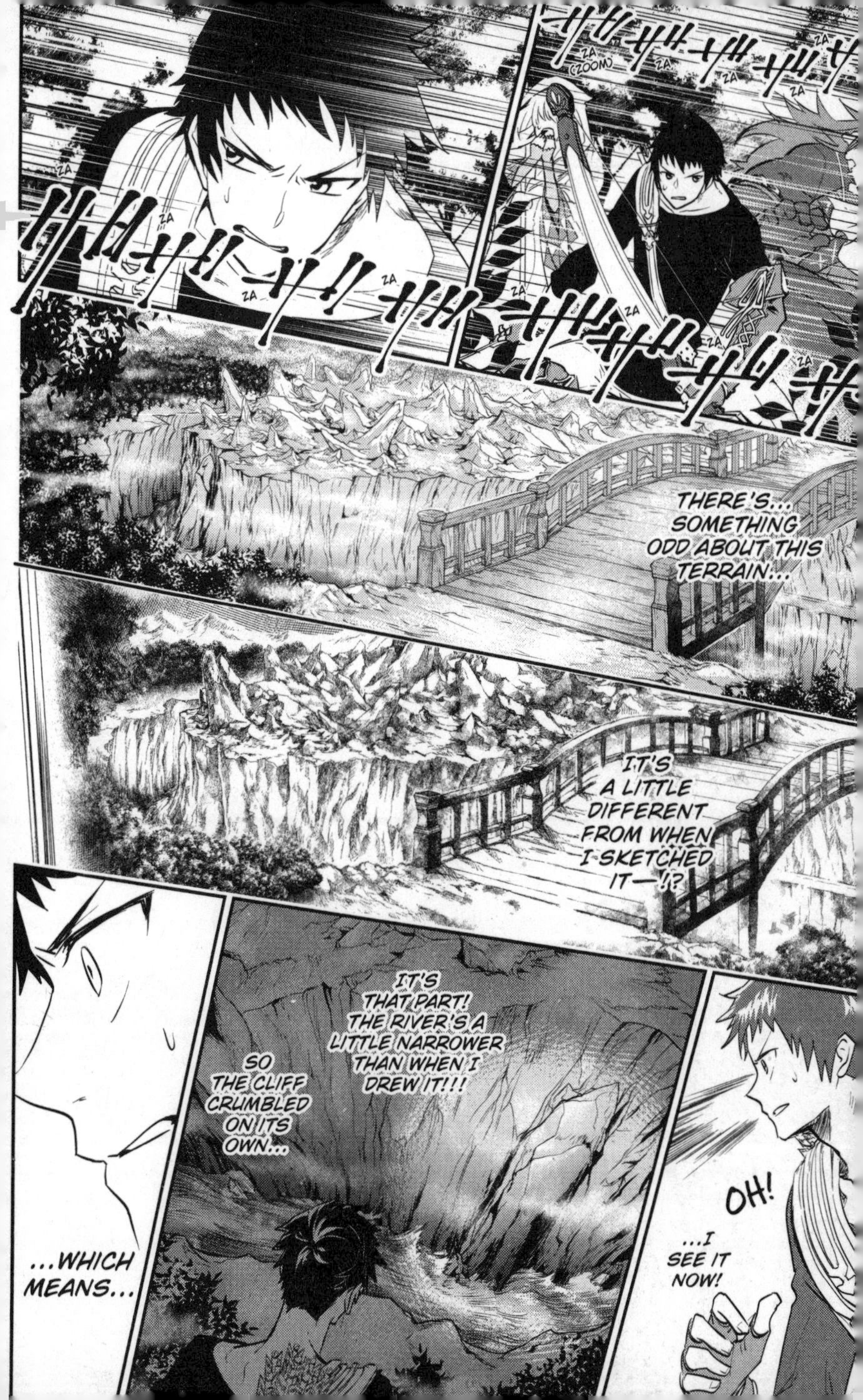
ZA
(ZOOM)
ZA
ZA
ZA
ZA
ZA
ZA
ZA
ZA
ZA
ZA
THERE'S... SOMETHING ODD ABOUT THIS TERRAIN...
IT'S A LITTLE DIFFERENT FROM WHEN I SKETCHED IT—!?
OH!
...I SEE IT NOW!
IT'S THAT PART! THE RIVER'S A LITTLE NARROWER THAN WHEN I DREW IT!!!
SO THE CLIFF CRUMBLED ON ITS OWN...
...WHICH MEANS...

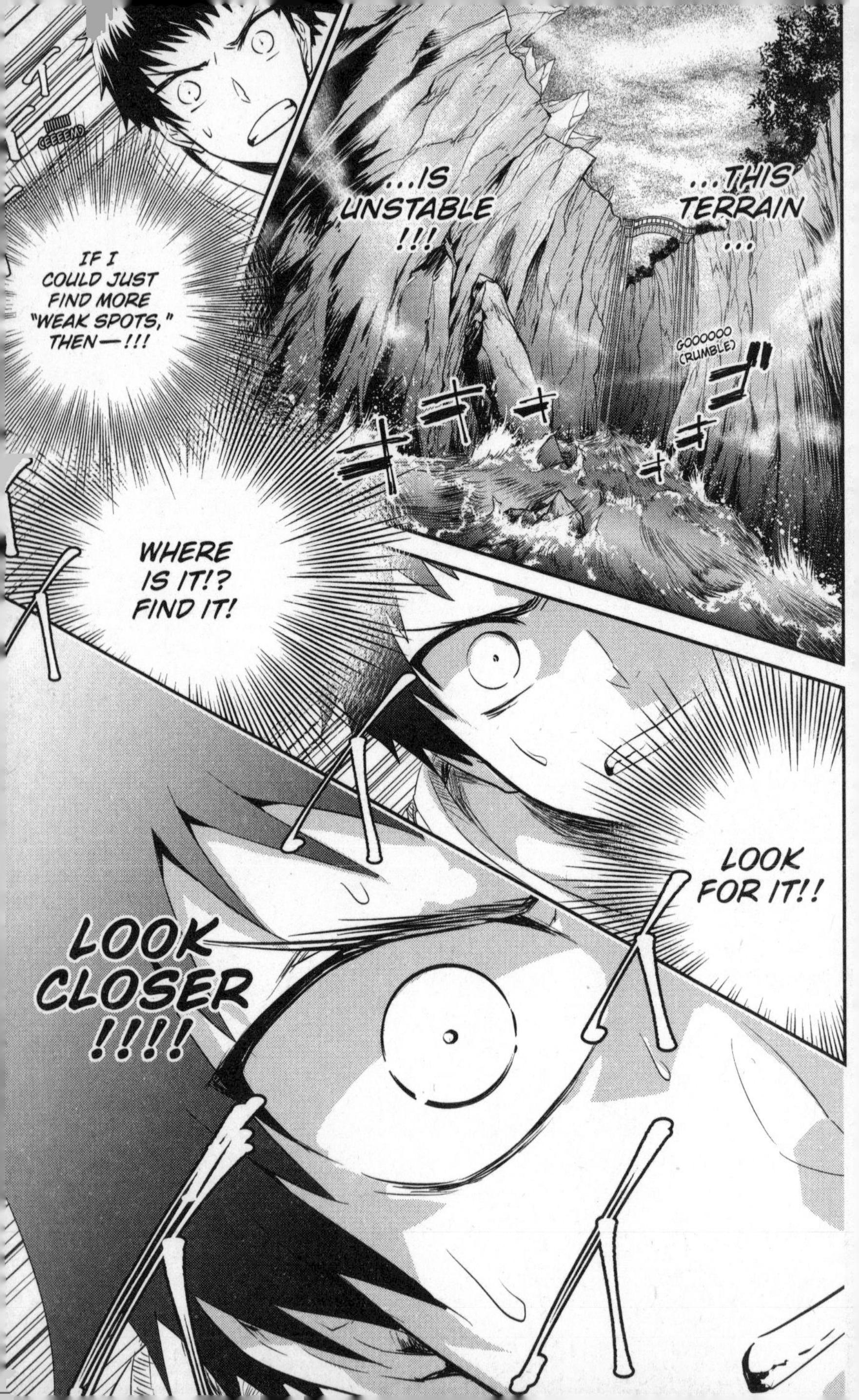
...THIS TERRAIN...
...IS UNSTABLE!!!
GOOOOOO (RUMBLE)
(EEEEM)
IF I COULD JUST FIND MORE "WEAK SPOTS," THEN—!!!
WHERE IS IT!? FIND IT!
LOOK FOR IT!!
LOOK CLOSER!!!!

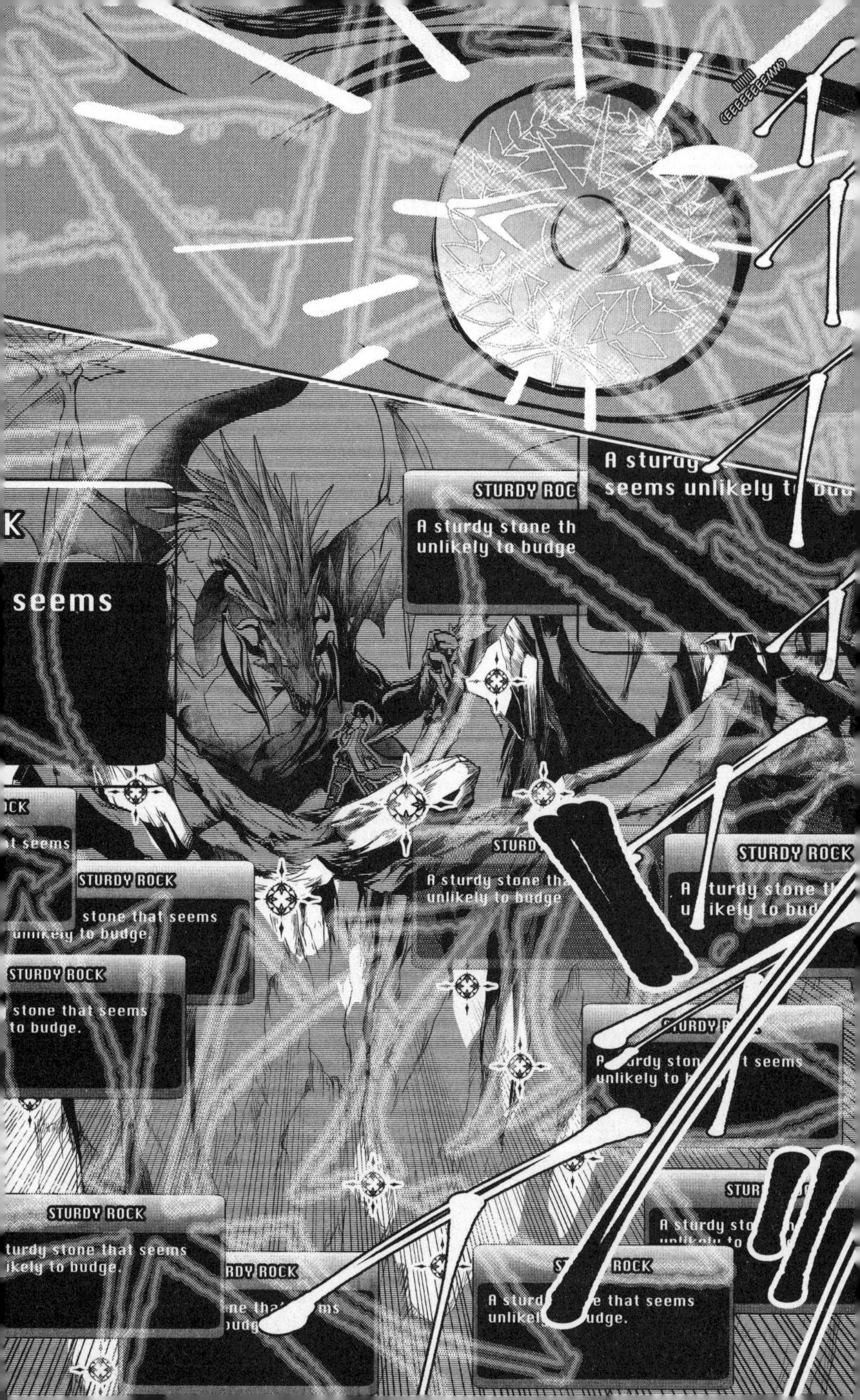
(EEEEEEEEW))
A sturdy
seems unlikely t
STURDY ROC
A sturdy stone th
unlikely to budge
K
seems
STURDY ROCK
A turdy stone th
u ikely to bud
STURD
A sturdy stone th
unlikely to budge
CK
t seems
STURDY ROCK
stone that seems
unlikely to budge.
URDY R
A sturdy ston t seems
unlikely to b
STURDY ROCK
stone that seems
to budge.
STUR
A sturdy sto
ROCK
A sturd e that seems
unlike udge.
RDY ROCK
ne tha ems
udge
STURDY ROCK
turdy stone that seems
likely to budge.

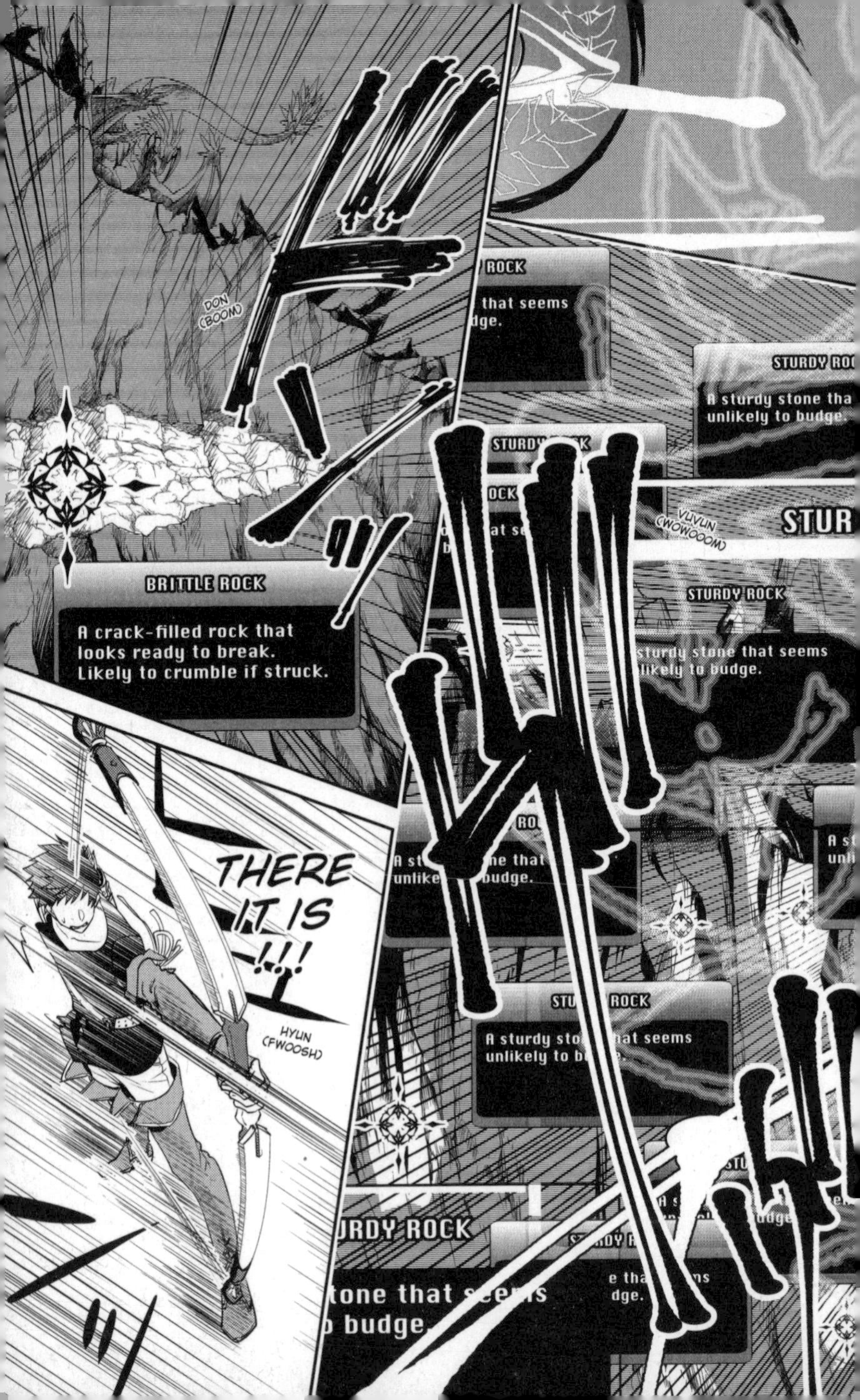
STURDY ROCK
A sturdy stone tha
unlikely to budge.
VUVUN
(WOWOOOM)
STURDY ROCK
sturdy stone that seems
likely to budge.
DON
(BOOM)
BRITTLE ROCK
A crack-filled rock that looks ready to break. Likely to crumble if struck.
THERE IT IS!!!
HYUN
(FWOOSH)
A sturdy sto hat seems
unlikely to bu
URDY ROCK
tone that seems
o budge.

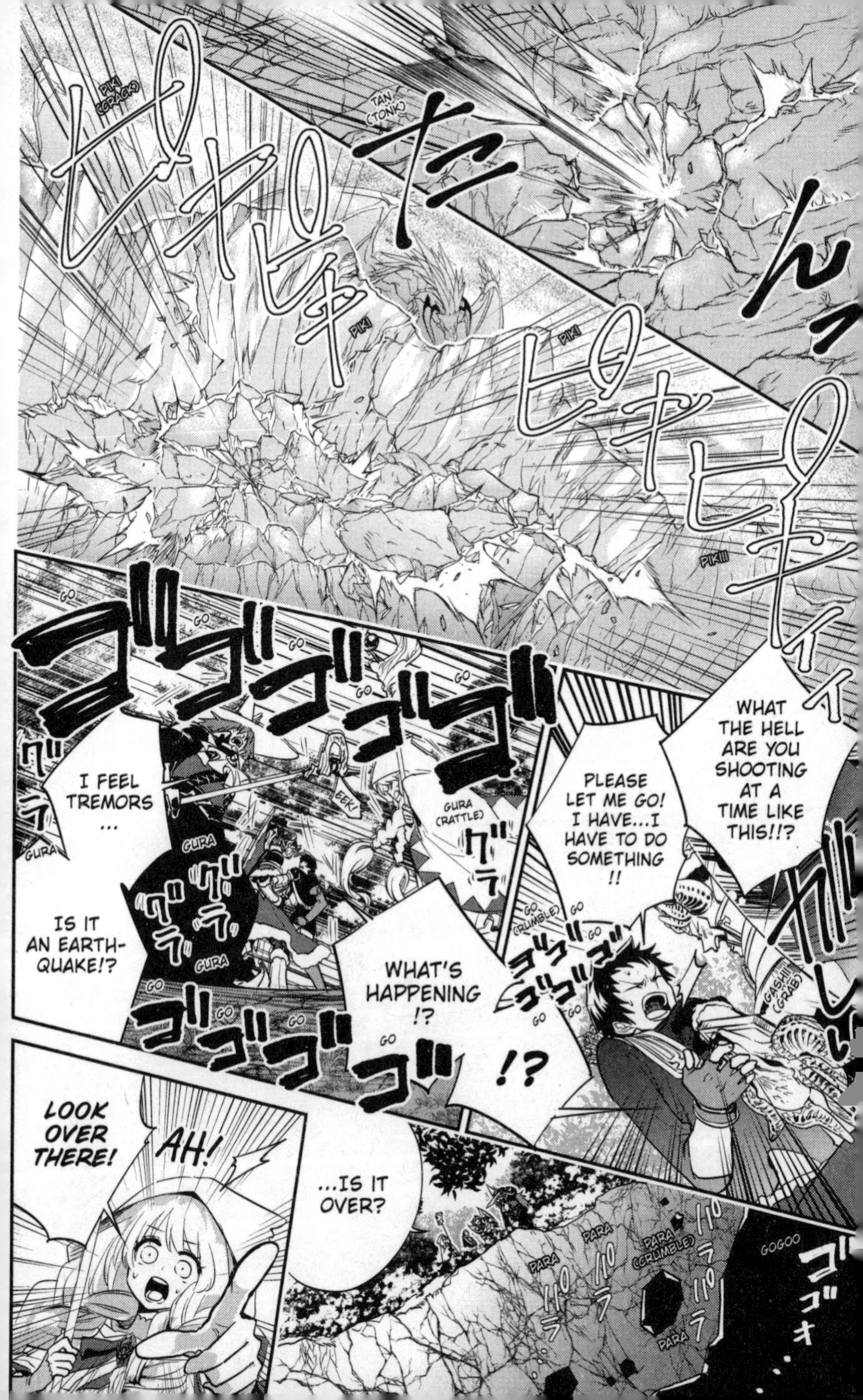
TAN (TONK)
PIKI (CRACK)
PIKI
PIKI
PIKIII
WHAT THE HELL ARE YOU SHOOTING AT A TIME LIKE THIS!!?
GASHIII (GRAB)
PLEASE LET ME GO! I HAVE...I HAVE TO DO SOMETHING!!
GO (CRUMBLE) GO
GO GO GO
!?
WHAT'S HAPPENING!?
GURA (RATTLE)
EEK!
GO GO GO
I FEEL TREMORS...
GURA
GURA
GURA
IS IT AN EARTHQUAKE!?
GO GO GO
GOGOO
PARA (CRUMBLE)
PARA
PARA
PARA
...IS IT OVER?
AH!
LOOK OVER THERE!

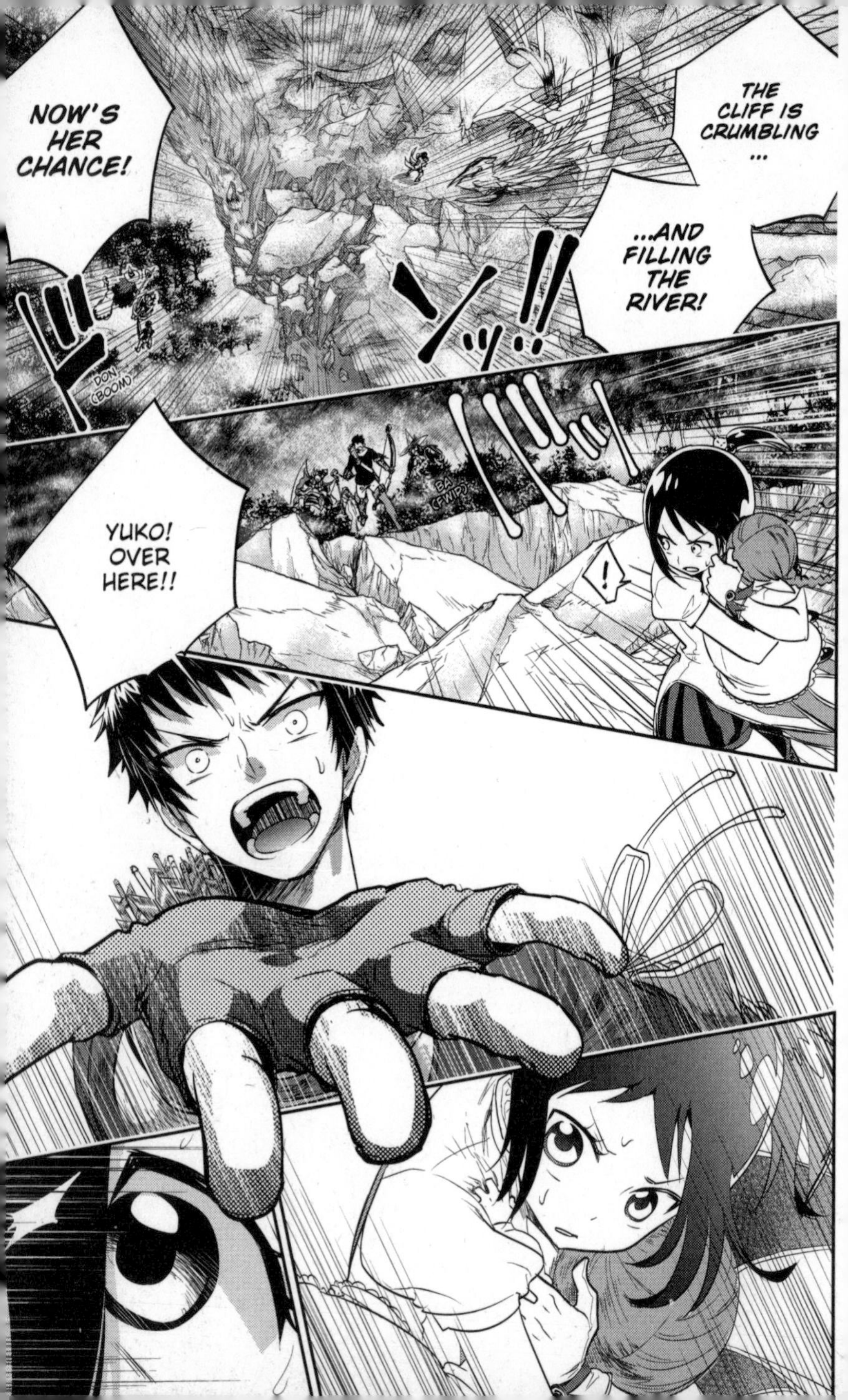
THE CLIFF IS CRUMBLING...
...AND FILLING THE RIVER!
NOW'S HER CHANCE!
DON (BOOM)
BA (FWIP)
!
YUKO! OVER HERE!!

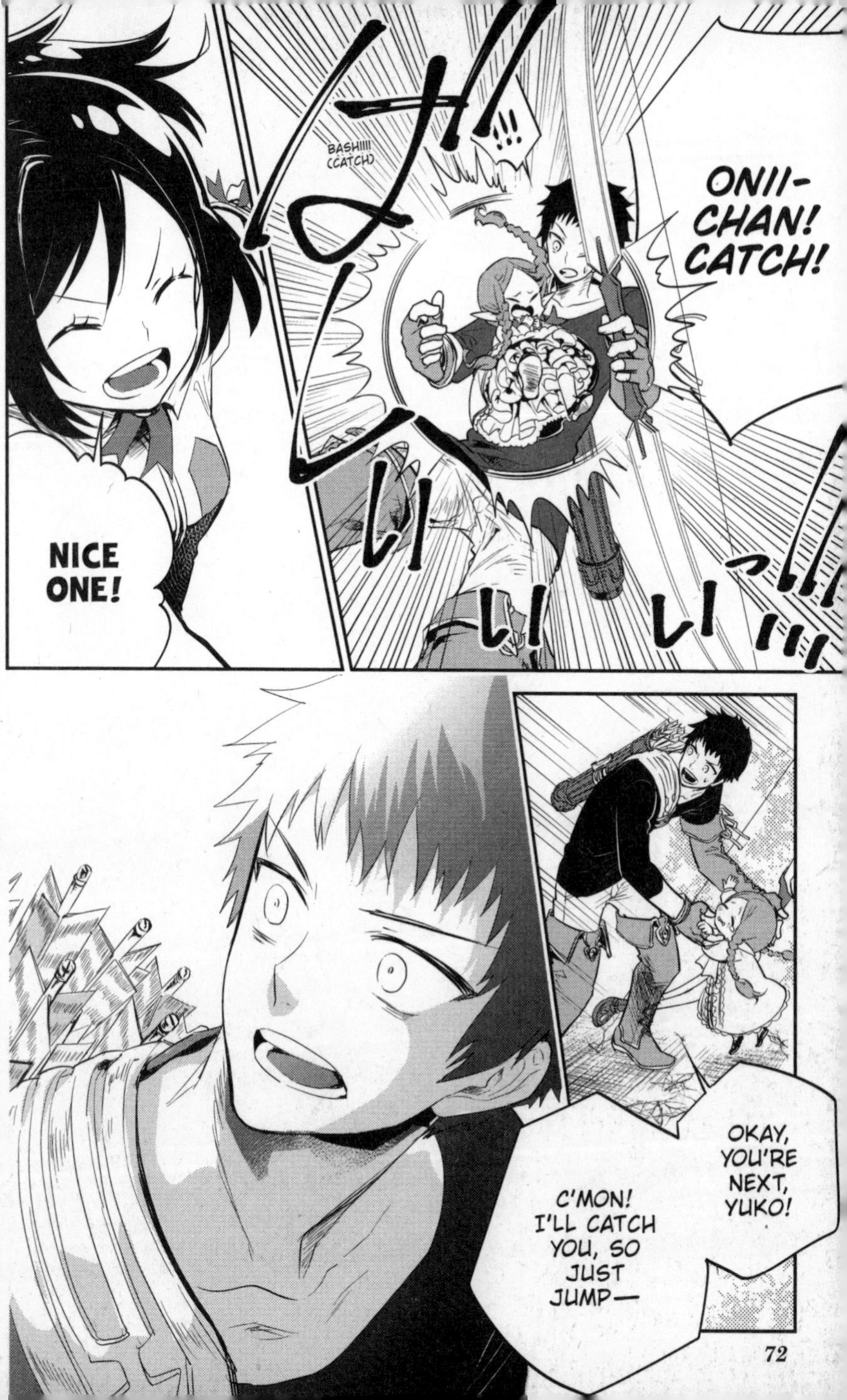
ONII-CHAN! CATCH!
BASHIIII (CATCH)
NICE ONE!
OKAY, YOU'RE NEXT, YUKO!
C'MON! I'LL CATCH YOU, SO JUST JUMP—

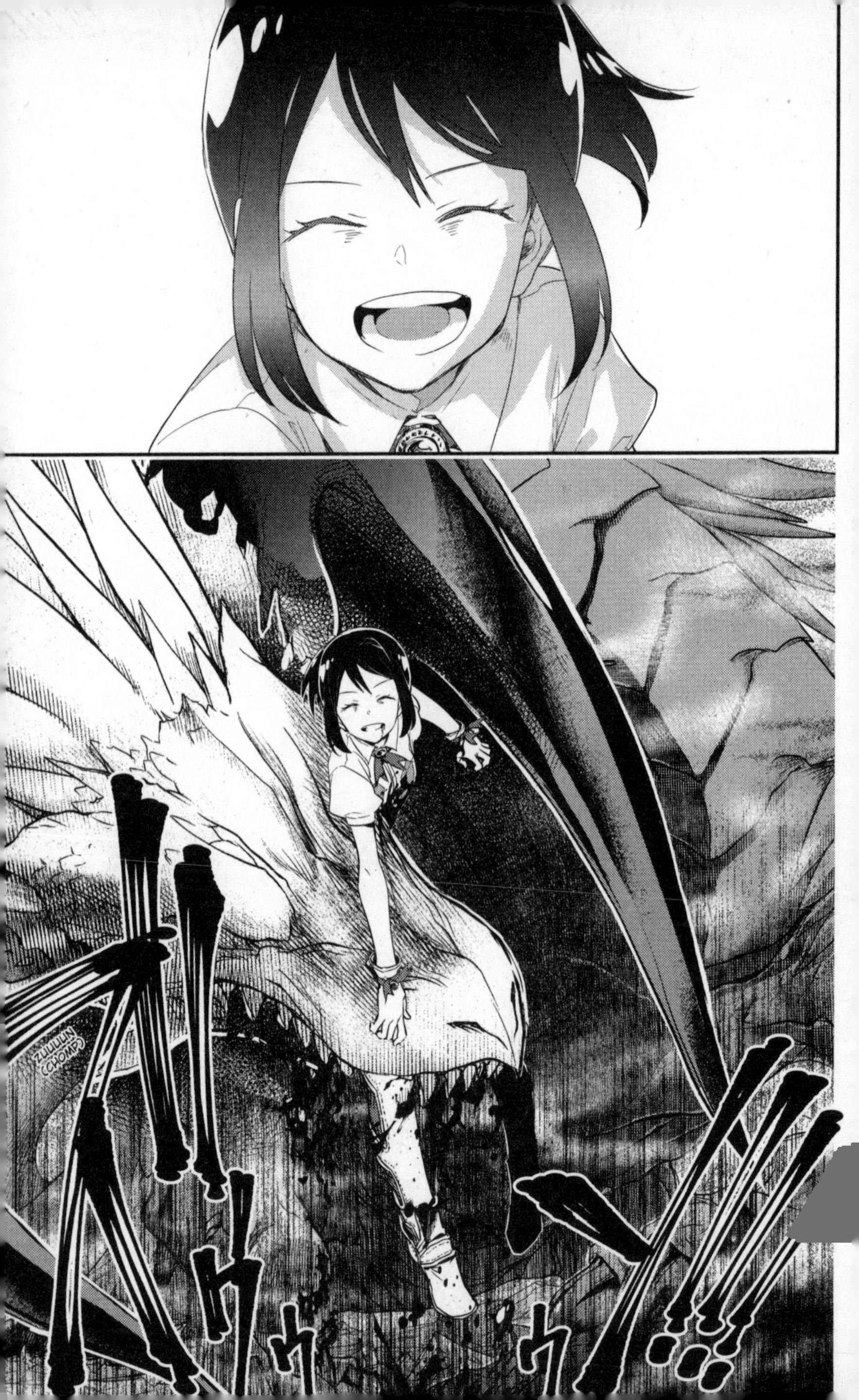
ZUUUUN
(CHOMP)

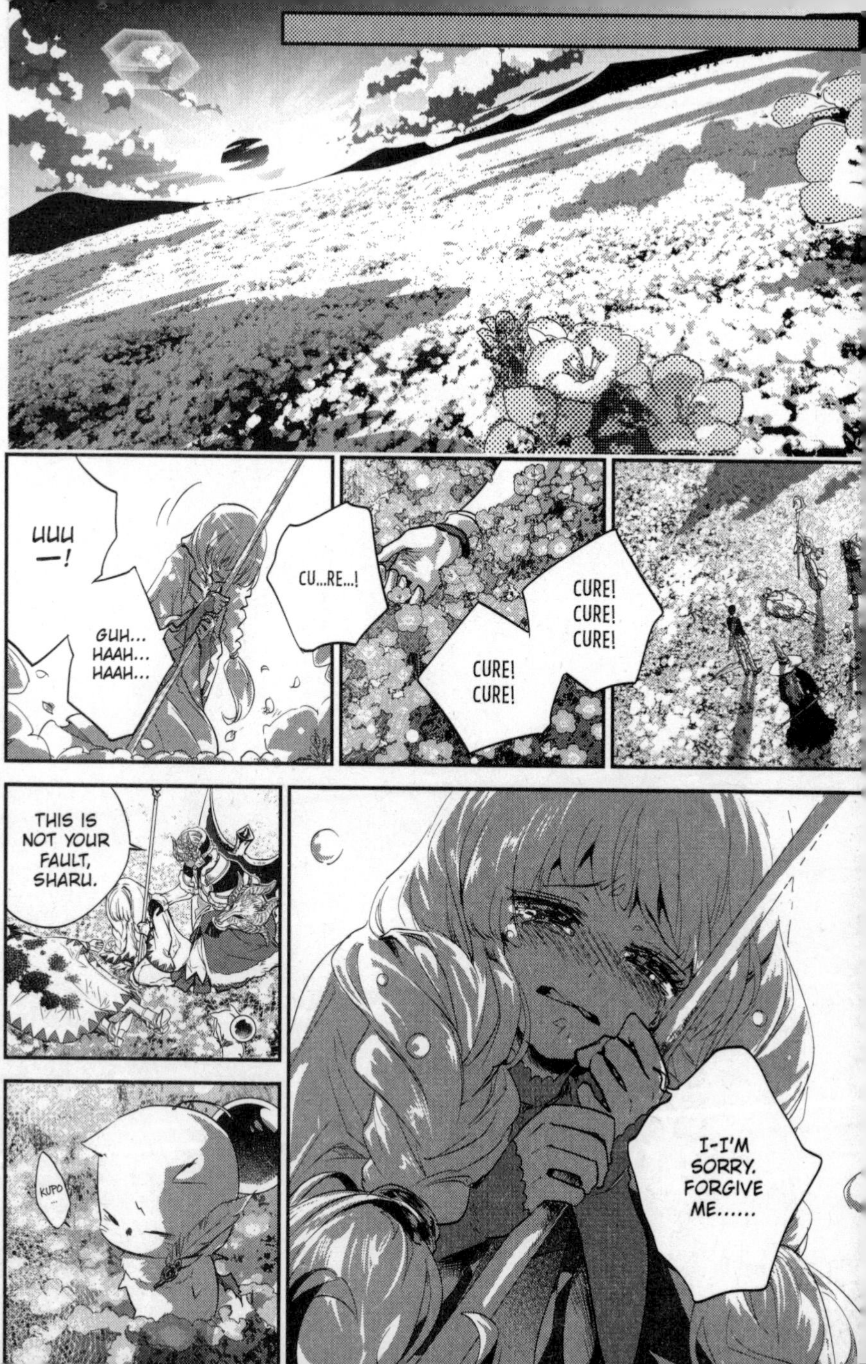
CU...RE...!
CURE! CURE! CURE!
CURE! CURE!
UUU—!
GUH... HAAH... HAAH...
I-I'M SORRY. FORGIVE ME......
THIS IS NOT YOUR FAULT, SHARU.
KUPO ...

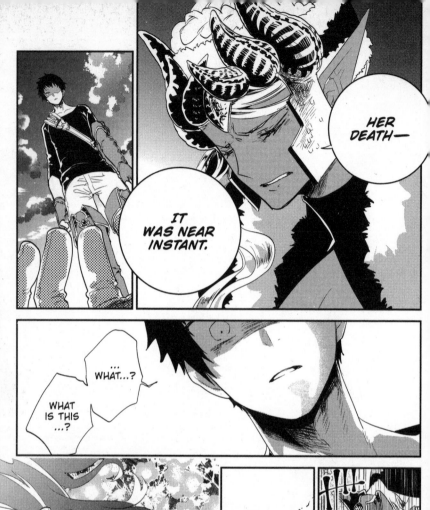

HER DEATH—

IT WAS NEAR INSTANT.

... WHAT...?

WHAT IS THIS ...?

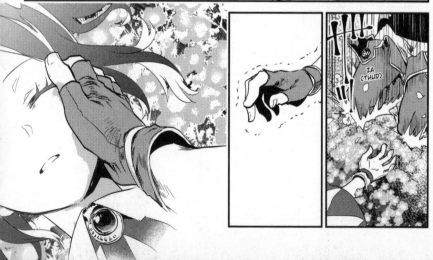

ZA
(THUD)

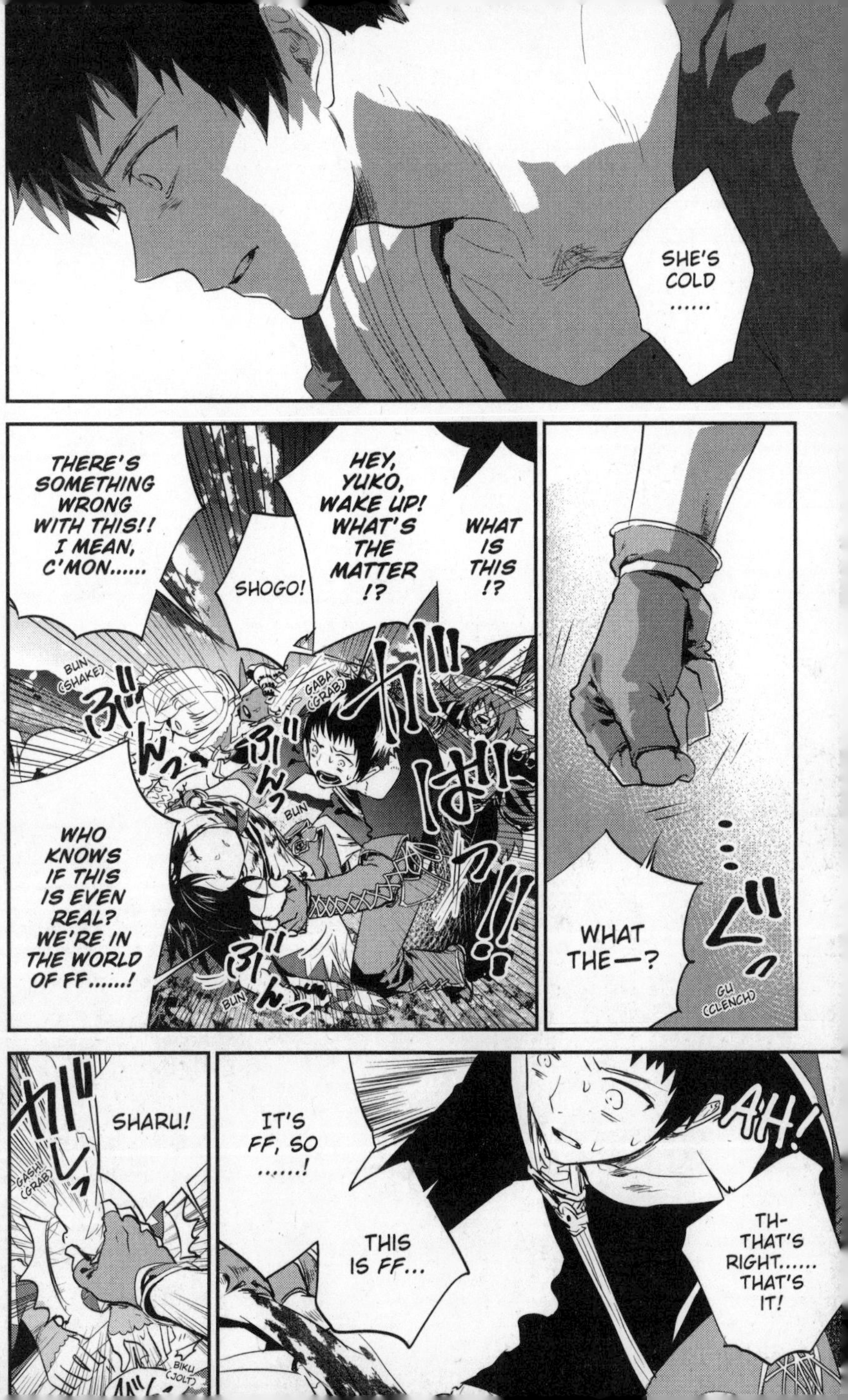
SHE'S COLD ......
......
WHAT THE—?
GU (CLENCH)
WHAT IS THIS !?
HEY, YUKO, WAKE UP! WHAT'S THE MATTER !?
SHOGO!
THERE'S SOMETHING WRONG WITH THIS!! I MEAN, C'MON......
GABA (GRAB)
BUN (SHAKE)
BUN
WHO KNOWS IF THIS IS EVEN REAL? WE'RE IN THE WORLD OF FF......!
BUN
AH!
TH-THAT'S RIGHT...... THAT'S IT!
IT'S FF, SO ......!
THIS IS FF...
SHARU!
GASH! (GRAB)
BIKU (JOLT)

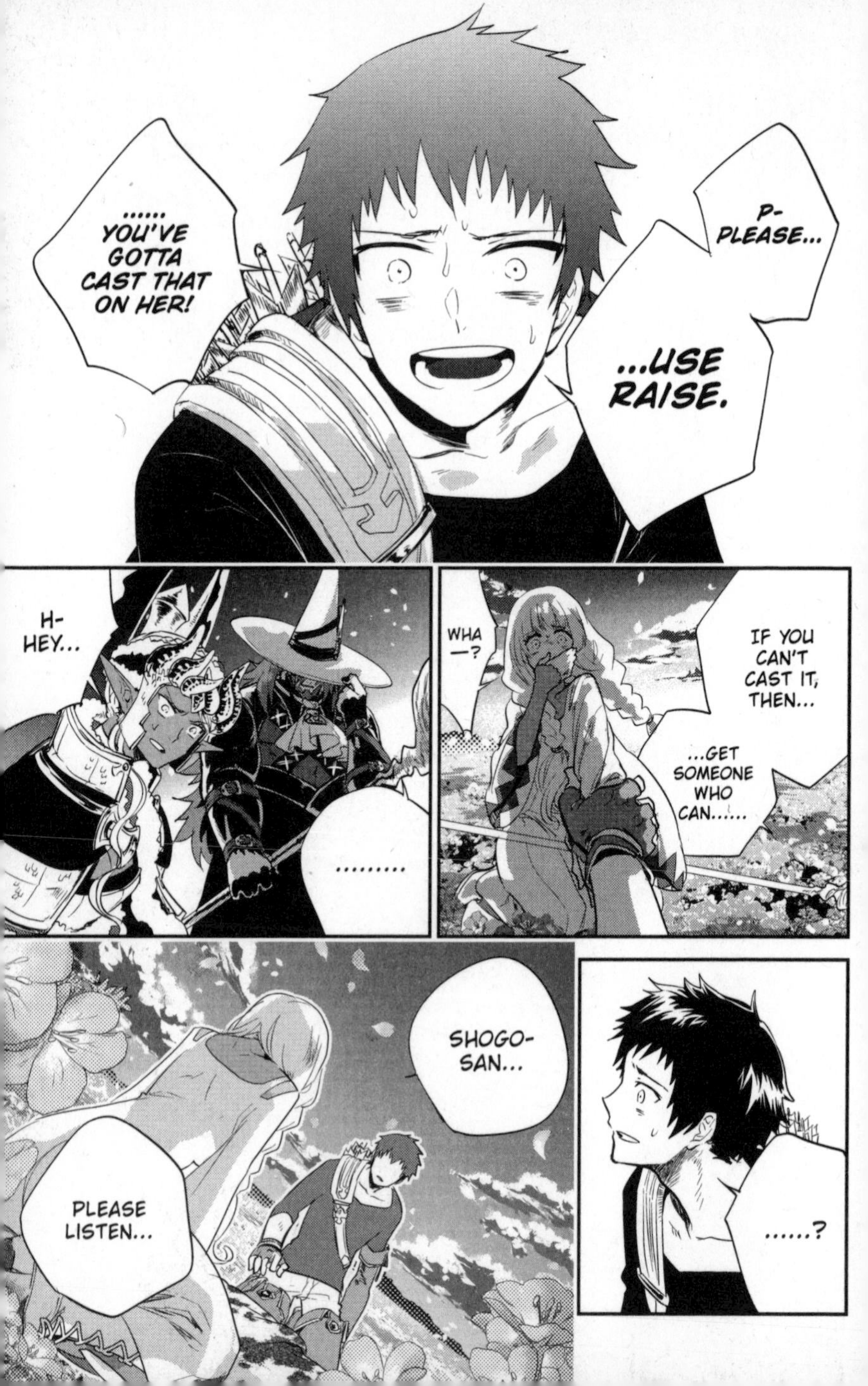
P-PLEASE...
...USE RAISE.
......YOU'VE GOTTA CAST THAT ON HER!
IF YOU CAN'T CAST IT, THEN...
WHA—?
...GET SOMEONE WHO CAN......
H-HEY...
....
......?
SHOGO-SAN...
PLEASE LISTEN...

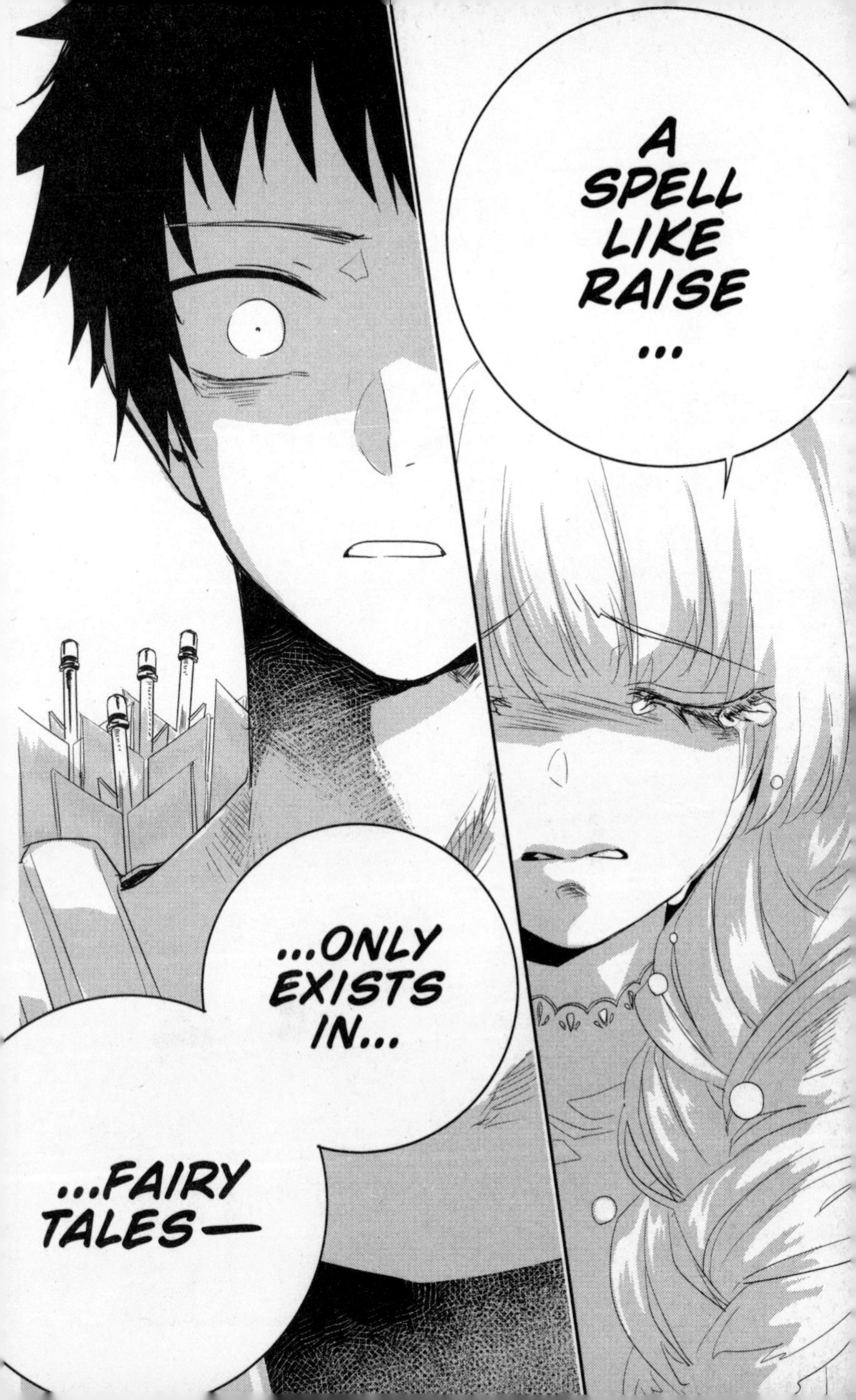
A SPELL LIKE RAISE...
...ONLY EXISTS IN...
...FAIRY TALES—

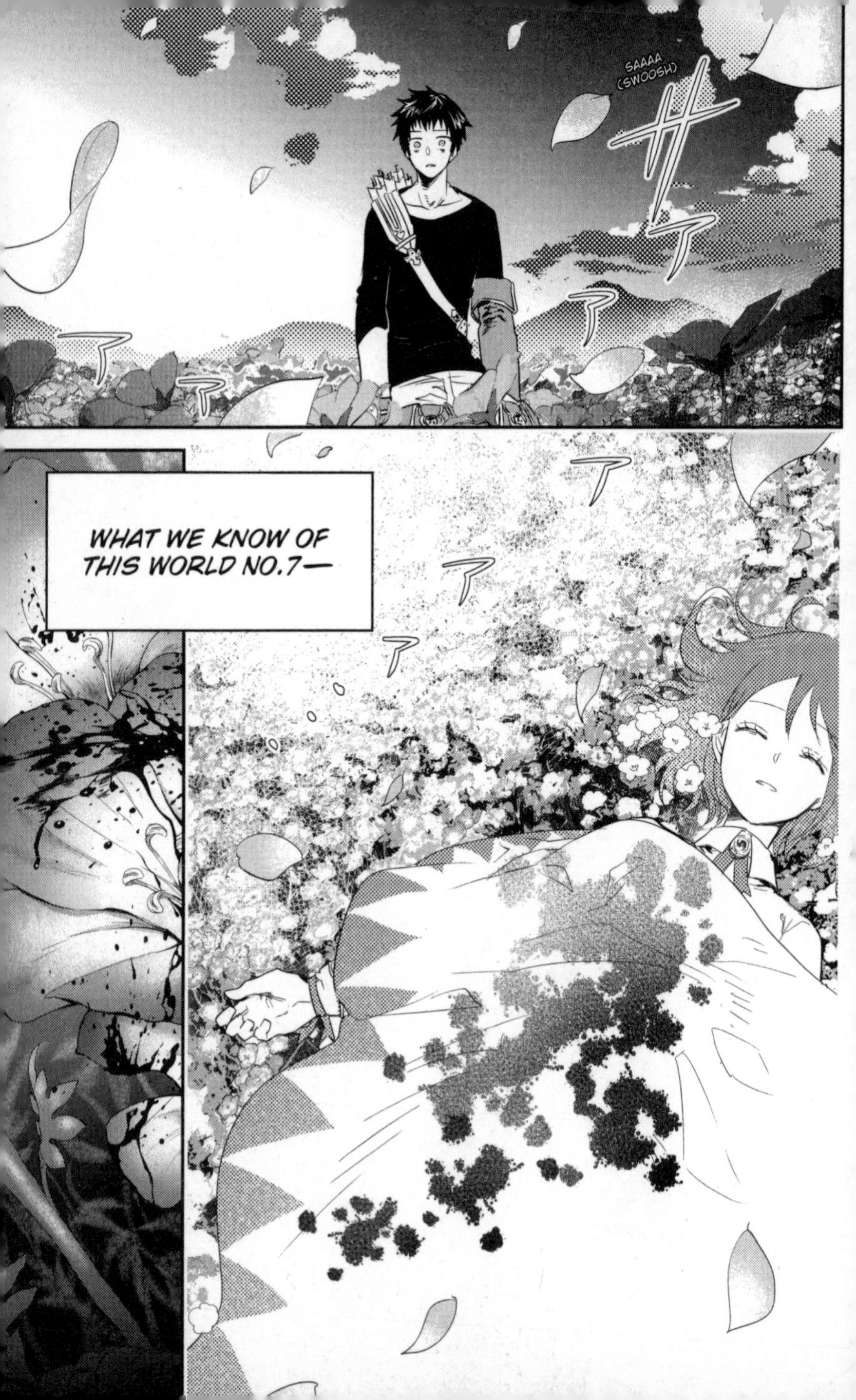
SAAAA
(SWOOSH)
サァァァ
ァァァ
WHAT WE KNOW OF THIS WORLD NO.7—

THERE'S NO SUCH THING AS RAISE...

FINAL FANTASY®

ファイナルファンタジー　ロスト・ストレンジャー

LOST STRANGER

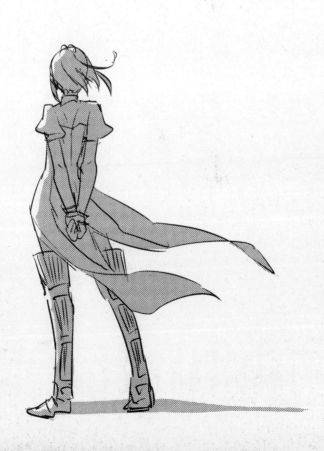

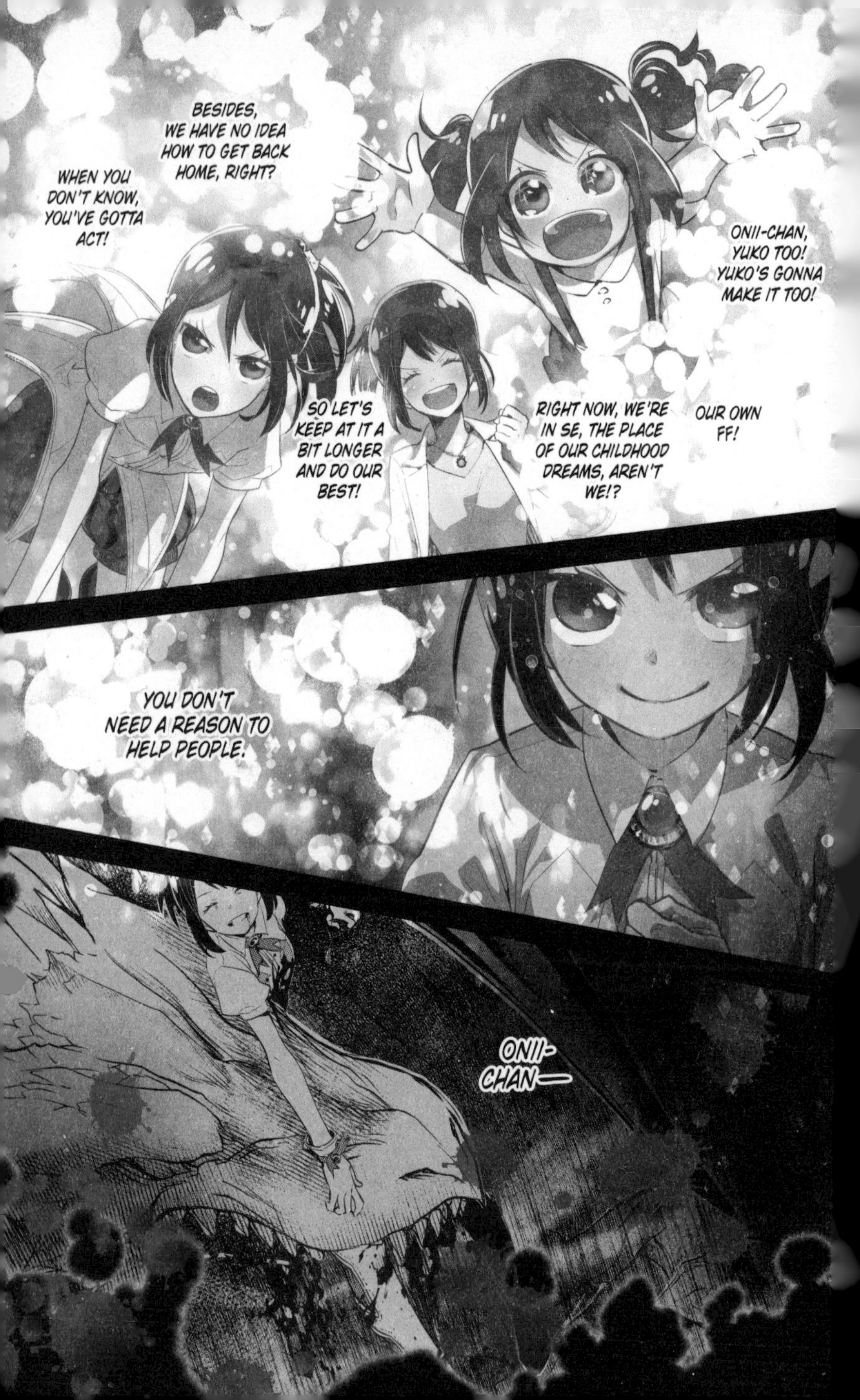
ONII-CHAN, YUKO TOO! YUKO'S GONNA MAKE IT TOO!
BESIDES, WE HAVE NO IDEA HOW TO GET BACK HOME, RIGHT?
WHEN YOU DON'T KNOW, YOU'VE GOTTA ACT!
RIGHT NOW, WE'RE IN SE, THE PLACE OF OUR CHILDHOOD DREAMS, AREN'T WE!?
OUR OWN FF!
SO LET'S KEEP AT IT A BIT LONGER AND DO OUR BEST!
YOU DON'T NEED A REASON TO HELP PEOPLE.
ONII-CHAN—

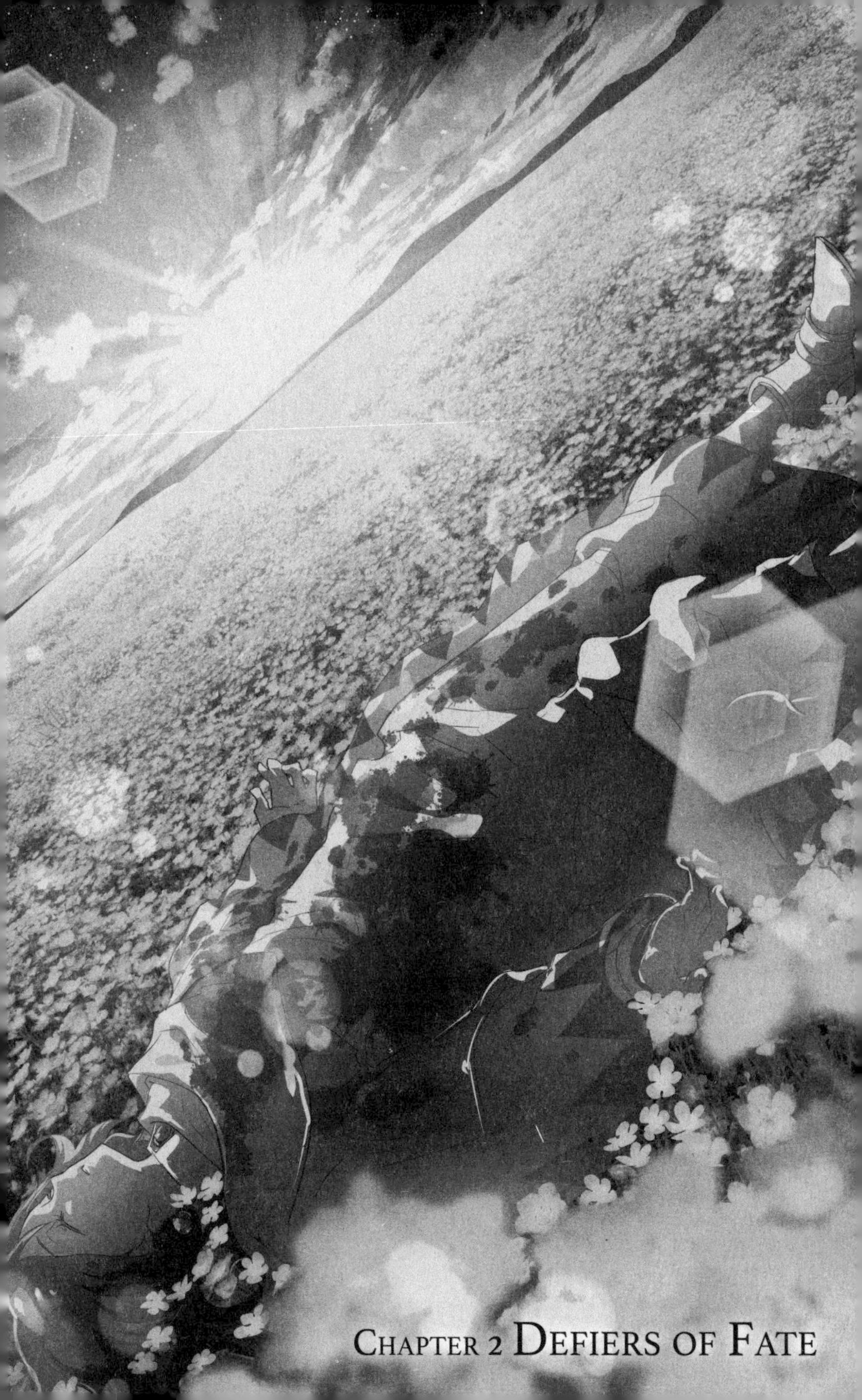

Chapter 2 Defiers of Fate

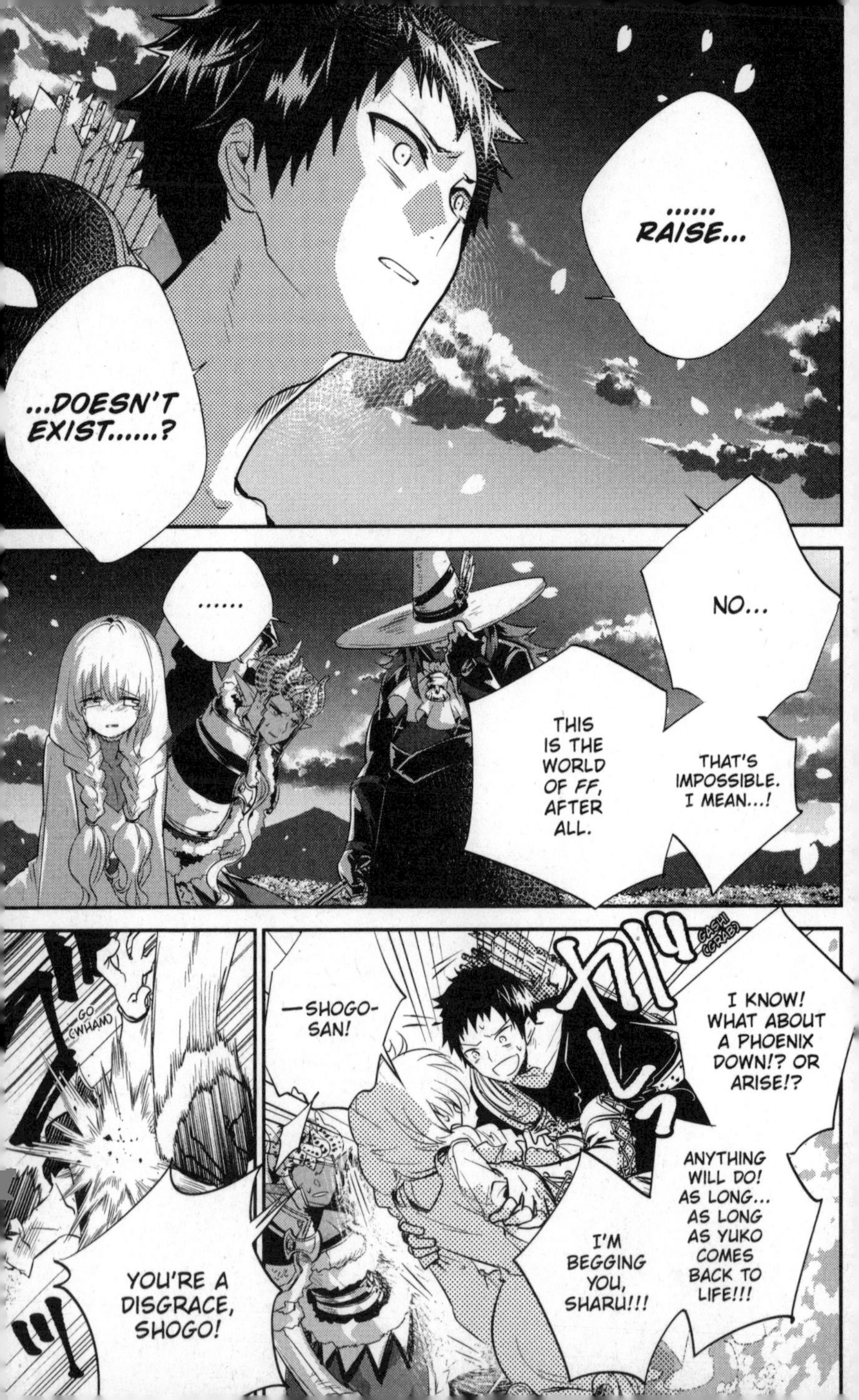
......RAISE...
...DOESN'T EXIST......?
NO...
THAT'S IMPOSSIBLE. I MEAN...!
THIS IS THE WORLD OF FF, AFTER ALL.
......
GASHI (GRAB)
I KNOW! WHAT ABOUT A PHOENIX DOWN!? OR ARISE!?
ANYTHING WILL DO! AS LONG... AS LONG AS YUKO COMES BACK TO LIFE!!!
I'M BEGGING YOU, SHARU!!!
—SHOGO-SAN!
GO (WHAM)
YOU'RE A DISGRACE, SHOGO!

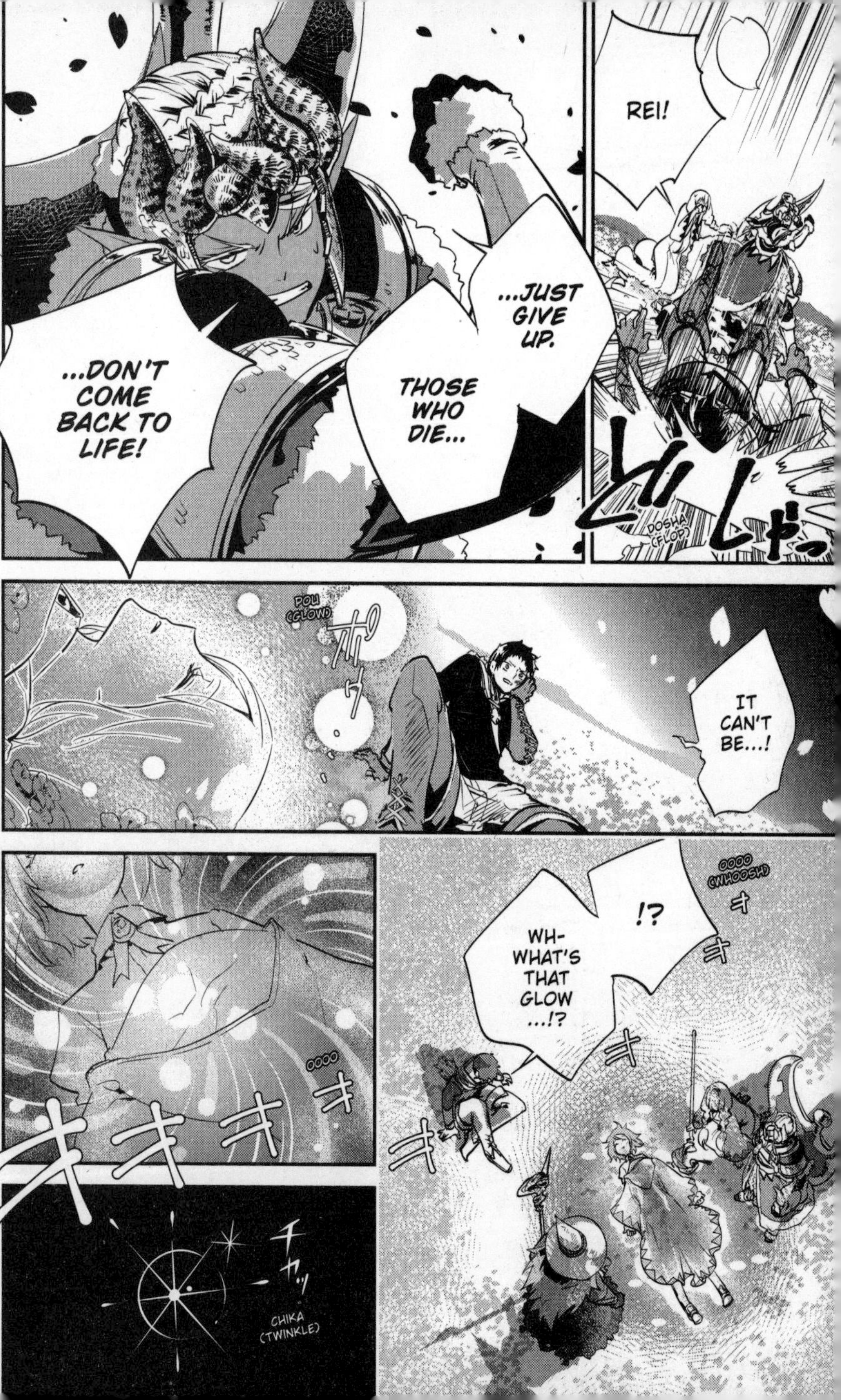
REI!
DOSHA (FLOP)
...JUST GIVE UP.
THOSE WHO DIE...
...DON'T COME BACK TO LIFE!
IT CAN'T BE...!
POU (GLOW)
OOOO (WHOOSH)
!?
WH-WHAT'S THAT GLOW ...!?
OOOO
CHIKA (TWINKLE)

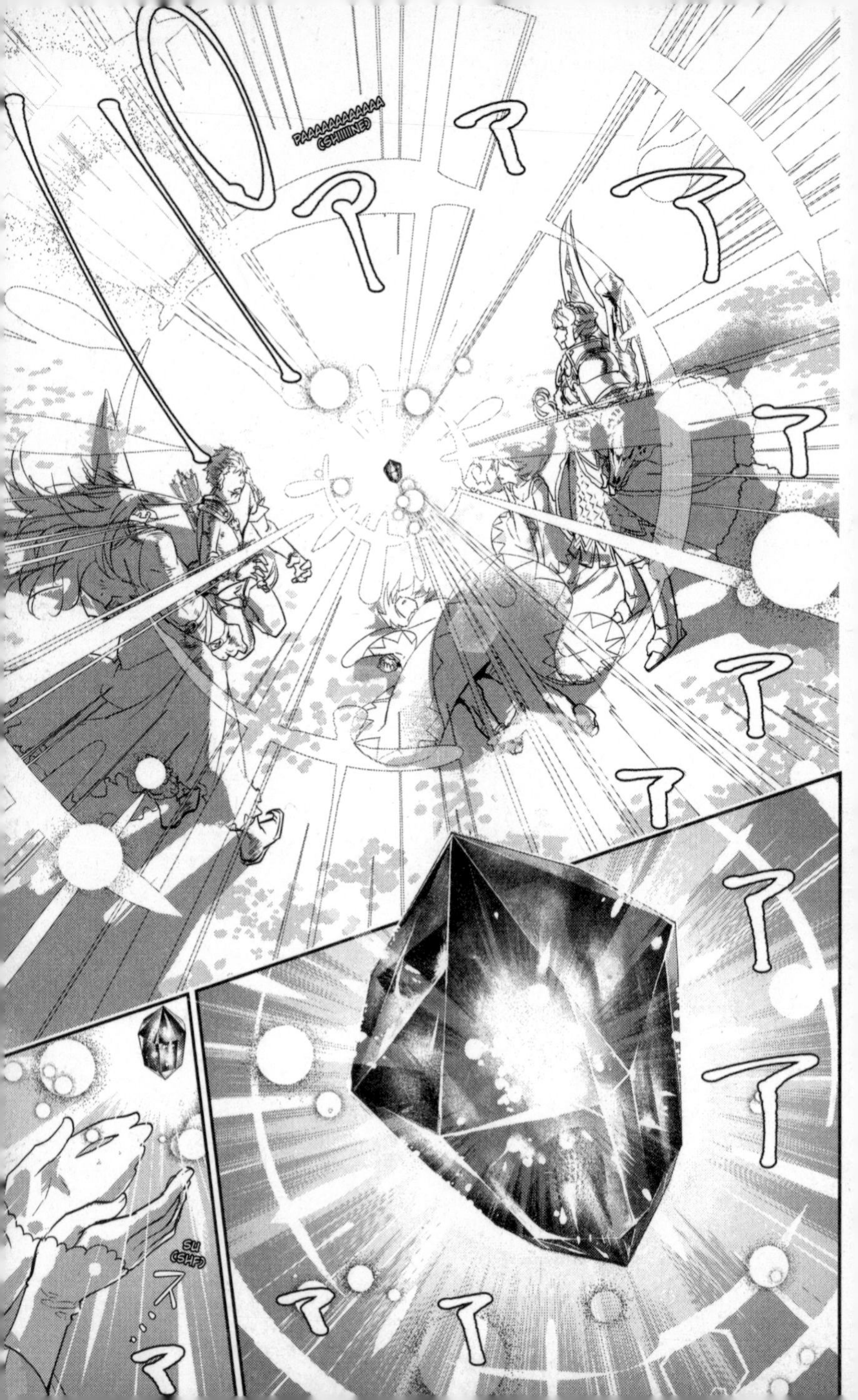
PAAAAAAAAAAAA
(SHIIIIINE)
SU
(SHF)

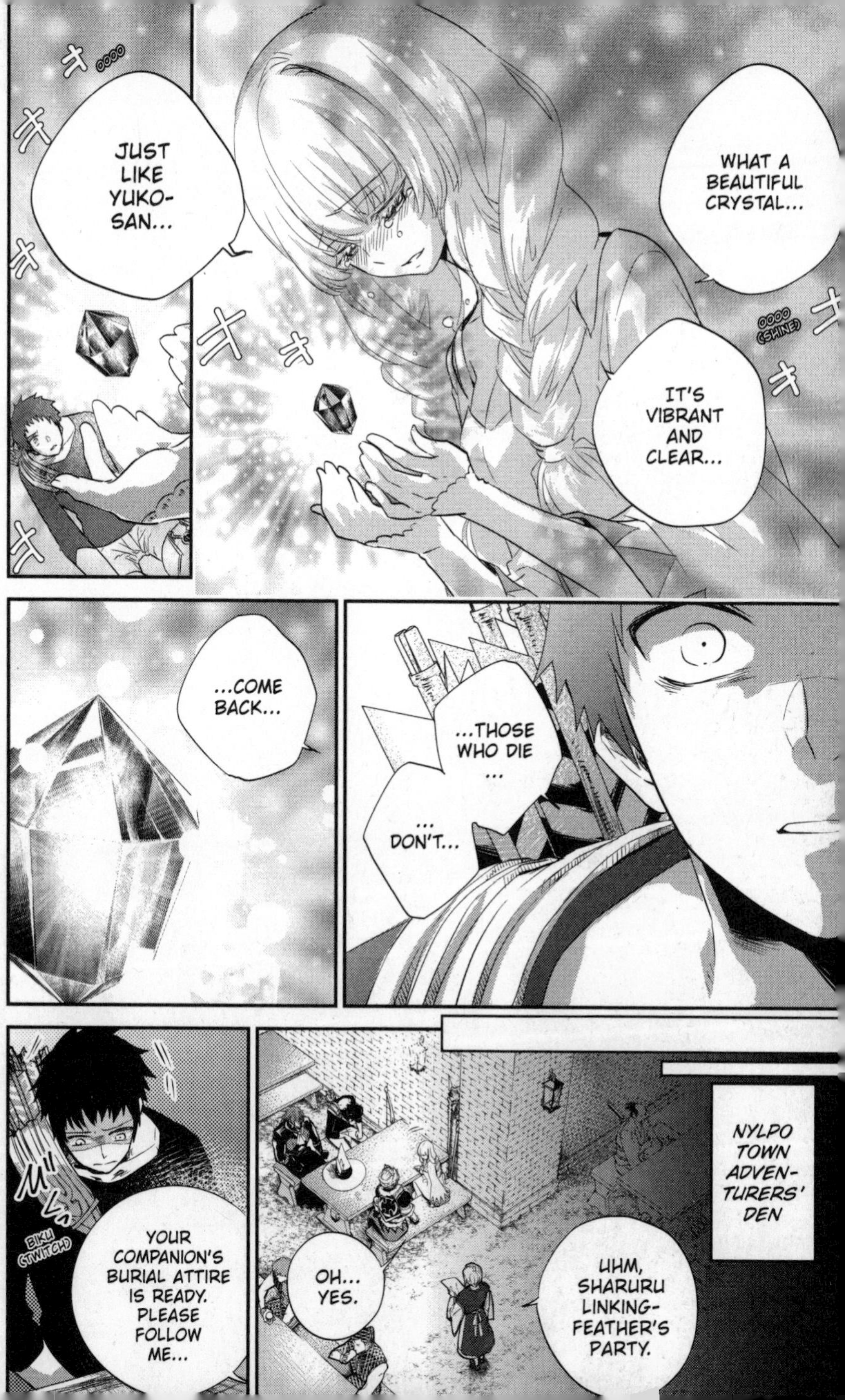
WHAT A BEAUTIFUL CRYSTAL...
OOOO (SHINE)
IT'S VIBRANT AND CLEAR...
OOOO
JUST LIKE YUKO-SAN...
...THOSE WHO DIE ...
... DON'T...
...COME BACK...
NYLPO TOWN ADVENTURERS' DEN
UHM, SHARURU LINKING-FEATHER'S PARTY.
OH... YES.
BIKU (TWITCH)
YOUR COMPANION'S BURIAL ATTIRE IS READY. PLEASE FOLLOW ME...

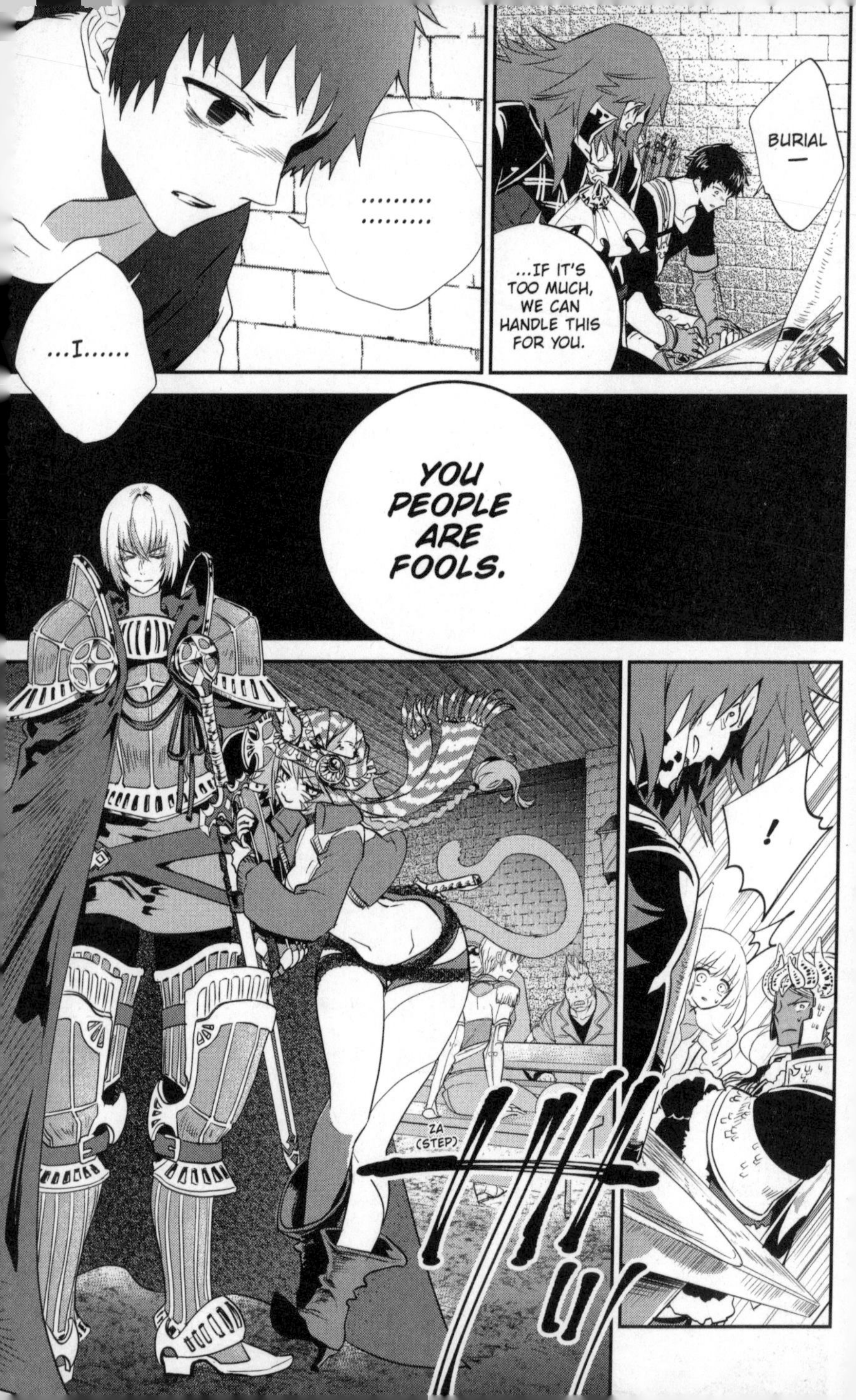
BURIAL —
...IF IT'S TOO MUCH, WE CAN HANDLE THIS FOR YOU.
....
....
...I......
YOU PEOPLE ARE FOOLS.
!
ZA (STEP)

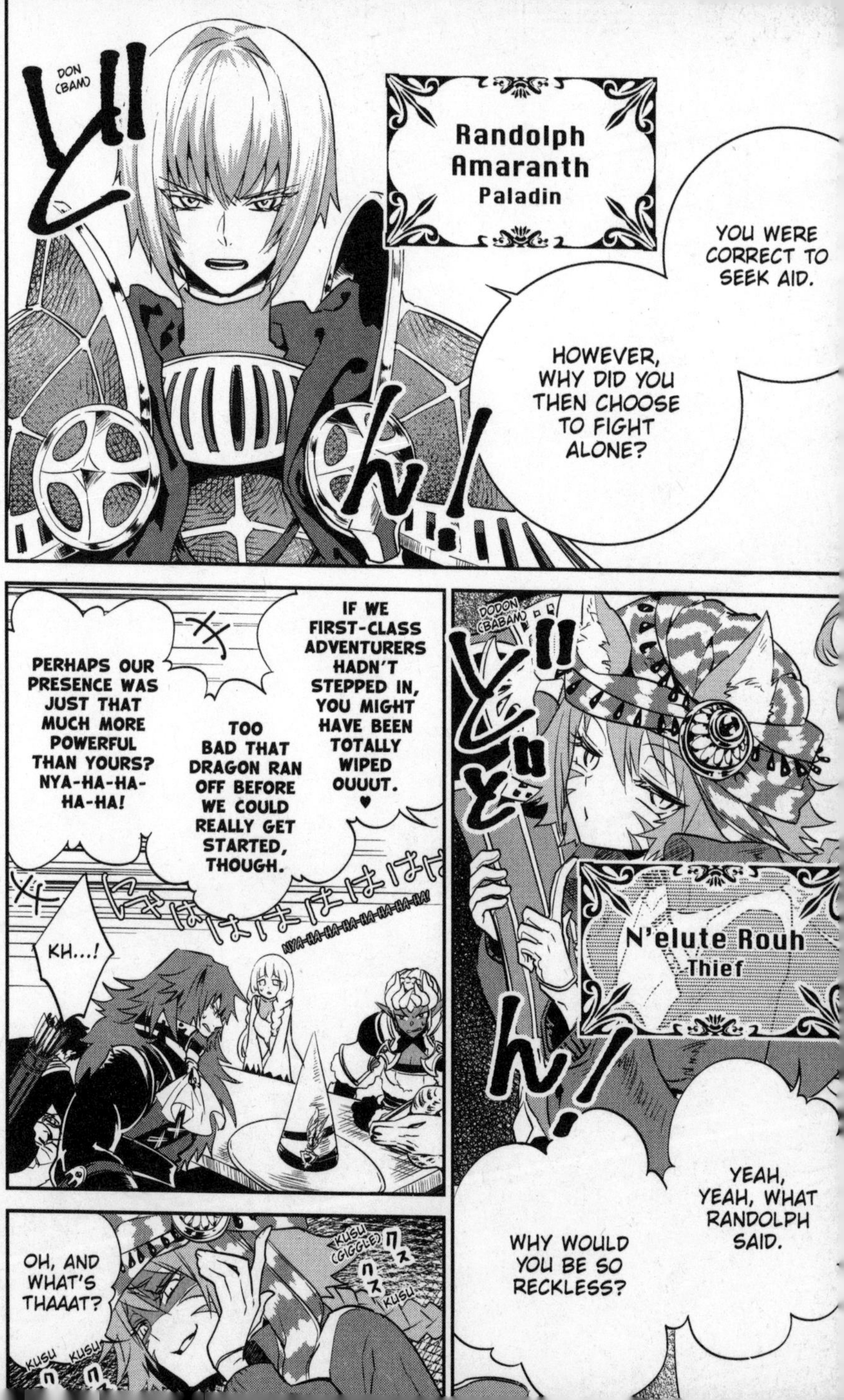
Randolph Amaranth
Paladin
YOU WERE CORRECT TO SEEK AID.
HOWEVER, WHY DID YOU THEN CHOOSE TO FIGHT ALONE?
DON (BAM)
DODON (BABAM)
N'elute Rouh
Thief
YEAH, YEAH, WHAT RANDOLPH SAID.
WHY WOULD YOU BE SO RECKLESS?
IF WE FIRST-CLASS ADVENTURERS HADN'T STEPPED IN, YOU MIGHT HAVE BEEN TOTALLY WIPED OUUUT. ♥
TOO BAD THAT DRAGON RAN OFF BEFORE WE COULD REALLY GET STARTED, THOUGH.
PERHAPS OUR PRESENCE WAS JUST THAT MUCH MORE POWERFUL THAN YOURS? NYA-HA-HA-HA-HA!
NYA-HA-HA-HA-HA-HA-HA-HA!
KH...!
KUSU (GIGGLE)
KUSU
OH, AND WHAT'S THAAAT?
KUSU KUSU

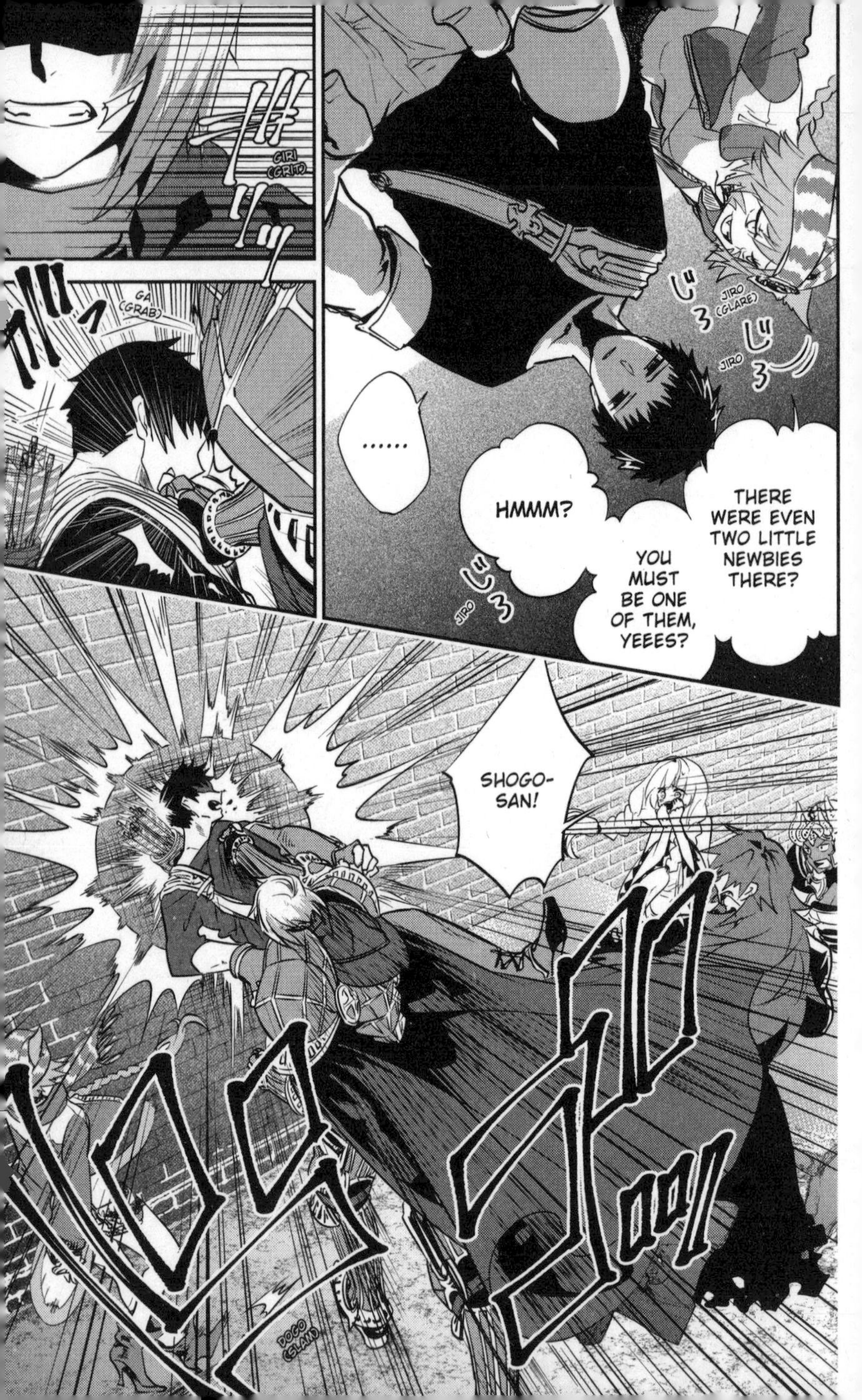
JIRO (GLARE)
JIRO
THERE WERE EVEN TWO LITTLE NEWBIES THERE?
YOU MUST BE ONE OF THEM, YEEES?
HMMM?
......
JIRO
GIRI (GRIT)
GA (GRAB)
SHOGO-SAN!
DOGO (SLAM)

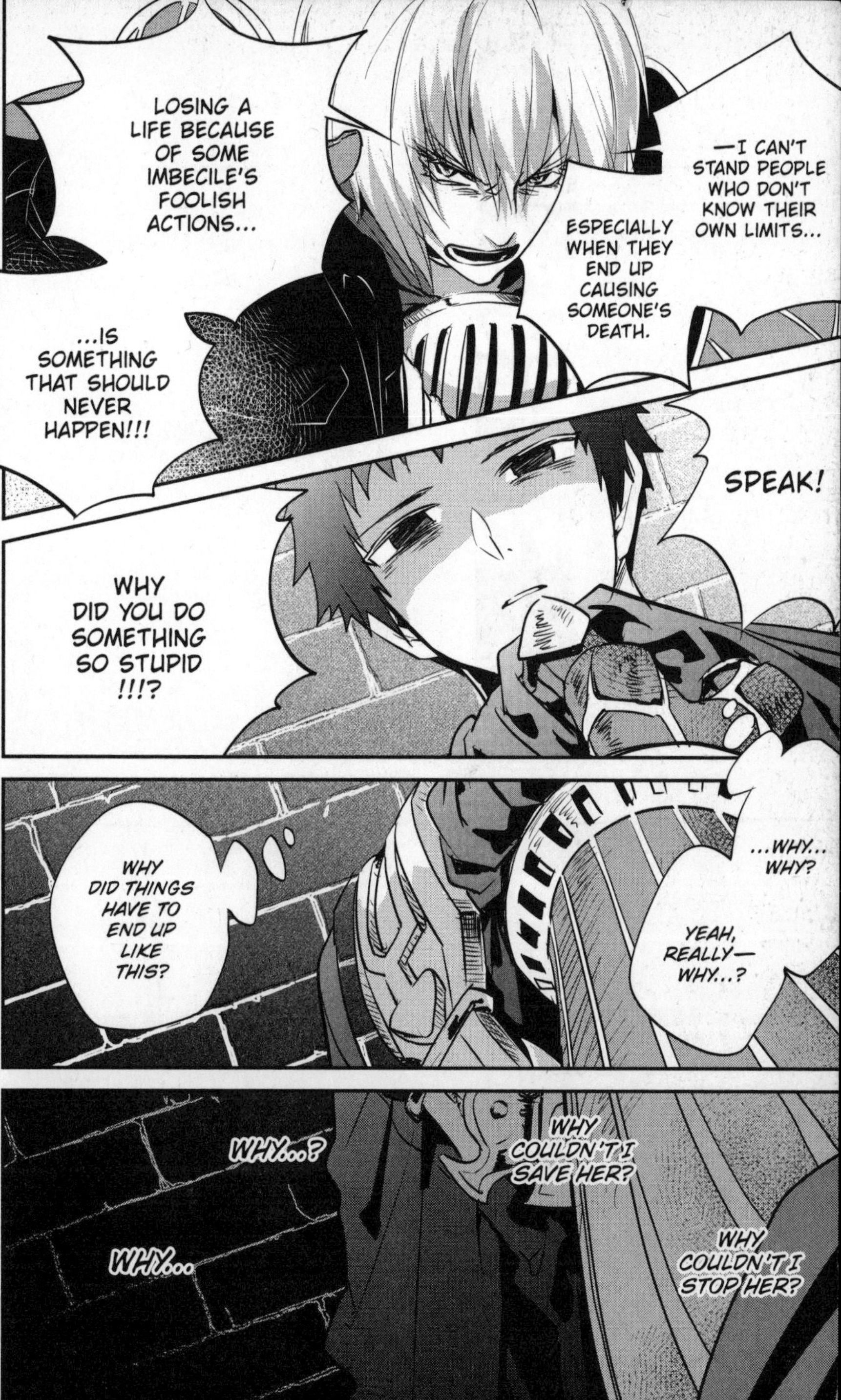
—I CAN'T STAND PEOPLE WHO DON'T KNOW THEIR OWN LIMITS...
ESPECIALLY WHEN THEY END UP CAUSING SOMEONE'S DEATH.
LOSING A LIFE BECAUSE OF SOME IMBECILE'S FOOLISH ACTIONS...
...IS SOMETHING THAT SHOULD NEVER HAPPEN!!!
SPEAK!
WHY DID YOU DO SOMETHING SO STUPID!!!?
...WHY... WHY?
YEAH, REALLY— WHY...?
WHY DID THINGS HAVE TO END UP LIKE THIS?
WHY COULDN'T I SAVE HER?
WHY COULDN'T I STOP HER?
WHY...?
WHY...

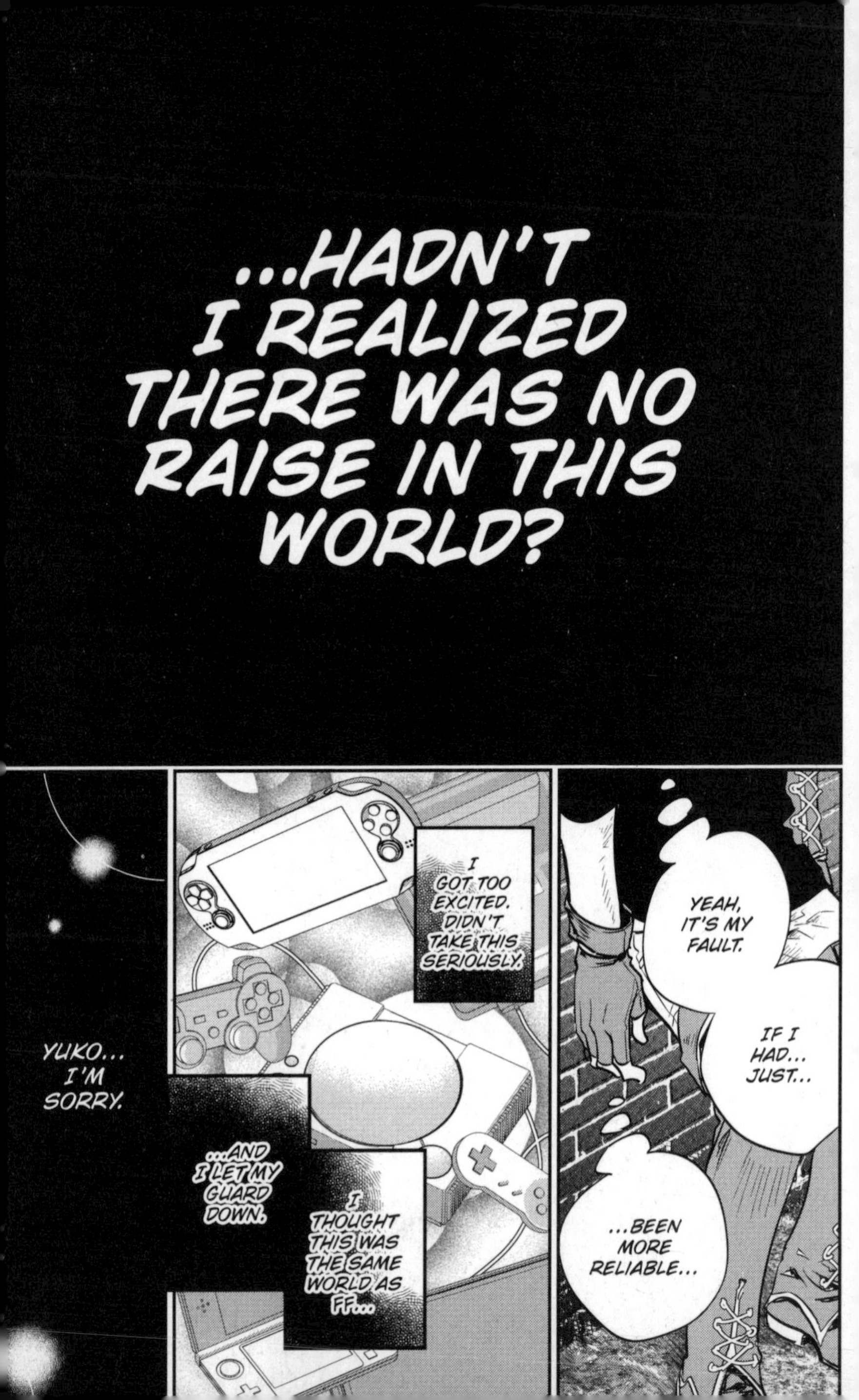
...HADN'T I REALIZED THERE WAS NO RAISE IN THIS WORLD?
YEAH, IT'S MY FAULT.
IF I HAD... JUST...
...BEEN MORE RELIABLE...
I GOT TOO EXCITED. DIDN'T TAKE THIS SERIOUSLY.
...AND I LET MY GUARD DOWN.
I THOUGHT THIS WAS THE SAME WORLD AS FF...
YUKO... I'M SORRY.

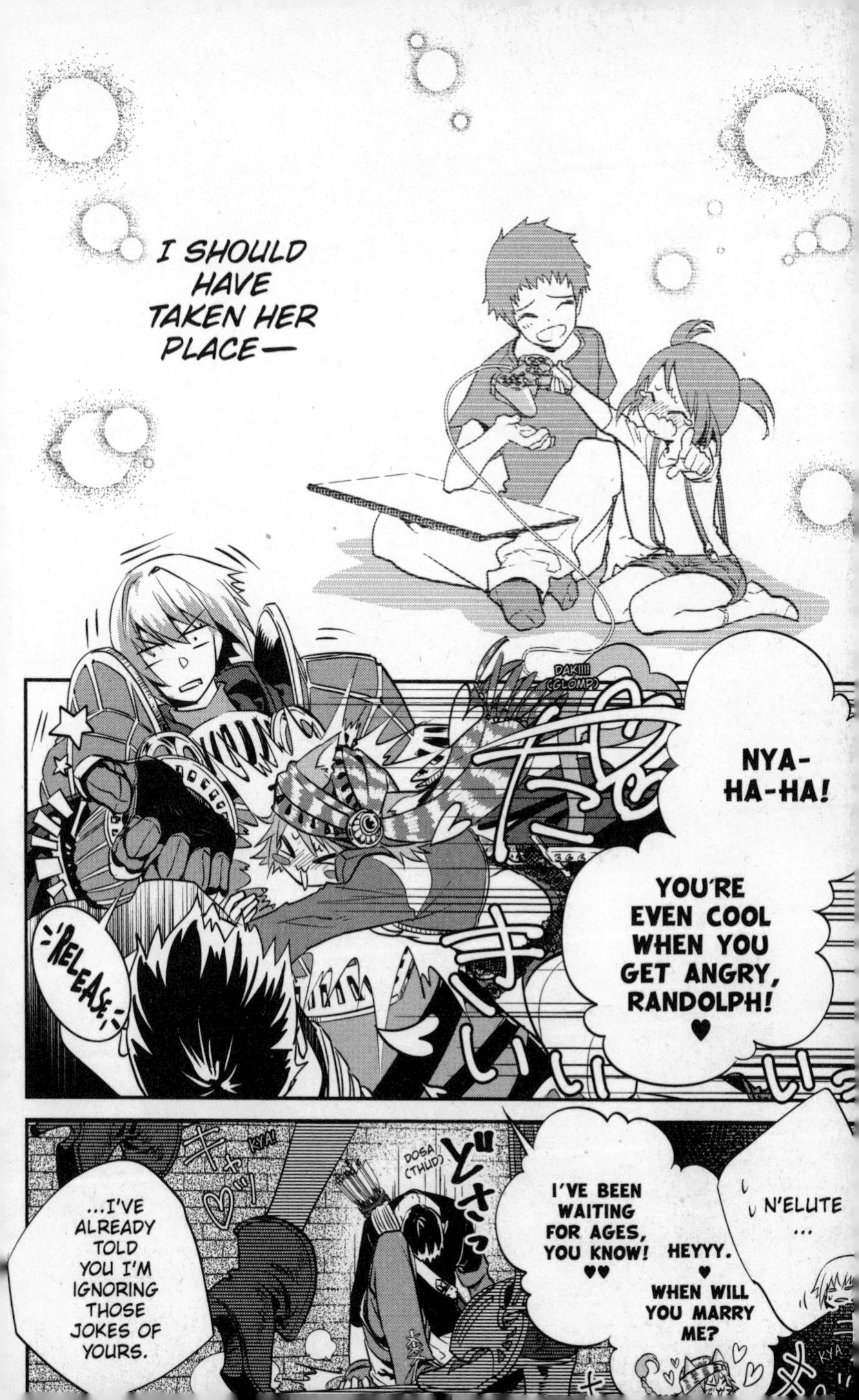

I SHOULD HAVE TAKEN HER PLACE—
NYA-HA-HA!
YOU'RE EVEN COOL WHEN YOU GET ANGRY, RANDOLPH! ♥
DAKIIII (GLOMP)
RELEASE
N'ELUTE ...
I'VE BEEN WAITING FOR AGES, YOU KNOW! ♥♥
HEYYY. ♥ WHEN WILL YOU MARRY ME?
DOSA (THUD)
KYA!
...I'VE ALREADY TOLD YOU I'M IGNORING THOSE JOKES OF YOURS.
KYA

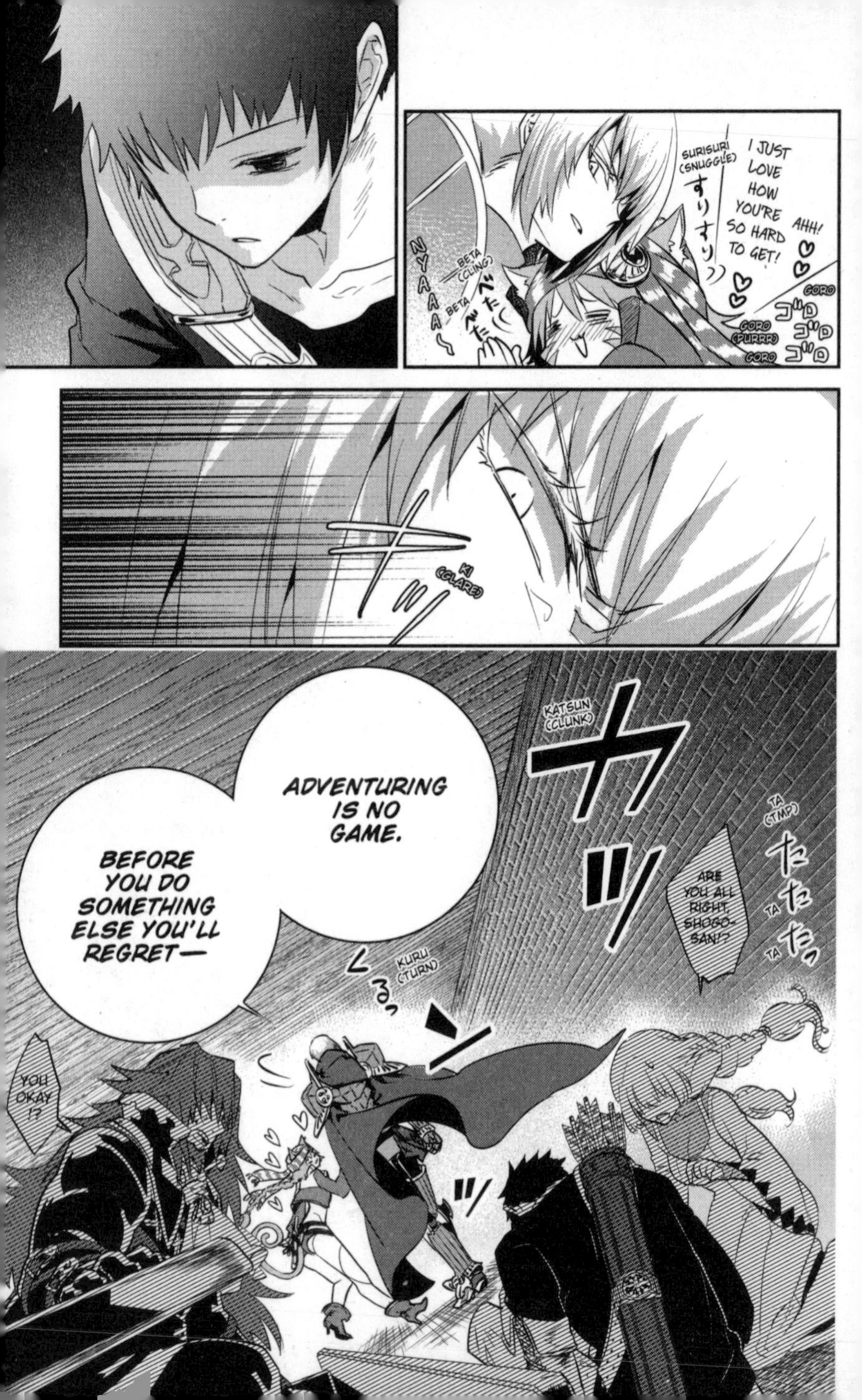
I JUST LOVE HOW YOU'RE SO HARD TO GET!
AHH!
SURISURI (SNUGGLE)
GORO GORO (PURRR) GORO
BETA (CLING) BETA
NYAAAA~
KI (GLARE)
KATSUN (CLUNK)
TA (TMP) TA TA
ARE YOU ALL RIGHT, SHOGO-SAN!?
ADVENTURING IS NO GAME.
BEFORE YOU DO SOMETHING ELSE YOU'LL REGRET—
KURU (TURN)
YOU OKAY!?

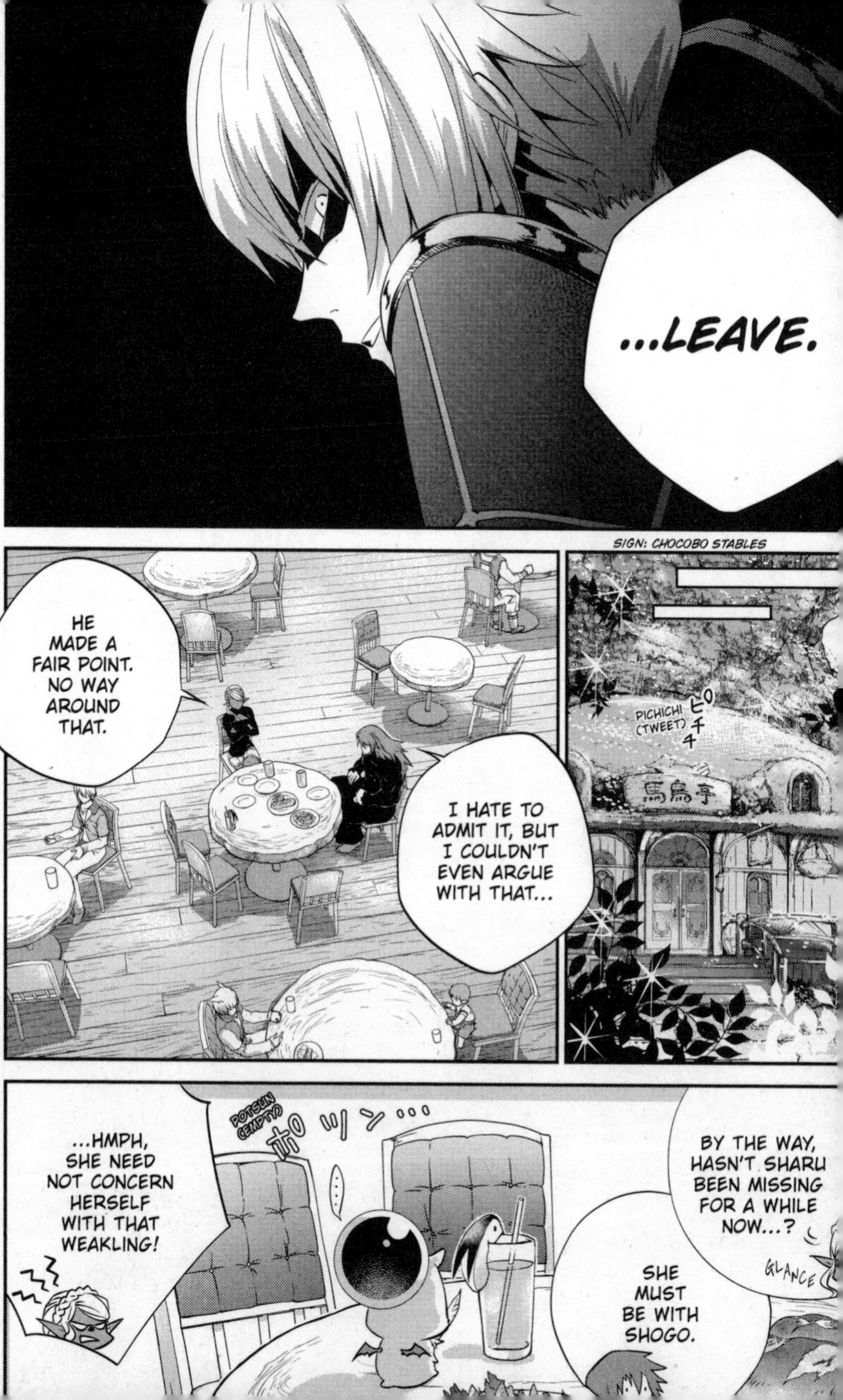
...LEAVE.
SIGN: CHOCOBO STABLES
馬鳥亭
ピチチ
PICHICHI (TWEET)
HE MADE A FAIR POINT. NO WAY AROUND THAT.
I HATE TO ADMIT IT, BUT I COULDN'T EVEN ARGUE WITH THAT...
BY THE WAY, HASN'T SHARU BEEN MISSING FOR A WHILE NOW...?
GLANCE
SHE MUST BE WITH SHOGO.
ポツン...
POTSUN (EMPTY)
...
...HMPH, SHE NEED NOT CONCERN HERSELF WITH THAT WEAKLING!

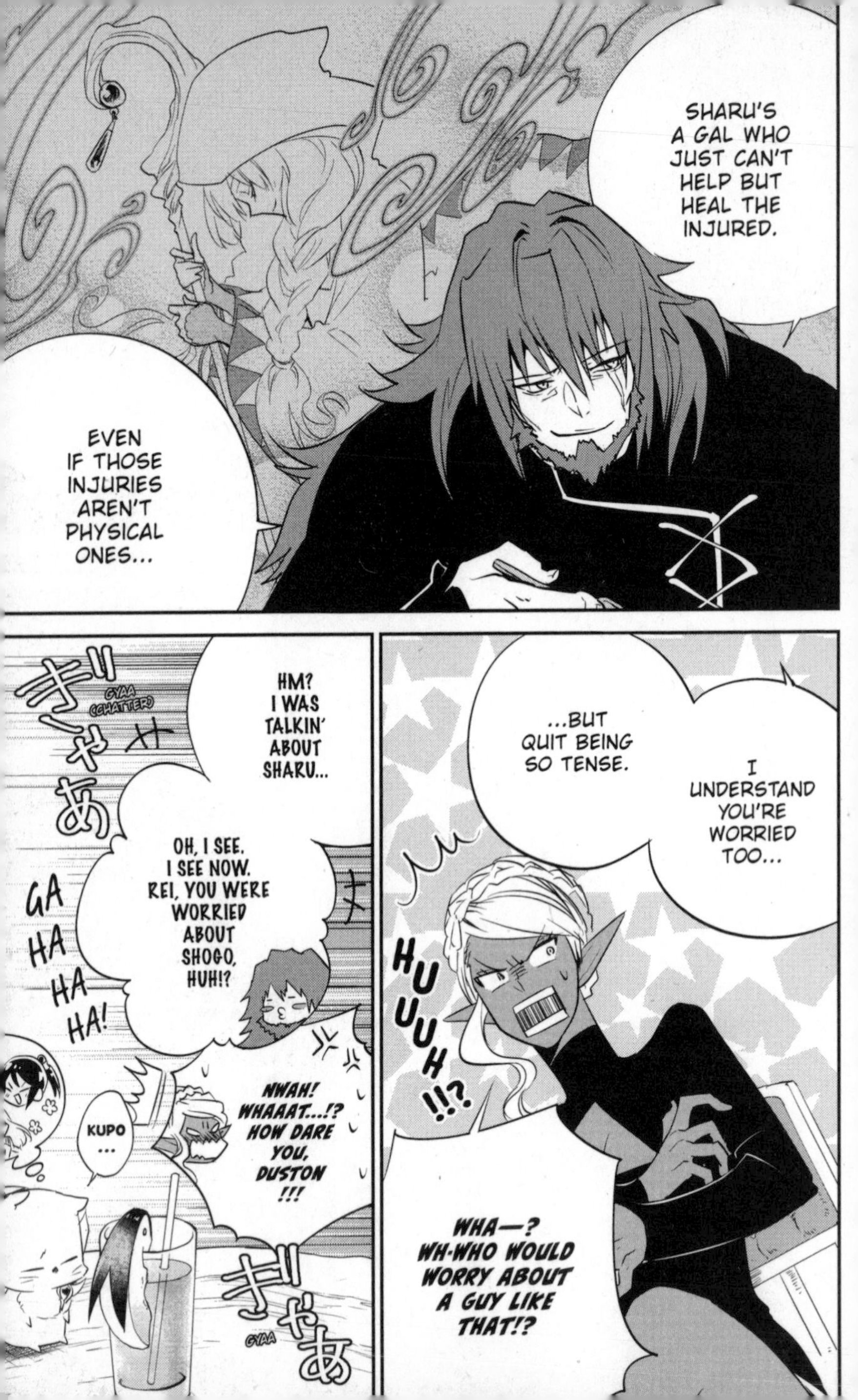
SHARU'S A GAL WHO JUST CAN'T HELP BUT HEAL THE INJURED.
EVEN IF THOSE INJURIES AREN'T PHYSICAL ONES...
I UNDERSTAND YOU'RE WORRIED TOO...
...BUT QUIT BEING SO TENSE.
HUUUH!!?
WHA—? WH-WHO WOULD WORRY ABOUT A GUY LIKE THAT!?
HM? I WAS TALKIN' ABOUT SHARU...
GYAA (CHATTER)
OH, I SEE. I SEE NOW. REI, YOU WERE WORRIED ABOUT SHOGO, HUH!?
GA HA HA HA!
NWAH! WHAAAT...!? HOW DARE YOU, DUSTON !!!
KUPO ...
GYAA

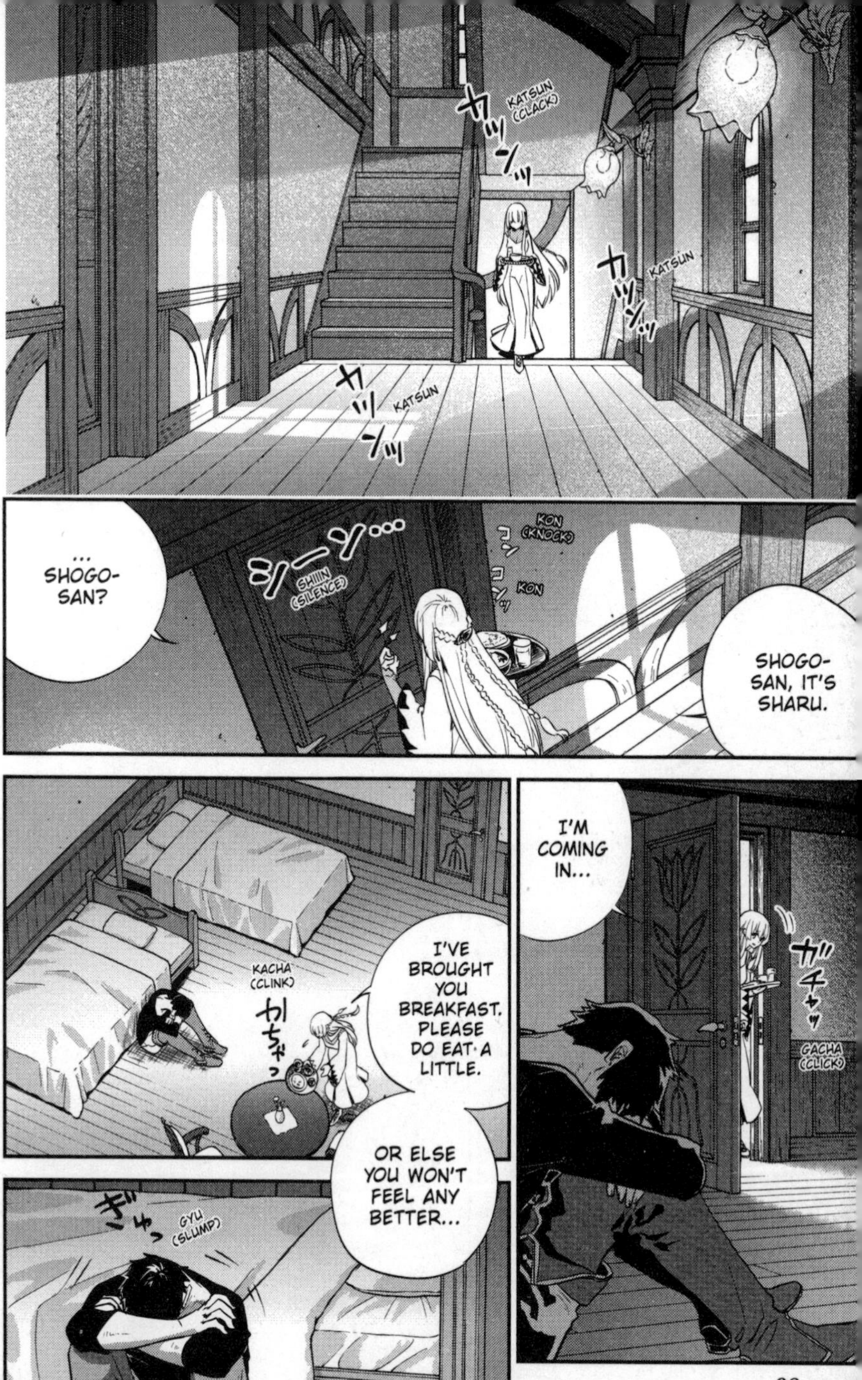
KATSUN (CLACK)
KATSUN
KATSUN
SHOGO-SAN, IT'S SHARU.
KON (KNOCK)
KON
SHIIIN (SILENCE)
... SHOGO-SAN?
I'M COMING IN...
GACHA (CLICK)
I'VE BROUGHT YOU BREAKFAST. PLEASE DO EAT A LITTLE.
KACHA (CLINK)
OR ELSE YOU WON'T FEEL ANY BETTER...
GYU (SLUMP)

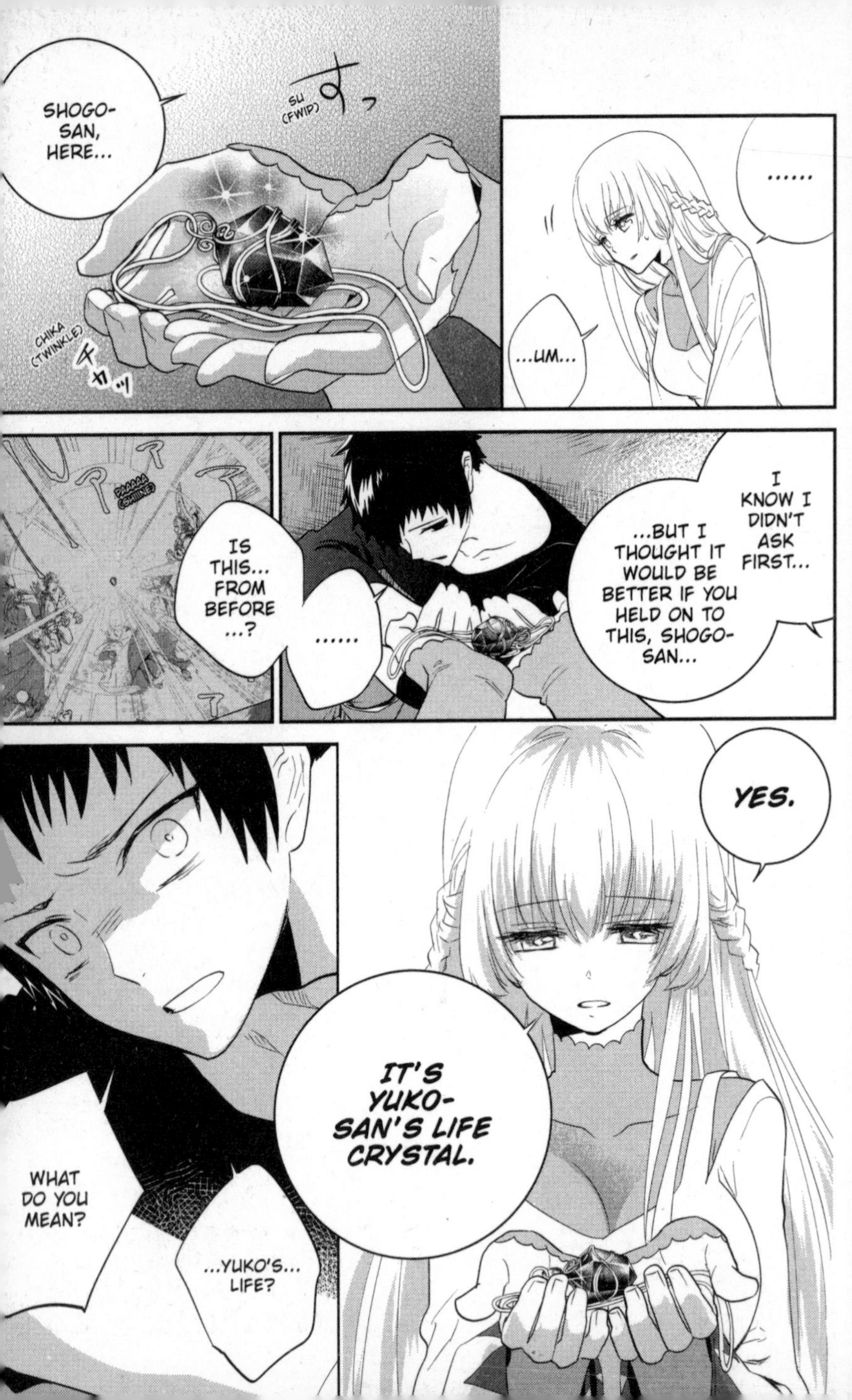
......
...UM...
SHOGO-SAN, HERE...
すっ
SU (FWIP)
チカッ
CHIKA (TWINKLE)
I KNOW I DIDN'T ASK FIRST...
...BUT I THOUGHT IT WOULD BE BETTER IF YOU HELD ON TO THIS, SHOGO-SAN...
......
IS THIS... FROM BEFORE...?
PAAAAA (SHIINE)
YES.
IT'S YUKO-SAN'S LIFE CRYSTAL.
...YUKO'S... LIFE?
WHAT DO YOU MEAN?

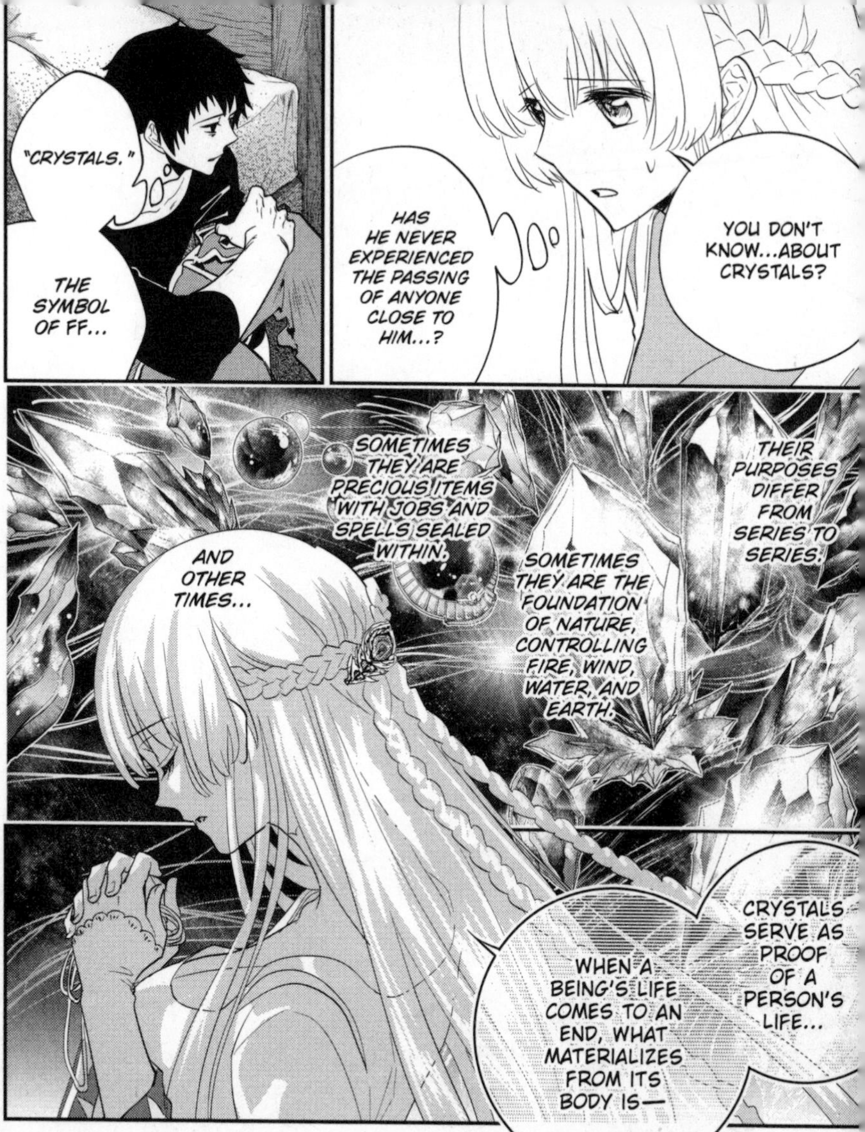
YOU DON'T KNOW...ABOUT CRYSTALS?
HAS HE NEVER EXPERIENCED THE PASSING OF ANYONE CLOSE TO HIM...?
"CRYSTALS."
THE SYMBOL OF FF...
THEIR PURPOSES DIFFER FROM SERIES TO SERIES.
SOMETIMES THEY ARE PRECIOUS ITEMS WITH JOBS AND SPELLS SEALED WITHIN.
SOMETIMES THEY ARE THE FOUNDATION OF NATURE, CONTROLLING FIRE, WIND, WATER, AND EARTH.
AND OTHER TIMES...
CRYSTALS SERVE AS PROOF OF A PERSON'S LIFE...
WHEN A BEING'S LIFE COMES TO AN END, WHAT MATERIALIZES FROM ITS BODY IS—
A SOUL CRYSTAL.

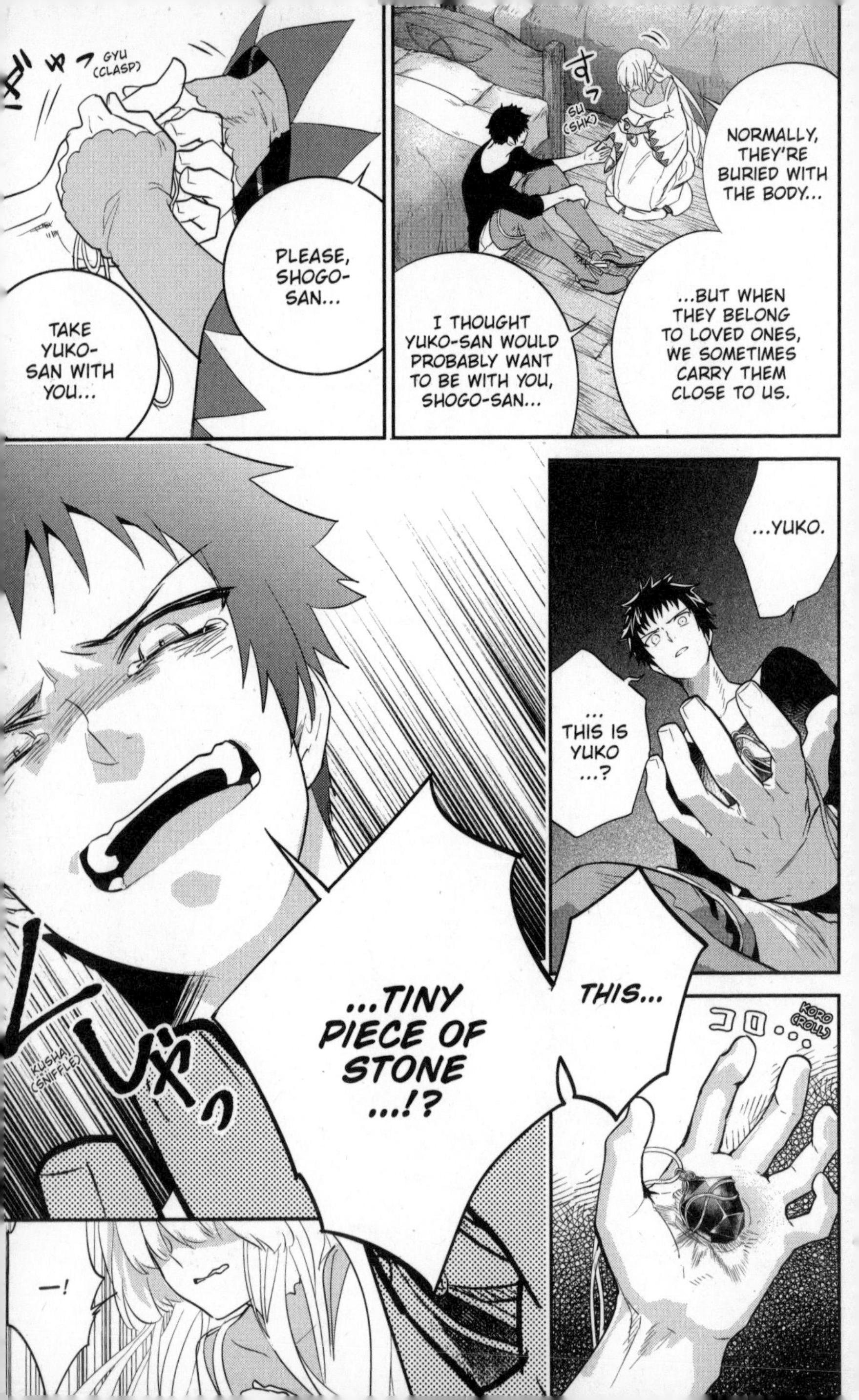
すっ
SU (SHK)
NORMALLY, THEY'RE BURIED WITH THE BODY...
...BUT WHEN THEY BELONG TO LOVED ONES, WE SOMETIMES CARRY THEM CLOSE TO US.
I THOUGHT YUKO-SAN WOULD PROBABLY WANT TO BE WITH YOU, SHOGO-SAN...
GYU (CLASP)
PLEASE, SHOGO-SAN...
TAKE YUKO-SAN WITH YOU...
...YUKO.
... THIS IS YUKO ...?
コロ...
KORO (ROLL)
THIS...
...TINY PIECE OF STONE ...!?
KUSHA (SNIFFLE)
—!

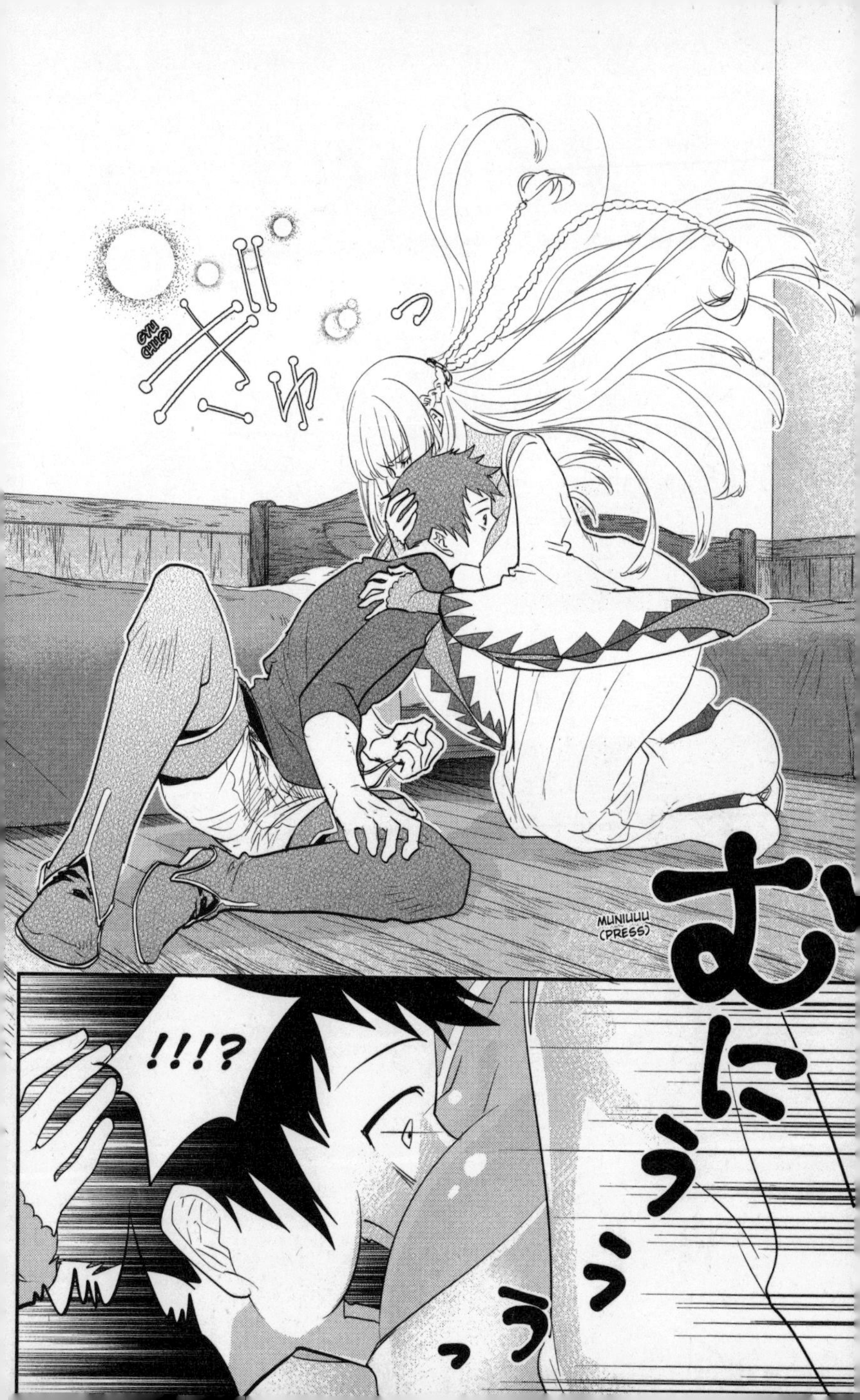
ぎゅっ
GYU (HUG)
むにうぅぅっ
MUNIUUU (PRESS)
!!!?

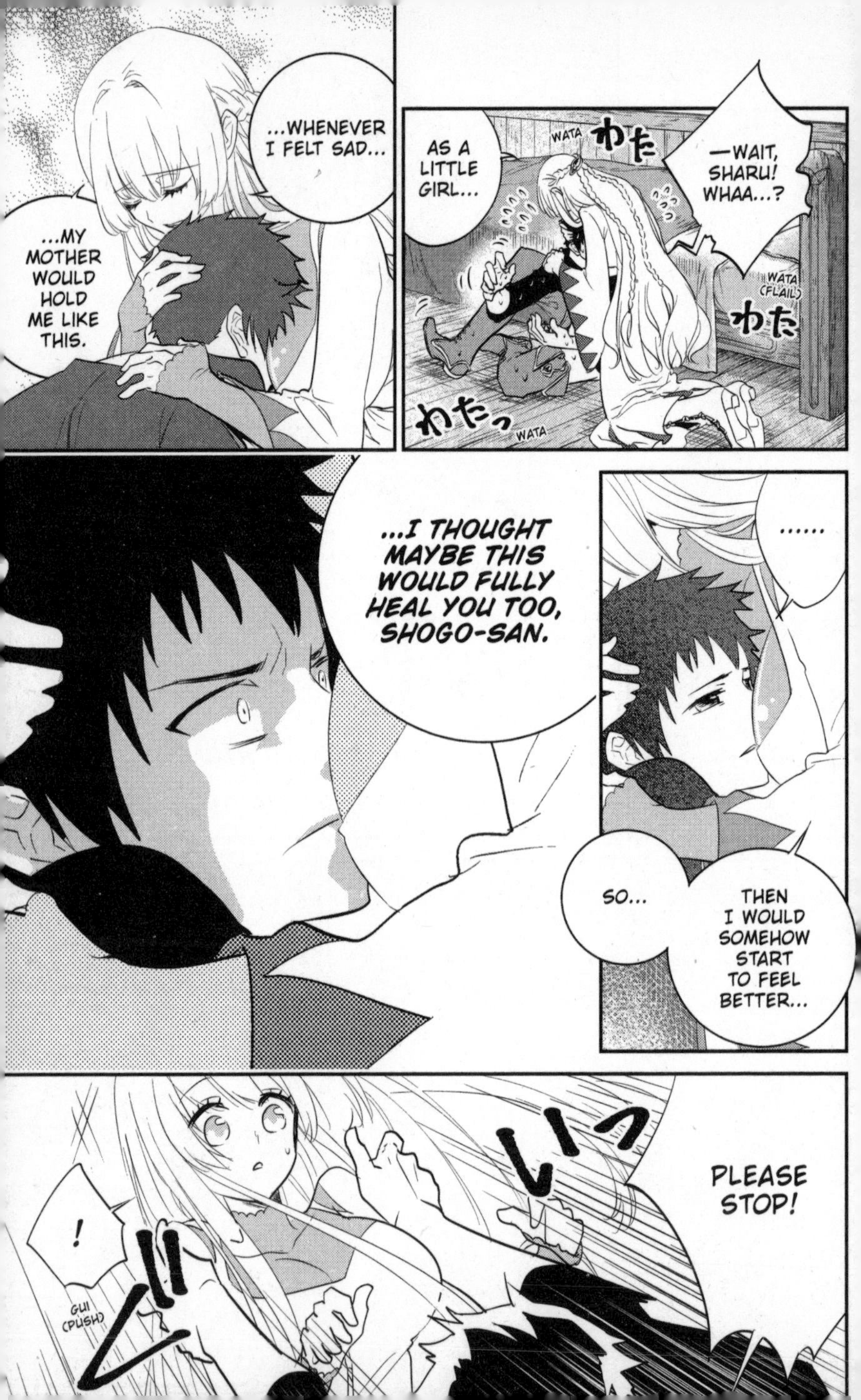
—WAIT, SHARU! WHAA...?
WATA わた
AS A LITTLE GIRL...
WATA (FLAIL) わた
わたっ WATA
...WHENEVER I FELT SAD...
...MY MOTHER WOULD HOLD ME LIKE THIS.
......
THEN I WOULD SOMEHOW START TO FEEL BETTER...
SO...
...I THOUGHT MAYBE THIS WOULD FULLY HEAL YOU TOO, SHOGO-SAN.
PLEASE STOP!
!
GUI (PUSH)

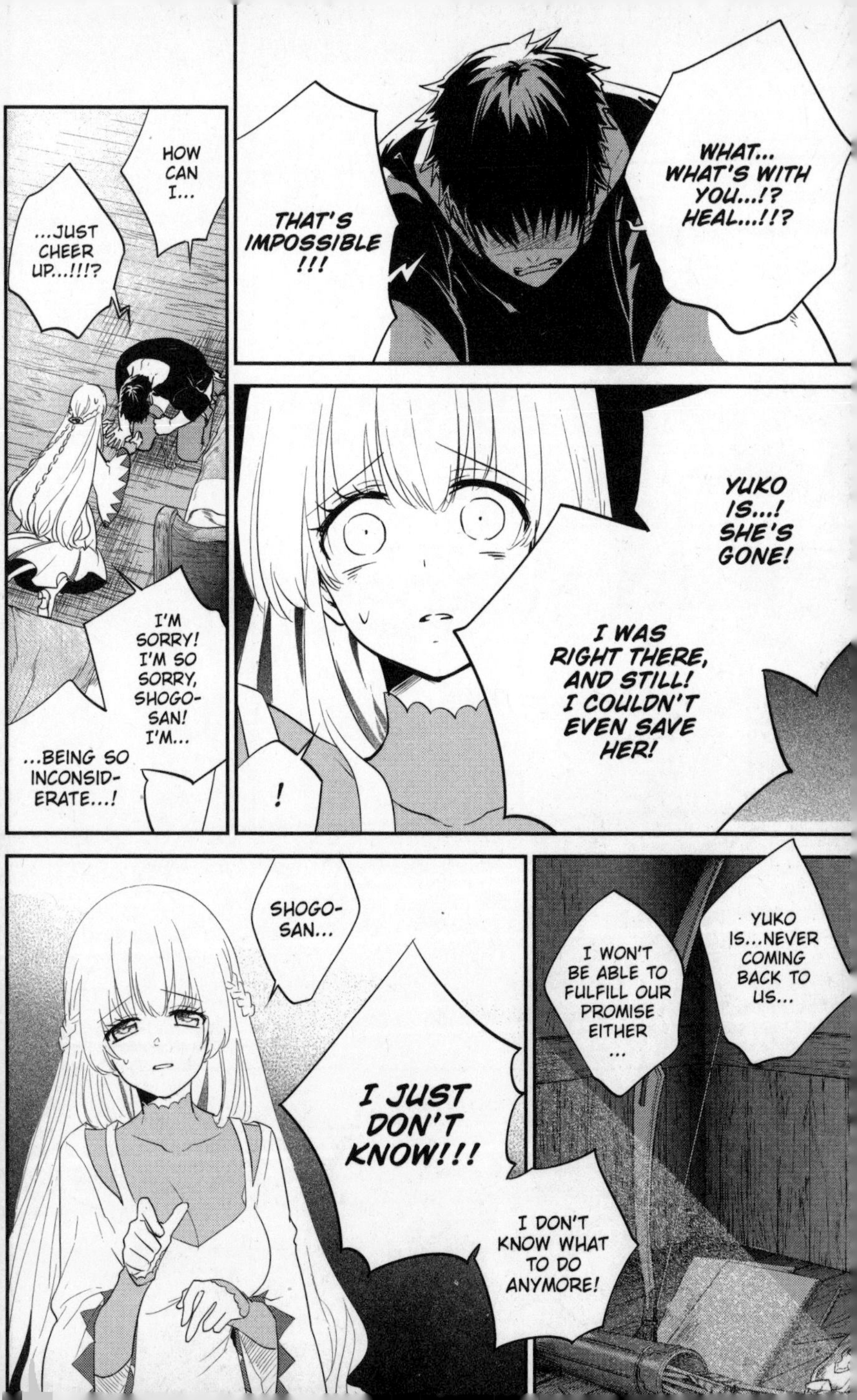
WHAT... WHAT'S WITH YOU...!? HEAL...!!?
THAT'S IMPOSSIBLE !!!
YUKO IS...! SHE'S GONE!
I WAS RIGHT THERE, AND STILL! I COULDN'T EVEN SAVE HER!
!
HOW CAN I...
...JUST CHEER UP...!!!?
I'M SORRY! I'M SO SORRY, SHOGO-SAN! I'M...
...BEING SO INCONSID-ERATE...!
YUKO IS...NEVER COMING BACK TO US...
I WON'T BE ABLE TO FULFILL OUR PROMISE EITHER ...
SHOGO-SAN...
I JUST DON'T KNOW!!!
I DON'T KNOW WHAT TO DO ANYMORE!

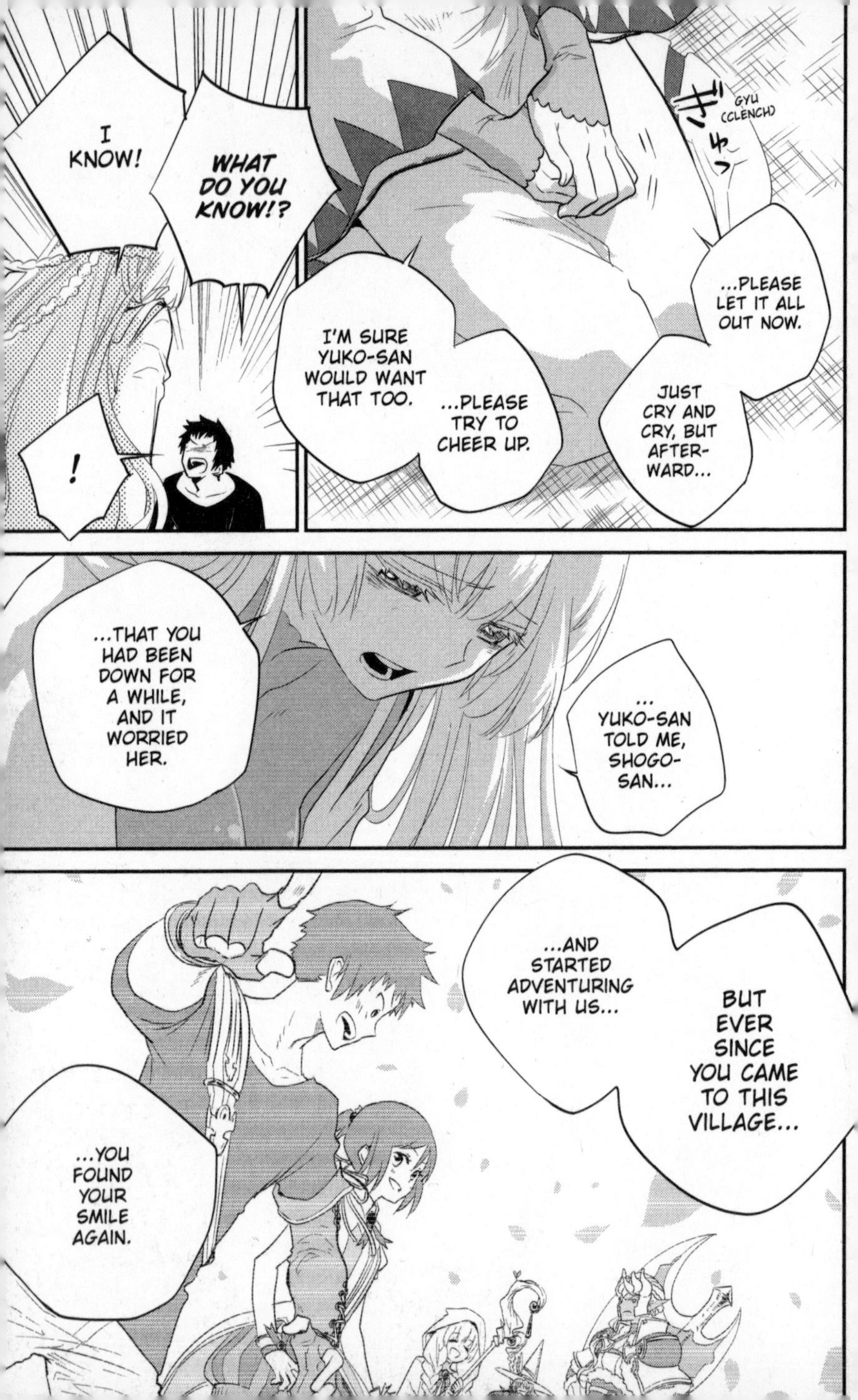
ぎゅっ
GYU (CLENCH)
...PLEASE LET IT ALL OUT NOW.
JUST CRY AND CRY, BUT AFTER-WARD...
...PLEASE TRY TO CHEER UP.
I'M SURE YUKO-SAN WOULD WANT THAT TOO.
WHAT DO YOU KNOW!?
I KNOW!
!
... YUKO-SAN TOLD ME, SHOGO-SAN...
...THAT YOU HAD BEEN DOWN FOR A WHILE, AND IT WORRIED HER.
BUT EVER SINCE YOU CAME TO THIS VILLAGE...
...AND STARTED ADVENTURING WITH US...
...YOU FOUND YOUR SMILE AGAIN.

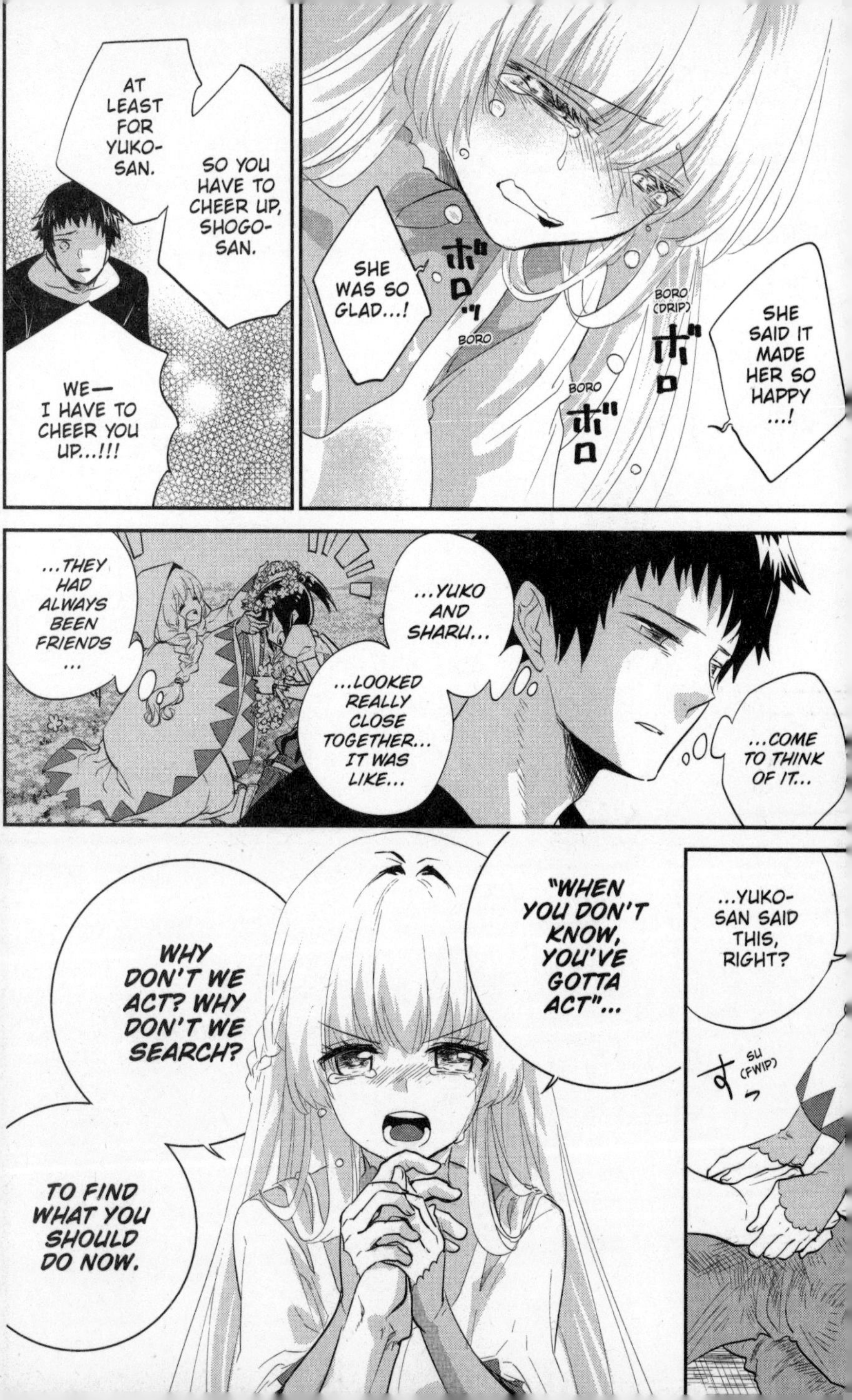
SHE SAID IT MADE HER SO HAPPY...!
BORO (DRIP)
ボロ
BORO
ボロ
SHE WAS SO GLAD...!
ボロッ
BORO
SO YOU HAVE TO CHEER UP, SHOGO-SAN.
AT LEAST FOR YUKO-SAN.
WE— I HAVE TO CHEER YOU UP...!!!
...COME TO THINK OF IT...
...YUKO AND SHARU...
...LOOKED REALLY CLOSE TOGETHER... IT WAS LIKE...
...THEY HAD ALWAYS BEEN FRIENDS...
...YUKO-SAN SAID THIS, RIGHT?
SU (FWIP)
す
"WHEN YOU DON'T KNOW, YOU'VE GOTTA ACT"...
WHY DON'T WE ACT? WHY DON'T WE SEARCH?
TO FIND WHAT YOU SHOULD DO NOW.

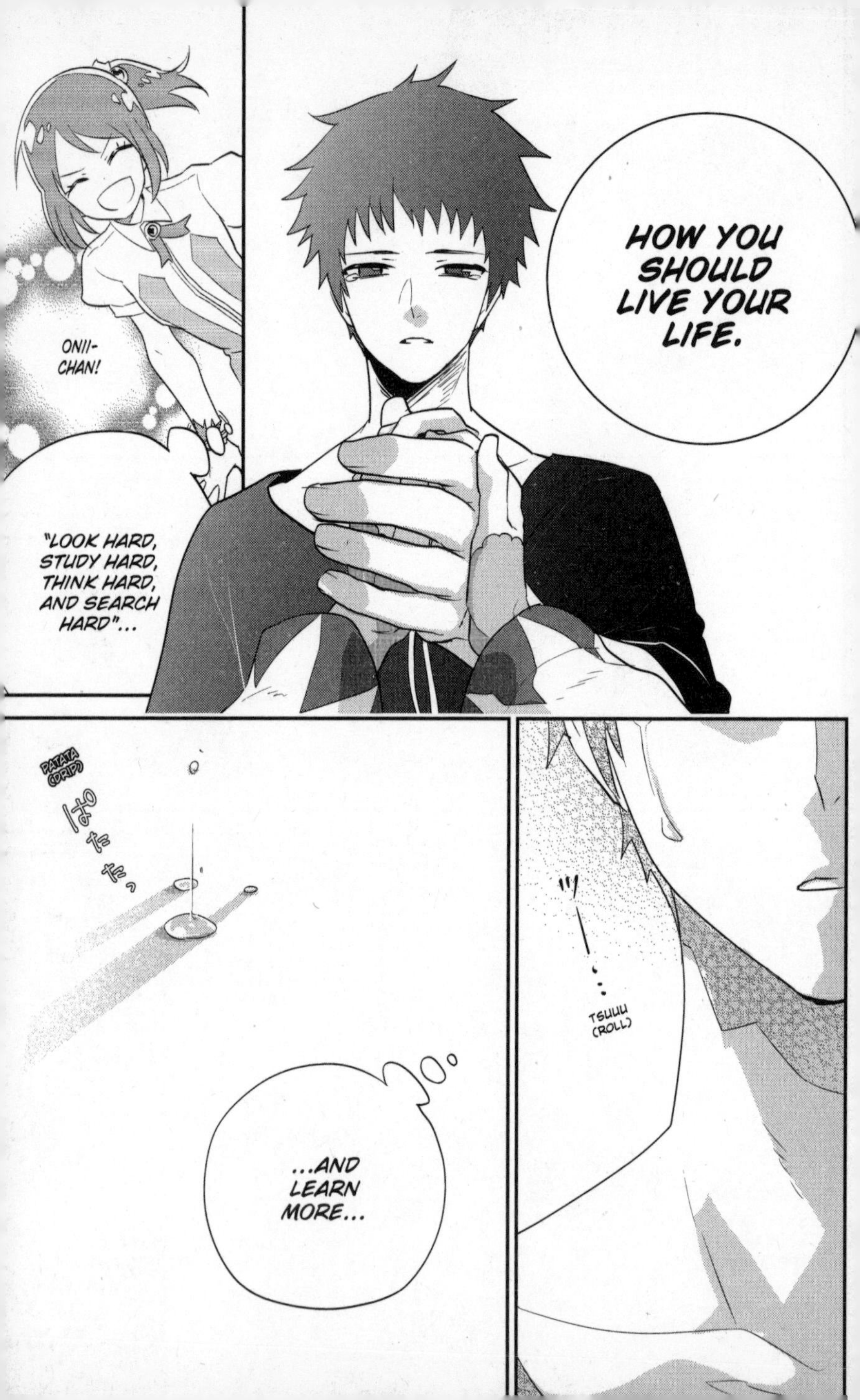
HOW YOU SHOULD LIVE YOUR LIFE.
ONII-CHAN!
"LOOK HARD, STUDY HARD, THINK HARD, AND SEARCH HARD"...
TSUUU (ROLL)
PATATA (DRIP)
ぱたたっ
...AND LEARN MORE...

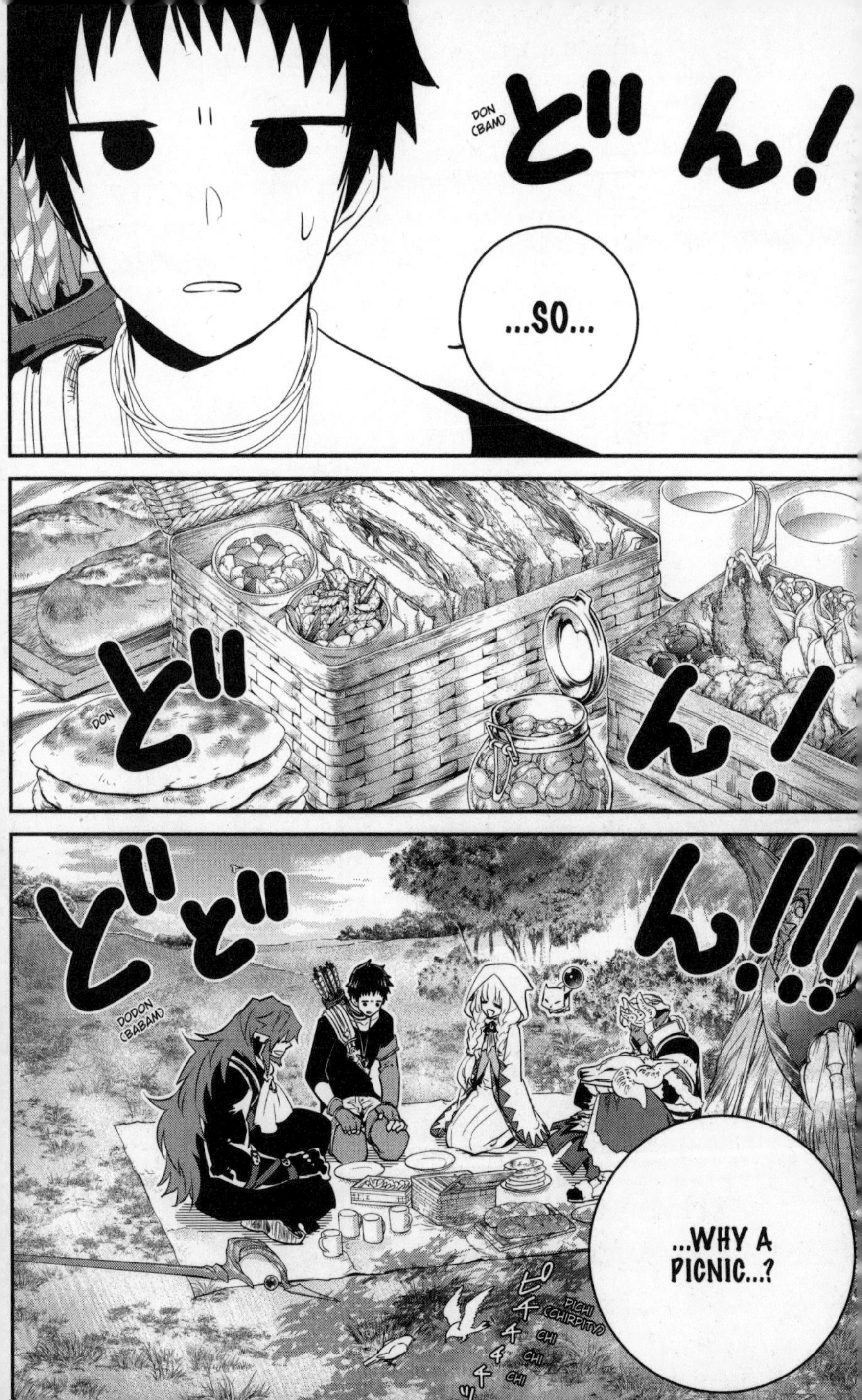
どん!
DON (BAM)
...SO...
どん!
DON
どどん!!!
DODON (BABAM)
...WHY A PICNIC...?
ピチチチチ
PICHI (CHIRPITY)
CHI
CHI
CHI

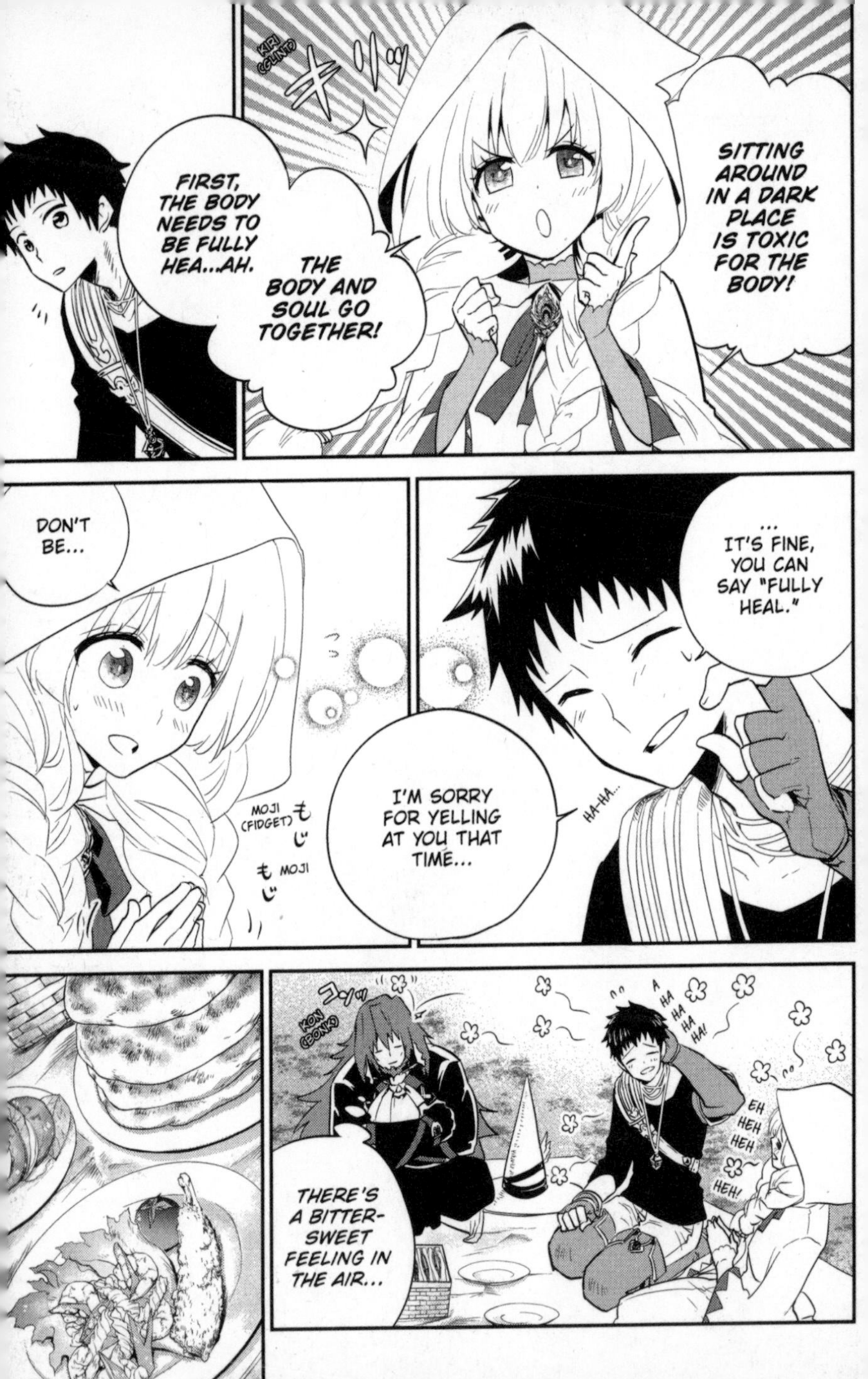
KIRI (GLINT)
SITTING AROUND IN A DARK PLACE IS TOXIC FOR THE BODY!
THE BODY AND SOUL GO TOGETHER!
FIRST, THE BODY NEEDS TO BE FULLY HEA...AH.
... IT'S FINE, YOU CAN SAY "FULLY HEAL."
HA-HA...
I'M SORRY FOR YELLING AT YOU THAT TIME...
DON'T BE...
MOJI (FIDGET) もじ
もじ MOJI
KON (BONK)
A HA HA HA HA!
EH HEH HEH HEH!
THERE'S A BITTER-SWEET FEELING IN THE AIR...

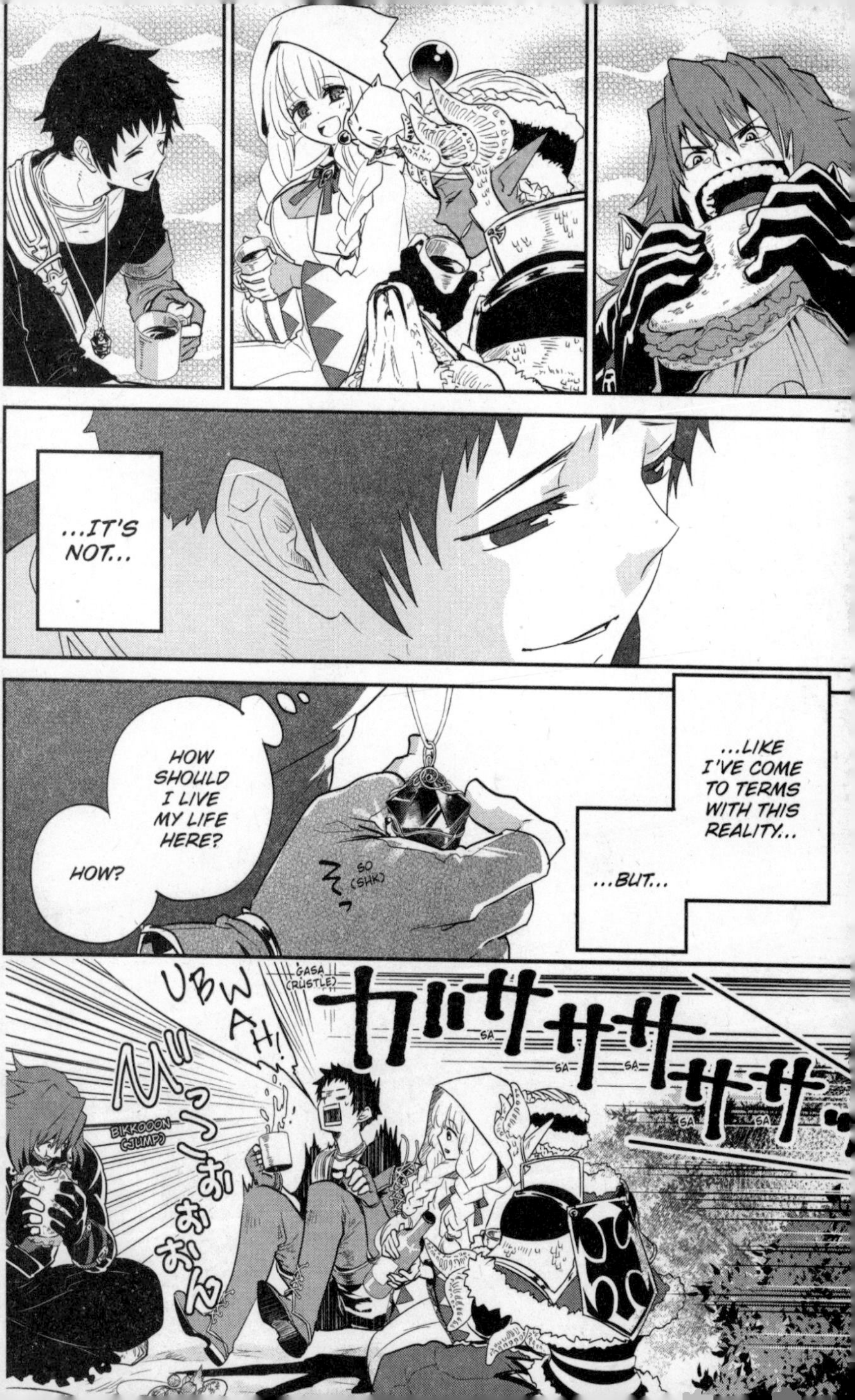
...IT'S NOT...
...LIKE I'VE COME TO TERMS WITH THIS REALITY...
...BUT...
SO (SHK)
HOW SHOULD I LIVE MY LIFE HERE?
HOW?
SA SA SA SA SA
GASA (RUSTLE)
UBWAH!
BIKKOOON (JUMP)

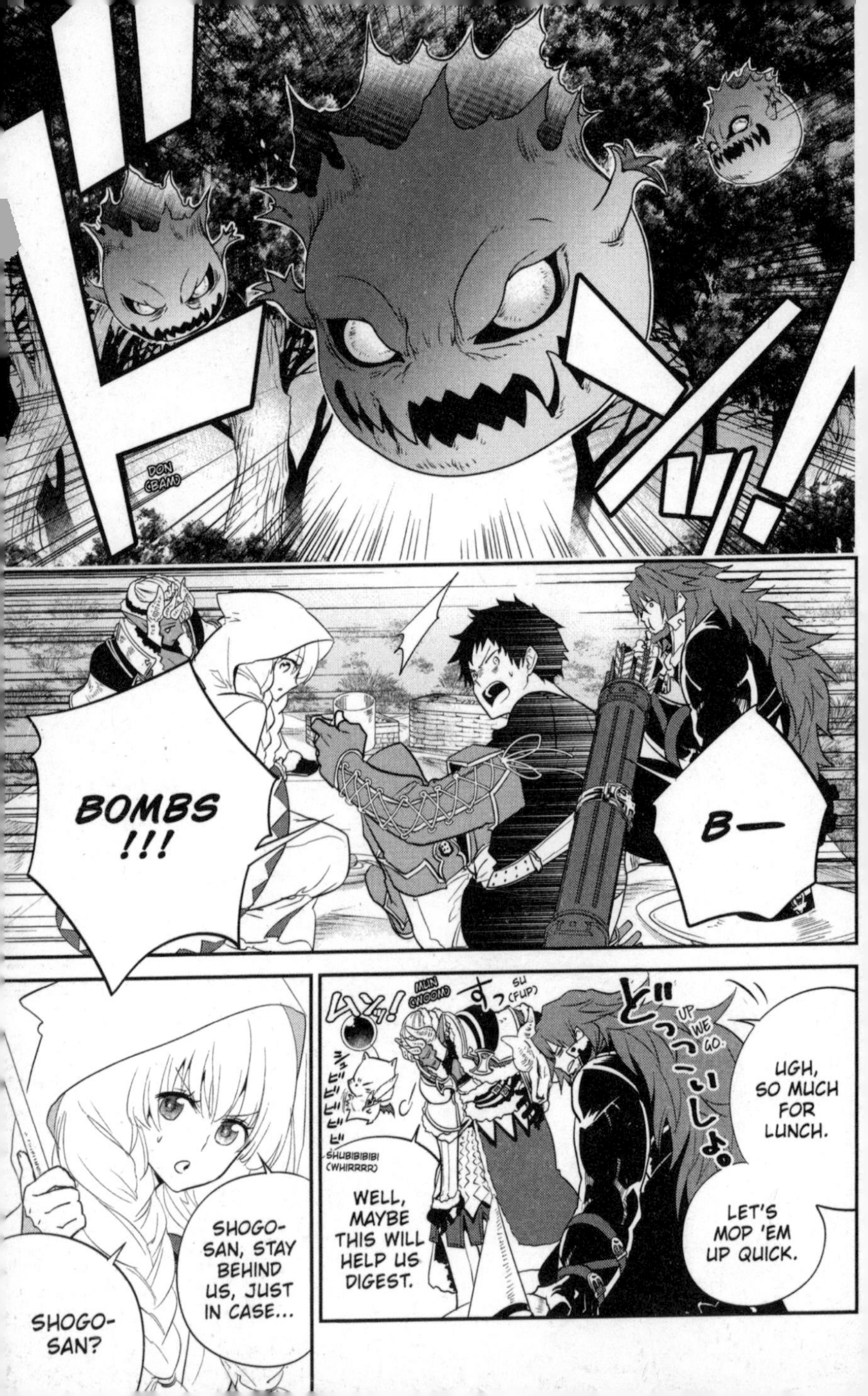
DON (BAM)
B—
BOMBS!!!
UP WE GO.
UGH, SO MUCH FOR LUNCH.
SU (FUP)
MUN (WOOM)
LET'S MOP 'EM UP QUICK.
SHUBIBIBIBI (WHIRRRR)
WELL, MAYBE THIS WILL HELP US DIGEST.
SHOGO-SAN, STAY BEHIND US, JUST IN CASE...
SHOGO-SAN?

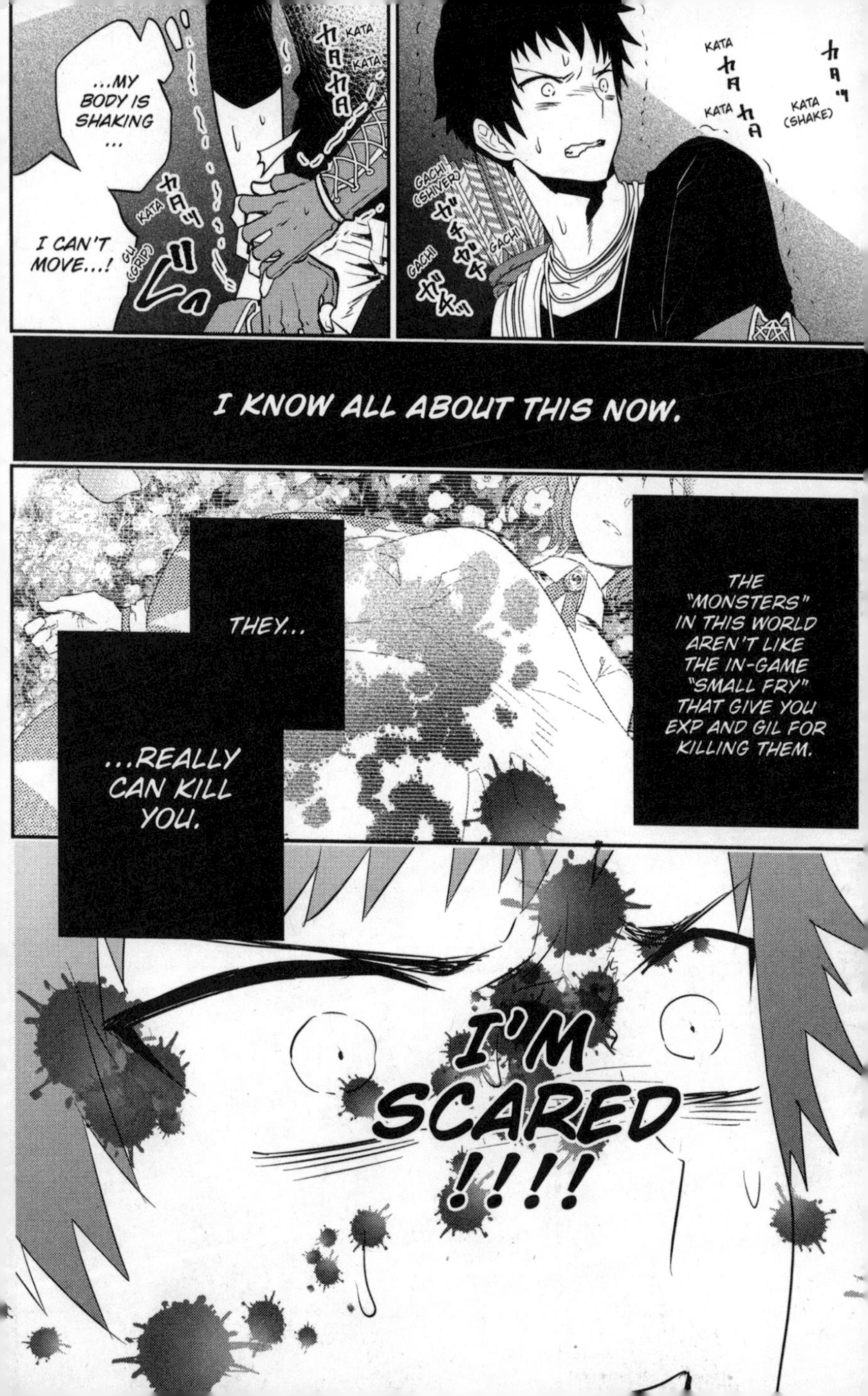
KATA
KATA
KATA (SHAKE)
GACHI (SHIVER)
GACHI
GACHI
KATA
KATA
...MY BODY IS SHAKING...
KATA
I CAN'T MOVE...!
GU (GRIP)
I KNOW ALL ABOUT THIS NOW.
THE "MONSTERS" IN THIS WORLD AREN'T LIKE THE IN-GAME "SMALL FRY" THAT GIVE YOU EXP AND GIL FOR KILLING THEM.
THEY...
...REALLY CAN KILL YOU.
I'M SCARED!!!!

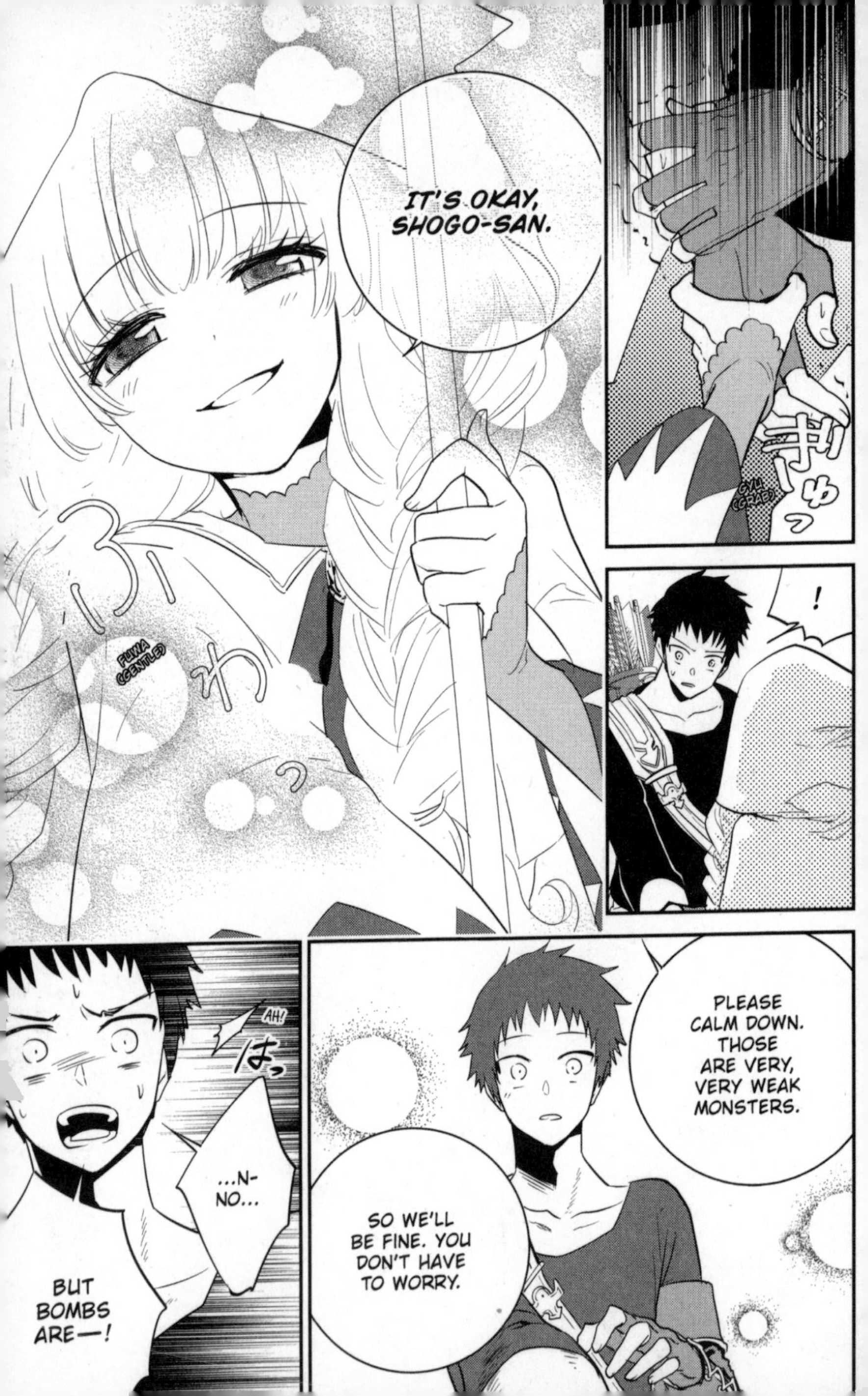
GYU (GRAB)
!
IT'S OKAY, SHOGO-SAN.
FUWA (GENTLE)
PLEASE CALM DOWN. THOSE ARE VERY, VERY WEAK MONSTERS.
SO WE'LL BE FINE. YOU DON'T HAVE TO WORRY.
AH!
...N-NO...
BUT BOMBS ARE—!

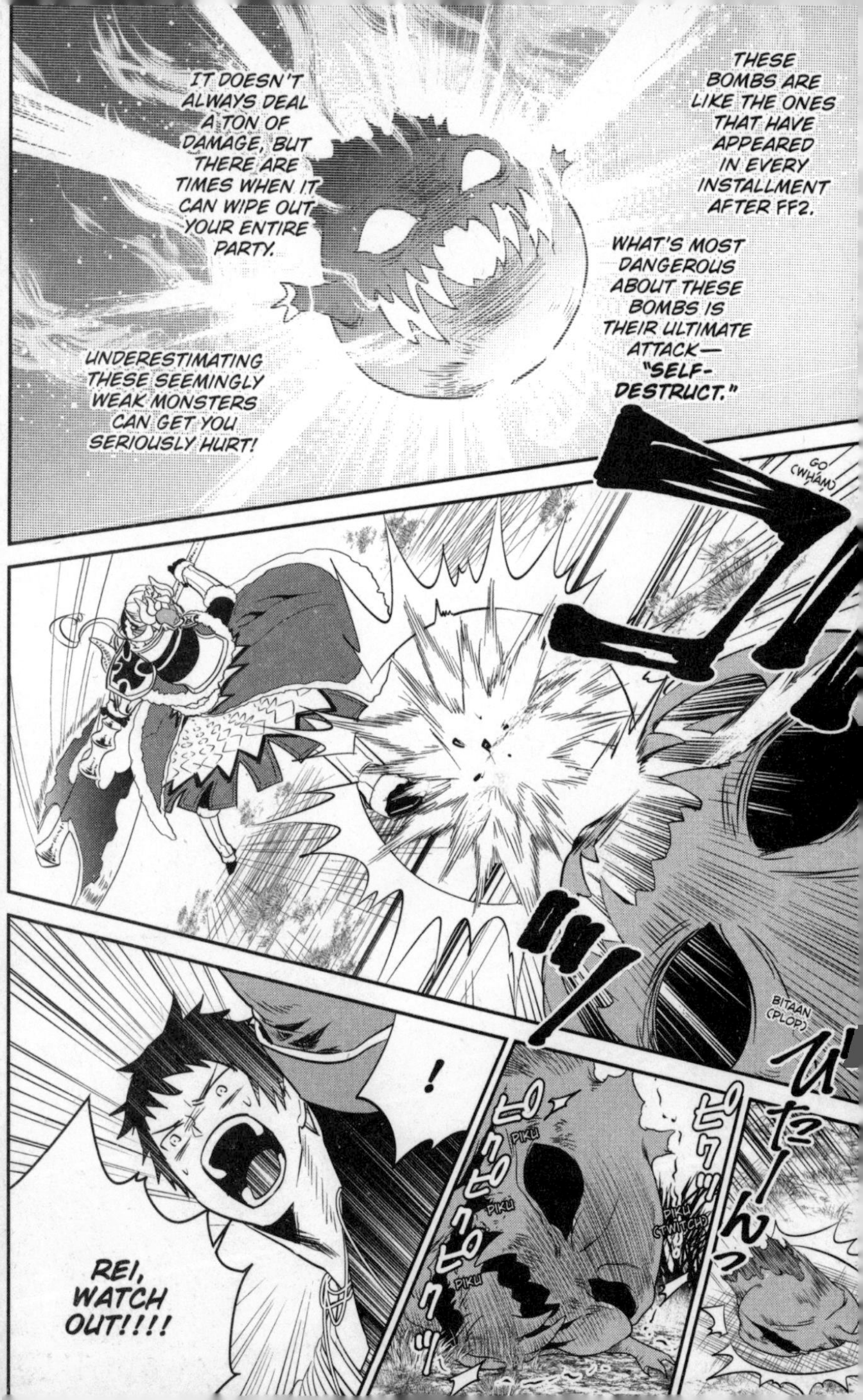
THESE BOMBS ARE LIKE THE ONES THAT HAVE APPEARED IN EVERY INSTALLMENT AFTER FF2.
WHAT'S MOST DANGEROUS ABOUT THESE BOMBS IS THEIR ULTIMATE ATTACK—"SELF-DESTRUCT."
IT DOESN'T ALWAYS DEAL A TON OF DAMAGE, BUT THERE ARE TIMES WHEN IT CAN WIPE OUT YOUR ENTIRE PARTY.
UNDERESTIMATING THESE SEEMINGLY WEAK MONSTERS CAN GET YOU SERIOUSLY HURT!
GO (WHAM)
BITAAN (PLOP)
PIKU (TWITCH)
PIKU
PIKU
PIKU
!
REI, WATCH OUT!!!!

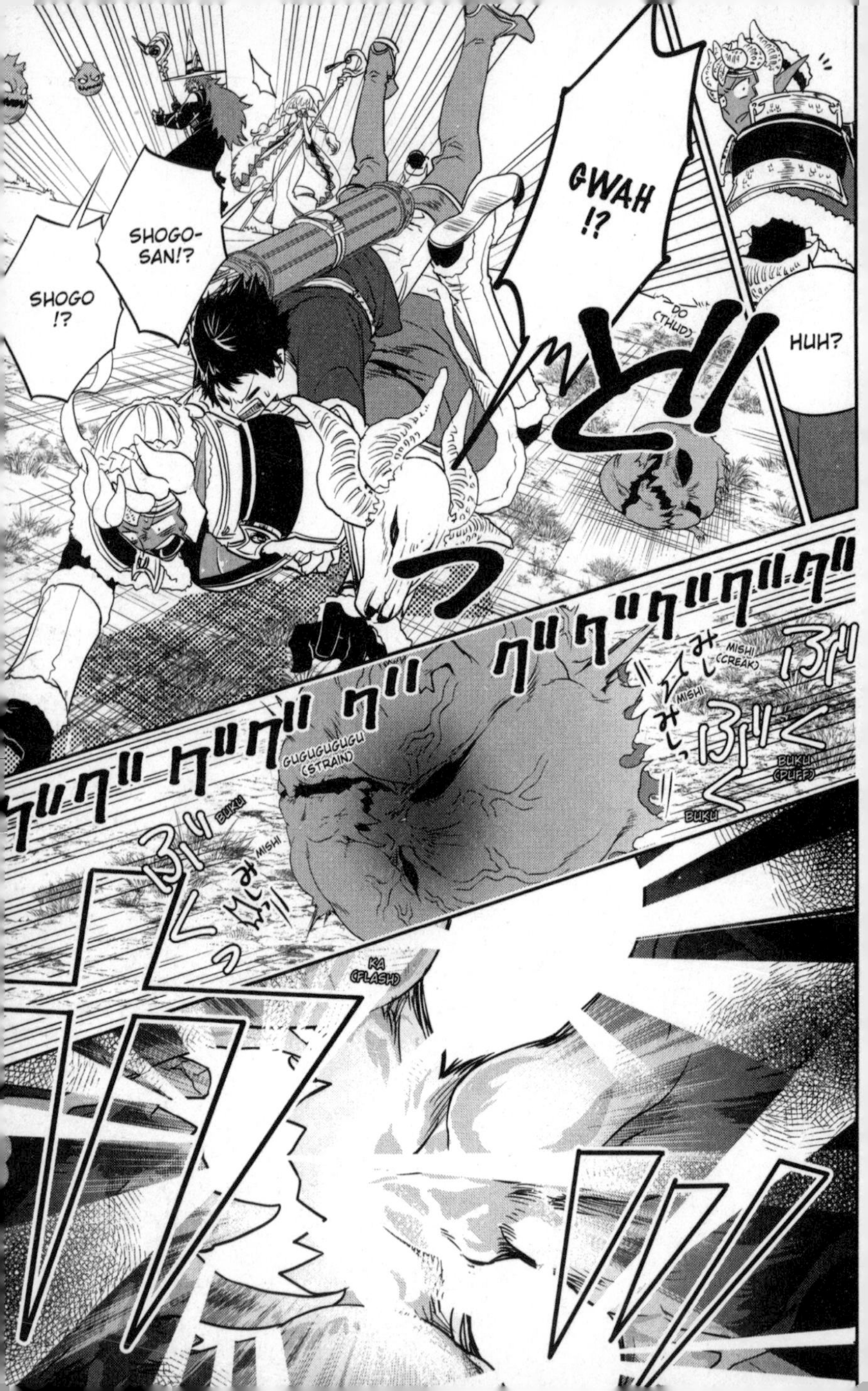
HUH?
GWAH !?
DO (THUD)
SHOGO-SAN!?
SHOGO !?
MISHI (CREAK)
MISHI
BUKU (PUFF)
BUKU
GUGUGUGUGU (STRAIN)
BUKU
MISHI
KA (FLASH)

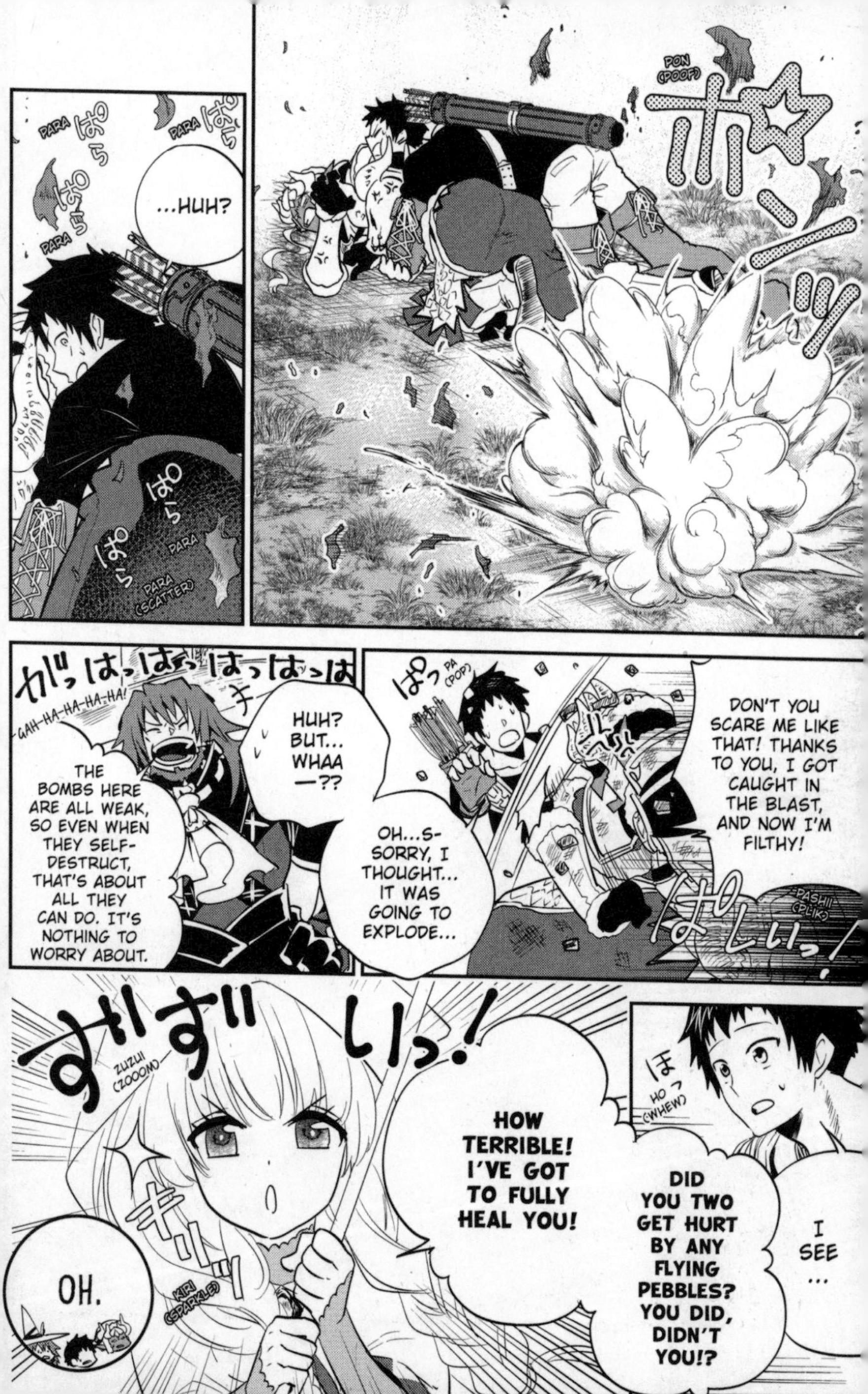
PON (POOF)
PARA
PARA
PARA
...HUH?
PARA
PARA (SCATTER)
DON'T YOU SCARE ME LIKE THAT! THANKS TO YOU, I GOT CAUGHT IN THE BLAST, AND NOW I'M FILTHY!
PA (POP)
PASHII (PLIK)
HUH? BUT... WHAA—??
OH...S-SORRY, I THOUGHT... IT WAS GOING TO EXPLODE...
GAH-HA-HA-HA-HA!
THE BOMBS HERE ARE ALL WEAK, SO EVEN WHEN THEY SELF-DESTRUCT, THAT'S ABOUT ALL THEY CAN DO. IT'S NOTHING TO WORRY ABOUT.
HO (WHEW)
I SEE...
ZUZUI (ZOOOM)
HOW TERRIBLE! I'VE GOT TO FULLY HEAL YOU!
DID YOU TWO GET HURT BY ANY FLYING PEBBLES? YOU DID, DIDN'T YOU!?
KIRI (SPARKLE)
OH.

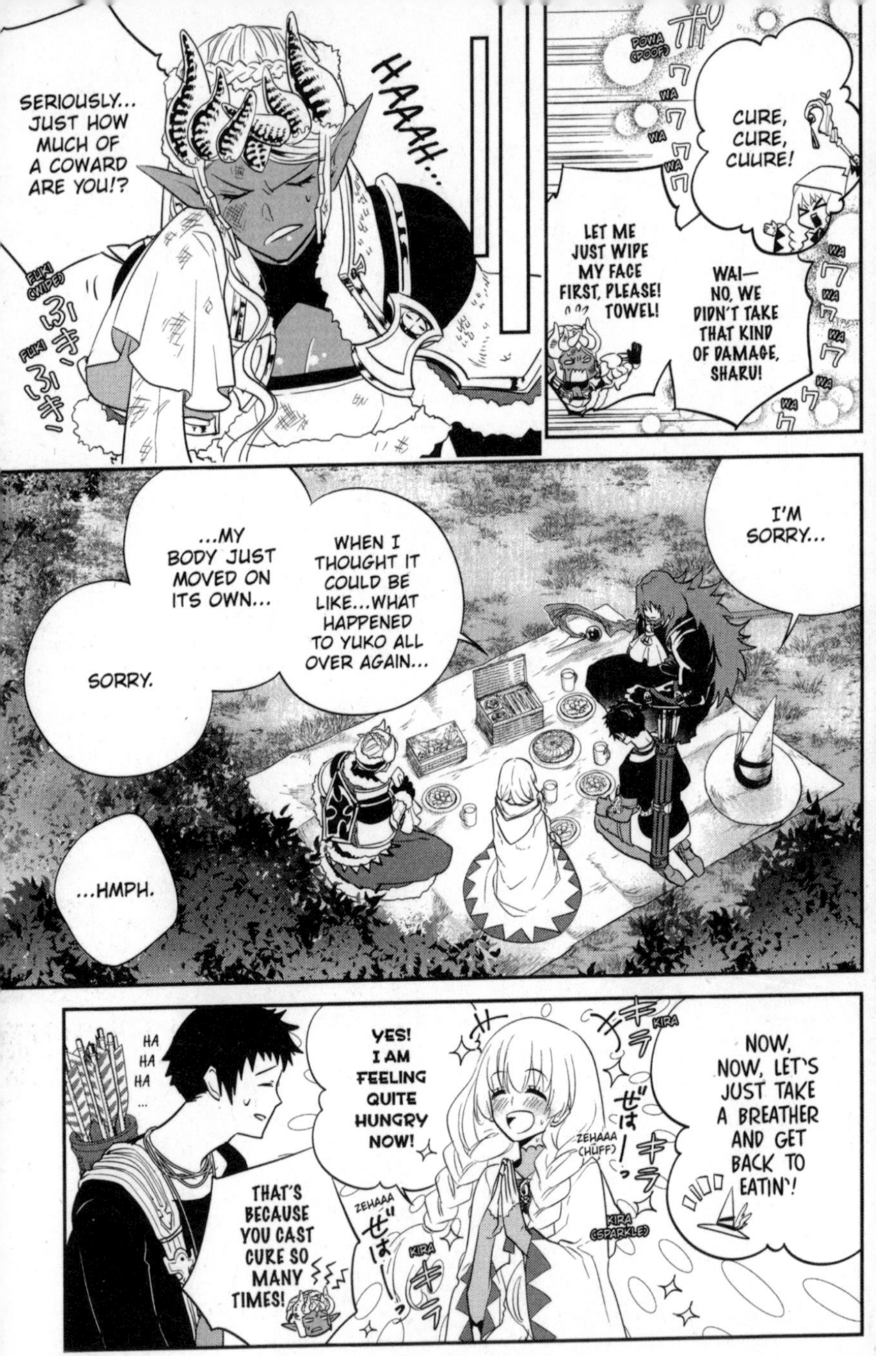
POWA (POOF)
WA WA WA
CURE, CURE, CUURE!
WA WA WA WA WA
WAI— NO, WE DIDN'T TAKE THAT KIND OF DAMAGE, SHARU!
LET ME JUST WIPE MY FACE FIRST, PLEASE! TOWEL!
HAAAH...
SERIOUSLY... JUST HOW MUCH OF A COWARD ARE YOU!?
FUKI (WIPE)
FUKI
I'M SORRY...
WHEN I THOUGHT IT COULD BE LIKE...WHAT HAPPENED TO YUKO ALL OVER AGAIN...
...MY BODY JUST MOVED ON ITS OWN...
SORRY.
...HMPH.
NOW, NOW, LET'S JUST TAKE A BREATHER AND GET BACK TO EATIN'!
KIRA
ZEHAAA (HUFF)
KIRA (SPARKLE)
YES! I AM FEELING QUITE HUNGRY NOW!
ZEHAAA
KIRA
THAT'S BECAUSE YOU CAST CURE SO MANY TIMES!
HA HA HA ...

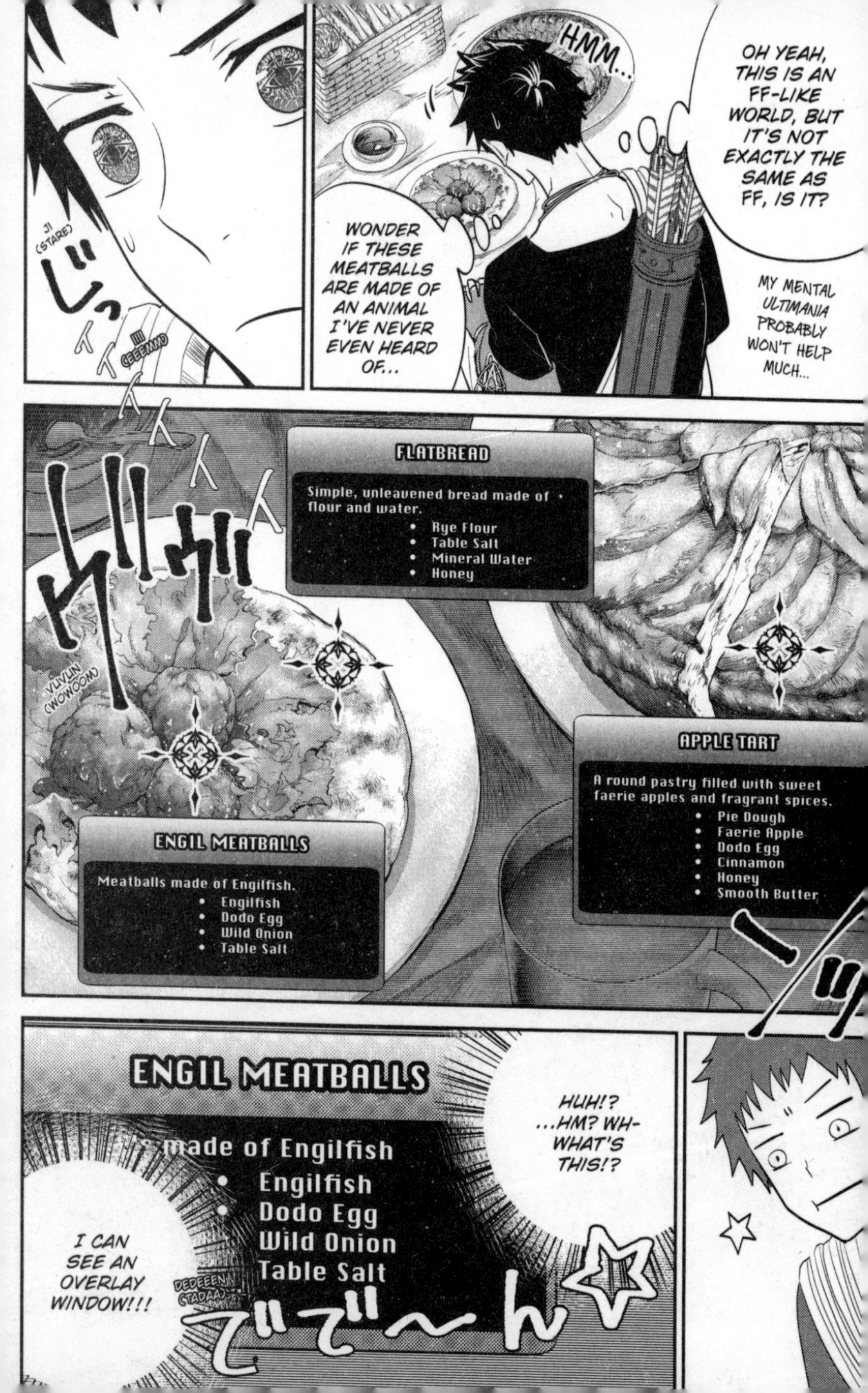
OH YEAH, THIS IS AN FF-LIKE WORLD, BUT IT'S NOT EXACTLY THE SAME AS FF, IS IT?
HMM...
MY MENTAL ULTIMANIA PROBABLY WON'T HELP MUCH...
WONDER IF THESE MEATBALLS ARE MADE OF AN ANIMAL I'VE NEVER EVEN HEARD OF...
JI (STARE)
IIII (EEEMMM)
FLATBREAD
Simple, unleavened bread made of flour and water.
• Rye Flour
• Table Salt
• Mineral Water
• Honey
APPLE TART
A round pastry filled with sweet faerie apples and fragrant spices.
• Pie Dough
• Faerie Apple
• Dodo Egg
• Cinnamon
• Honey
• Smooth Butter
ENGIL MEATBALLS
Meatballs made of Engilfish.
• Engilfish
• Dodo Egg
• Wild Onion
• Table Salt
VUVUN (WOWOOM)
HUH!? ...HM? WH-WHAT'S THIS!?
ENGIL MEATBALLS
made of Engilfish
• Engilfish
• Dodo Egg
Wild Onion
Table Salt
I CAN SEE AN OVERLAY WINDOW!!!
DEDEEEN (TADAA)

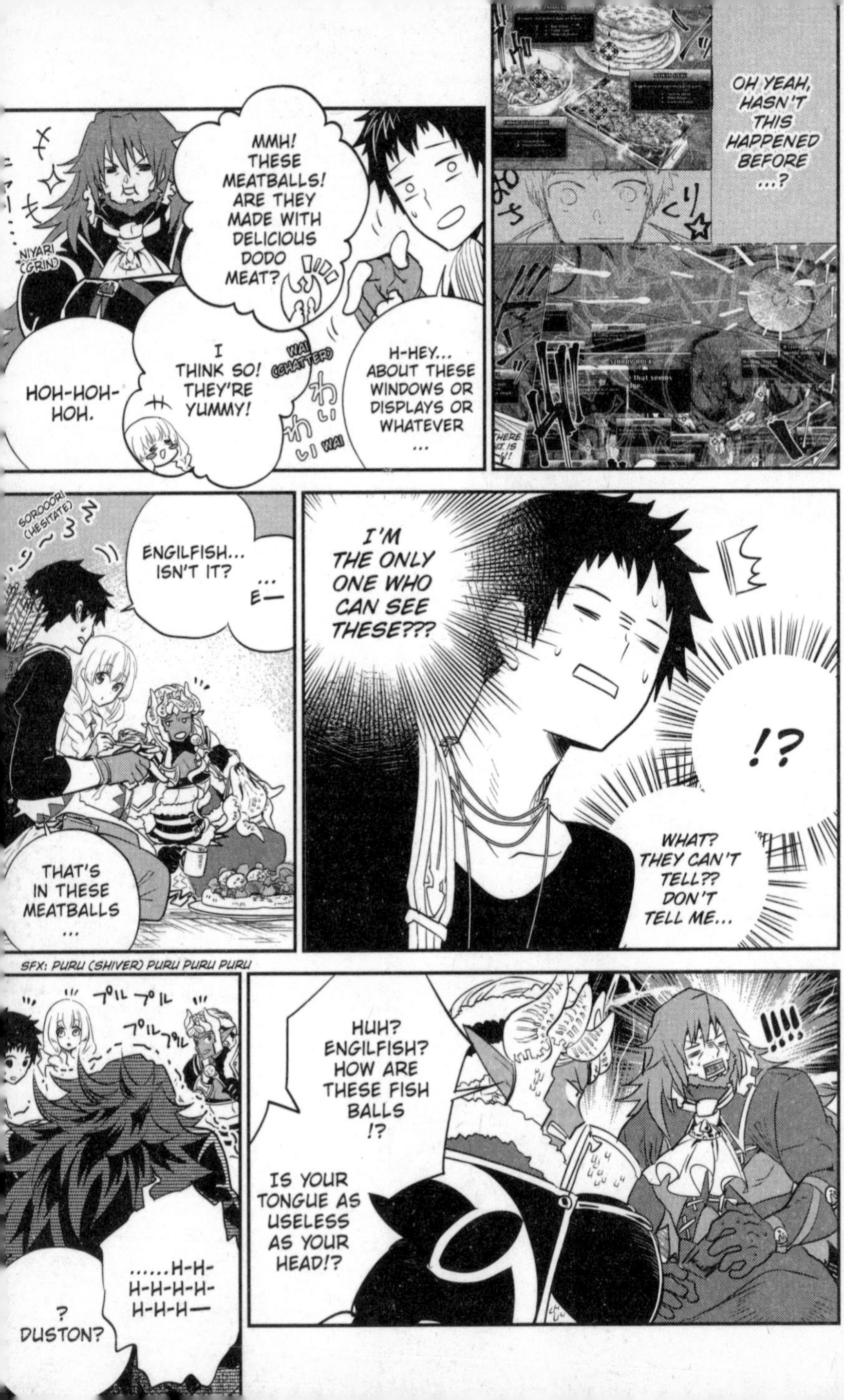
OH YEAH, HASN'T THIS HAPPENED BEFORE ...?
STURDY ROCK
MMH! THESE MEATBALLS! ARE THEY MADE WITH DELICIOUS DODO MEAT?
NIYARI (GRIN)
H-HEY... ABOUT THESE WINDOWS OR DISPLAYS OR WHATEVER ...
WAI (CHATTER)
WAI WAI
I THINK SO! THEY'RE YUMMY!
HOH-HOH-HOH.
I'M THE ONLY ONE WHO CAN SEE THESE???
!?
WHAT? THEY CAN'T TELL?? DON'T TELL ME...
SOROOORI (HESITATE)
ENGILFISH... ISN'T IT?
... E—
THAT'S IN THESE MEATBALLS ...
SFX: PURU (SHIVER) PURU PURU PURU
!!!!
HUH? ENGILFISH? HOW ARE THESE FISH BALLS !?
IS YOUR TONGUE AS USELESS AS YOUR HEAD!?
......H-H-H-H-H-H-H-H-H—
? DUSTON?

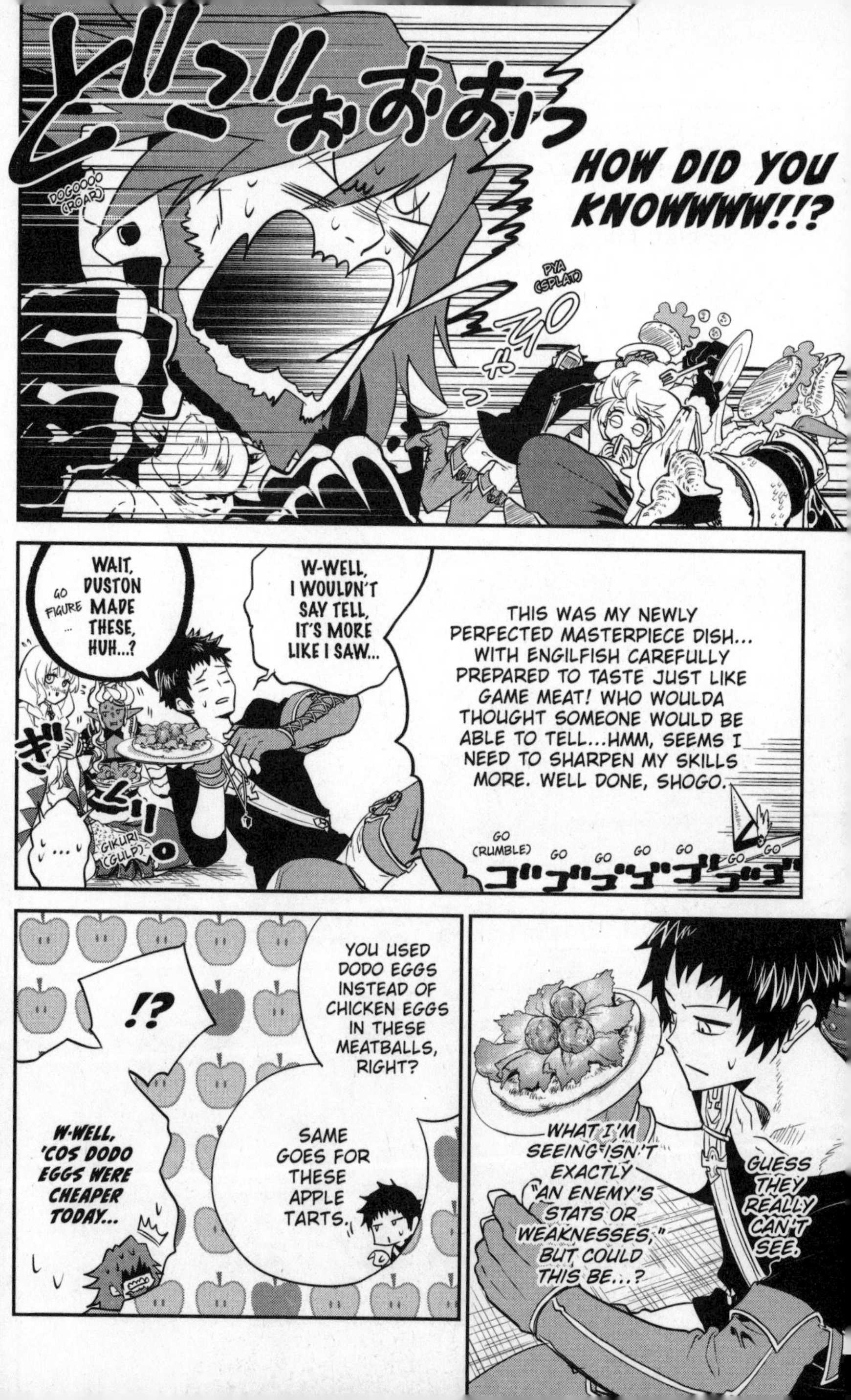
HOW DID YOU KNOWWWW!!?
DOGOOOO (ROAR)
PYA (SPLAT)
THIS WAS MY NEWLY PERFECTED MASTERPIECE DISH... WITH ENGILFISH CAREFULLY PREPARED TO TASTE JUST LIKE GAME MEAT! WHO WOULDA THOUGHT SOMEONE WOULD BE ABLE TO TELL...HMM, SEEMS I NEED TO SHARPEN MY SKILLS MORE. WELL DONE, SHOGO.
GO (RUMBLE) GO GO GO GO GO GO
W-WELL, I WOULDN'T SAY TELL, IT'S MORE LIKE I SAW...
WAIT, DUSTON MADE THESE, HUH...?
GO FIGURE...
GIKURI (GULP)
...
WHAT I'M SEEING ISN'T EXACTLY "AN ENEMY'S STATS OR WEAKNESSES," BUT COULD THIS BE...?
GUESS THEY REALLY CAN'T SEE.
YOU USED DODO EGGS INSTEAD OF CHICKEN EGGS IN THESE MEATBALLS, RIGHT?
!?
SAME GOES FOR THESE APPLE TARTS.
W-WELL, 'COS DODO EGGS WERE CHEAPER TODAY...

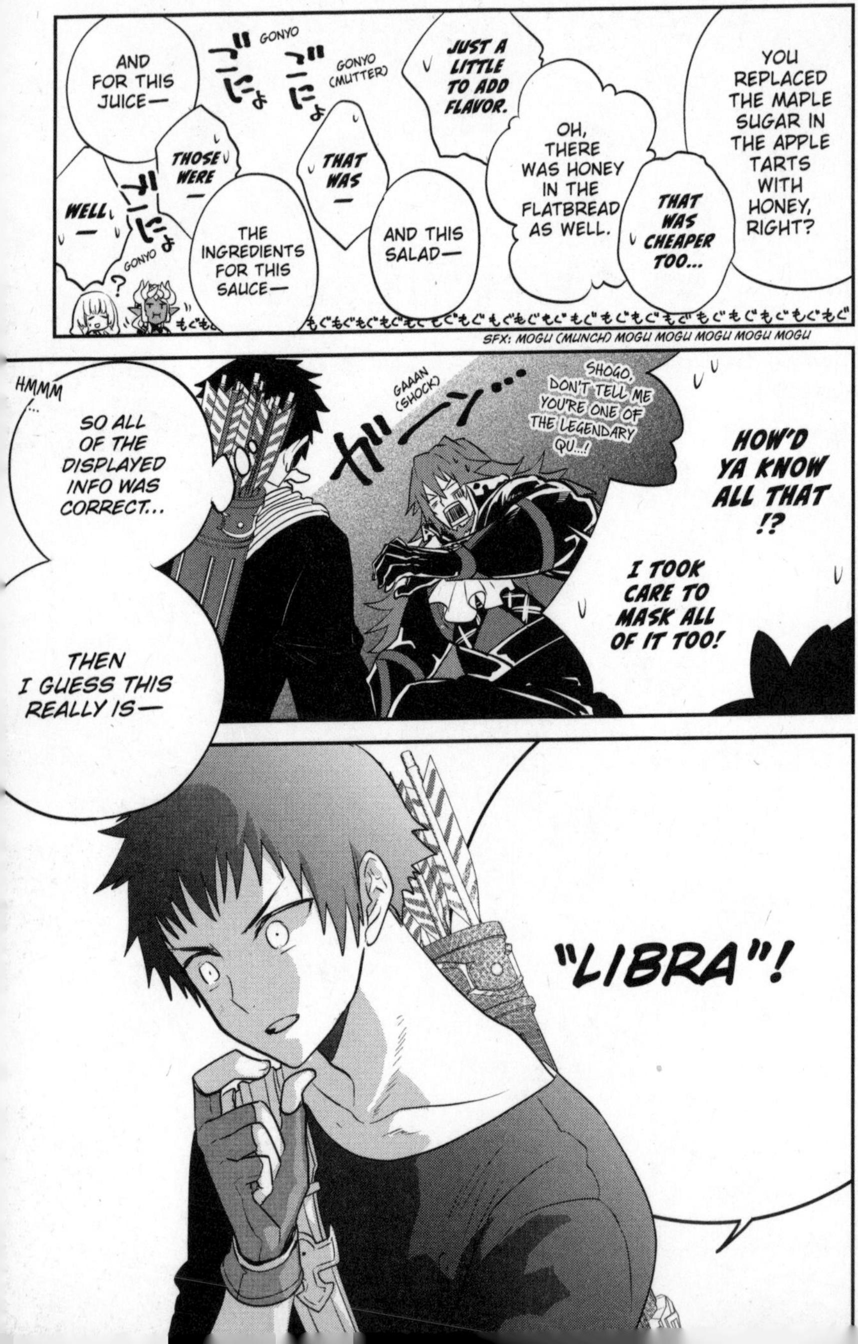
YOU REPLACED THE MAPLE SUGAR IN THE APPLE TARTS WITH HONEY, RIGHT?
THAT WAS CHEAPER TOO...
OH, THERE WAS HONEY IN THE FLATBREAD AS WELL.
JUST A LITTLE TO ADD FLAVOR.
AND THIS SALAD—
THAT WAS—
GONYO (MUTTER)
GONYO
THE INGREDIENTS FOR THIS SAUCE—
THOSE WERE—
AND FOR THIS JUICE—
WELL—
GONYO
SFX: MOGU (MUNCH) MOGU MOGU MOGU MOGU MOGU
HOW'D YA KNOW ALL THAT!?
I TOOK CARE TO MASK ALL OF IT TOO!
SHOGO, DON'T TELL ME YOU'RE ONE OF THE LEGENDARY QU...!
GAAAN (SHOCK)
HMMM...
SO ALL OF THE DISPLAYED INFO WAS CORRECT...
THEN I GUESS THIS REALLY IS—
"LIBRA"!

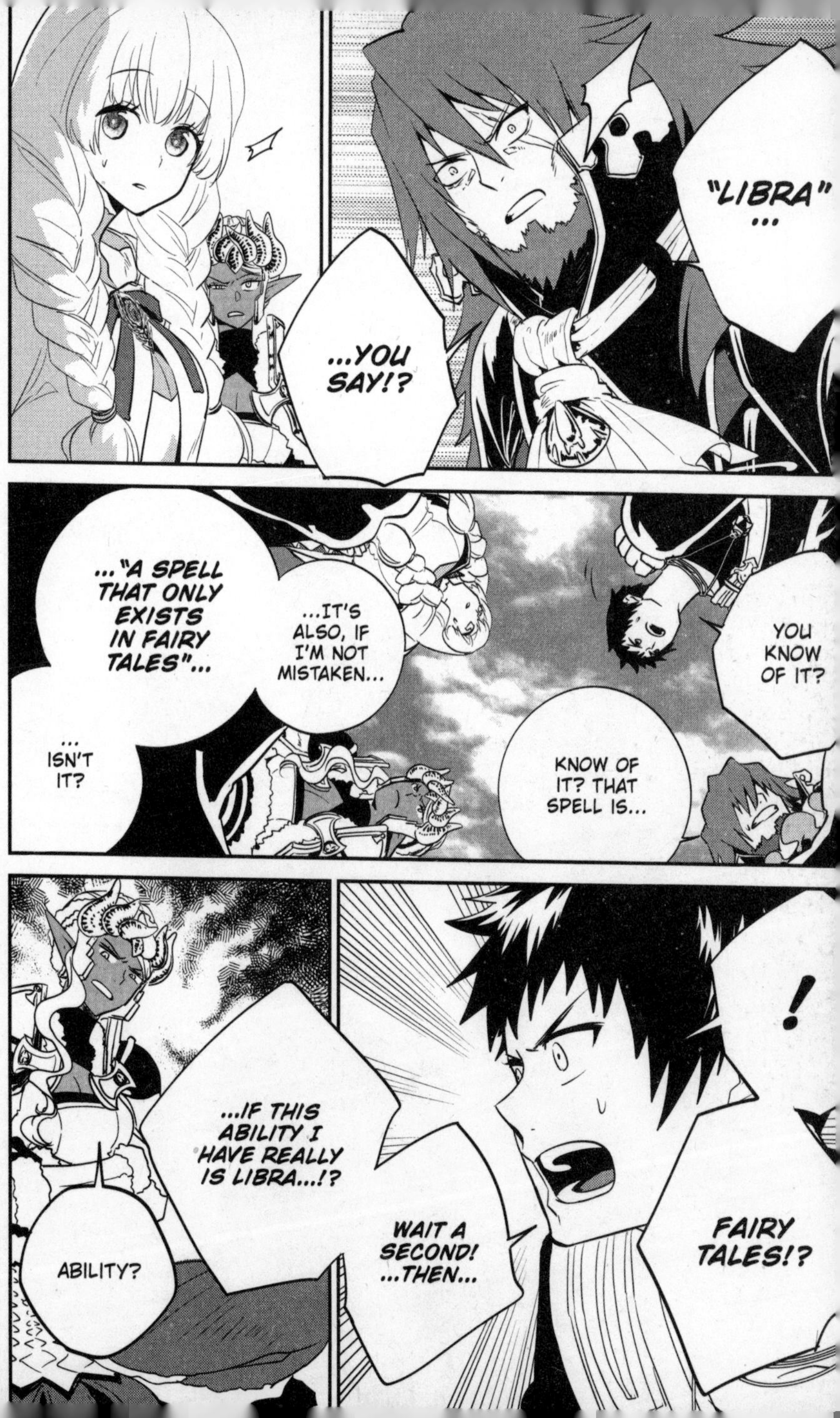
"LIBRA" ...
...YOU SAY!?
YOU KNOW OF IT?
KNOW OF IT? THAT SPELL IS...
...IT'S ALSO, IF I'M NOT MISTAKEN...
..."A SPELL THAT ONLY EXISTS IN FAIRY TALES"...
... ISN'T IT?
!
FAIRY TALES!?
WAIT A SECOND! ...THEN...
...IF THIS ABILITY I HAVE REALLY IS LIBRA...!?
ABILITY?

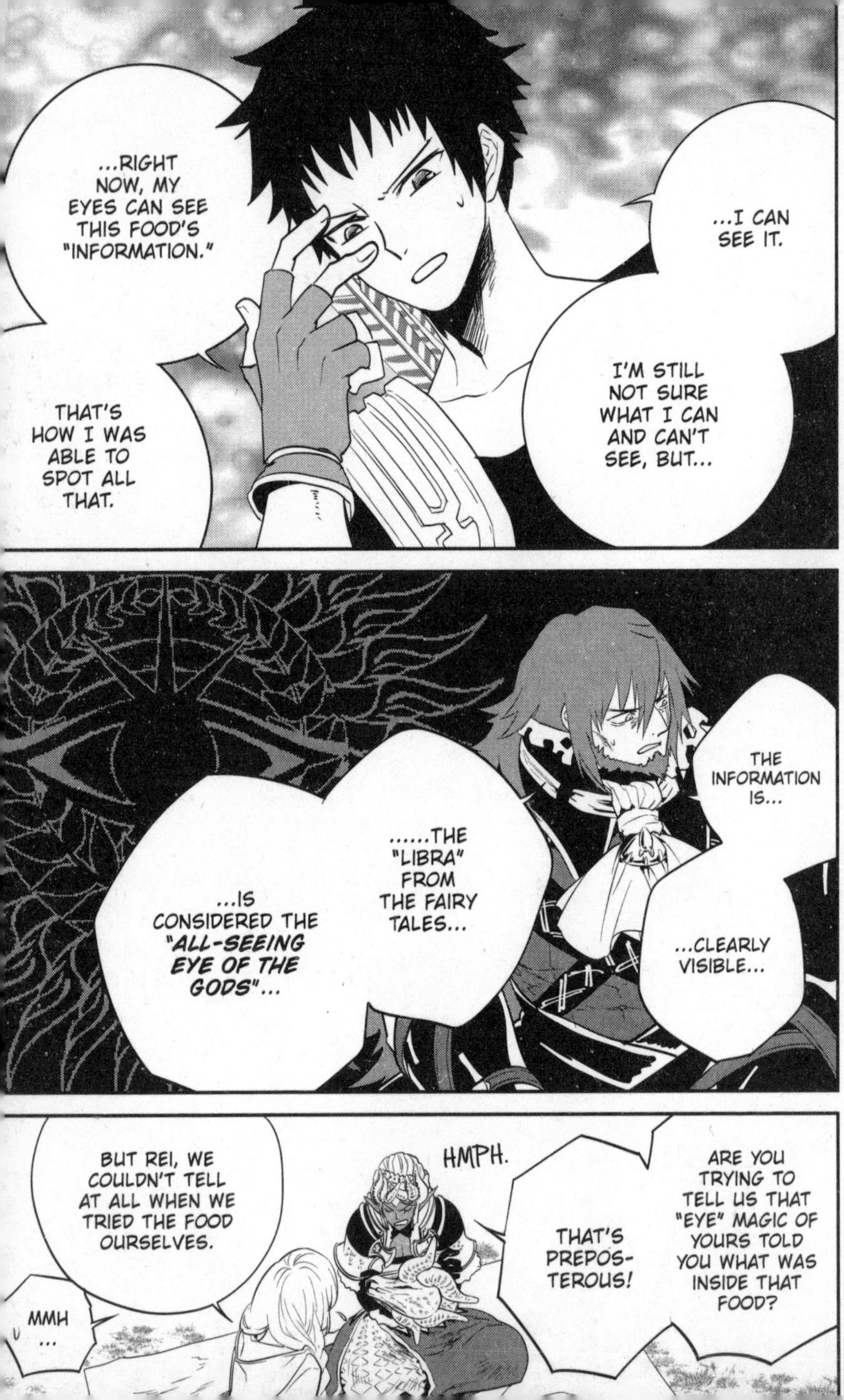
...I CAN SEE IT.
I'M STILL NOT SURE WHAT I CAN AND CAN'T SEE, BUT...
...RIGHT NOW, MY EYES CAN SEE THIS FOOD'S "INFORMATION."
THAT'S HOW I WAS ABLE TO SPOT ALL THAT.
THE INFORMATION IS...
...CLEARLY VISIBLE...
......THE "LIBRA" FROM THE FAIRY TALES...
...IS CONSIDERED THE "*ALL-SEEING EYE OF THE GODS*"...
ARE YOU TRYING TO TELL US THAT "EYE" MAGIC OF YOURS TOLD YOU WHAT WAS INSIDE THAT FOOD?
THAT'S PREPOSTEROUS!
HMPH.
BUT REI, WE COULDN'T TELL AT ALL WHEN WE TRIED THE FOOD OURSELVES.
MMH...

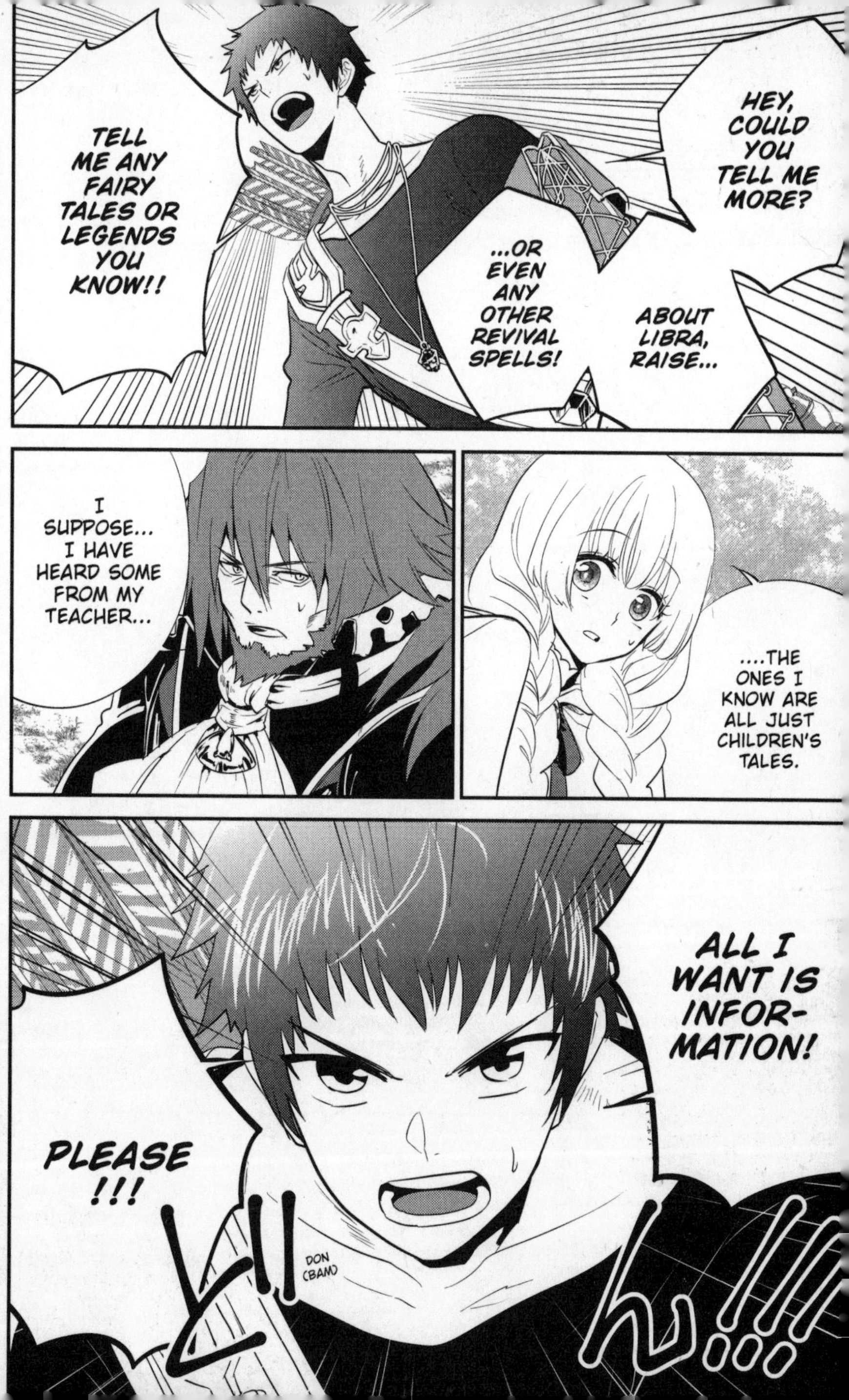
HEY, COULD YOU TELL ME MORE?
ABOUT LIBRA, RAISE...
...OR EVEN ANY OTHER REVIVAL SPELLS!
TELL ME ANY FAIRY TALES OR LEGENDS YOU KNOW!!
....THE ONES I KNOW ARE ALL JUST CHILDREN'S TALES.
I SUPPOSE... I HAVE HEARD SOME FROM MY TEACHER...
ALL I WANT IS INFOR-MATION!
PLEASE !!!
DON (BAM)

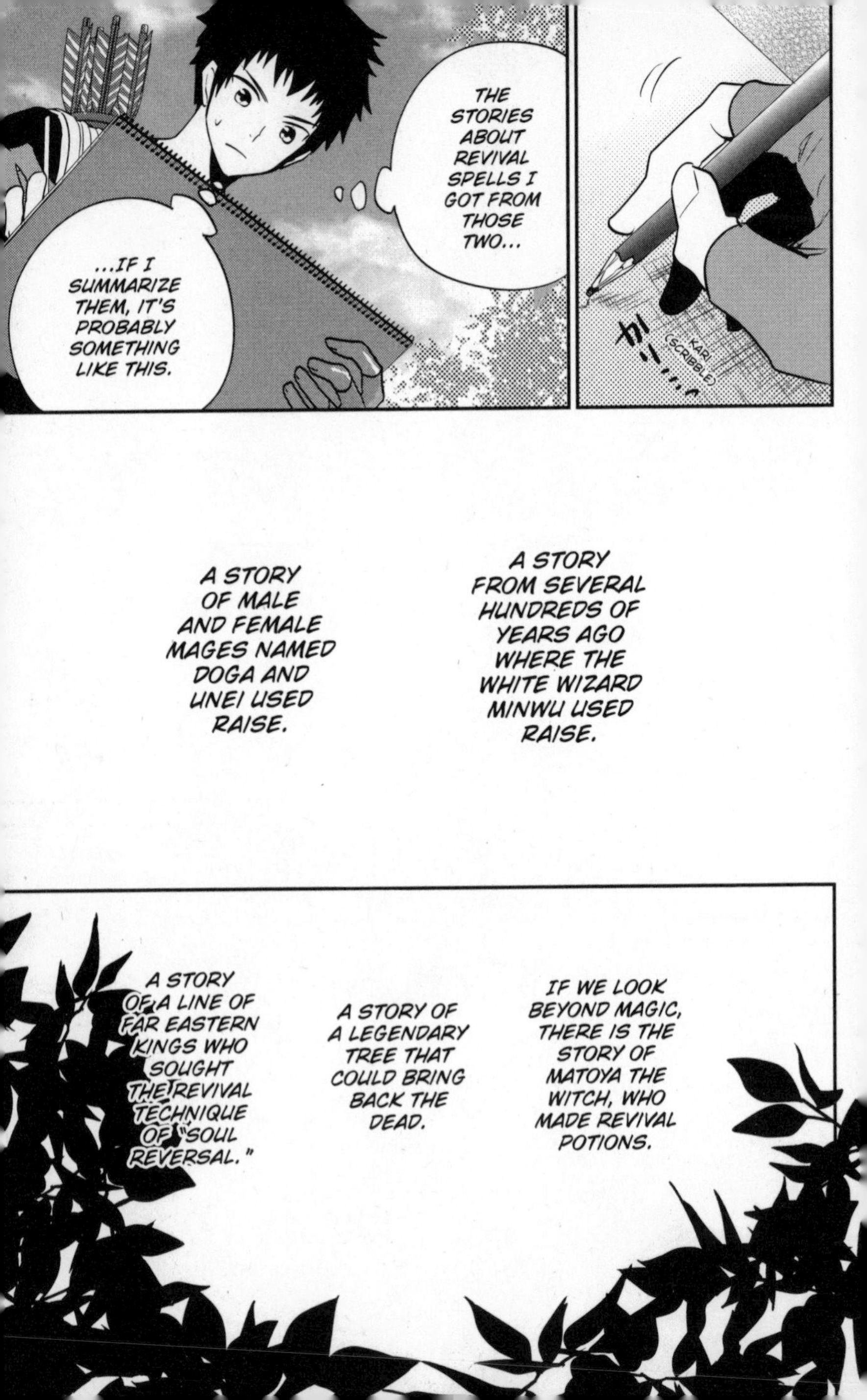
KARI (SCRIBBLE)
THE STORIES ABOUT REVIVAL SPELLS I GOT FROM THOSE TWO...
...IF I SUMMARIZE THEM, IT'S PROBABLY SOMETHING LIKE THIS.
A STORY FROM SEVERAL HUNDREDS OF YEARS AGO WHERE THE WHITE WIZARD MINWU USED RAISE.
A STORY OF MALE AND FEMALE MAGES NAMED DOGA AND UNEI USED RAISE.
IF WE LOOK BEYOND MAGIC, THERE IS THE STORY OF MATOYA THE WITCH, WHO MADE REVIVAL POTIONS.
A STORY OF A LEGENDARY TREE THAT COULD BRING BACK THE DEAD.
A STORY OF A LINE OF FAR EASTERN KINGS WHO SOUGHT THE REVIVAL TECHNIQUE OF "SOUL REVERSAL."

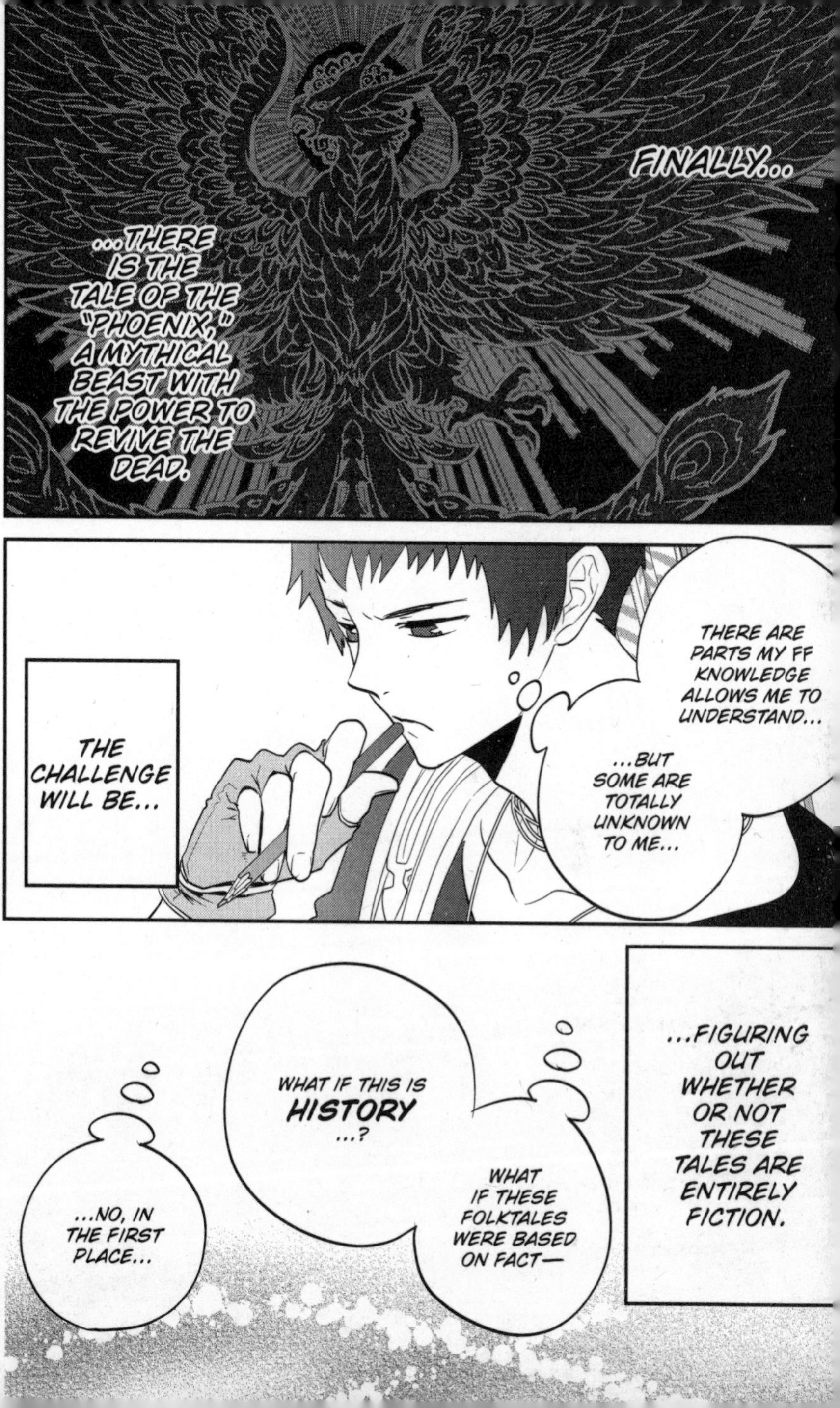
FINALLY...
...THERE IS THE TALE OF THE "PHOENIX," A MYTHICAL BEAST WITH THE POWER TO REVIVE THE DEAD.
THERE ARE PARTS MY FF KNOWLEDGE ALLOWS ME TO UNDERSTAND...
...BUT SOME ARE TOTALLY UNKNOWN TO ME...
THE CHALLENGE WILL BE...
...FIGURING OUT WHETHER OR NOT THESE TALES ARE ENTIRELY FICTION.
WHAT IF THIS IS HISTORY ...?
WHAT IF THESE FOLKTALES WERE BASED ON FACT—
...NO, IN THE FIRST PLACE...

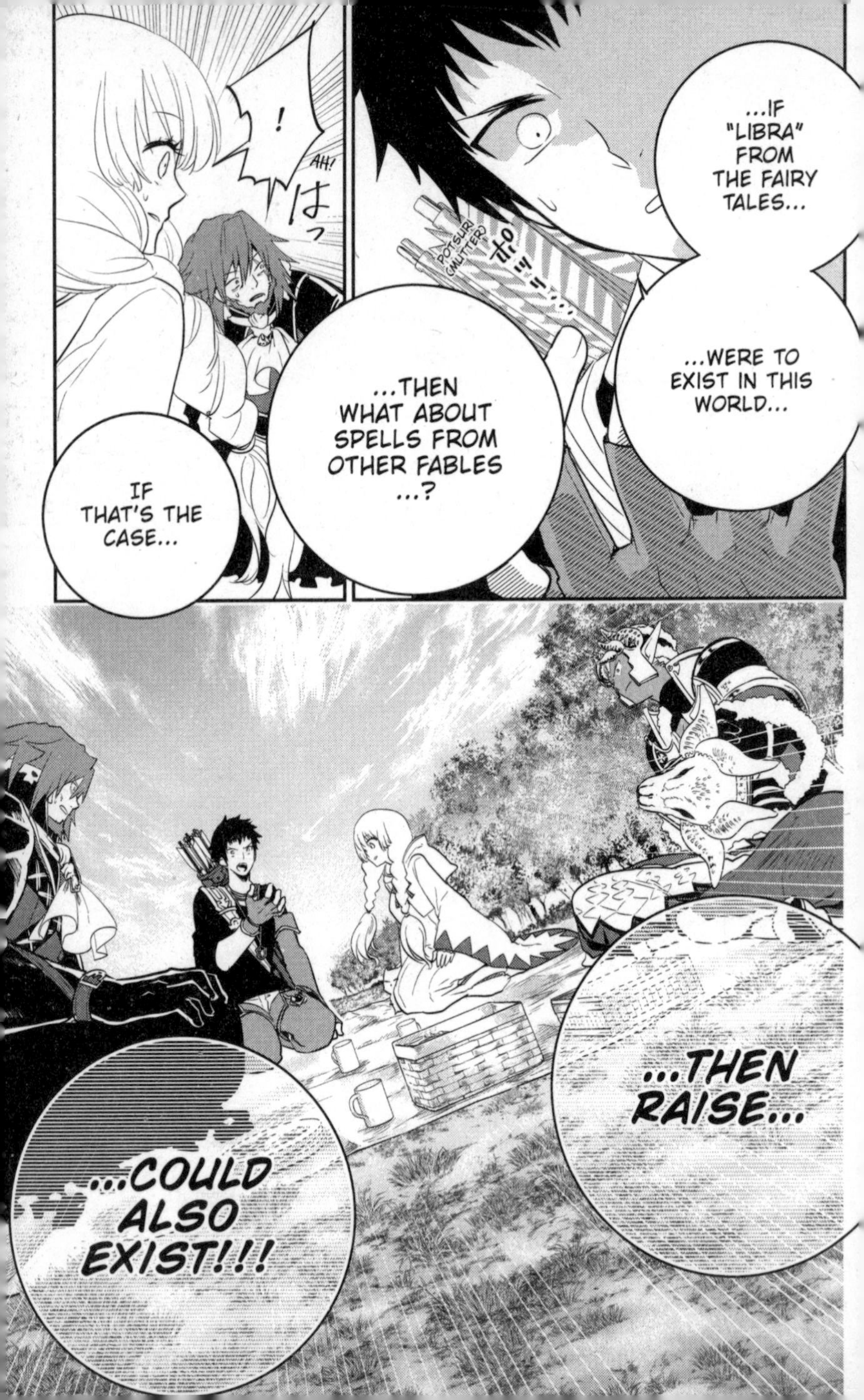

...IF "LIBRA" FROM THE FAIRY TALES...
POTSURI (MUTTER)
...WERE TO EXIST IN THIS WORLD...
...THEN WHAT ABOUT SPELLS FROM OTHER FABLES ...?
!
AH!
はっ
IF THAT'S THE CASE...
...THEN RAISE...
...COULD ALSO EXIST!!!

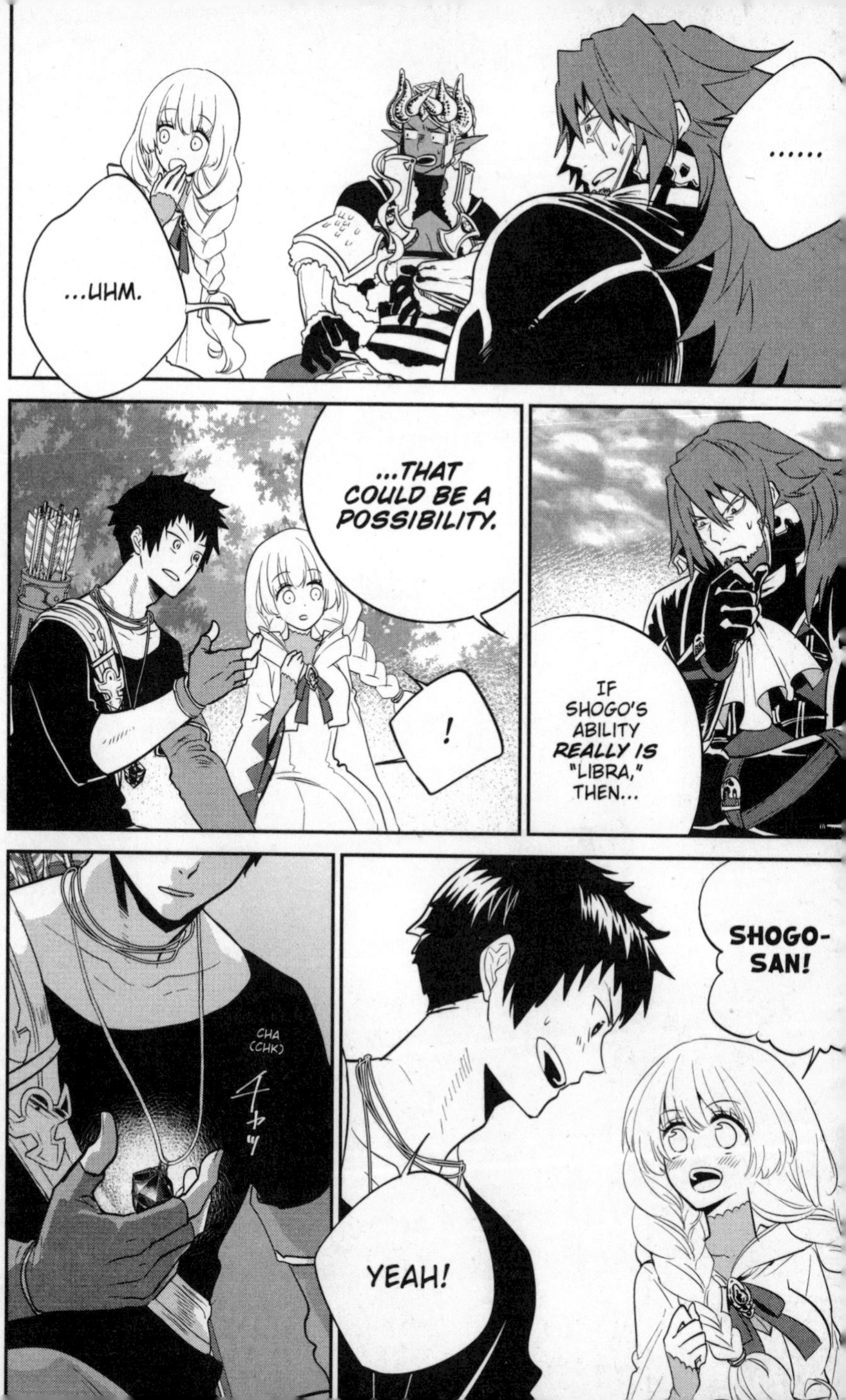

......
...UHM.
IF SHOGO'S ABILITY REALLY IS "LIBRA," THEN...
...THAT COULD BE A POSSIBILITY.
!
SHOGO-SAN!
YEAH!
チャッ
CHA (CHK)

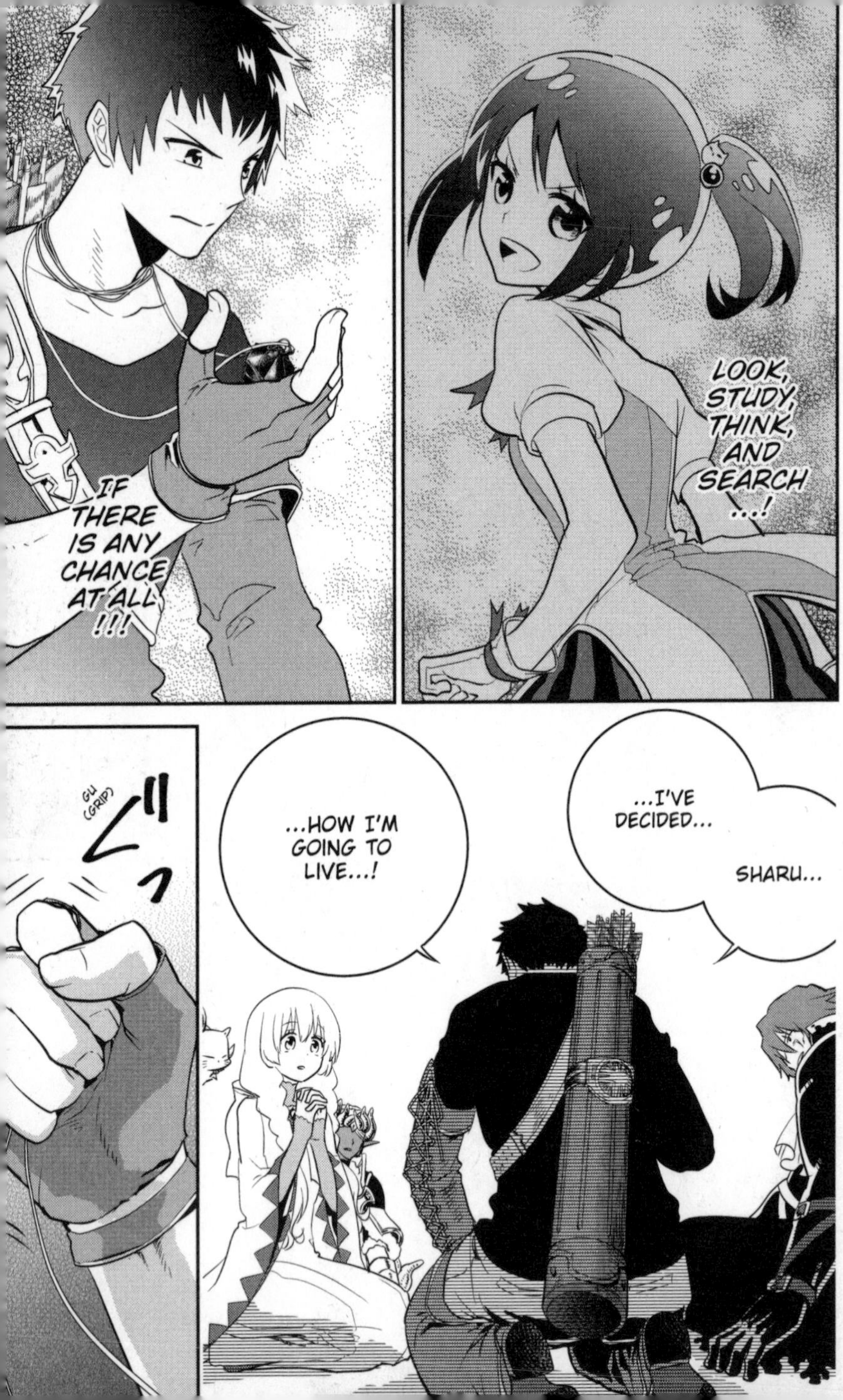
LOOK, STUDY, THINK, AND SEARCH ...!
IF THERE IS ANY CHANCE AT ALL !!!
...I'VE DECIDED... SHARU...
...HOW I'M GOING TO LIVE...!
GU (GRIP)

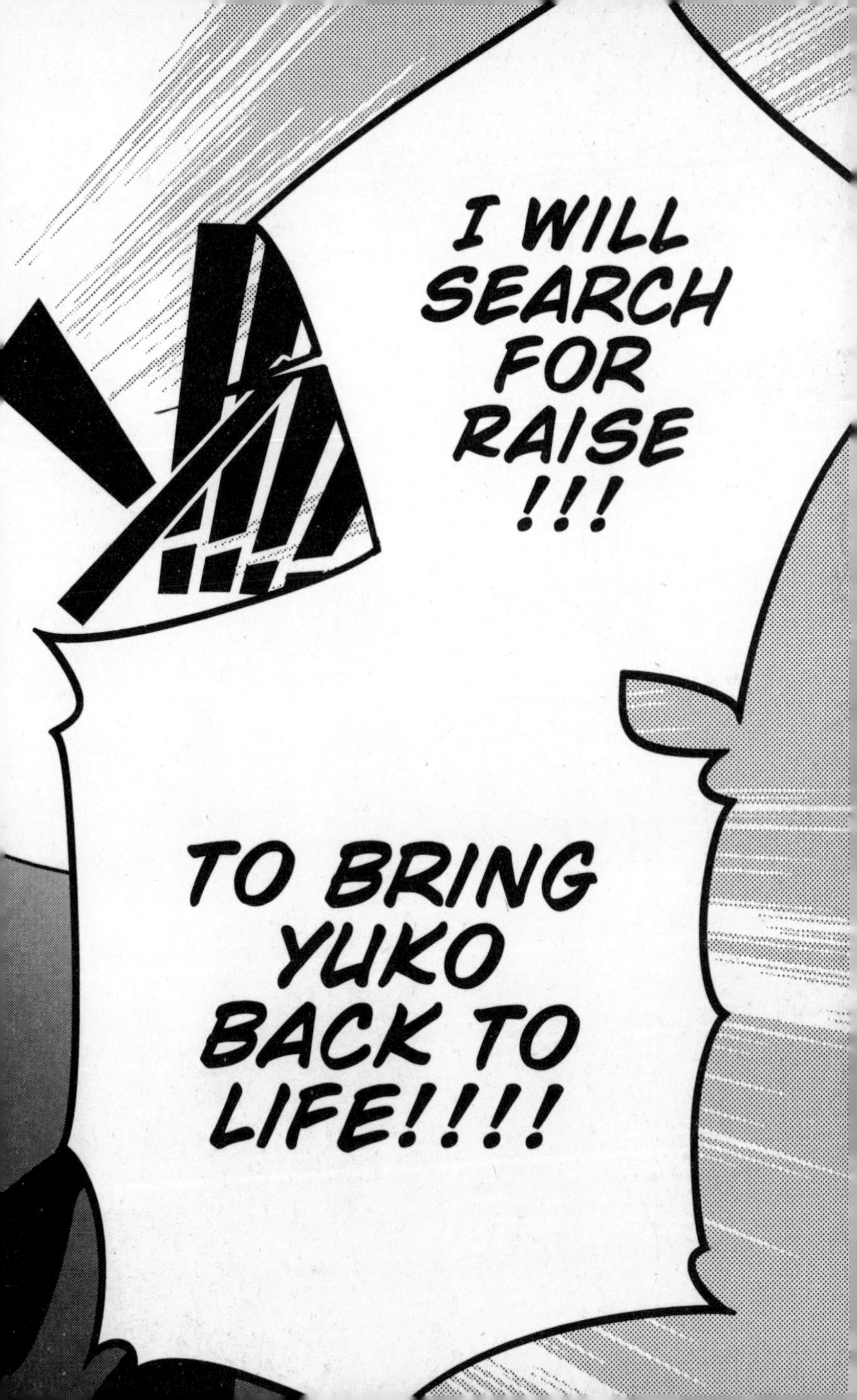
!!
I WILL SEARCH FOR RAISE !!!
TO BRING YUKO BACK TO LIFE!!!!

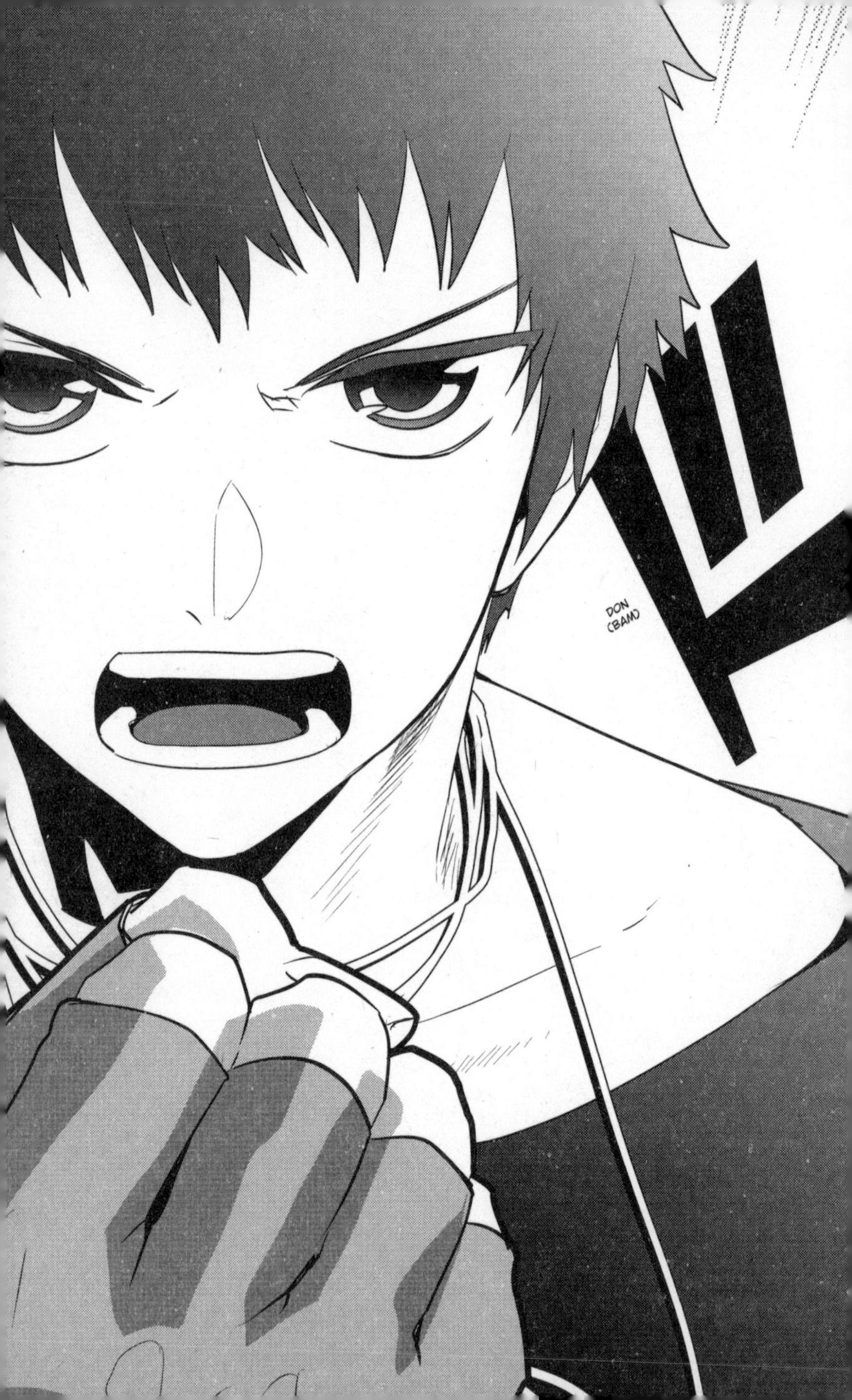
DON
(BAM)

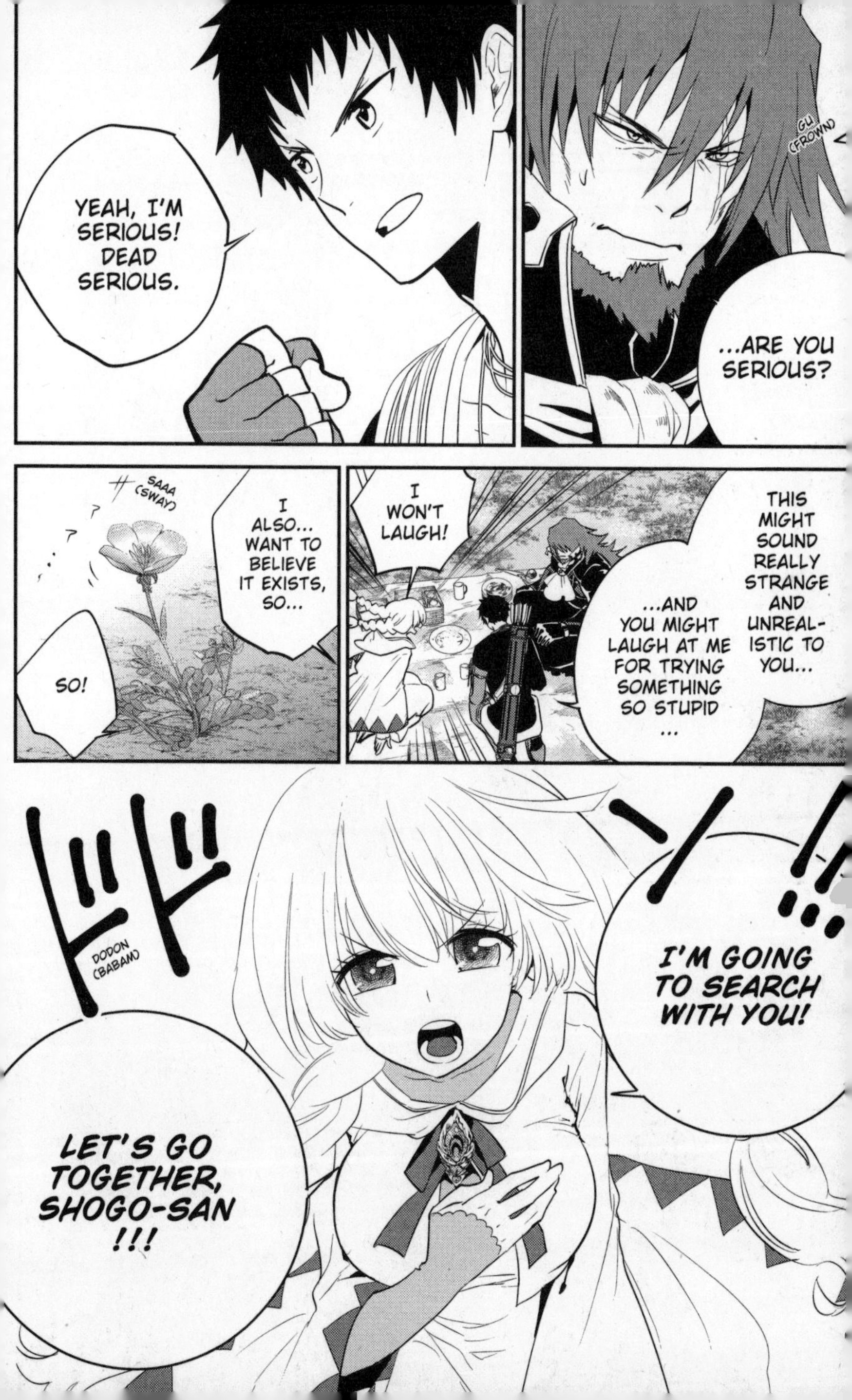
GU (FROWN)
...ARE YOU SERIOUS?
YEAH, I'M SERIOUS! DEAD SERIOUS.
THIS MIGHT SOUND REALLY STRANGE AND UNREAL-ISTIC TO YOU...
...AND YOU MIGHT LAUGH AT ME FOR TRYING SOMETHING SO STUPID ...
I WON'T LAUGH!
I ALSO... WANT TO BELIEVE IT EXISTS, SO...
SAAA (SWAY)
SO!
I'M GOING TO SEARCH WITH YOU!
DODON (BABAM)
LET'S GO TOGETHER, SHOGO-SAN !!!

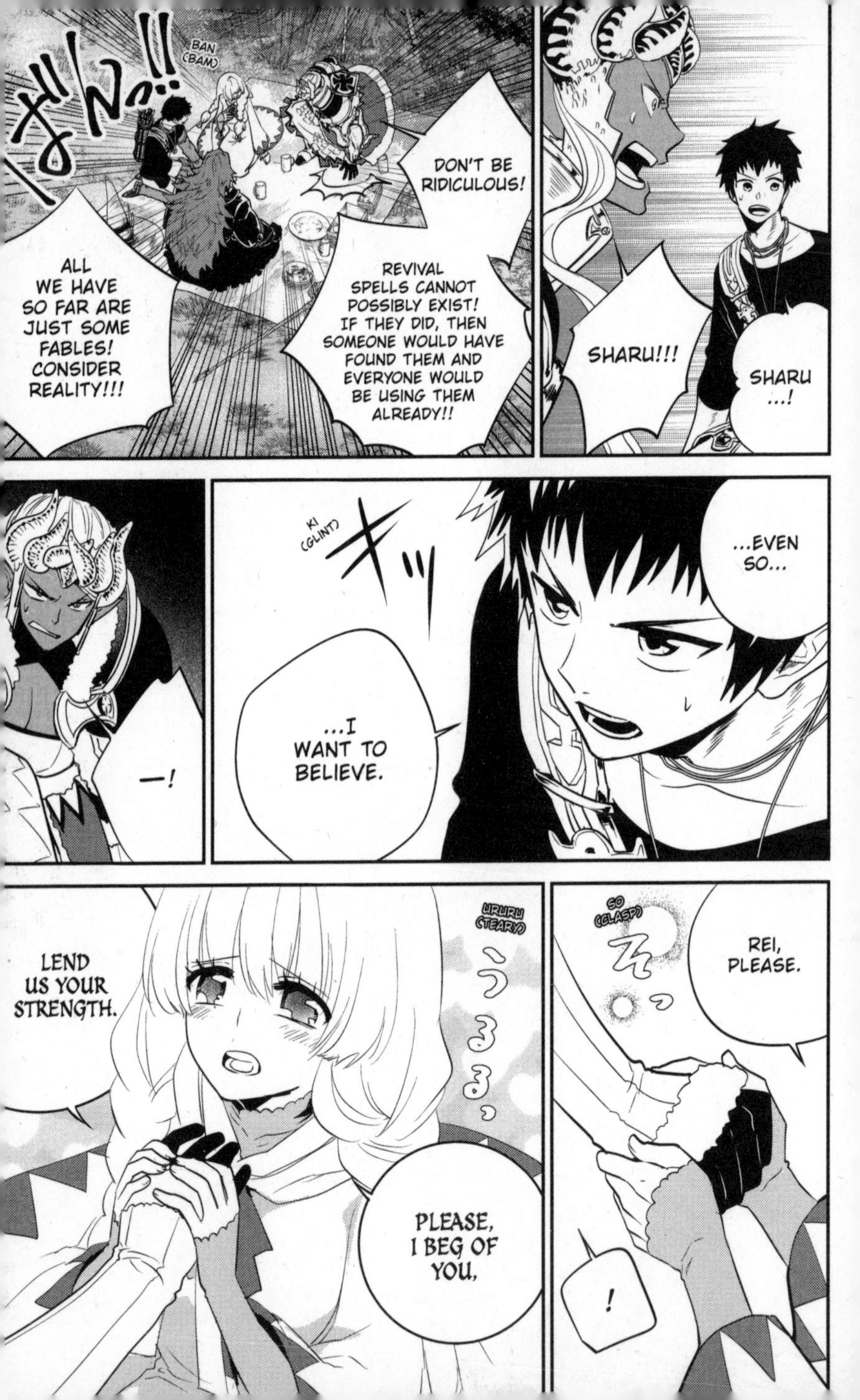
SHARU ...!
SHARU!!!
BAN (BAM)
DON'T BE RIDICULOUS!
REVIVAL SPELLS CANNOT POSSIBLY EXIST! IF THEY DID, THEN SOMEONE WOULD HAVE FOUND THEM AND EVERYONE WOULD BE USING THEM ALREADY!!
ALL WE HAVE SO FAR ARE JUST SOME FABLES! CONSIDER REALITY!!!
...EVEN SO...
KI (GLINT)
...I WANT TO BELIEVE.
—!
SO (CLASP)
REI, PLEASE.
!
URURU (TEARY)
PLEASE, I BEG OF YOU,
LEND US YOUR STRENGTH.

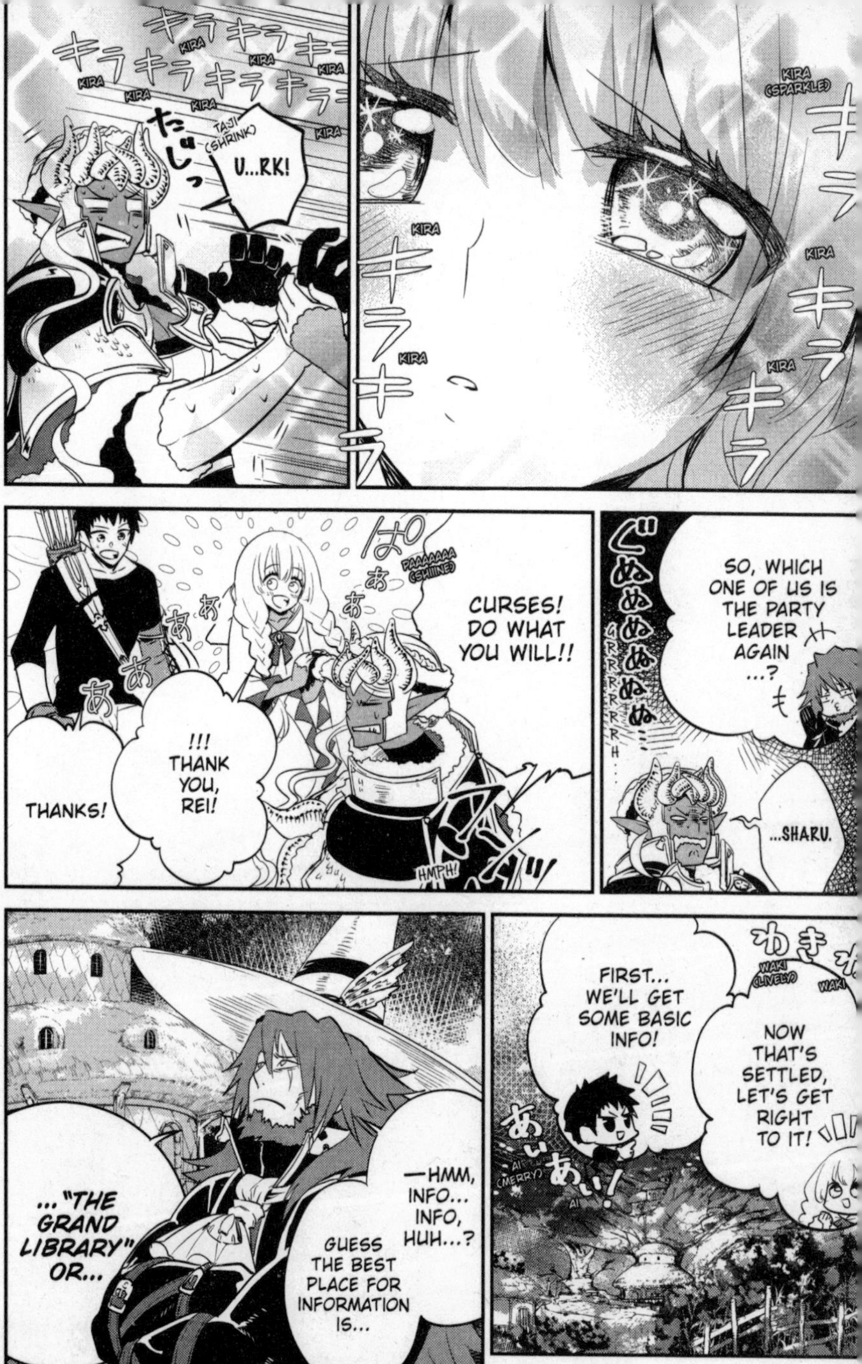
KIRA (SPARKLE)
KIRA
KIRA
KIRA
KIRA
KIRA
KIRA
KIRA
KIRA
KIRA
TAJI (SHRINK)
U...RK!
SO, WHICH ONE OF US IS THE PARTY LEADER AGAIN ...?
GRRRRRRH...
...SHARU.
PAAAAAAA (SHIIINE)
CURSES! DO WHAT YOU WILL!!
HMPH!
!!! THANK YOU, REI!
THANKS!
WAKI (LIVELY) WAKI
NOW THAT'S SETTLED, LET'S GET RIGHT TO IT!
FIRST... WE'LL GET SOME BASIC INFO!
AI (MERRY) AI
—HMM, INFO... INFO, HUH...?
GUESS THE BEST PLACE FOR INFORMATION IS...
..."THE GRAND LIBRARY" OR...

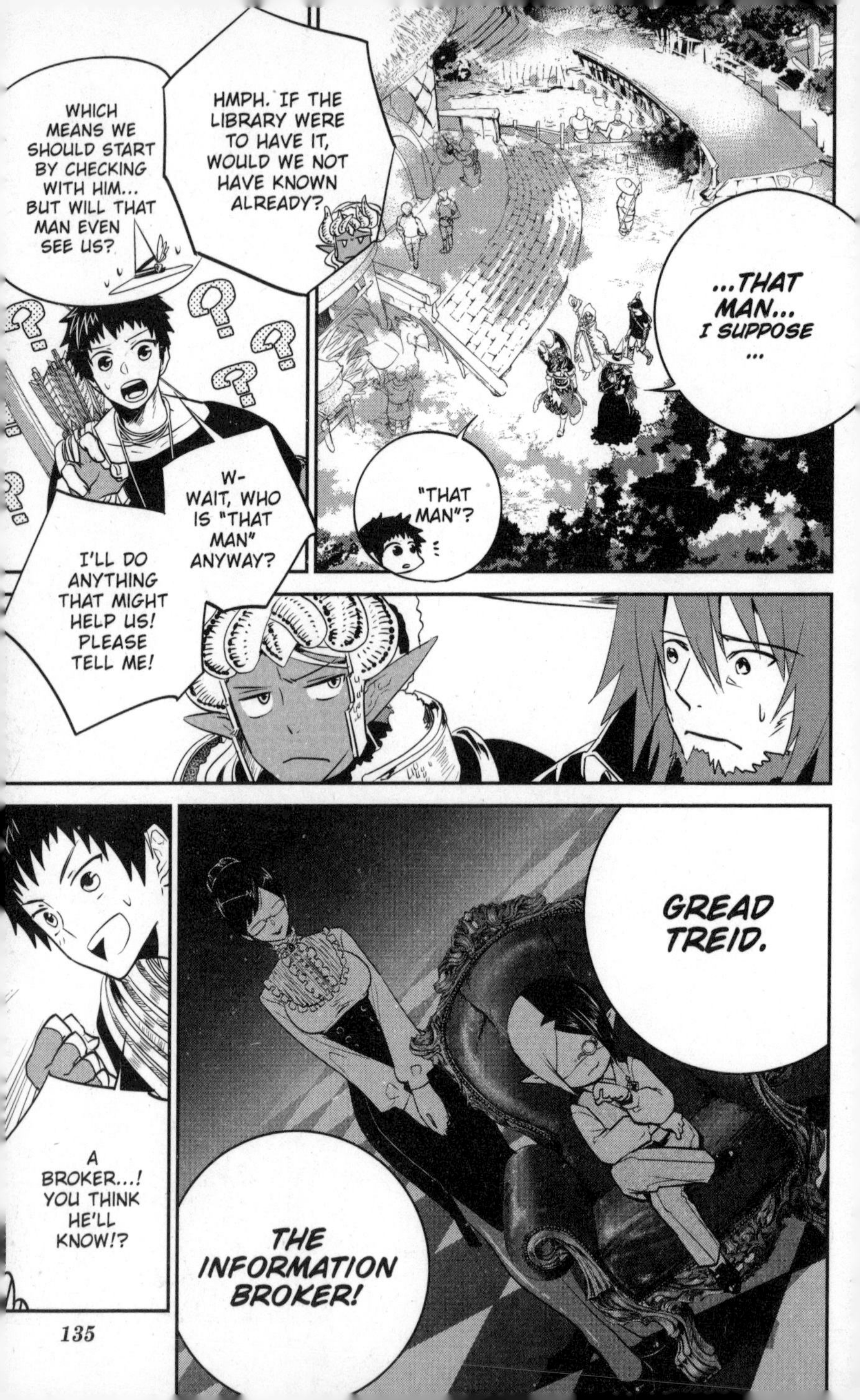
HMPH. IF THE LIBRARY WERE TO HAVE IT, WOULD WE NOT HAVE KNOWN ALREADY?
...THAT MAN... I SUPPOSE ...
"THAT MAN"?
WHICH MEANS WE SHOULD START BY CHECKING WITH HIM... BUT WILL THAT MAN EVEN SEE US?
W-WAIT, WHO IS "THAT MAN" ANYWAY?
I'LL DO ANYTHING THAT MIGHT HELP US! PLEASE TELL ME!
GREAD TREID.
THE INFORMATION BROKER!
A BROKER...! YOU THINK HE'LL KNOW!?

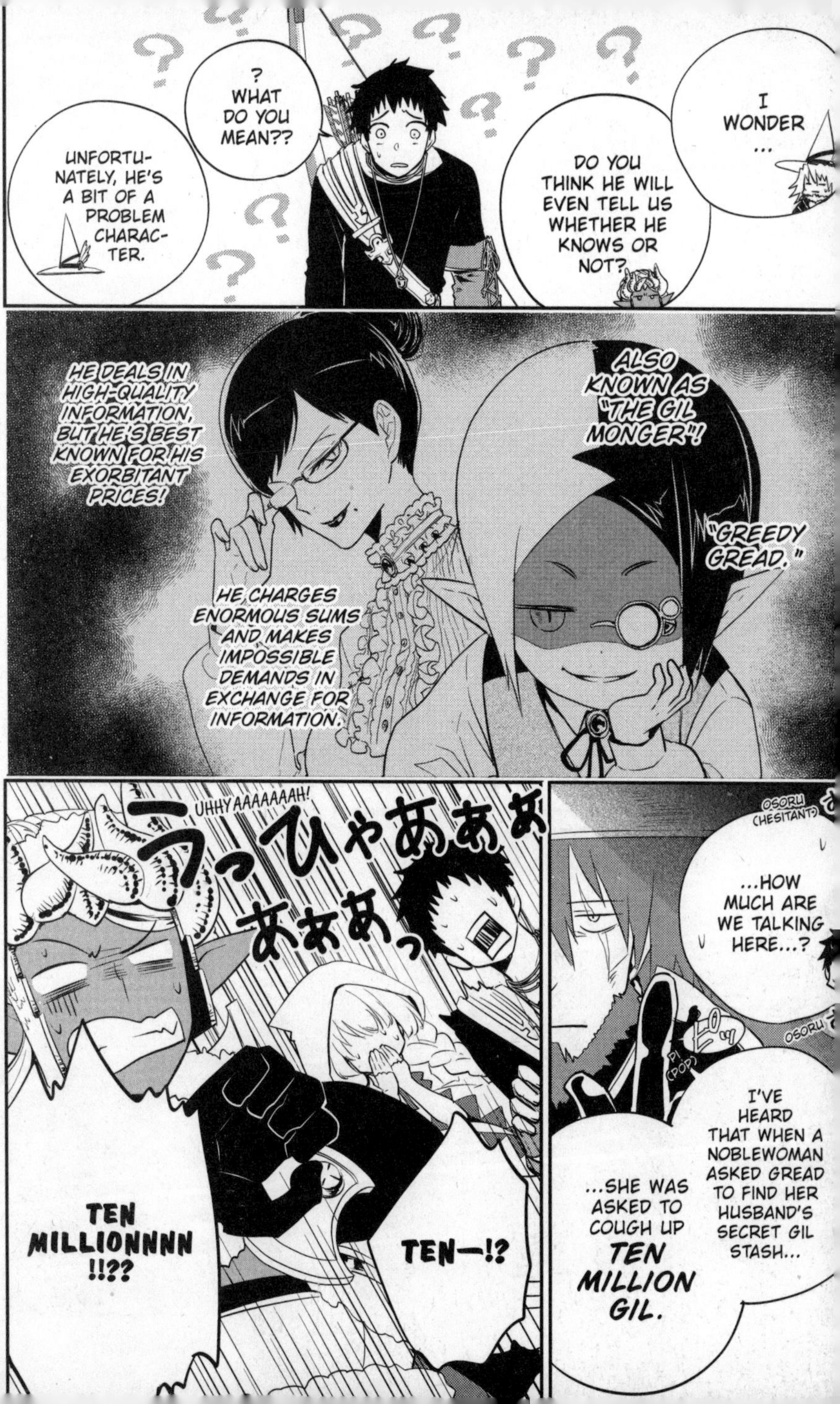
I WONDER ...
DO YOU THINK HE WILL EVEN TELL US WHETHER HE KNOWS OR NOT?
? WHAT DO YOU MEAN??
UNFORTUNATELY, HE'S A BIT OF A PROBLEM CHARACTER.
ALSO KNOWN AS "THE GIL MONGER"!
"GREEDY GREAD."
HE DEALS IN HIGH-QUALITY INFORMATION, BUT HE'S BEST KNOWN FOR HIS EXORBITANT PRICES!
HE CHARGES ENORMOUS SUMS AND MAKES IMPOSSIBLE DEMANDS IN EXCHANGE FOR INFORMATION.
OSORU (HESITANT)
...HOW MUCH ARE WE TALKING HERE...?
PI (POP)
OSORU
I'VE HEARD THAT WHEN A NOBLEWOMAN ASKED GREAD TO FIND HER HUSBAND'S SECRET GIL STASH...
...SHE WAS ASKED TO COUGH UP TEN MILLION GIL.
UHHYAAAAAAAH!
うっひゃあああああっ
TEN—!?
TEN MILLIONNNN !!??

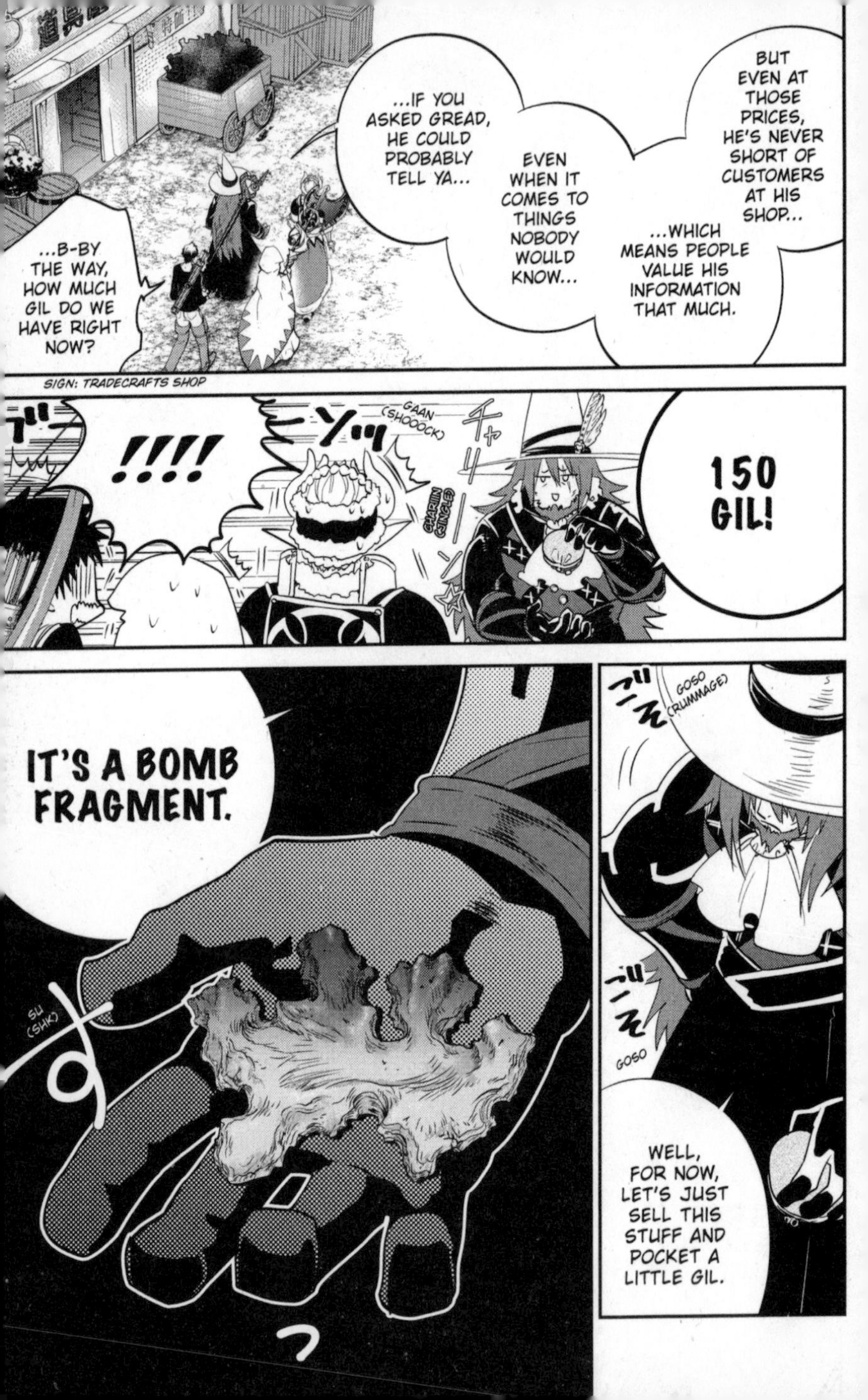

BUT EVEN AT THOSE PRICES, HE'S NEVER SHORT OF CUSTOMERS AT HIS SHOP...
...WHICH MEANS PEOPLE VALUE HIS INFORMATION THAT MUCH.
EVEN WHEN IT COMES TO THINGS NOBODY WOULD KNOW...
...IF YOU ASKED GREAD, HE COULD PROBABLY TELL YA...
...B-BY THE WAY, HOW MUCH GIL DO WE HAVE RIGHT NOW?
SIGN: TRADECRAFTS SHOP
150 GIL!
CHARIIN (JINGLE)
GAAN (SHOOOCK)
!!!!
GOSO (RUMMAGE)
GOSO
WELL, FOR NOW, LET'S JUST SELL THIS STUFF AND POCKET A LITTLE GIL.
IT'S A BOMB FRAGMENT.
SU (SHK)

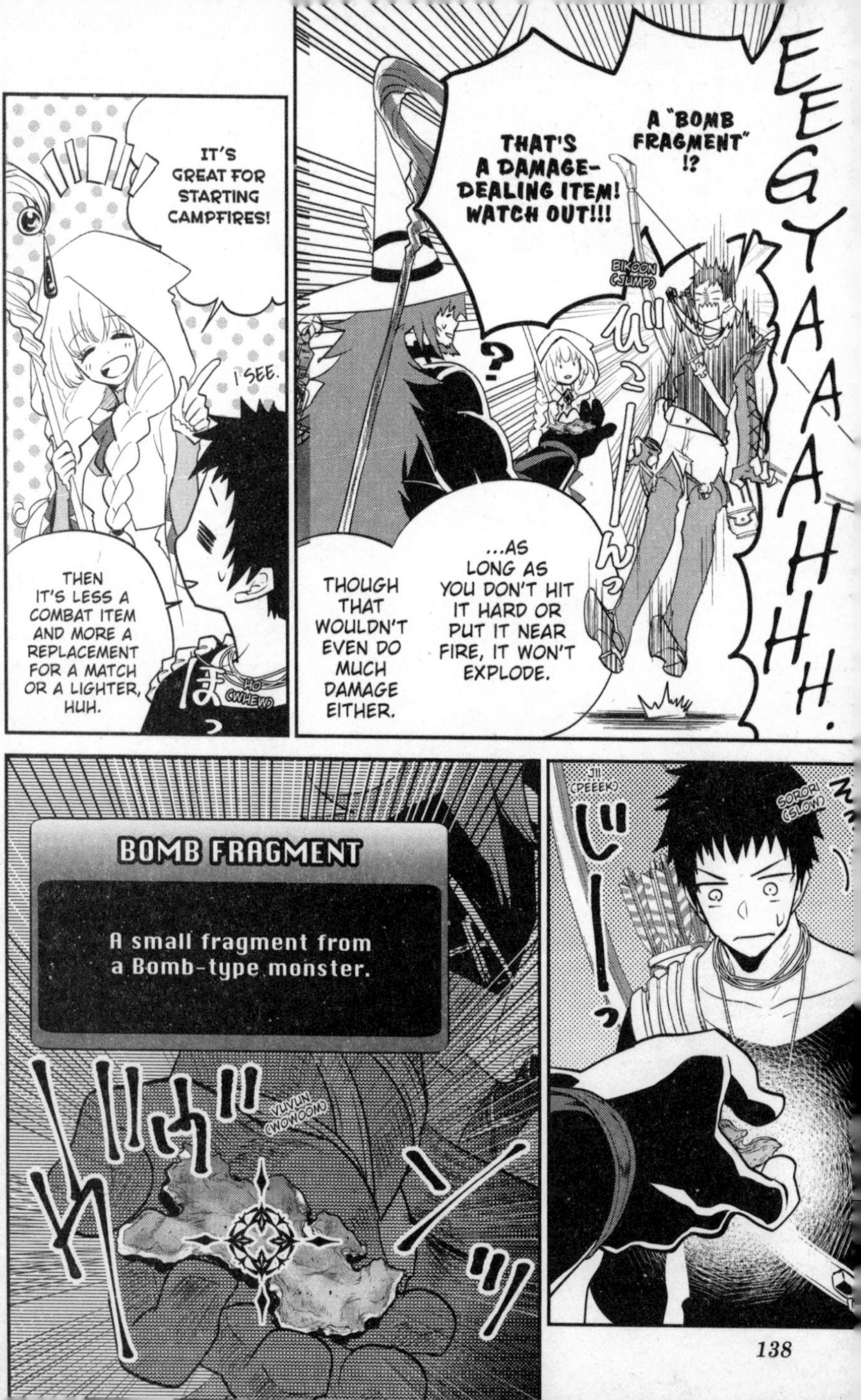
EEGYAAAHHH.
A "BOMB FRAGMENT" !?
THAT'S A DAMAGE-DEALING ITEM! WATCH OUT!!!
BIKOON (JUMP)
?
...AS LONG AS YOU DON'T HIT IT HARD OR PUT IT NEAR FIRE, IT WON'T EXPLODE.
THOUGH THAT WOULDN'T EVEN DO MUCH DAMAGE EITHER.
IT'S GREAT FOR STARTING CAMPFIRES!
I SEE.
THEN IT'S LESS A COMBAT ITEM AND MORE A REPLACEMENT FOR A MATCH OR A LIGHTER, HUH.
HO (WHEW)
JII (PEEEK)
SORORI (SLOW)
BOMB FRAGMENT
A small fragment from a Bomb-type monster.
VUVUN (WOWOOM)

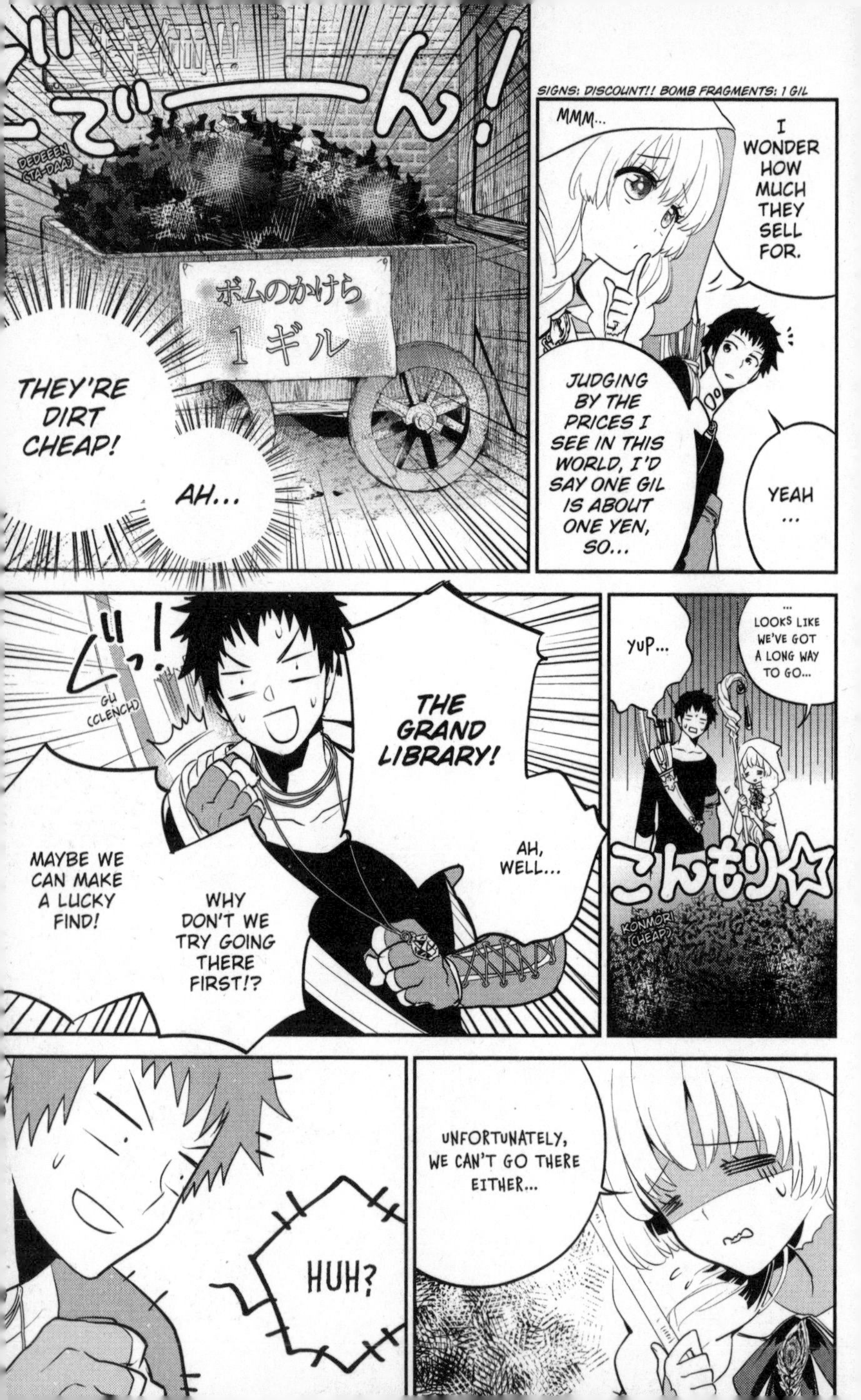
SIGNS: DISCOUNT!! BOMB FRAGMENTS: 1 GIL
MMM...
I WONDER HOW MUCH THEY SELL FOR.
YEAH...
JUDGING BY THE PRICES I SEE IN THIS WORLD, I'D SAY ONE GIL IS ABOUT ONE YEN, SO...
DEDEEEN (TA-DAA)
ボムのかけら
1ギル
AH...
THEY'RE DIRT CHEAP!
...LOOKS LIKE WE'VE GOT A LONG WAY TO GO...
YUP...
こんもり☆
KONMORI (CHEAP)
THE GRAND LIBRARY!
AH, WELL...
WHY DON'T WE TRY GOING THERE FIRST!?
MAYBE WE CAN MAKE A LUCKY FIND!
GU (CLENCH)
UNFORTUNATELY, WE CAN'T GO THERE EITHER...
HUH?

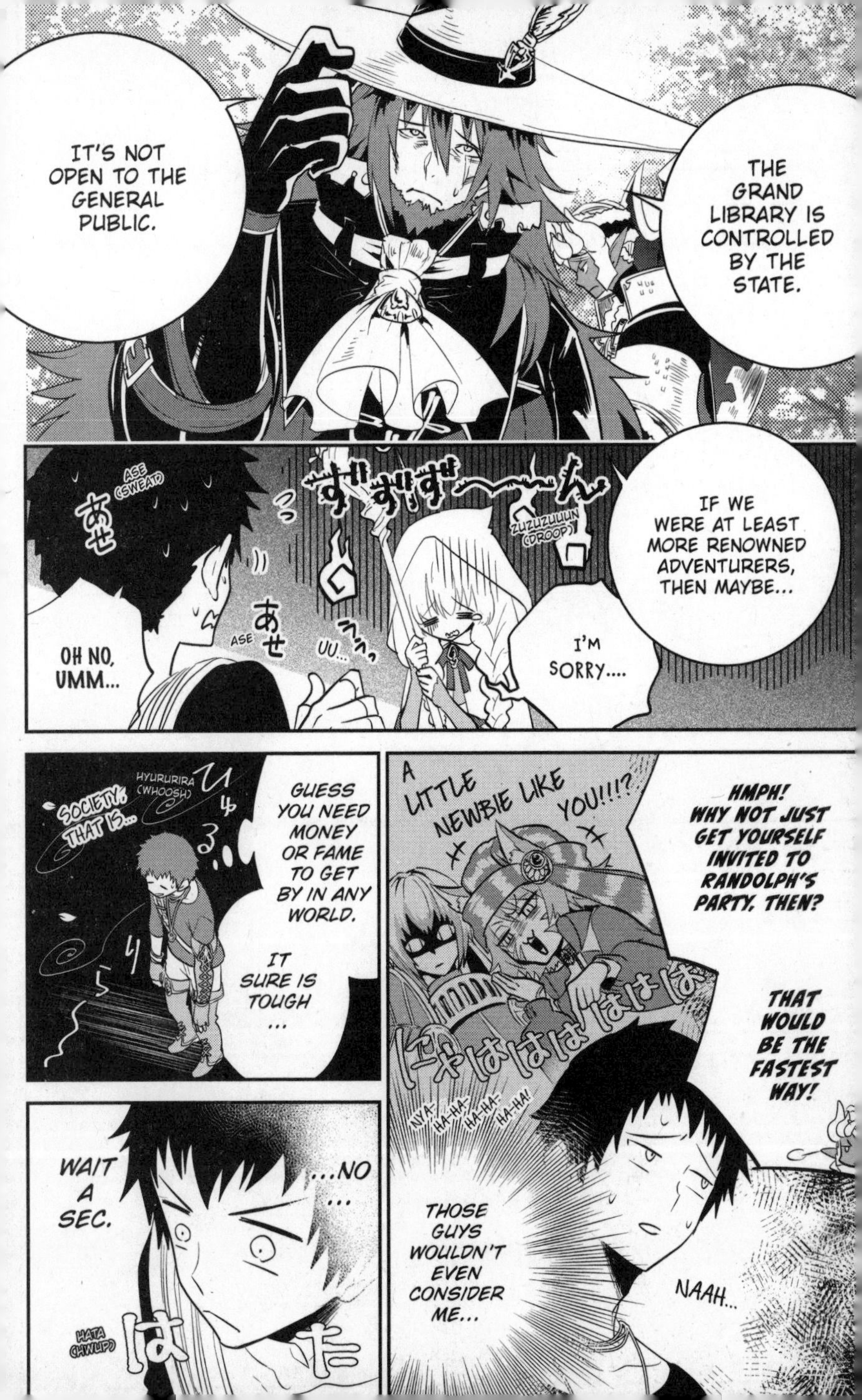
THE GRAND LIBRARY IS CONTROLLED BY THE STATE.
IT'S NOT OPEN TO THE GENERAL PUBLIC.
IF WE WERE AT LEAST MORE RENOWNED ADVENTURERS, THEN MAYBE...
ZUZUZUUUN (DROOP)
I'M SORRY....
UU...
ASE
ASE (SWEAT)
OH NO, UMM...
HMPH! WHY NOT JUST GET YOURSELF INVITED TO RANDOLPH'S PARTY, THEN?
A LITTLE NEWBIE LIKE YOU!!!?
THAT WOULD BE THE FASTEST WAY!
NYA-HA-HA-HA-HA-HA!
NAAH...
THOSE GUYS WOULDN'T EVEN CONSIDER ME...
HYURURIRA (WHOOSH)
SOCIETY, THAT IS...
GUESS YOU NEED MONEY OR FAME TO GET BY IN ANY WORLD.
IT SURE IS TOUGH...
...NO...
WAIT A SEC.
HATA (HWUP)

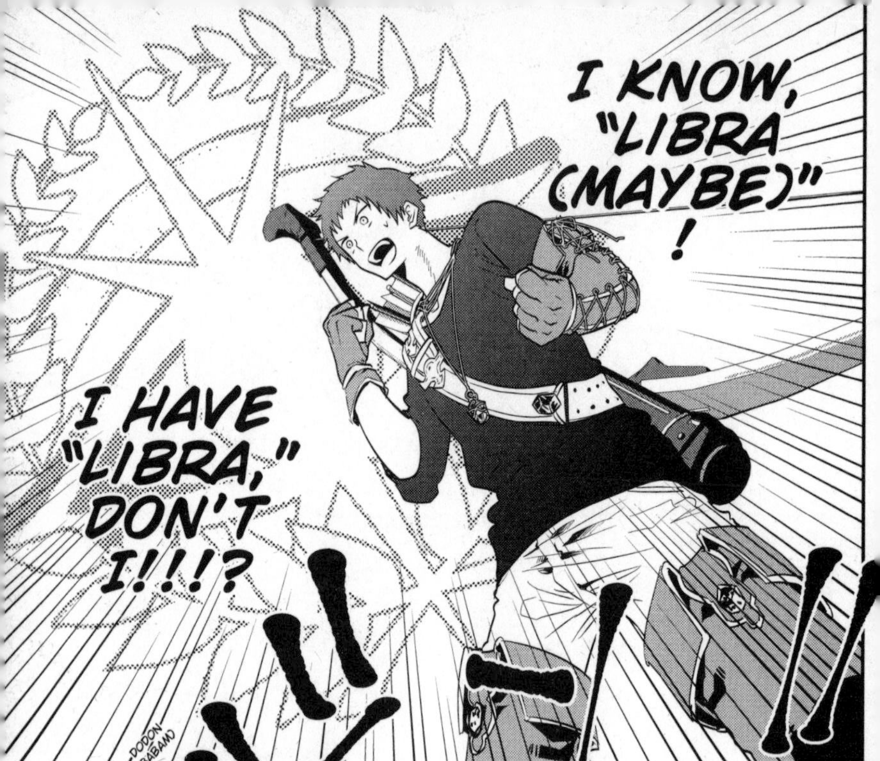
I KNOW, "LIBRA (MAYBE)"!
I HAVE "LIBRA," DON'T I!!!?
DODON (BABAM)

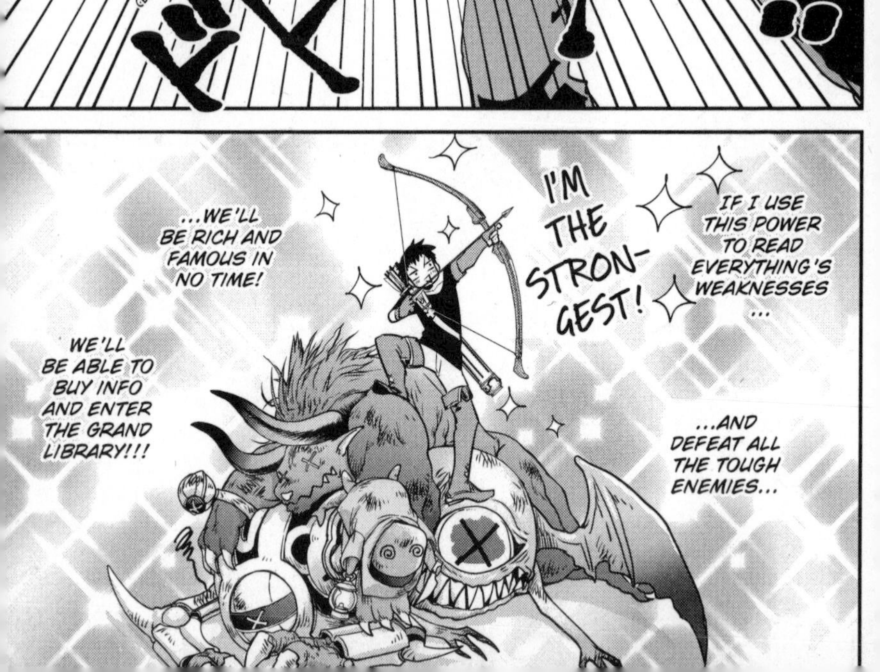
IF I USE THIS POWER TO READ EVERYTHING'S WEAKNESSES...
...AND DEFEAT ALL THE TOUGH ENEMIES...
I'M THE STRON-GEST!
...WE'LL BE RICH AND FAMOUS IN NO TIME!
WE'LL BE ABLE TO BUY INFO AND ENTER THE GRAND LIBRARY!!!

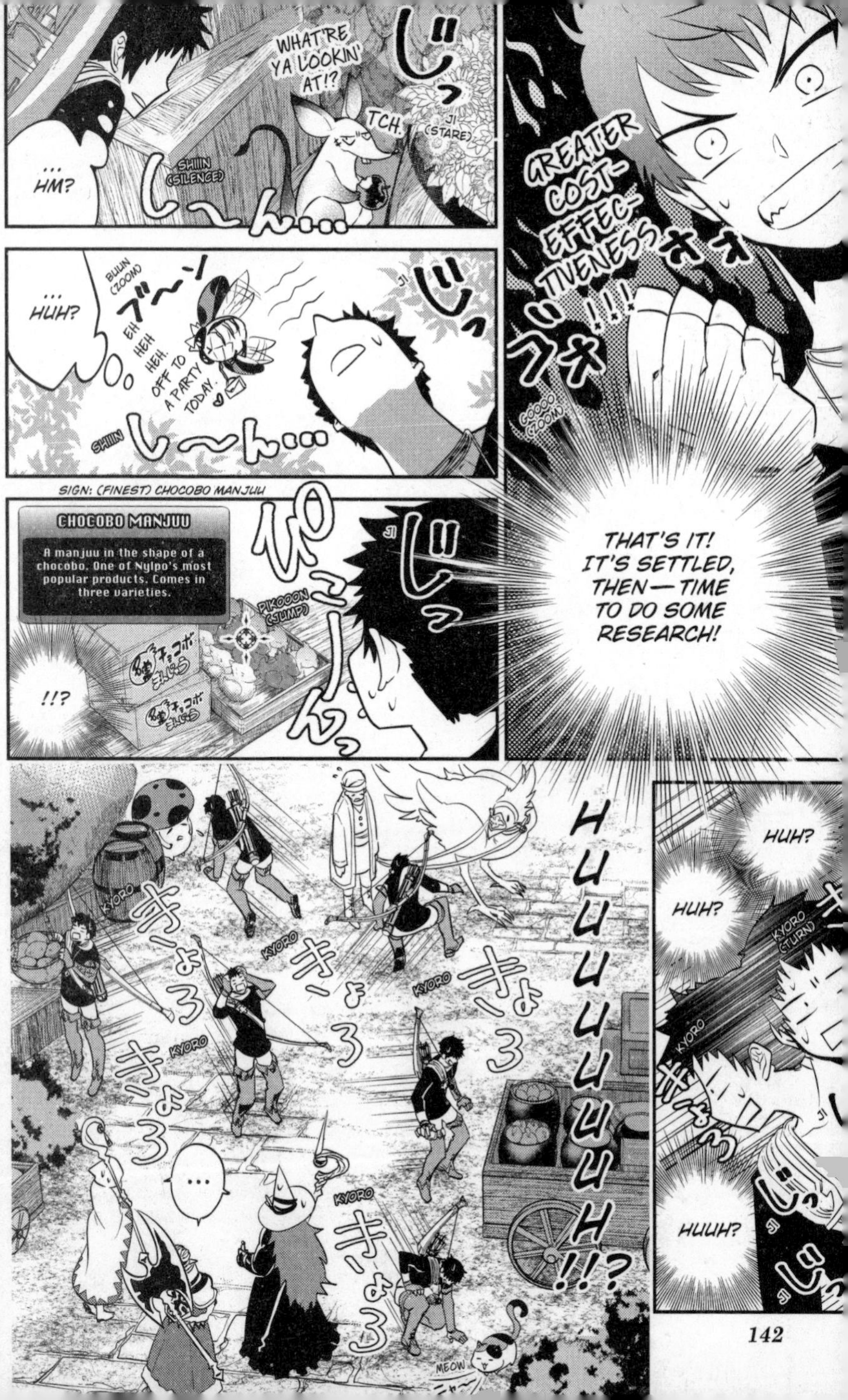
GREATER COST-EFFECTIVENESS
GOOOO (ZOOM)
THAT'S IT! IT'S SETTLED, THEN—TIME TO DO SOME RESEARCH!
WHAT'RE YA LOOKIN' AT!?
JI (STARE)
TCH.
SHIIN (SILENCE)
... HM?
JI
BUUN (ZOOM)
EH HEH HEH. OFF TO A PARTY TODAY.
... HUH?
SHIIN
SIGN: (FINEST) CHOCOBO MANJUU
JI
PIKOOON (JUMP)
CHOCOBO MANJUU
A manjuu in the shape of a chocobo. One of Nylpo's most popular products. Comes in three varieties.
!!?
HUH?
KYORO (TURN)
HUH?
KYORO
JI
HUUH?
HUUUUUUUUUH!!?
KYORO
KYORO
KYORO
KYORO
KYORO
...
KYORO
MEOW

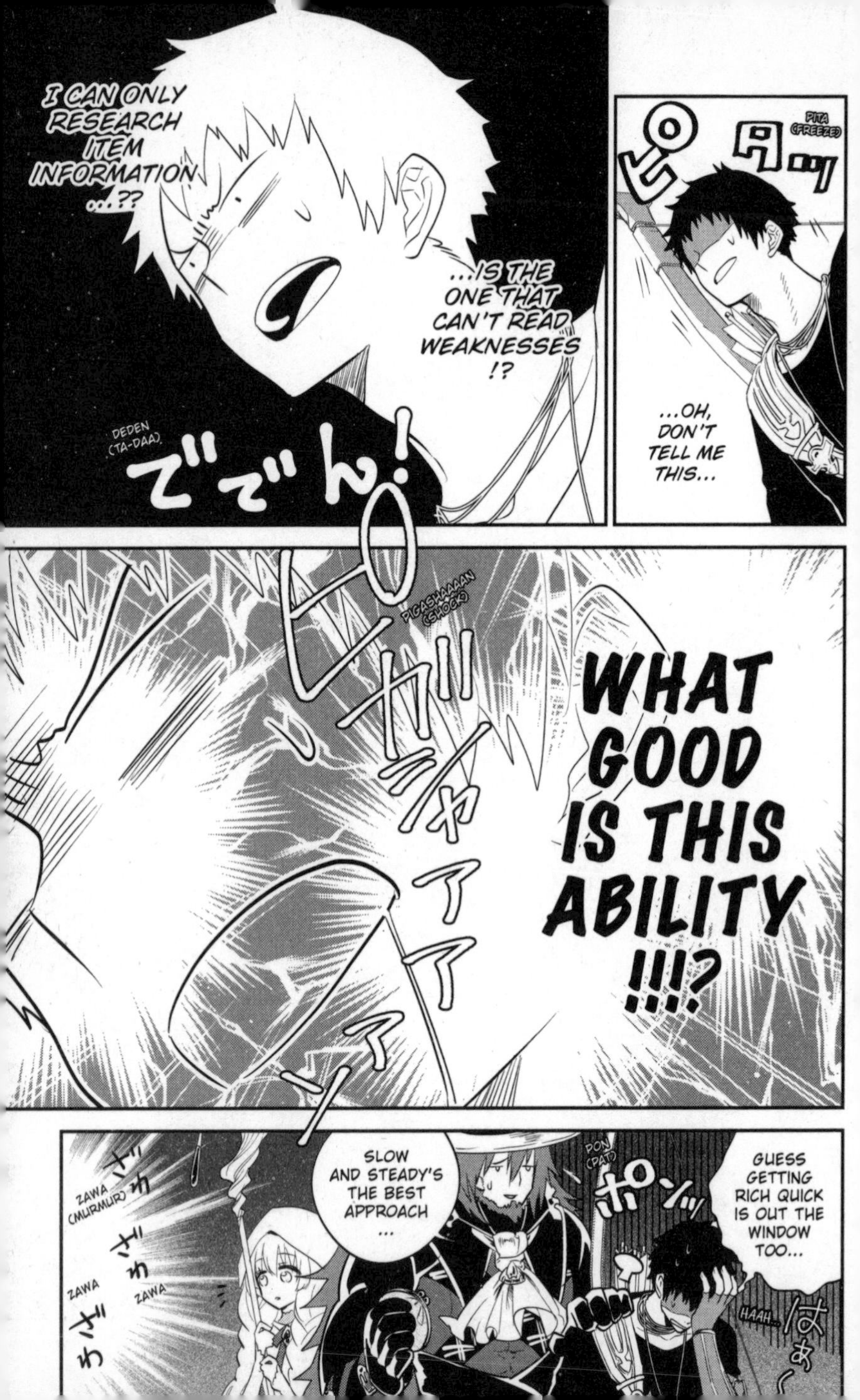
PITA (FREEZE)
ピタッ
...OH, DON'T TELL ME THIS...
I CAN ONLY RESEARCH ITEM INFORMATION ...??
...IS THE ONE THAT CAN'T READ WEAKNESSES !?
DEDEN (TA-DAA)
ででん!
PIGASHAAAAN (SHOCK)
WHAT GOOD IS THIS ABILITY !!!?
GUESS GETTING RICH QUICK IS OUT THE WINDOW TOO...
HAAH...
PON (PAT)
ポンッ
SLOW AND STEADY'S THE BEST APPROACH ...
ZAWA (MURMUR)
ZAWA
ZAWA

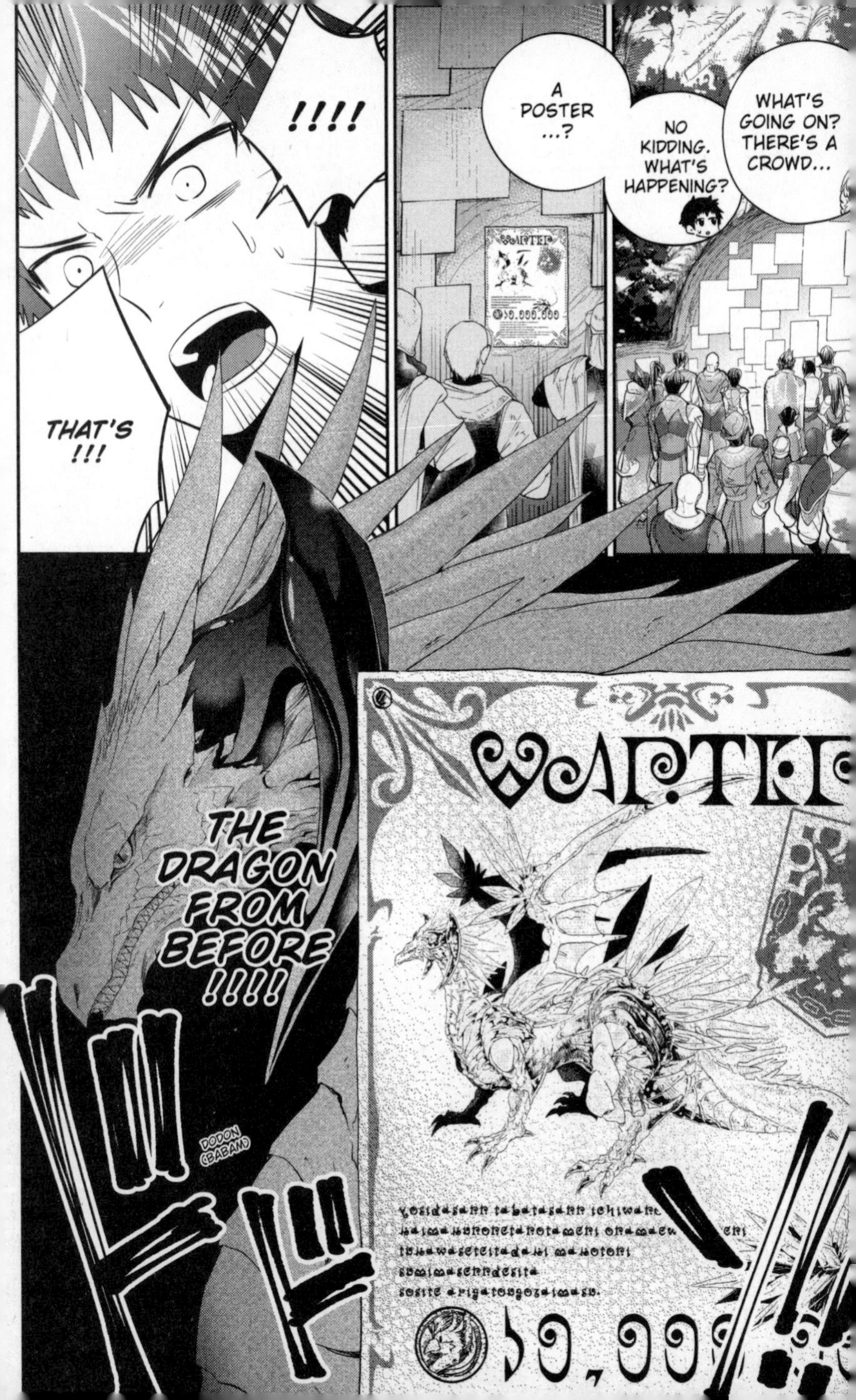
WHAT'S GOING ON? THERE'S A CROWD...
NO KIDDING. WHAT'S HAPPENING?
A POSTER ...?
!!!!
THAT'S !!!
THE DRAGON FROM BEFORE !!!!
DODON (BABAM)

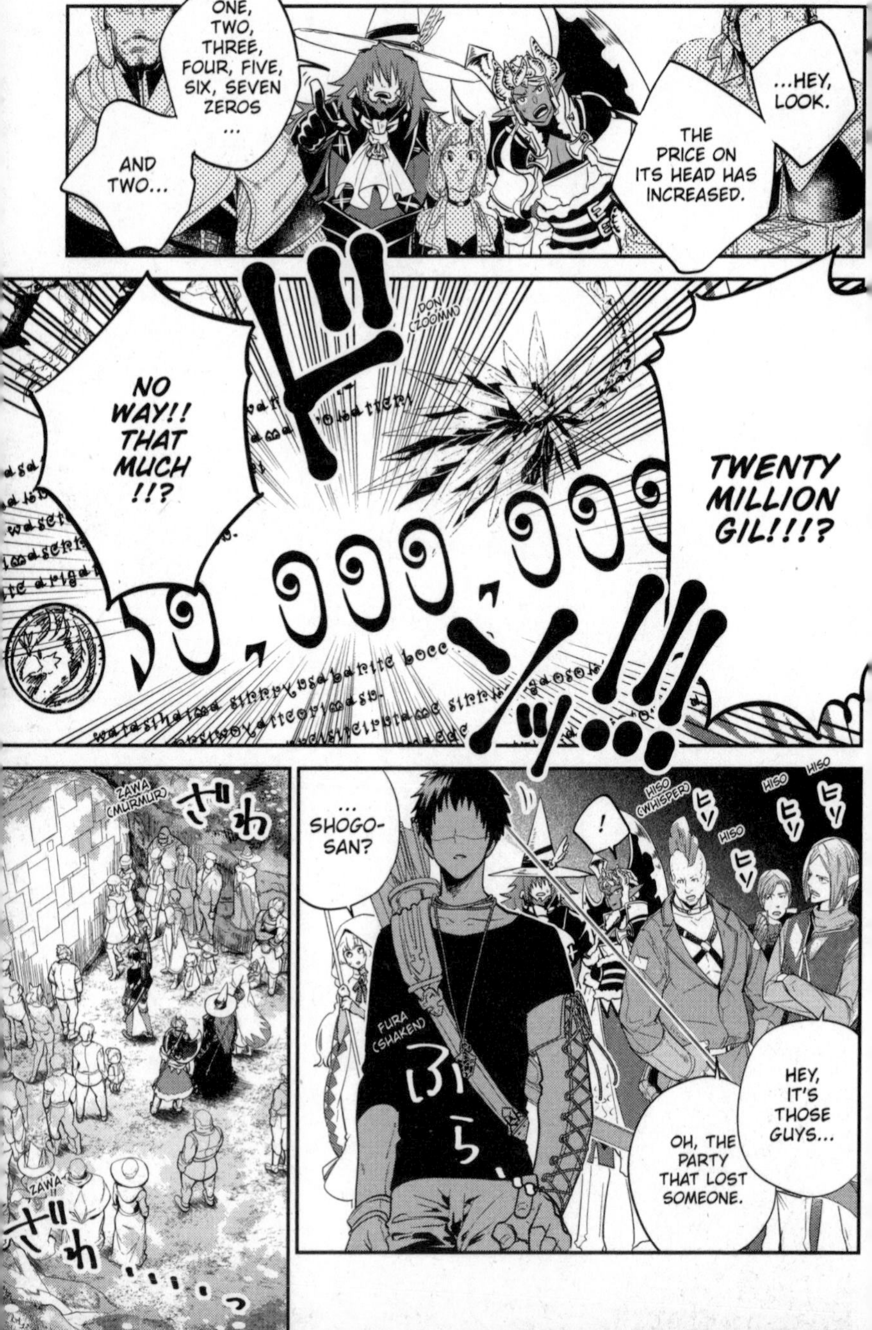
...HEY, LOOK.
THE PRICE ON ITS HEAD HAS INCREASED.
ONE, TWO, THREE, FOUR, FIVE, SIX, SEVEN ZEROS ...
AND TWO...
TWENTY MILLION GIL!!!?
DON (ZOOMM)
NO WAY!! THAT MUCH!!?
HISO HISO
HISO
HISO (WHISPER)
!
... SHOGO-SAN?
FURA (SHAKEN)
HEY, IT'S THOSE GUYS...
OH, THE PARTY THAT LOST SOMEONE.
ZAWA (MURMUR)
ZAWA

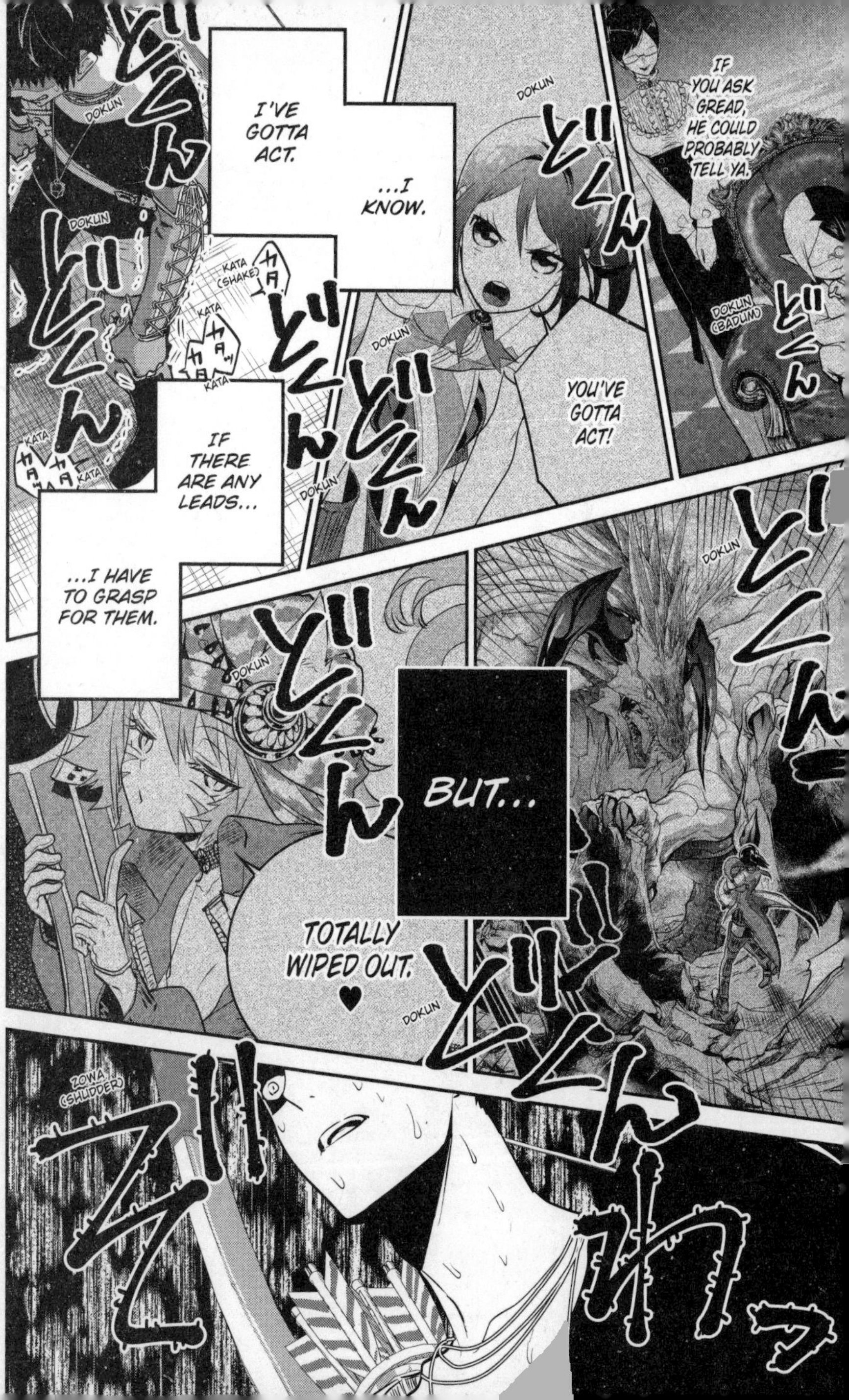
IF YOU ASK GREAD, HE COULD PROBABLY TELL YA.
DOKUN (BADUM)
DOKUN
DOKUN
YOU'VE GOTTA ACT!
...I KNOW.
I'VE GOTTA ACT.
DOKUN
KATA (SHAKE)
KATA
KATA
DOKUN
KATA
KATA
IF THERE ARE ANY LEADS...
DOKUN
...I HAVE TO GRASP FOR THEM.
DOKUN
BUT...
DOKUN
TOTALLY WIPED OUT. ♥
DOKUN
ZOWA (SHUDDER)

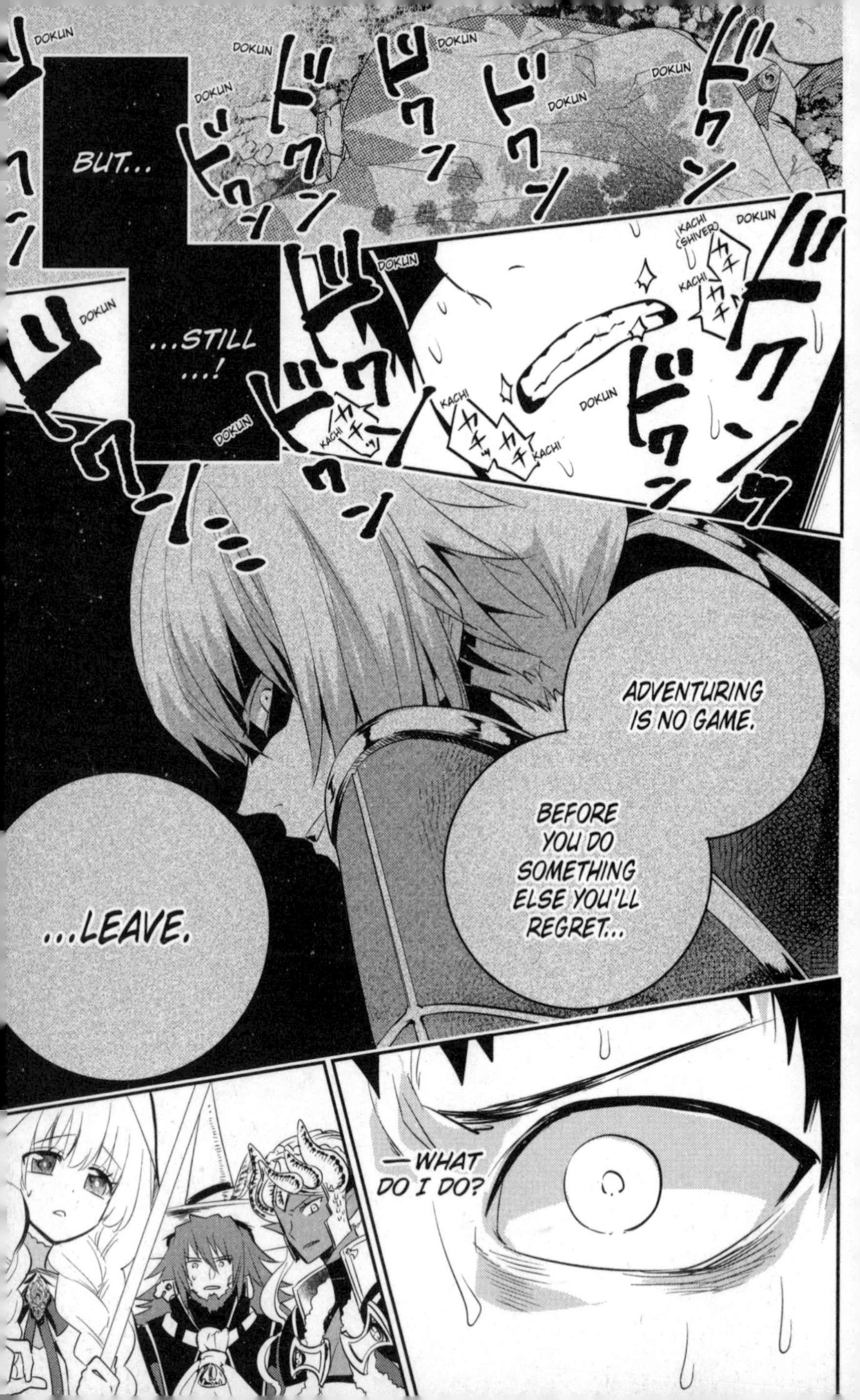
DOKUN
DOKUN
DOKUN
DOKUN
DOKUN
BUT...
DOKUN
KACHI (SHIVER)
KACHI
DOKUN
KACHI
KACHI
KACHI
DOKUN
DOKUN
...STILL ...!
DOKUN
ADVENTURING IS NO GAME.
BEFORE YOU DO SOMETHING ELSE YOU'LL REGRET...
...LEAVE.
—WHAT DO I DO?

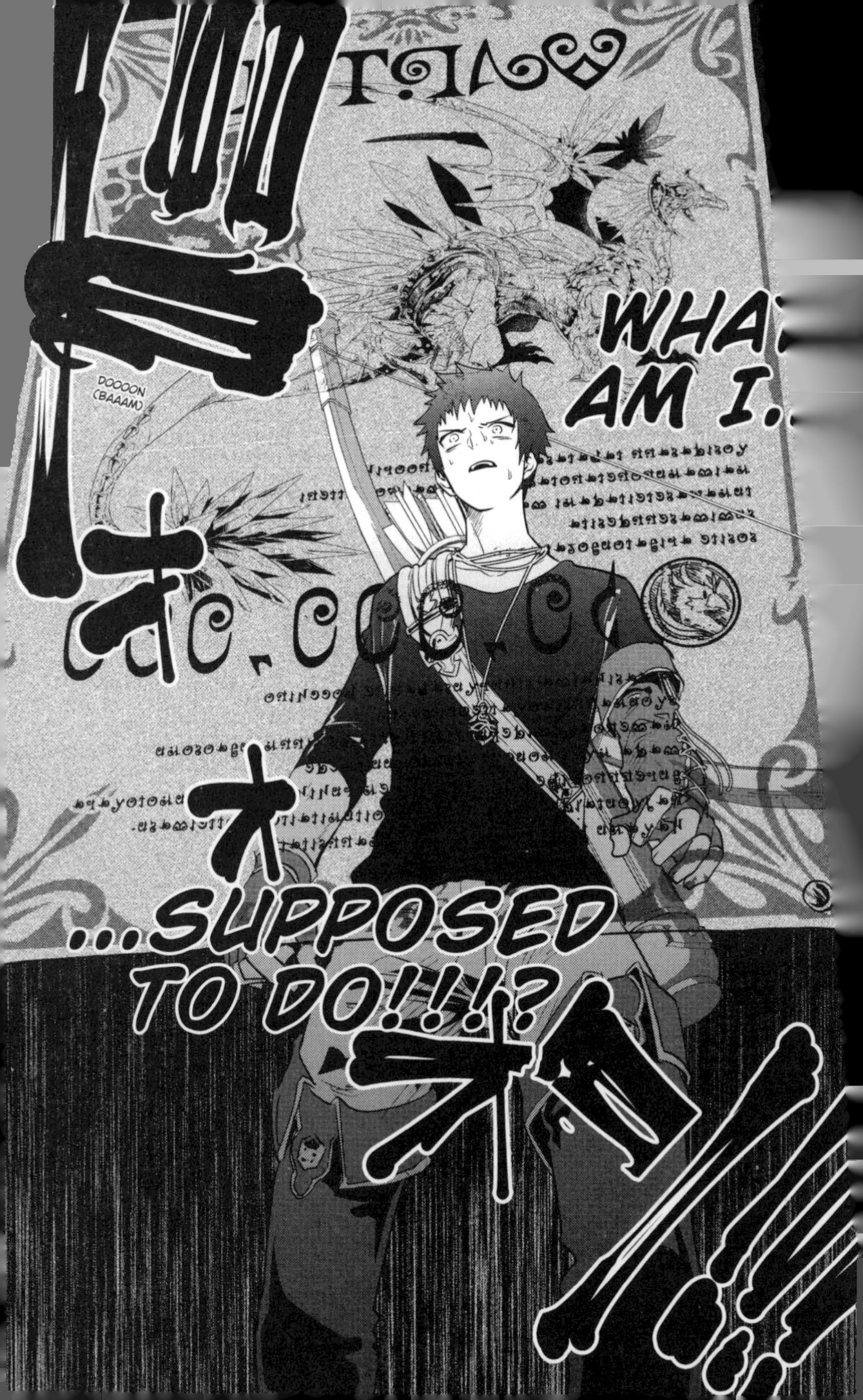
WHA
AM I..
DOOOON
(BAAAM)
...SUPPOSED
TO DO!!!?

FINAL FANTASY®
ファイナルファンタジー　ロスト・ストレンジャー
LOST STRANGER

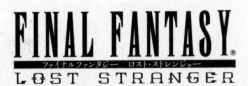

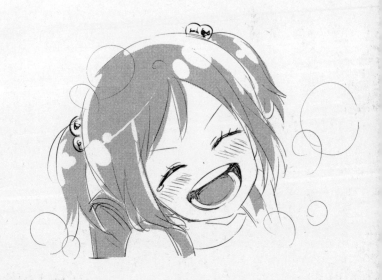

Chapter 3 Challenge

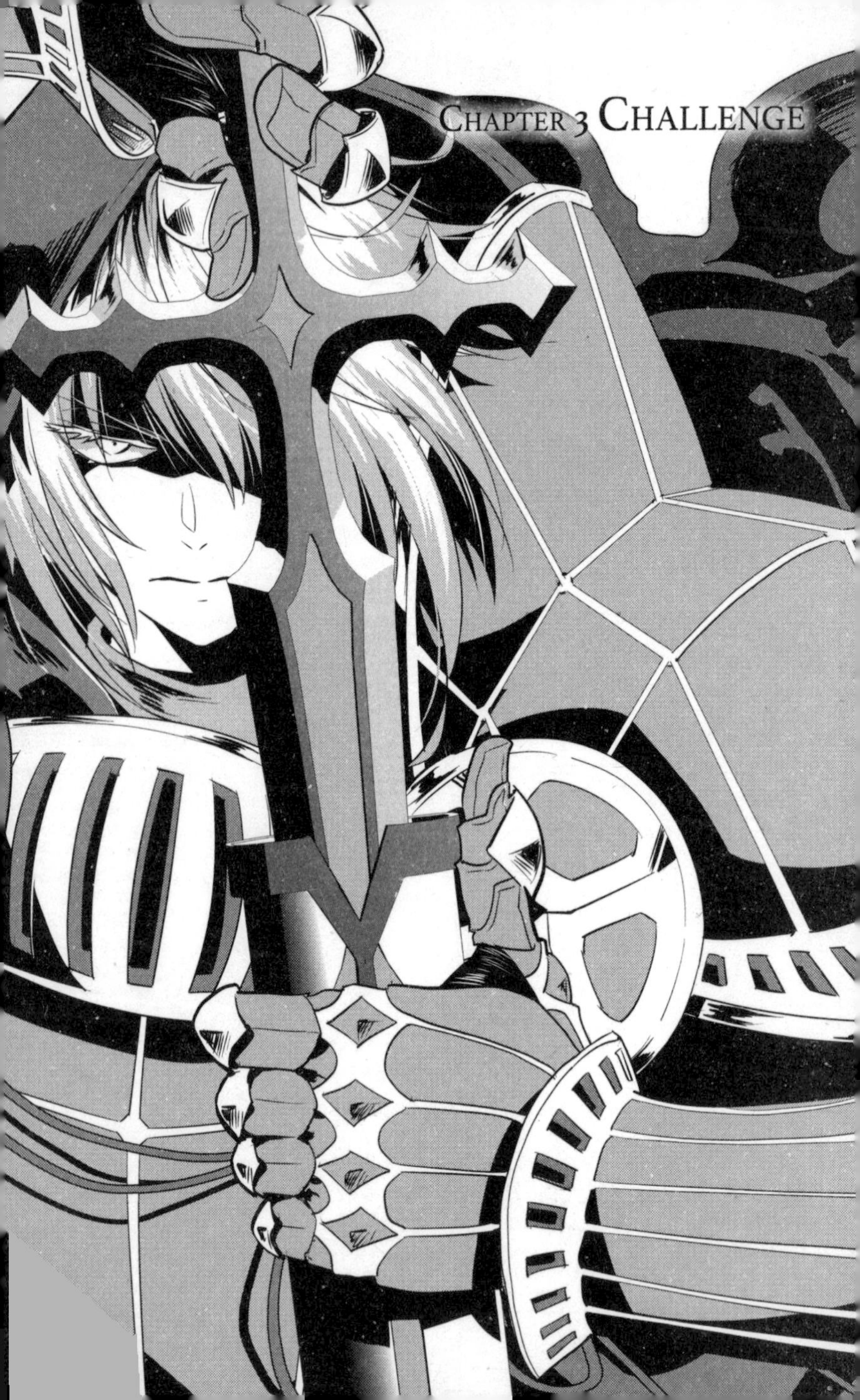

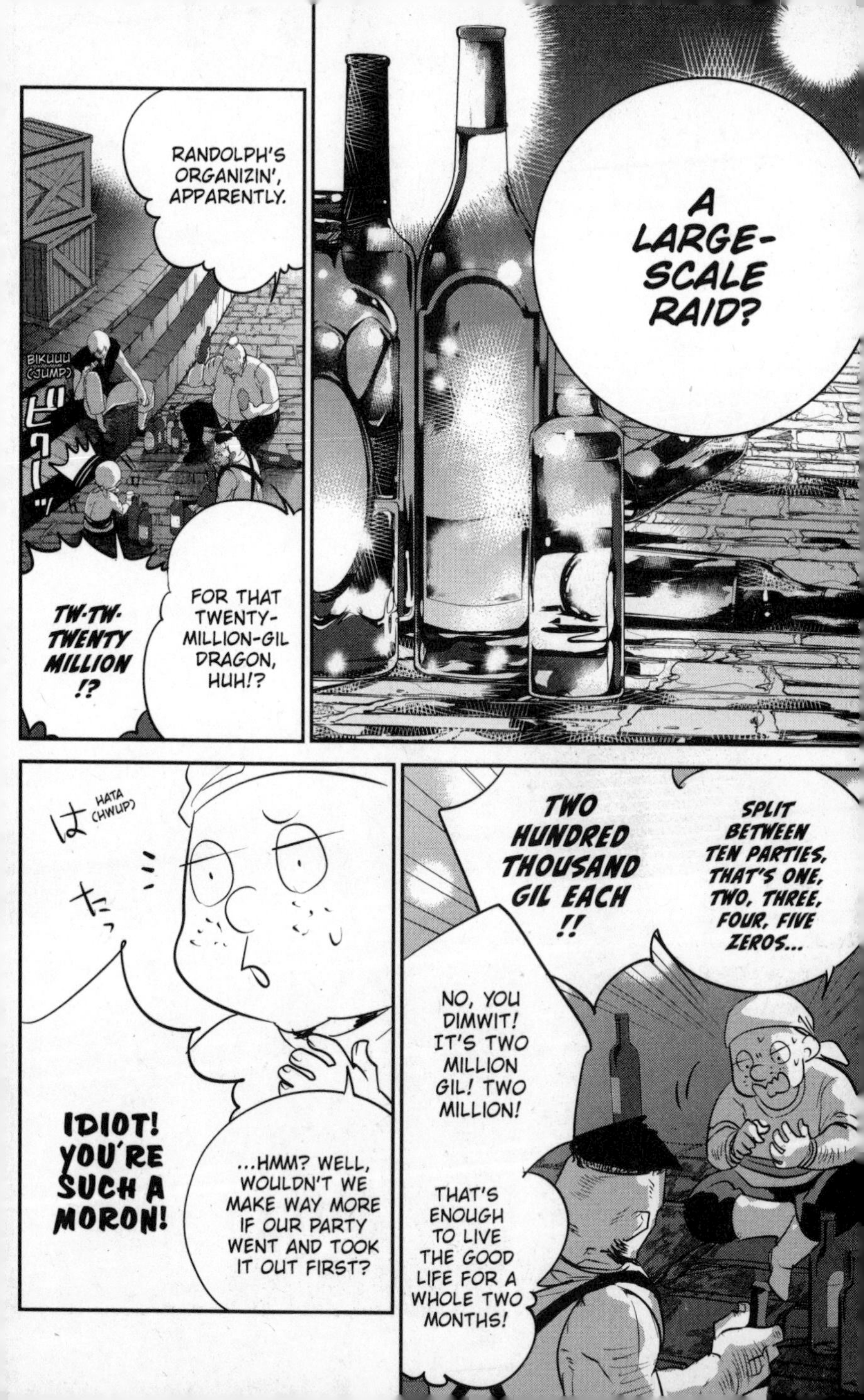

A LARGE-SCALE RAID?
RANDOLPH'S ORGANIZIN', APPARENTLY.
BIKUUU (JUMP)
FOR THAT TWENTY-MILLION-GIL DRAGON, HUH!?
TW-TW-TWENTY MILLION !?
SPLIT BETWEEN TEN PARTIES, THAT'S ONE, TWO, THREE, FOUR, FIVE ZEROS...
TWO HUNDRED THOUSAND GIL EACH !!
NO, YOU DIMWIT! IT'S TWO MILLION GIL! TWO MILLION!
THAT'S ENOUGH TO LIVE THE GOOD LIFE FOR A WHOLE TWO MONTHS!
はたっ
HATA (HWUP)
...HMM? WELL, WOULDN'T WE MAKE WAY MORE IF OUR PARTY WENT AND TOOK IT OUT FIRST?
IDIOT! YOU'RE SUCH A MORON!

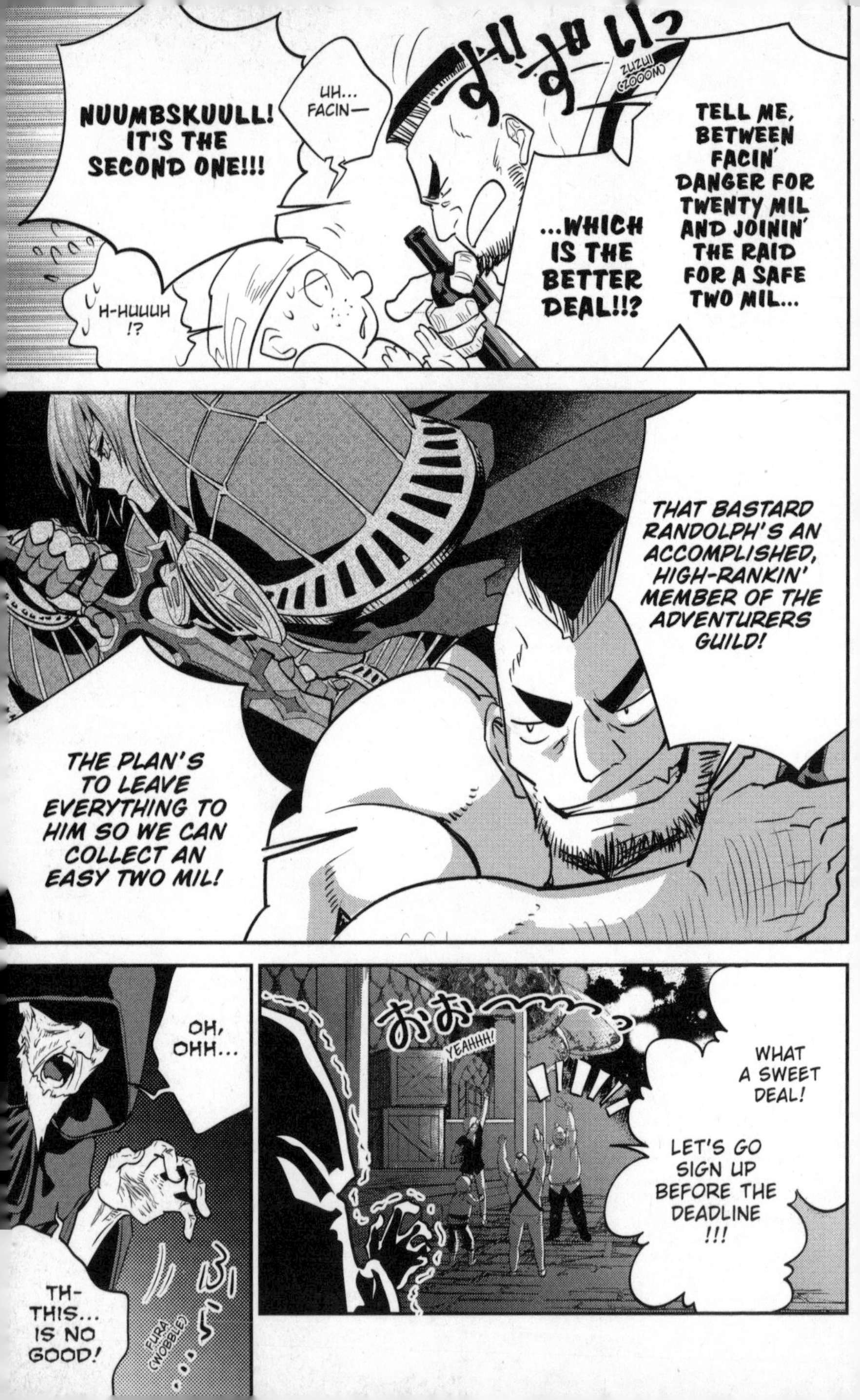
TELL ME, BETWEEN FACIN' DANGER FOR TWENTY MIL AND JOININ' THE RAID FOR A SAFE TWO MIL...
...WHICH IS THE BETTER DEAL!!?
ZUZUI! (ZOOOM)
UH... FACIN—
NUUMBSKUULL! IT'S THE SECOND ONE!!!
H-HUUUH!?
THAT BASTARD RANDOLPH'S AN ACCOMPLISHED, HIGH-RANKIN' MEMBER OF THE ADVENTURERS GUILD!
THE PLAN'S TO LEAVE EVERYTHING TO HIM SO WE CAN COLLECT AN EASY TWO MIL!
おお～～っ
YEAHHH!
WHAT A SWEET DEAL!
LET'S GO SIGN UP BEFORE THE DEADLINE!!!
OH, OHH...
TH-THIS... IS NO GOOD!
ふら...
FURA (WOBBLE)

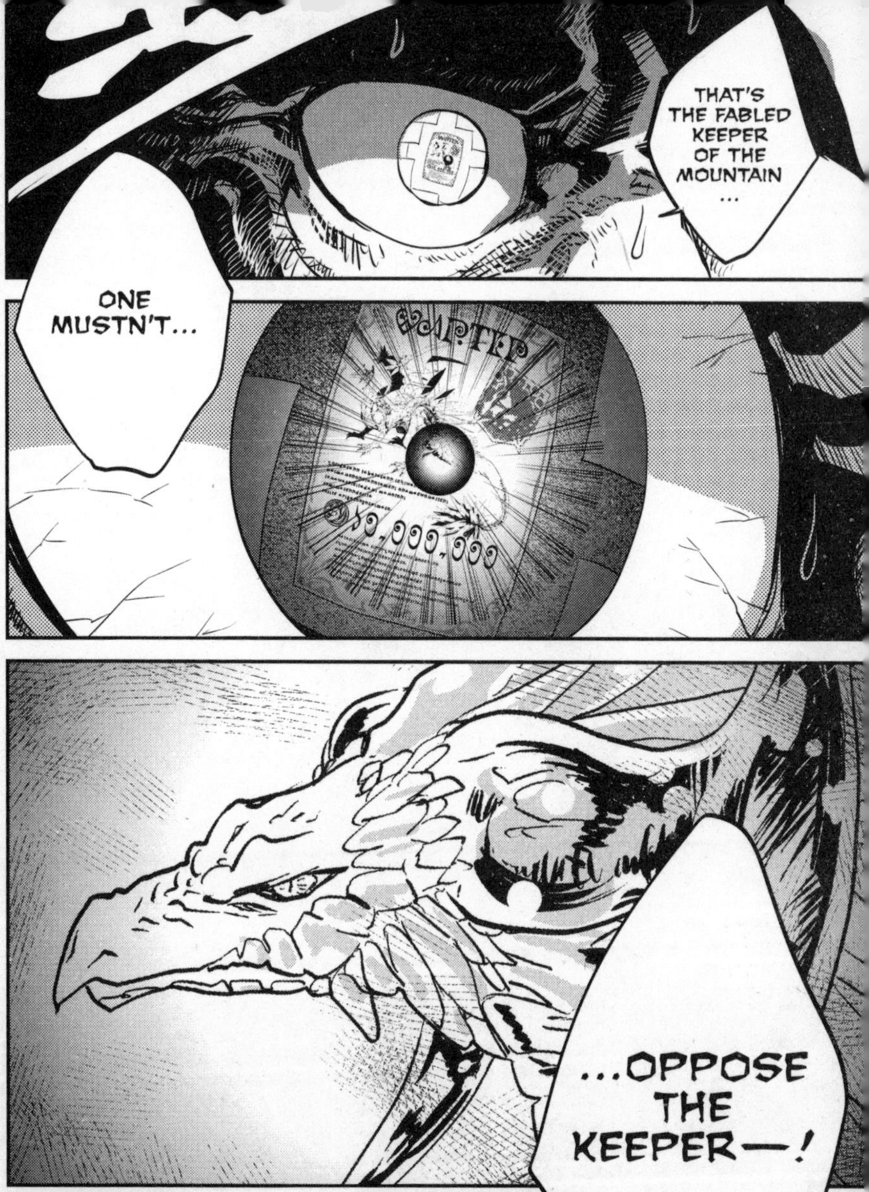
THAT'S THE FABLED KEEPER OF THE MOUNTAIN...
ONE MUSTN'T...
...OPPOSE THE KEEPER—!

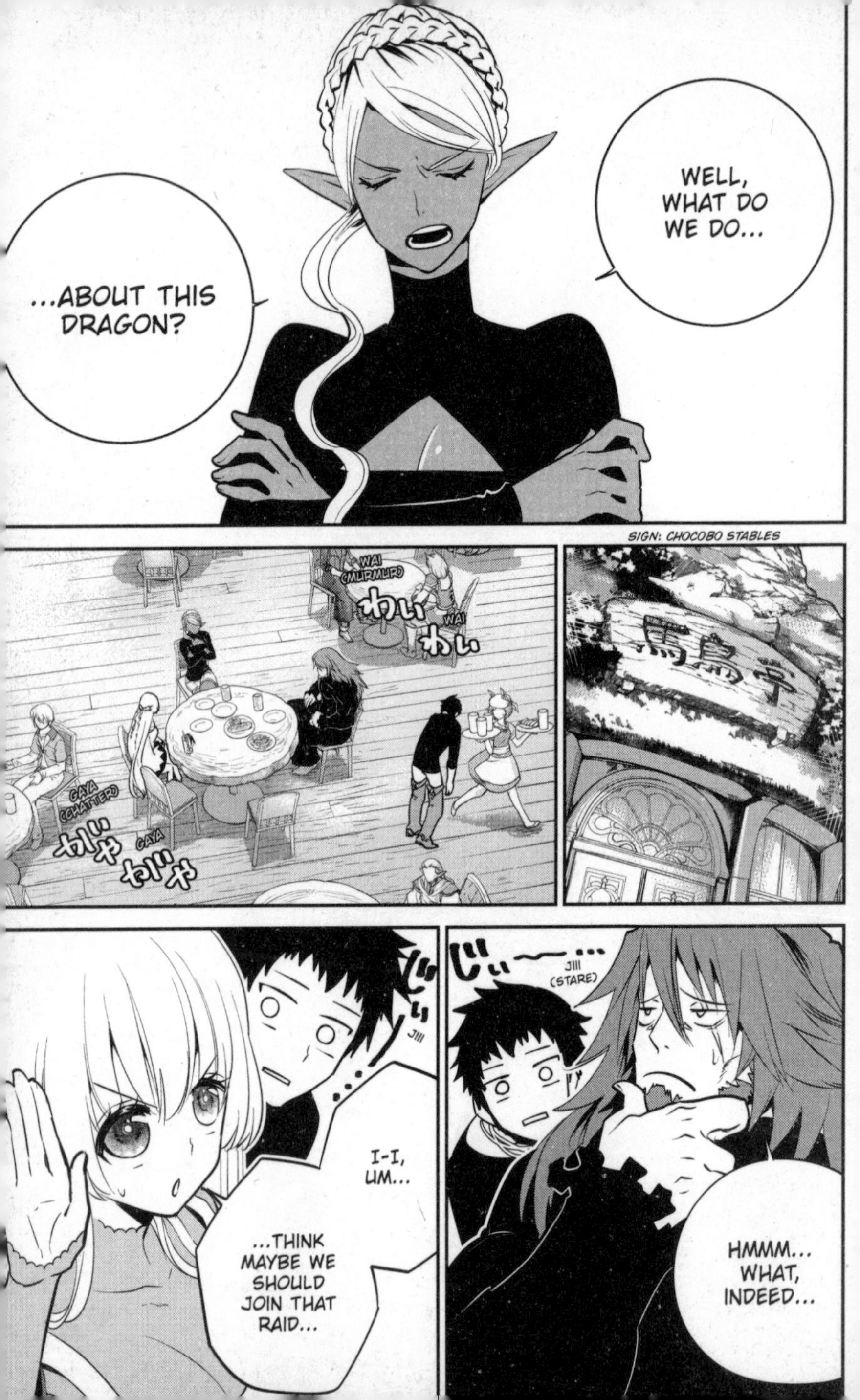
WELL, WHAT DO WE DO...
...ABOUT THIS DRAGON?
SIGN: CHOCOBO STABLES
馬鳥亭
わいわい
WAI (MURMUR)
WAI
わいわい
がやがや
GAYA (CHATTER)
GAYA
がやがや
じぃ~...
JIII (STARE)
HMMM... WHAT, INDEED...
じぃ
JIII
...
I-I, UM...
...THINK MAYBE WE SHOULD JOIN THAT RAID...

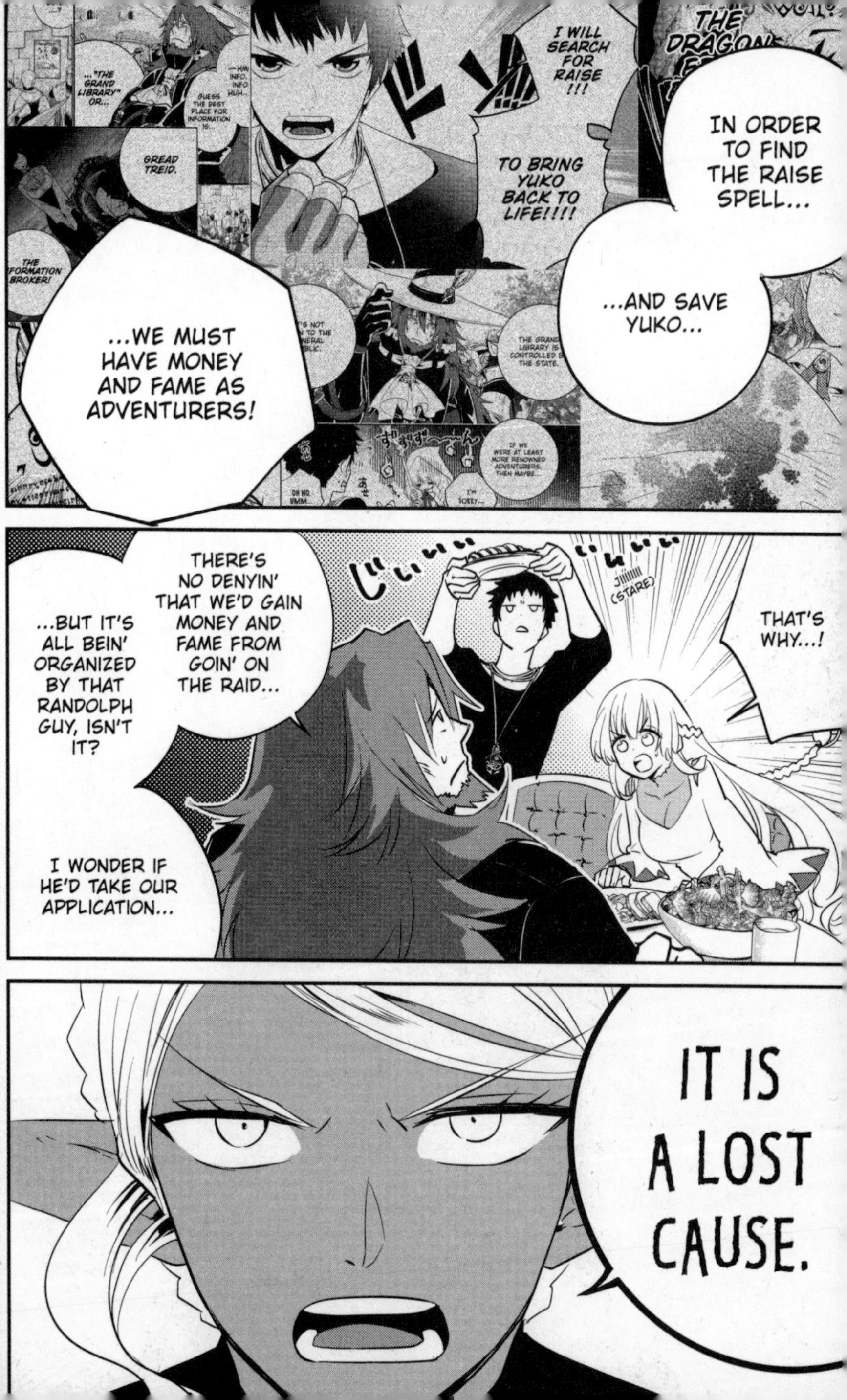
IN ORDER TO FIND THE RAISE SPELL...
...AND SAVE YUKO...
I WILL SEARCH FOR RAISE!!!
TO BRING YUKO BACK TO LIFE!!!!
—HM INFO. INFO HUH...
GUESS THE BEST PLACE FOR INFORMATION IS...
..."THE GRAND LIBRARY" OR...
GREAD TREID.
IF WE WERE AT LEAST MORE RENOWNED ADVENTURERS, THEN MAYBE...
I'M SORRY...
OH NO. UMM...
...WE MUST HAVE MONEY AND FAME AS ADVENTURERS!
THAT'S WHY...!
JIIIIIII (STARE)
THERE'S NO DENYIN' THAT WE'D GAIN MONEY AND FAME FROM GOIN' ON THE RAID...
...BUT IT'S ALL BEIN' ORGANIZED BY THAT RANDOLPH GUY, ISN'T IT?
I WONDER IF HE'D TAKE OUR APPLICATION...
IT IS A LOST CAUSE.

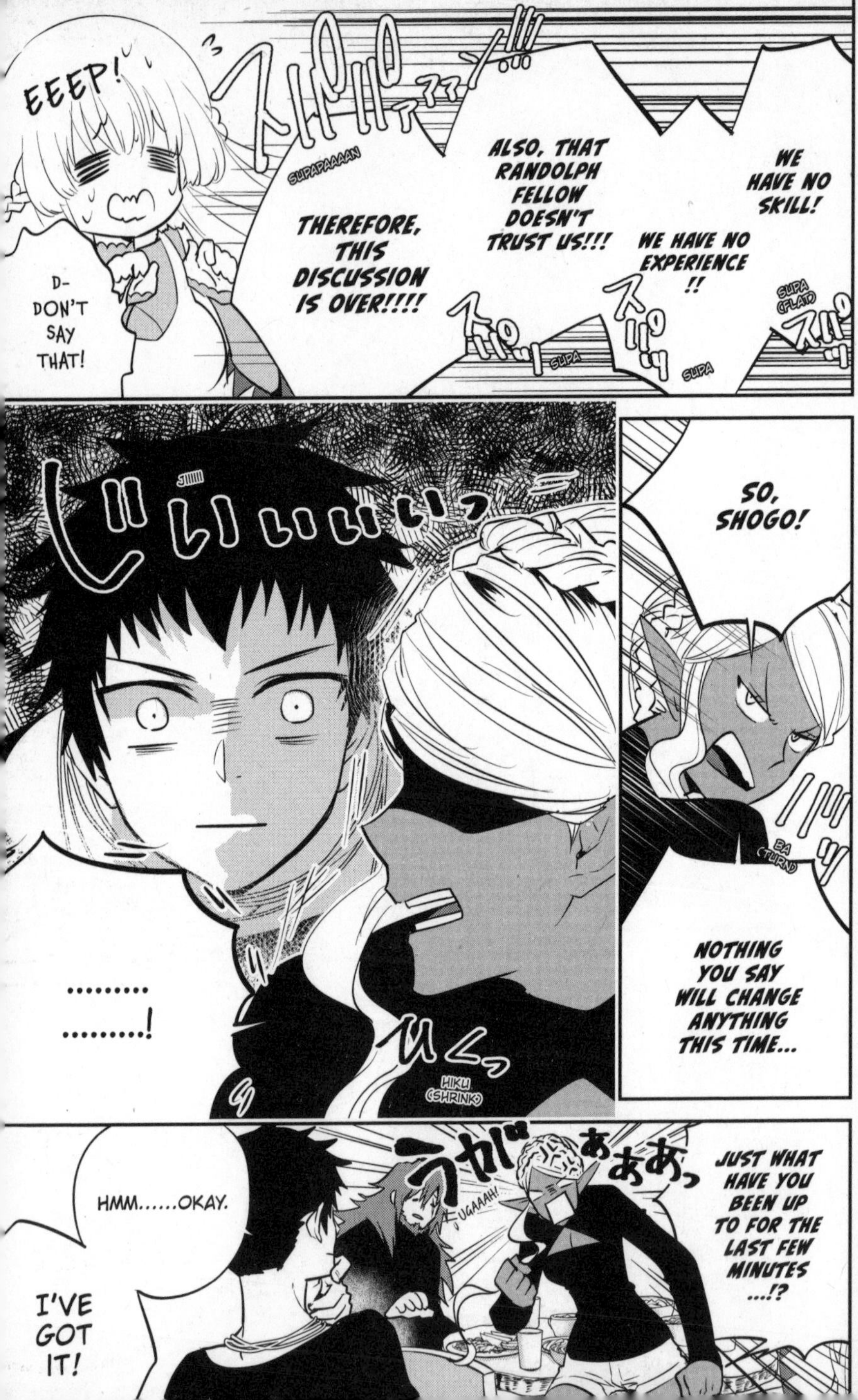
WE HAVE NO SKILL!
SUPA (FLAT)
WE HAVE NO EXPERIENCE!!
SUPA
ALSO, THAT RANDOLPH FELLOW DOESN'T TRUST US!!!
SUPA
THEREFORE, THIS DISCUSSION IS OVER!!!!
SUPAPAAAAN
EEEP!
D- DON'T SAY THAT!
SO, SHOGO!
BA (TURN)
NOTHING YOU SAY WILL CHANGE ANYTHING THIS TIME...
JIIIIII
HIKU (SHRINK)
....
.........!
JUST WHAT HAVE YOU BEEN UP TO FOR THE LAST FEW MINUTES ...!?
UGAAAH!
HMM......OKAY.
I'VE GOT IT!

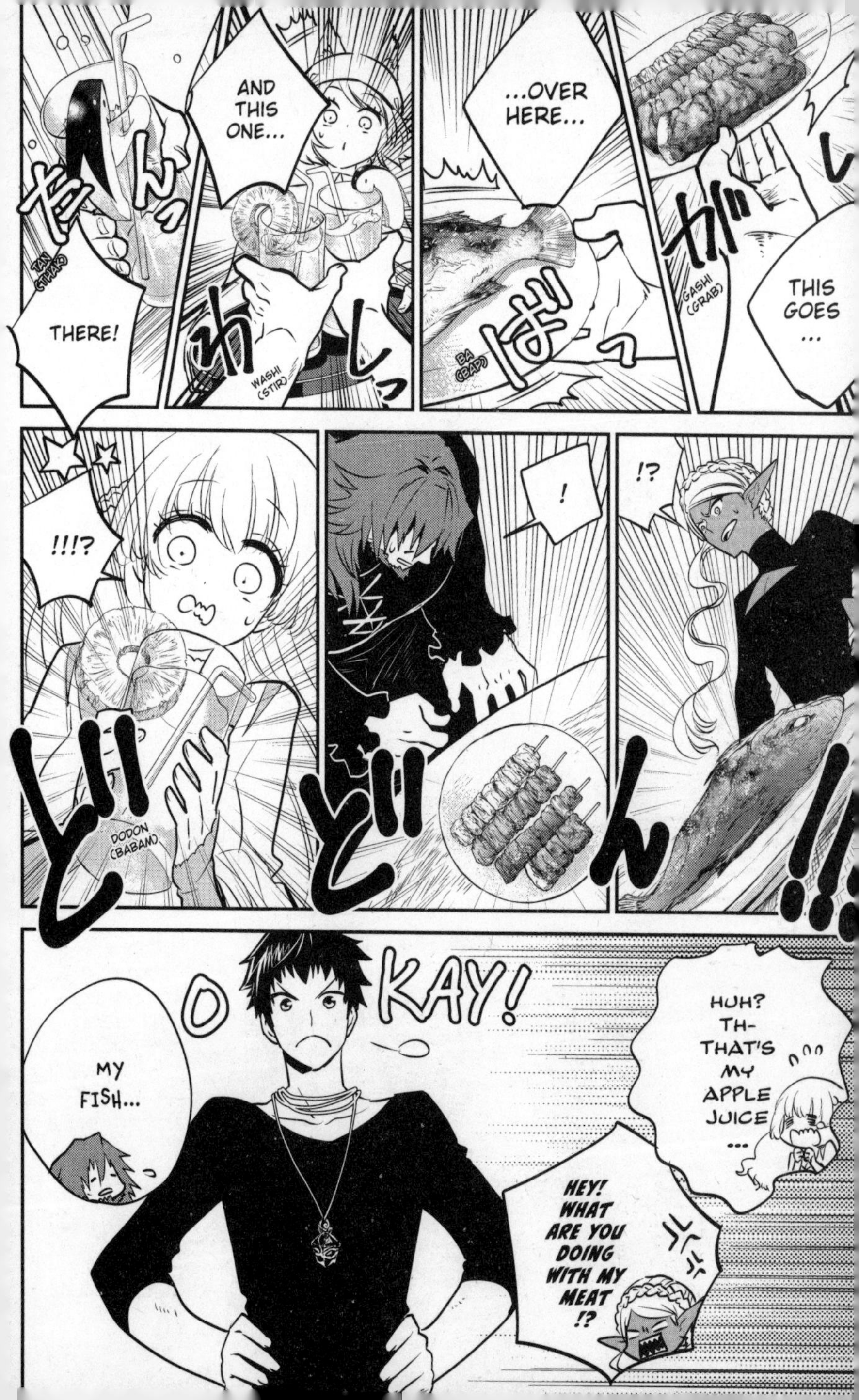
THIS GOES ...
がしっ
GASHI (GRAB)
...OVER HERE...
ばっ
BA (BAP)
AND THIS ONE...
わしっ
WASHI (STIR)
たんっ
TAN (THAP)
THERE!
!?
!
!!!?
どどん!!!
DODON (BABAM)
HUH? TH-THAT'S MY APPLE JUICE ...
OKAY!
HEY! WHAT ARE YOU DOING WITH MY MEAT !?
MY FISH...

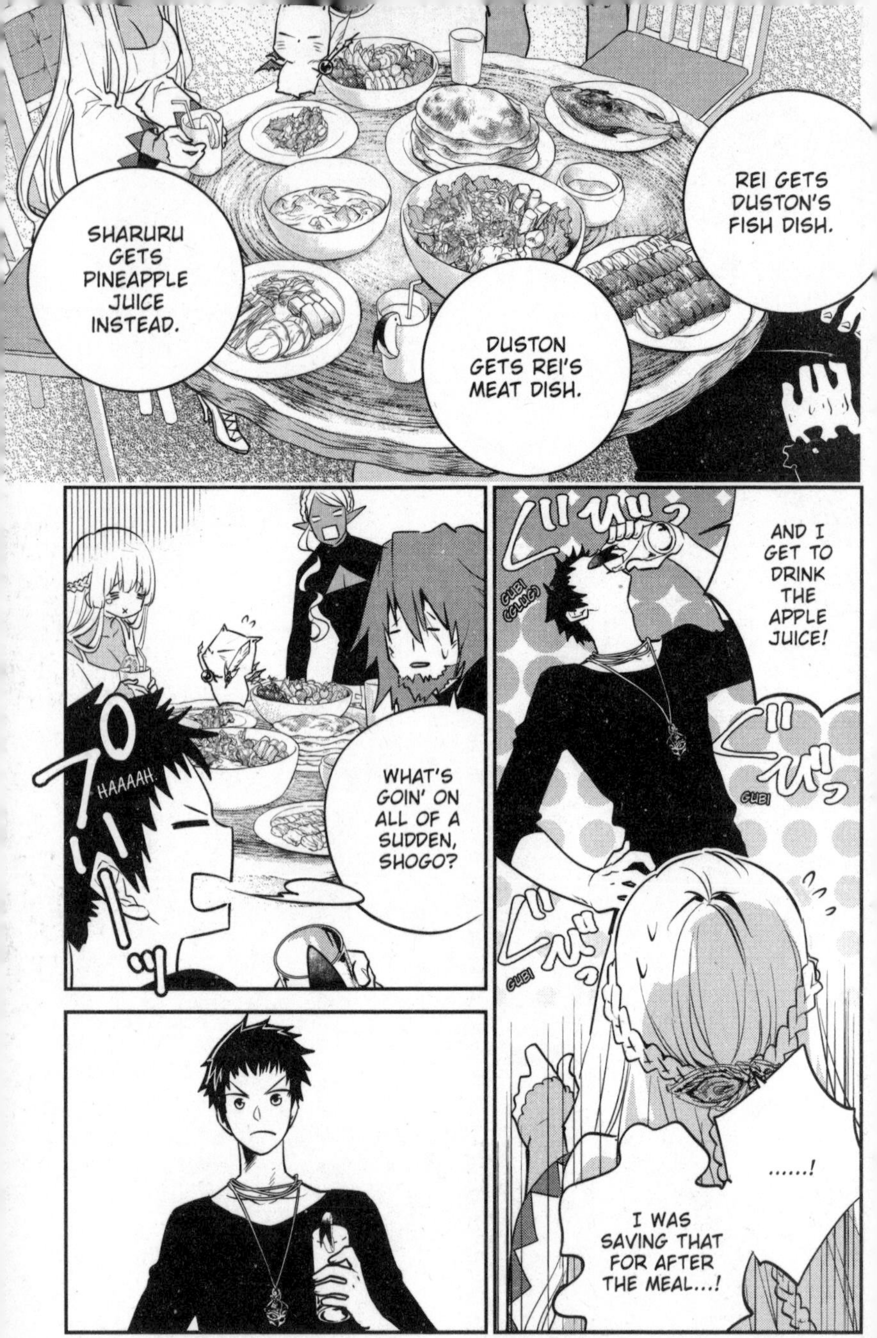
REI GETS DUSTON'S FISH DISH.
DUSTON GETS REI'S MEAT DISH.
SHARURU GETS PINEAPPLE JUICE INSTEAD.
GUBI (GLUG)
AND I GET TO DRINK THE APPLE JUICE!
GUBI
GUBI
......!
I WAS SAVING THAT FOR AFTER THE MEAL...!
HAAAAH.
WHAT'S GOIN' ON ALL OF A SUDDEN, SHOGO?

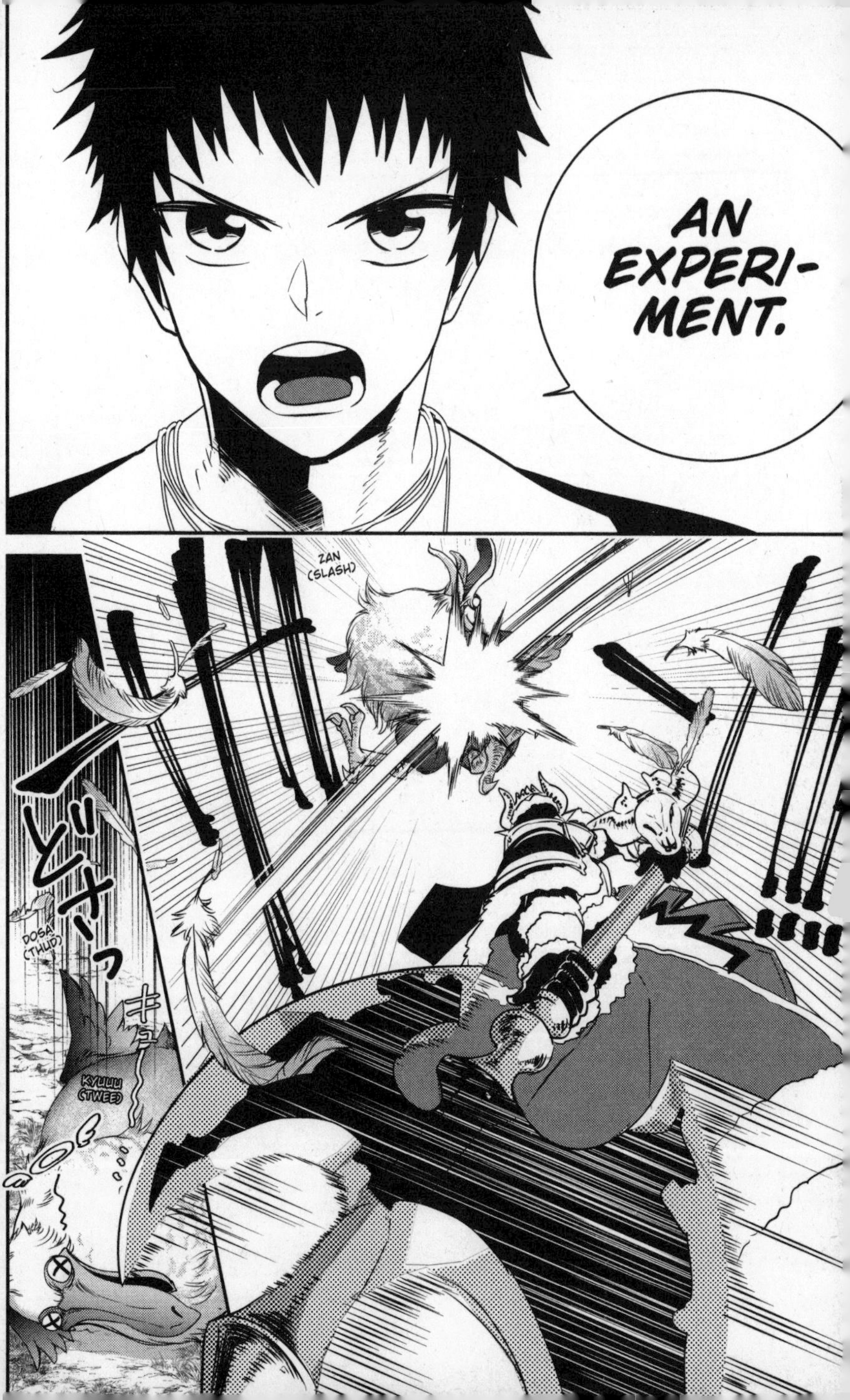
AN EXPERIMENT.
ZAN (SLASH)
どさっ
DOSA (THUD)
キュ
KYUUU (TWEE)

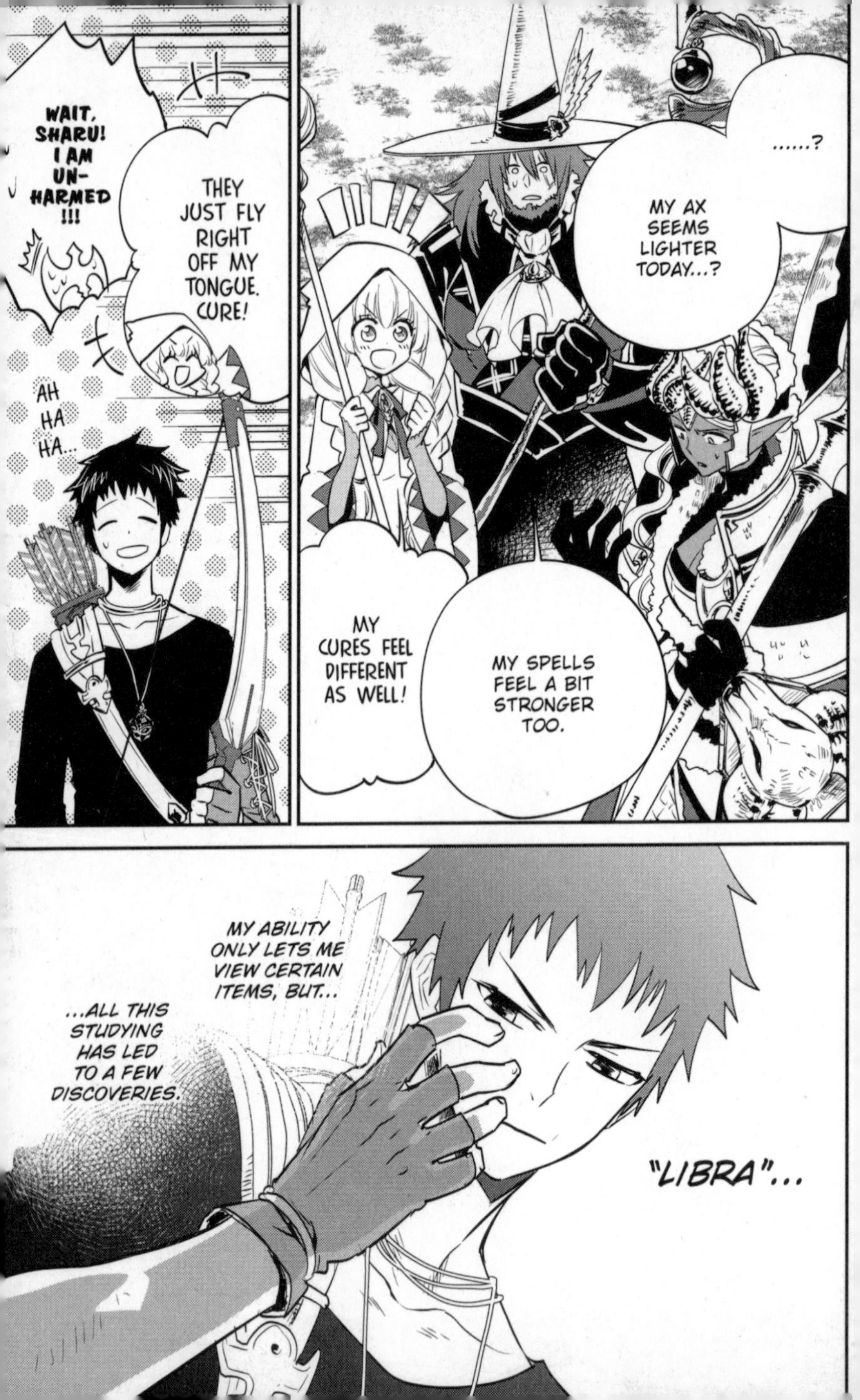
......?
MY AX SEEMS LIGHTER TODAY...?
MY SPELLS FEEL A BIT STRONGER TOO.
MY CURES FEEL DIFFERENT AS WELL!
THEY JUST FLY RIGHT OFF MY TONGUE. CURE!
WAIT, SHARU! I AM UN-HARMED!!!
AH HA HA...
MY ABILITY ONLY LETS ME VIEW CERTAIN ITEMS, BUT...
...ALL THIS STUDYING HAS LED TO A FEW DISCOVERIES.
"LIBRA"...

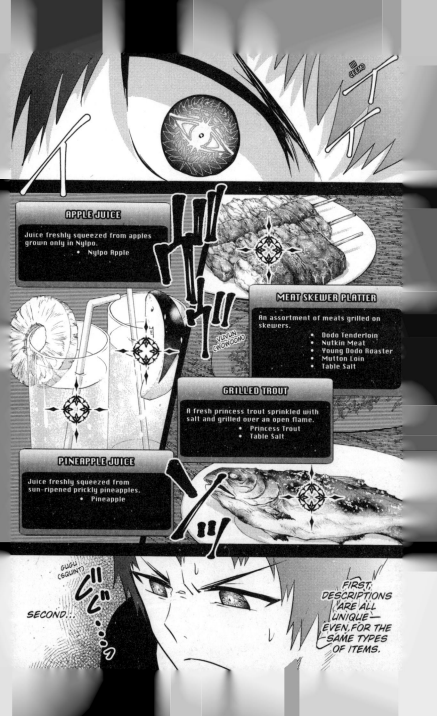

APPLE JUICE

Juice freshly squeezed from apples grown only in Nylpo.
- Nylpo Apple

MEAT SKEWER PLATTER

An assortment of meats grilled on skewers.
- Dodo Tenderloin
- Nutkin Meat
- Young Dodo Roaster
- Mutton Loin
- Table Salt

GRILLED TROUT

A fresh princess trout sprinkled with salt and grilled over an open flame.
- Princess Trout
- Table Salt

PINEAPPLE JUICE

Juice freshly squeezed from sun-ripened prickly pineapples.
- Pineapple

VUVUN (WOWOOM)

GUGU (SQUINT)

SECOND...

FIRST: DESCRIPTIONS ARE ALL UNIQUE— EVEN FOR THE SAME TYPES OF ITEMS.

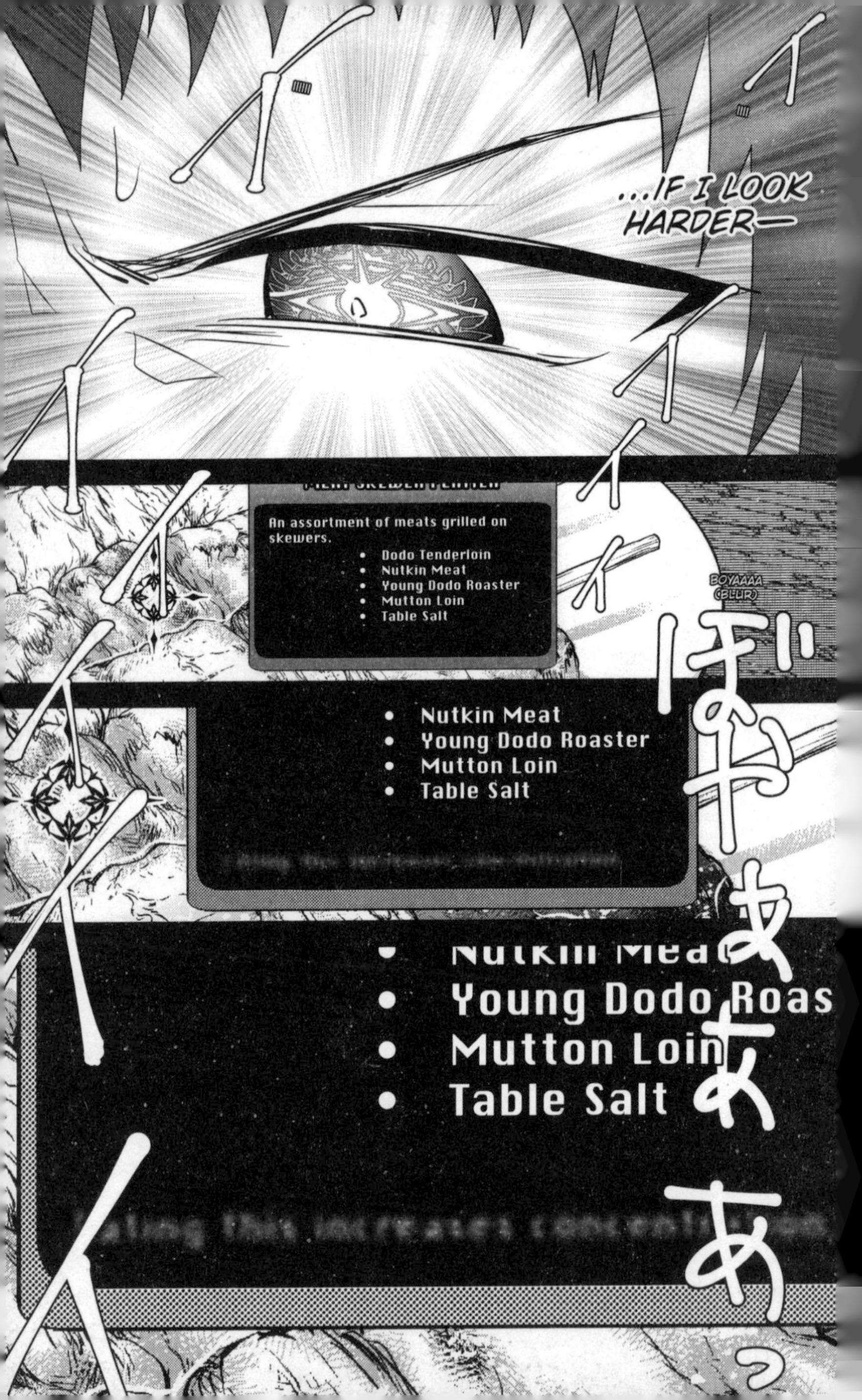

...IF I LOOK HARDER—

MEAT SKEWER PLATTER

An assortment of meats grilled on skewers.

- Dodo Tenderloin
- Nutkin Meat
- Young Dodo Roaster
- Mutton Loin
- Table Salt

BOYAAAA
(BLUR)

- Nutkin Meat
- Young Dodo Roaster
- Mutton Loin
- Table Salt

- Nutkin Meat
- Young Dodo Roas
- Mutton Loin
- Table Salt

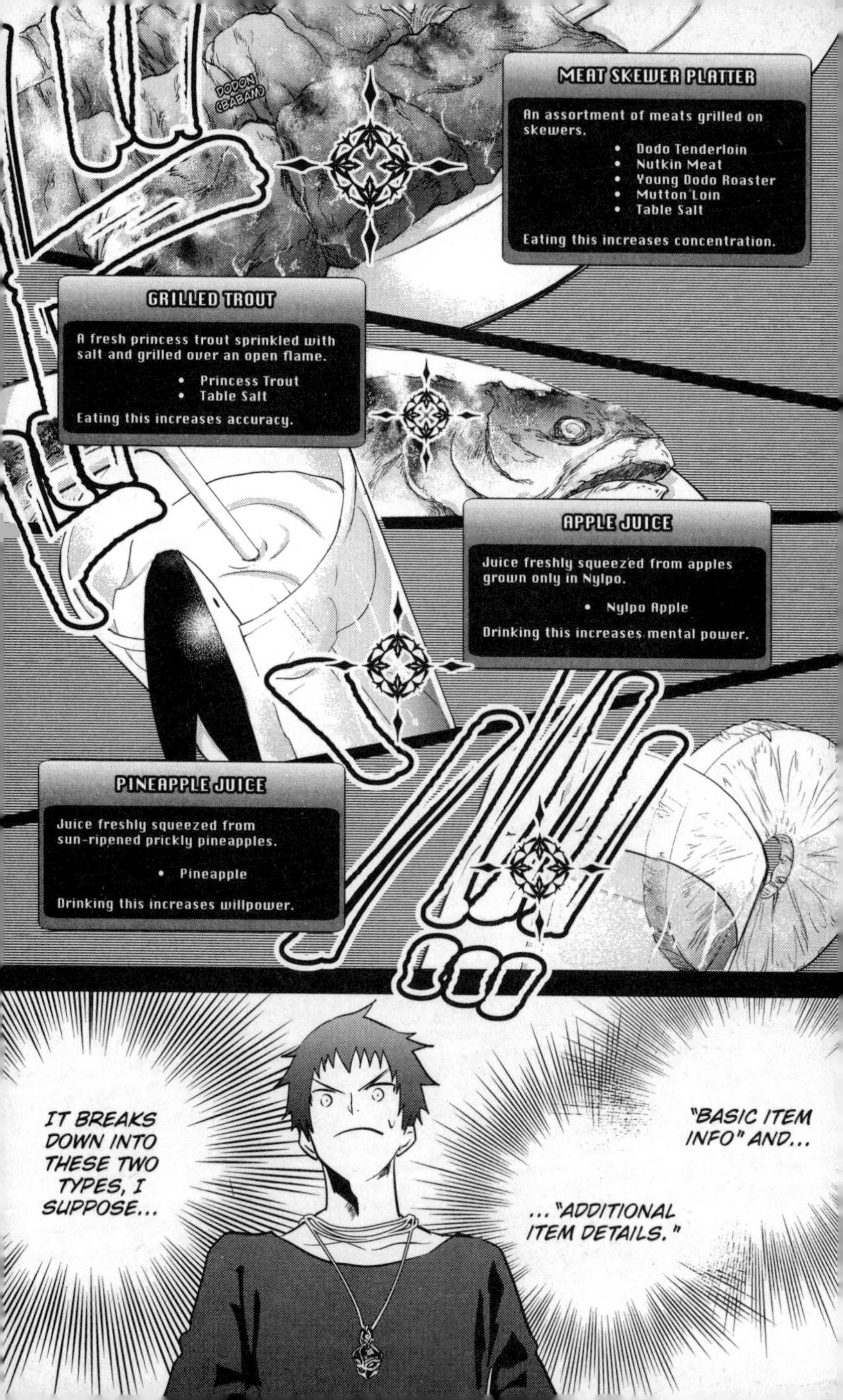
MEAT SKEWER PLATTER
An assortment of meats grilled on skewers.
• Dodo Tenderloin
• Nutkin Meat
• Young Dodo Roaster
• Mutton Loin
• Table Salt
Eating this increases concentration.
DODON (BABAN)
GRILLED TROUT
A fresh princess trout sprinkled with salt and grilled over an open flame.
• Princess Trout
• Table Salt
Eating this increases accuracy.
APPLE JUICE
Juice freshly squeezed from apples grown only in Nylpo.
• Nylpo Apple
Drinking this increases mental power.
PINEAPPLE JUICE
Juice freshly squeezed from sun-ripened prickly pineapples.
• Pineapple
Drinking this increases willpower.
"BASIC ITEM INFO" AND...
..."ADDITIONAL ITEM DETAILS."
IT BREAKS DOWN INTO THESE TWO TYPES, I SUPPOSE...

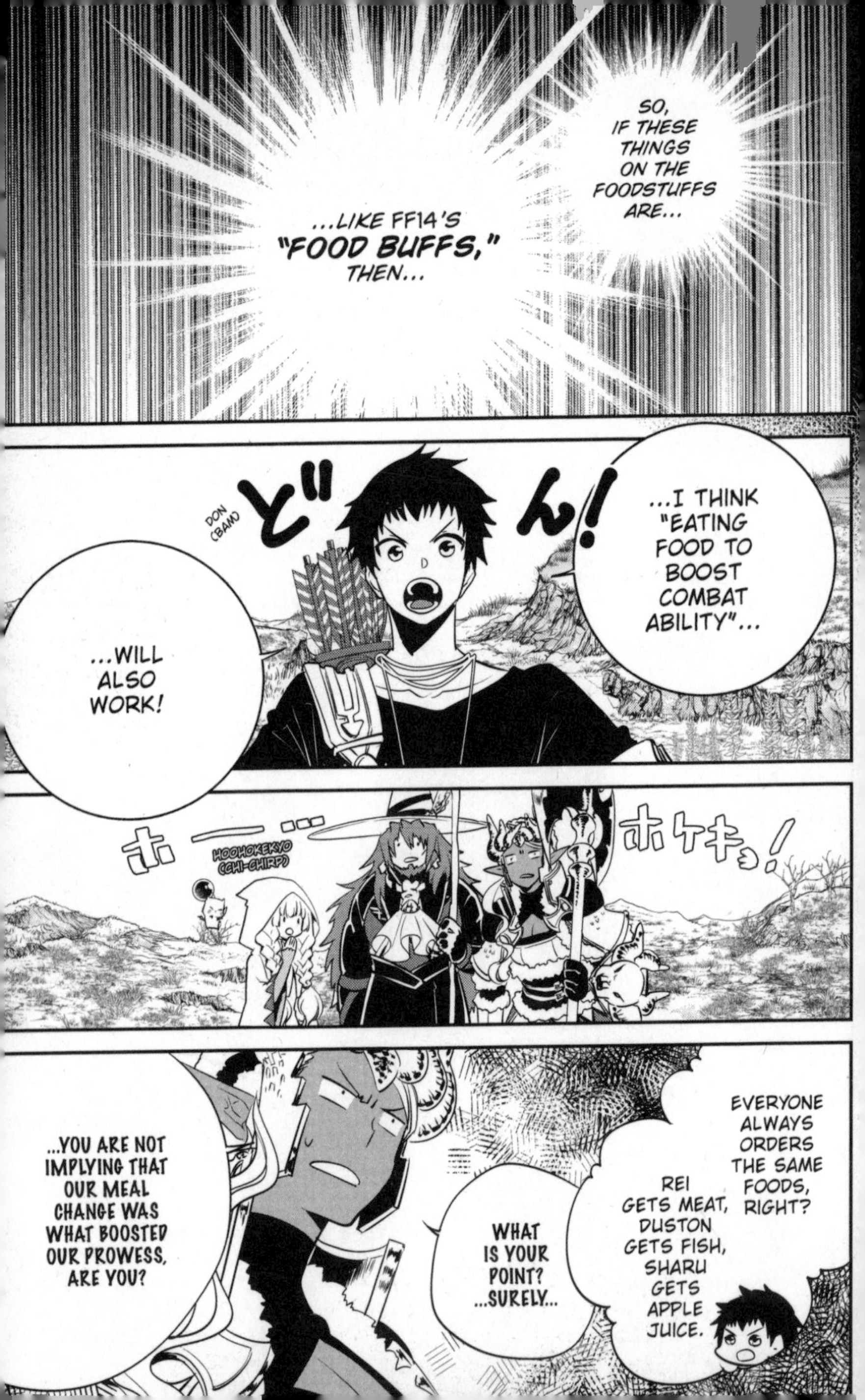
SO, IF THESE THINGS ON THE FOODSTUFFS ARE...
...LIKE FF14'S "FOOD BUFFS," THEN...
...I THINK "EATING FOOD TO BOOST COMBAT ABILITY"...
どん!
DON (BAM)
...WILL ALSO WORK!
ホーー…ホケキョ!
HOOHOKEKYO (CHI-CHIRP)
EVERYONE ALWAYS ORDERS THE SAME FOODS, RIGHT?
REI GETS MEAT, DUSTON GETS FISH, SHARU GETS APPLE JUICE.
WHAT IS YOUR POINT? ...SURELY...
...YOU ARE NOT IMPLYING THAT OUR MEAL CHANGE WAS WHAT BOOSTED OUR PROWESS, ARE YOU?

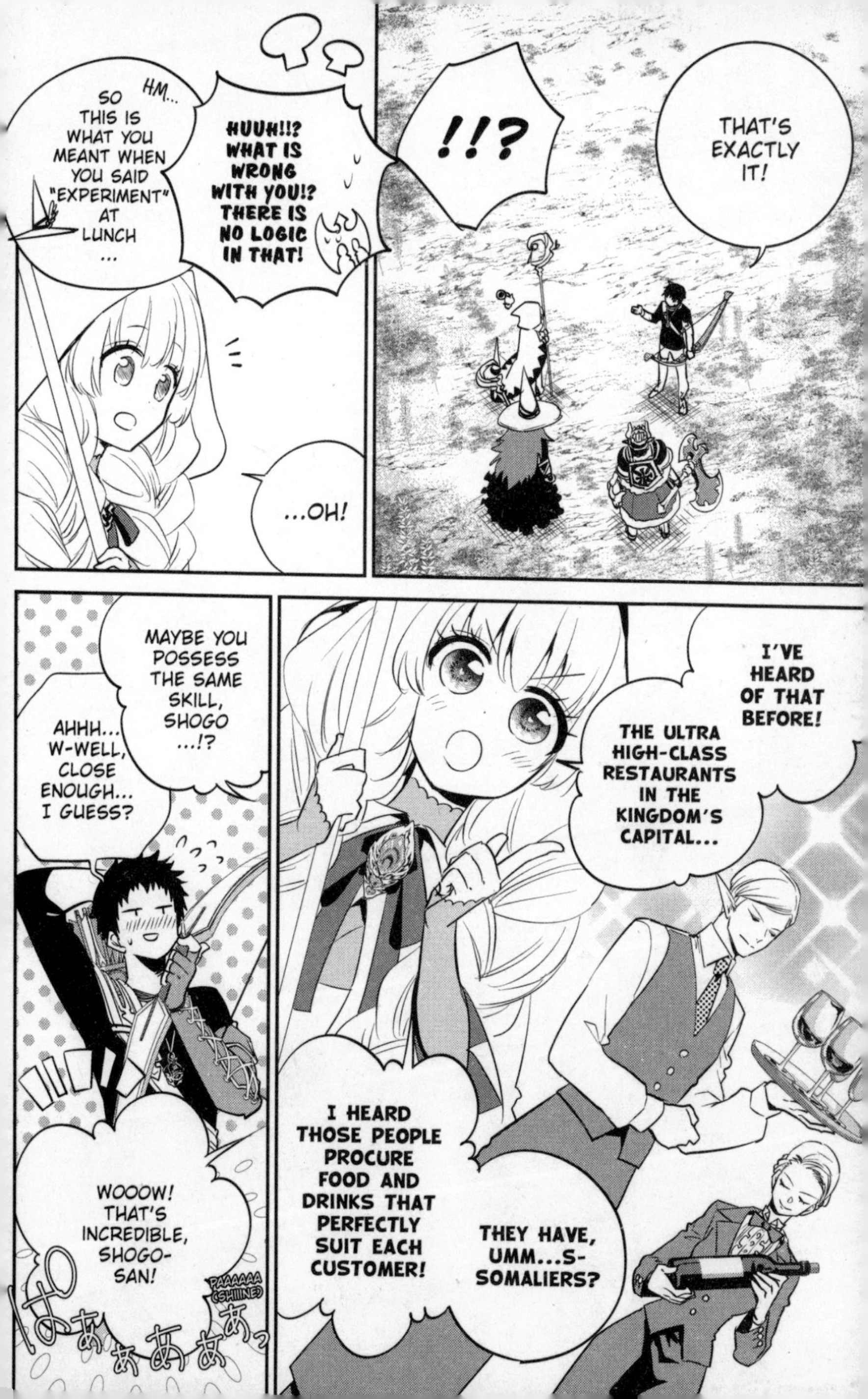
THAT'S EXACTLY IT!
!!?
HUUH!!? WHAT IS WRONG WITH YOU!? THERE IS NO LOGIC IN THAT!
HM...
SO THIS IS WHAT YOU MEANT WHEN YOU SAID "EXPERIMENT" AT LUNCH ...
...OH!
I'VE HEARD OF THAT BEFORE!
THE ULTRA HIGH-CLASS RESTAURANTS IN THE KINGDOM'S CAPITAL...
THEY HAVE, UMM...S-SOMALIERS?
I HEARD THOSE PEOPLE PROCURE FOOD AND DRINKS THAT PERFECTLY SUIT EACH CUSTOMER!
MAYBE YOU POSSESS THE SAME SKILL, SHOGO ...!?
AHHH... W-WELL, CLOSE ENOUGH... I GUESS?
WOOOW! THAT'S INCREDIBLE, SHOGO-SAN!
PAAAAAA (SHIIINED)
はぁぁぁぁあっ

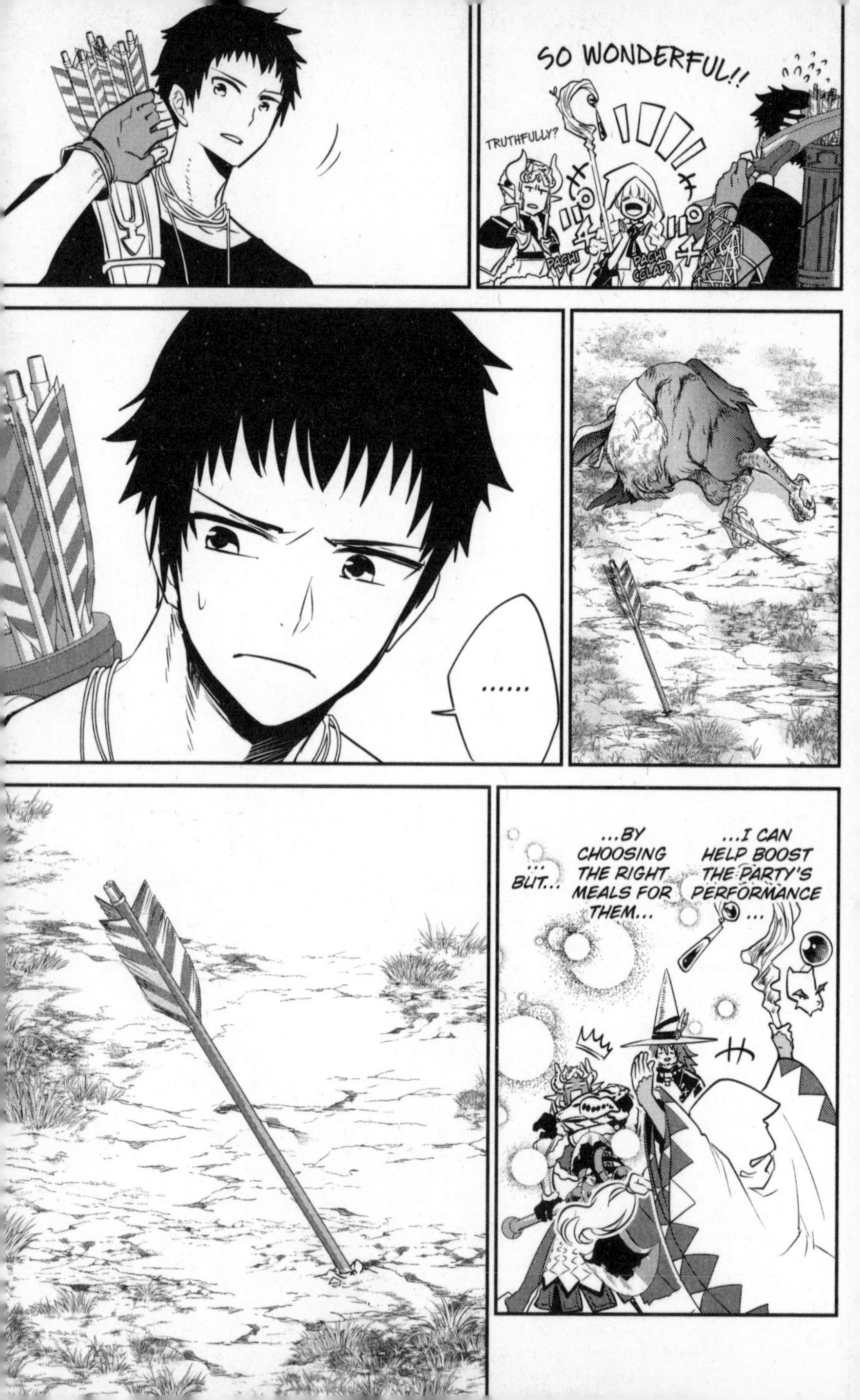
SO WONDERFUL!!
TRUTHFULLY?
PACHI
PACHI (CLAP)
......
...BUT...
...BY CHOOSING THE RIGHT MEALS FOR THEM...
...I CAN HELP BOOST THE PARTY'S PERFORMANCE...

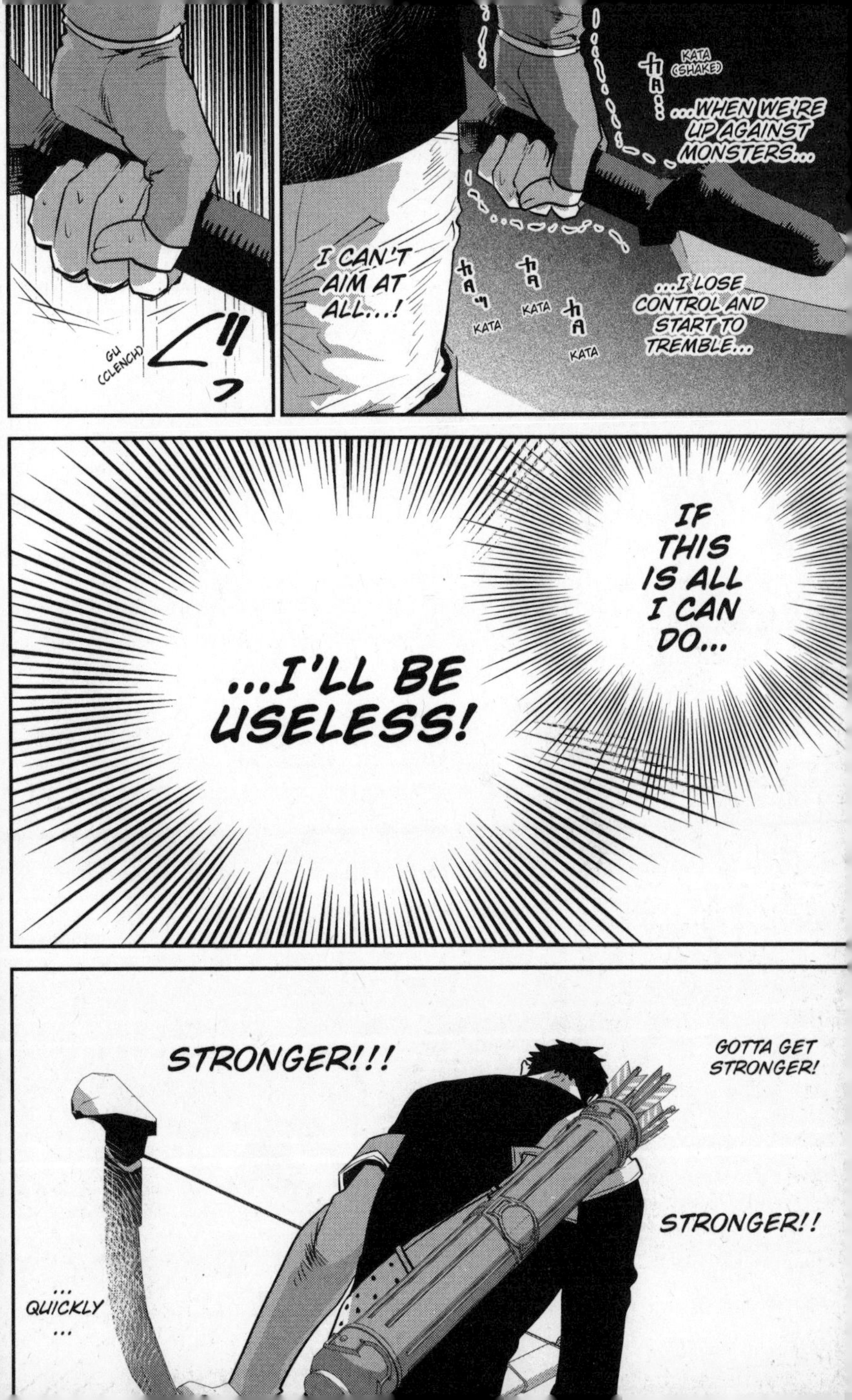
KATA (SHAKE)
...WHEN WE'RE UP AGAINST MONSTERS...
...I LOSE CONTROL AND START TO TREMBLE...
KATA
KATA
KATA
I CAN'T AIM AT ALL...!
GU (CLENCH)
IF THIS IS ALL I CAN DO...
...I'LL BE USELESS!
GOTTA GET STRONGER!
STRONGER!!!
STRONGER!!
...QUICKLY...

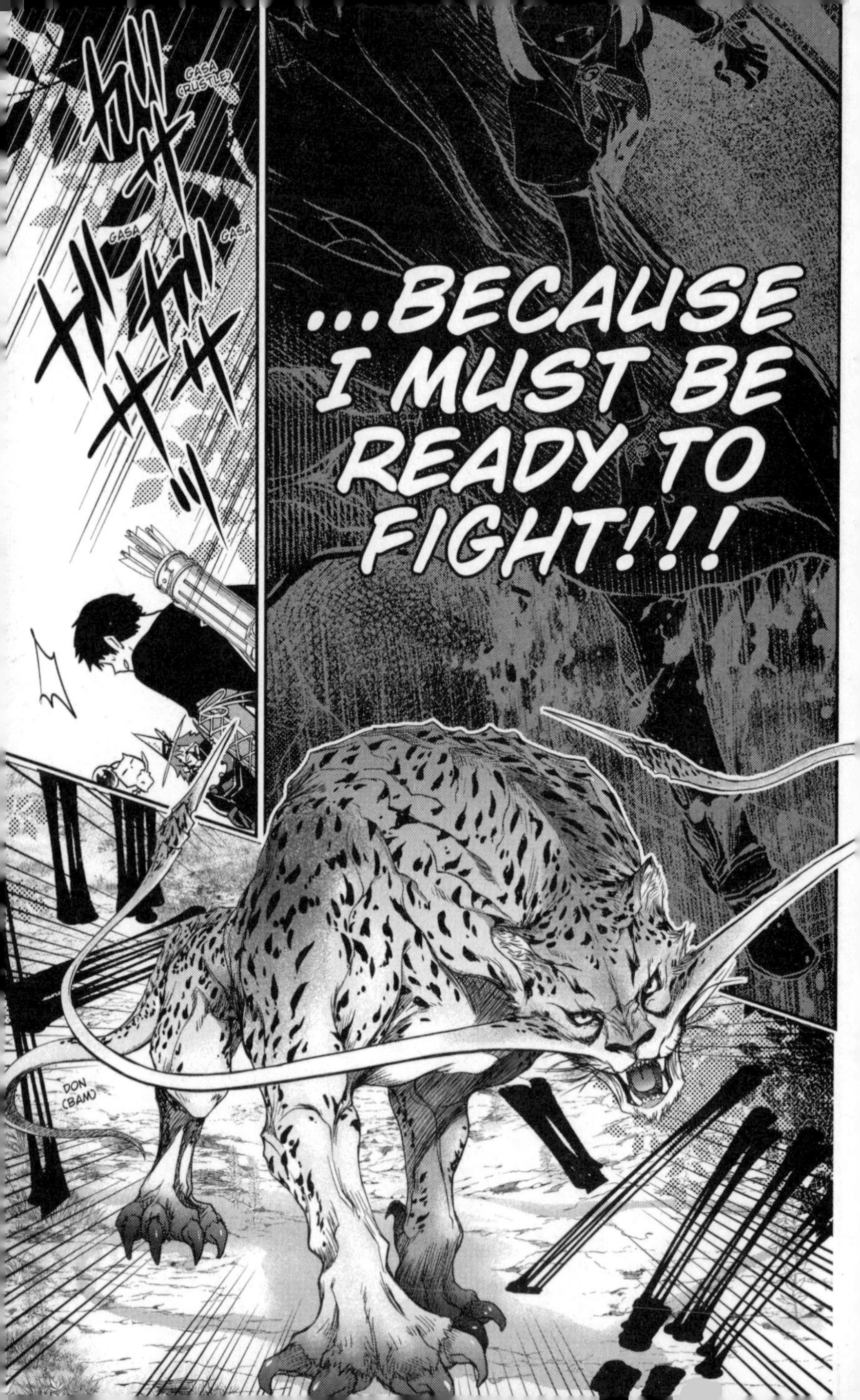
...BECAUSE I MUST BE READY TO FIGHT!!!
GASA (RUSTLE)
GASA
GASA
DON (BAM)

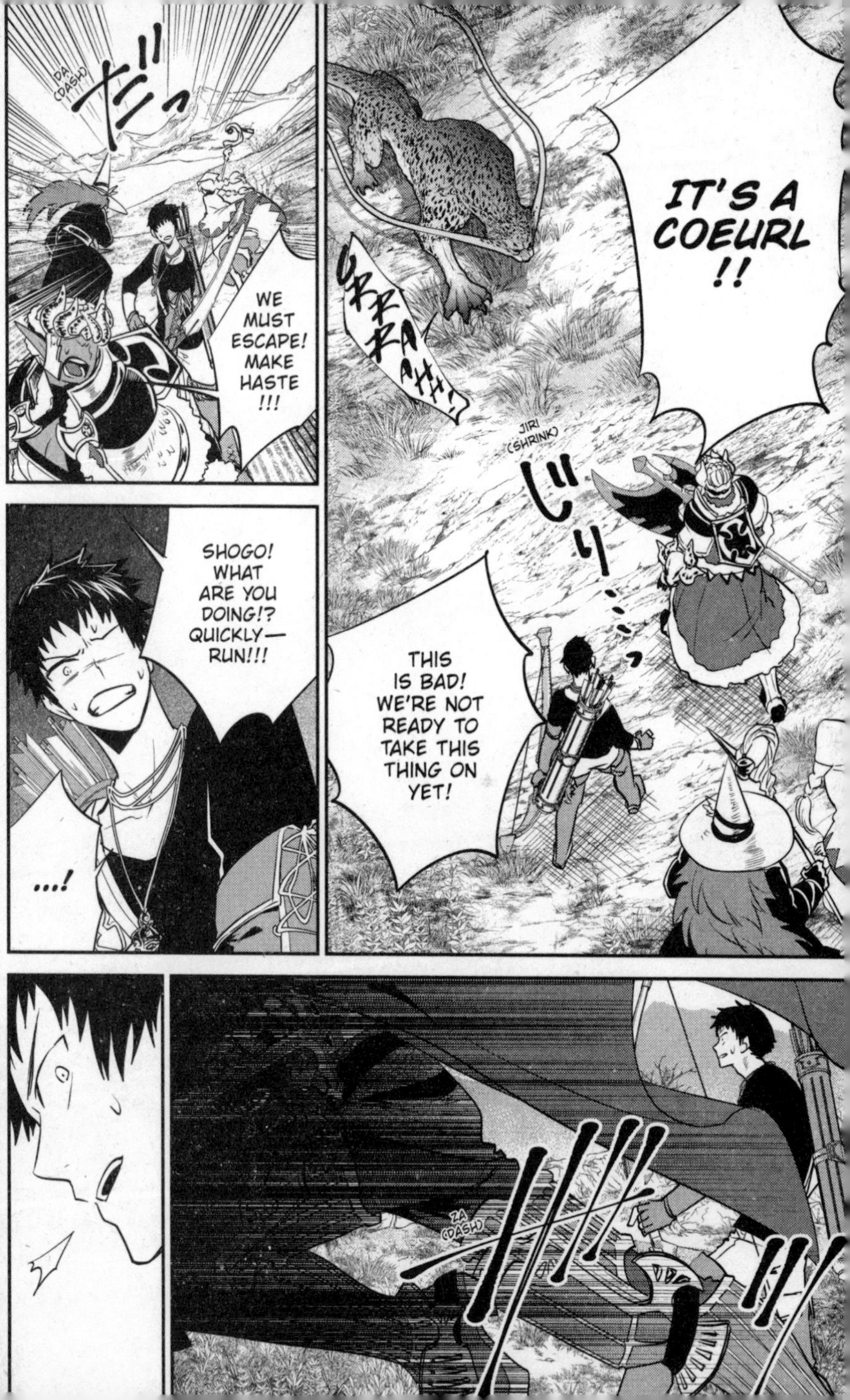
IT'S A COEURL!!
URRAAHH!
JIRI (SHRINK)
THIS IS BAD! WE'RE NOT READY TO TAKE THIS THING ON YET!
DA (DASH)
WE MUST ESCAPE! MAKE HASTE!!!
SHOGO! WHAT ARE YOU DOING!? QUICKLY—RUN!!!
...!
ZA (DASH)

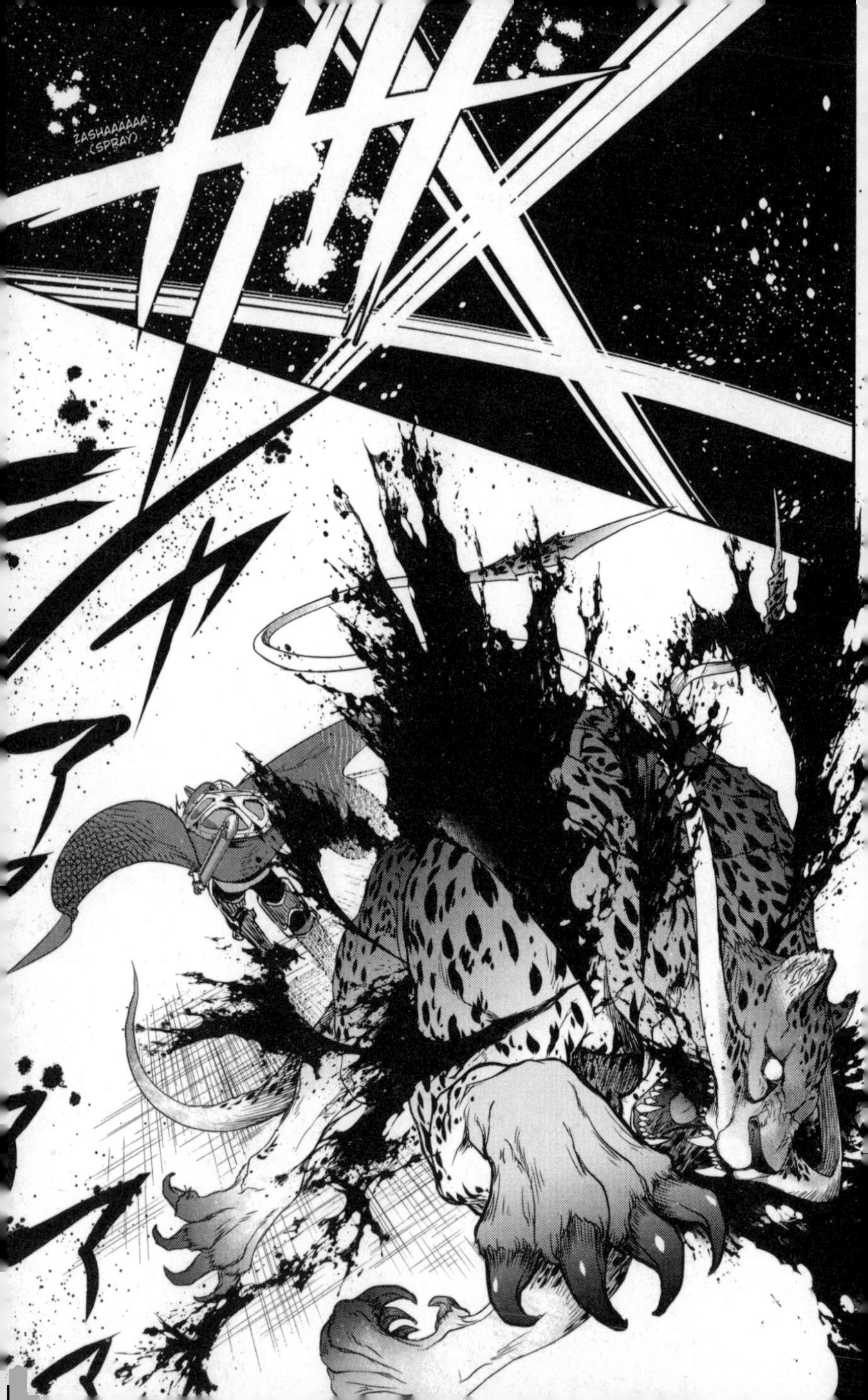
ZASHAAAAAAA (SPRAY)

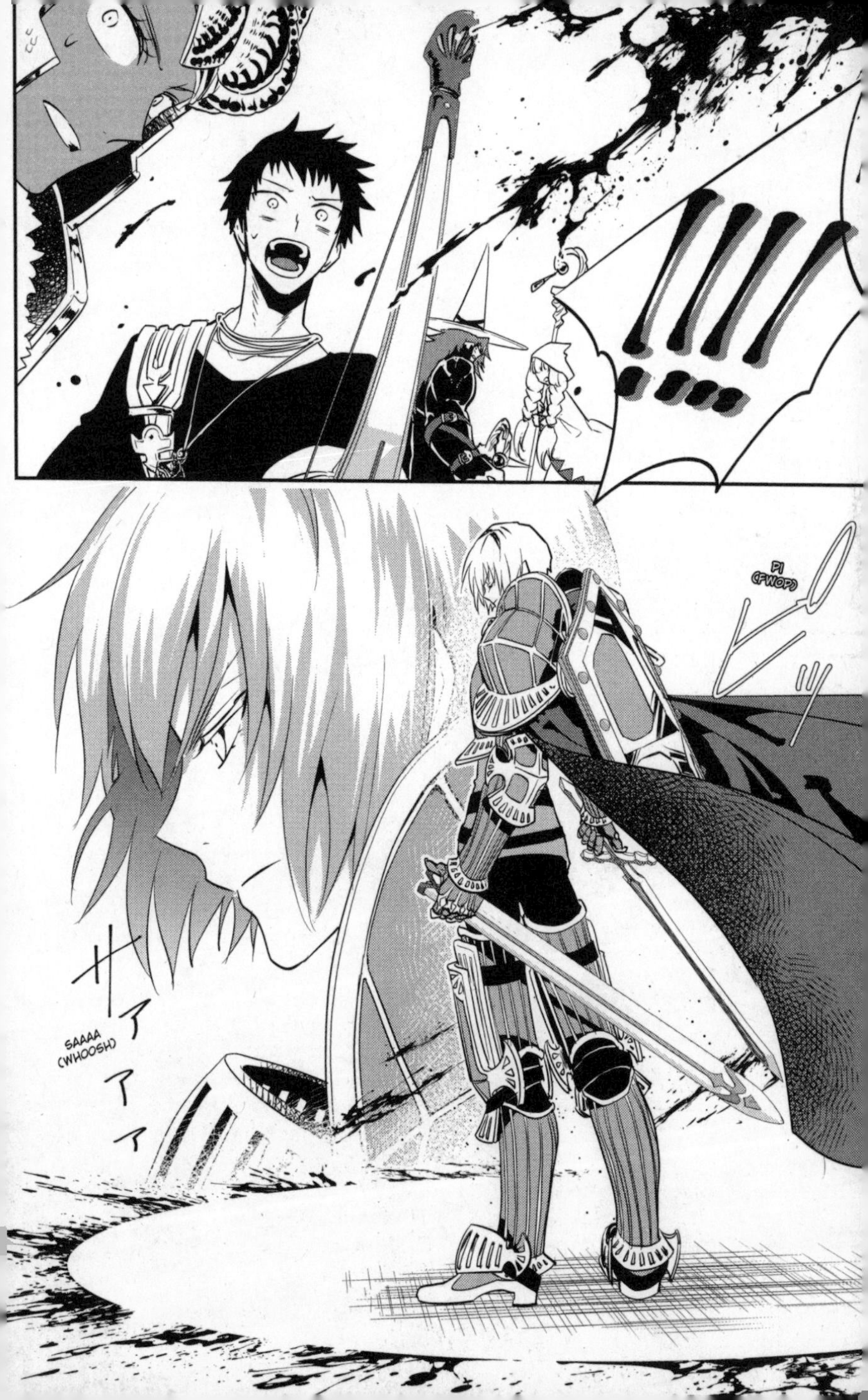
!!!!
PI
(FWOP)
SAAAA
(WHOOSH)

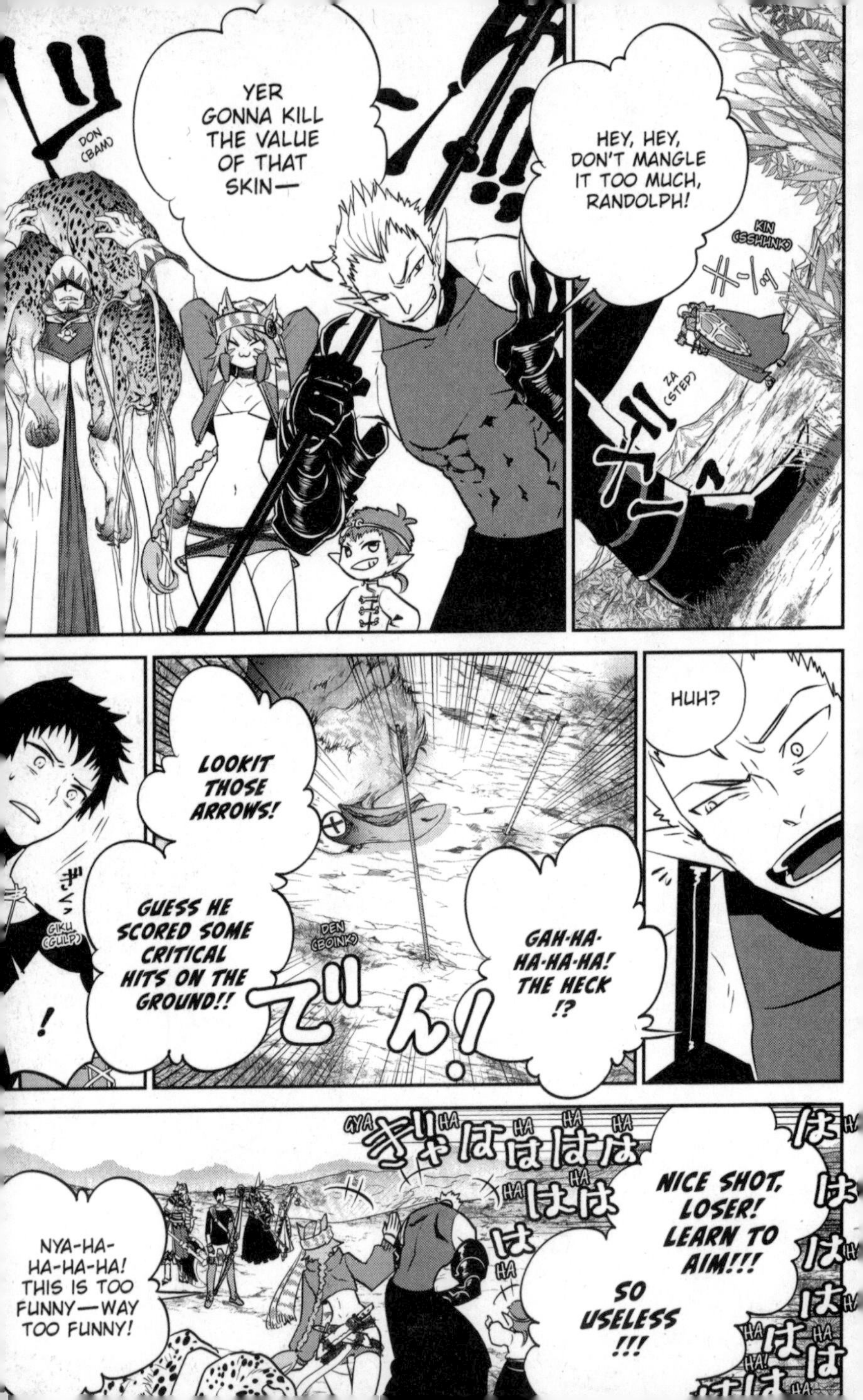
KIN (SSHHNK)
ZA (STEP)
HEY, HEY, DON'T MANGLE IT TOO MUCH, RANDOLPH!
YER GONNA KILL THE VALUE OF THAT SKIN—
DON (BAM)
HUH?
LOOKIT THOSE ARROWS!
GUESS HE SCORED SOME CRITICAL HITS ON THE GROUND!!
GAH-HA-HA-HA-HA! THE HECK!?
DEN (BOINK)
GIKU (GULP)
!
GYA HA HA HA HA
HA HA
HA
NICE SHOT, LOSER! LEARN TO AIM!!!
SO USELESS!!!
HA HA HA HA
NYA-HA-HA-HA-HA! THIS IS TOO FUNNY—WAY TOO FUNNY!

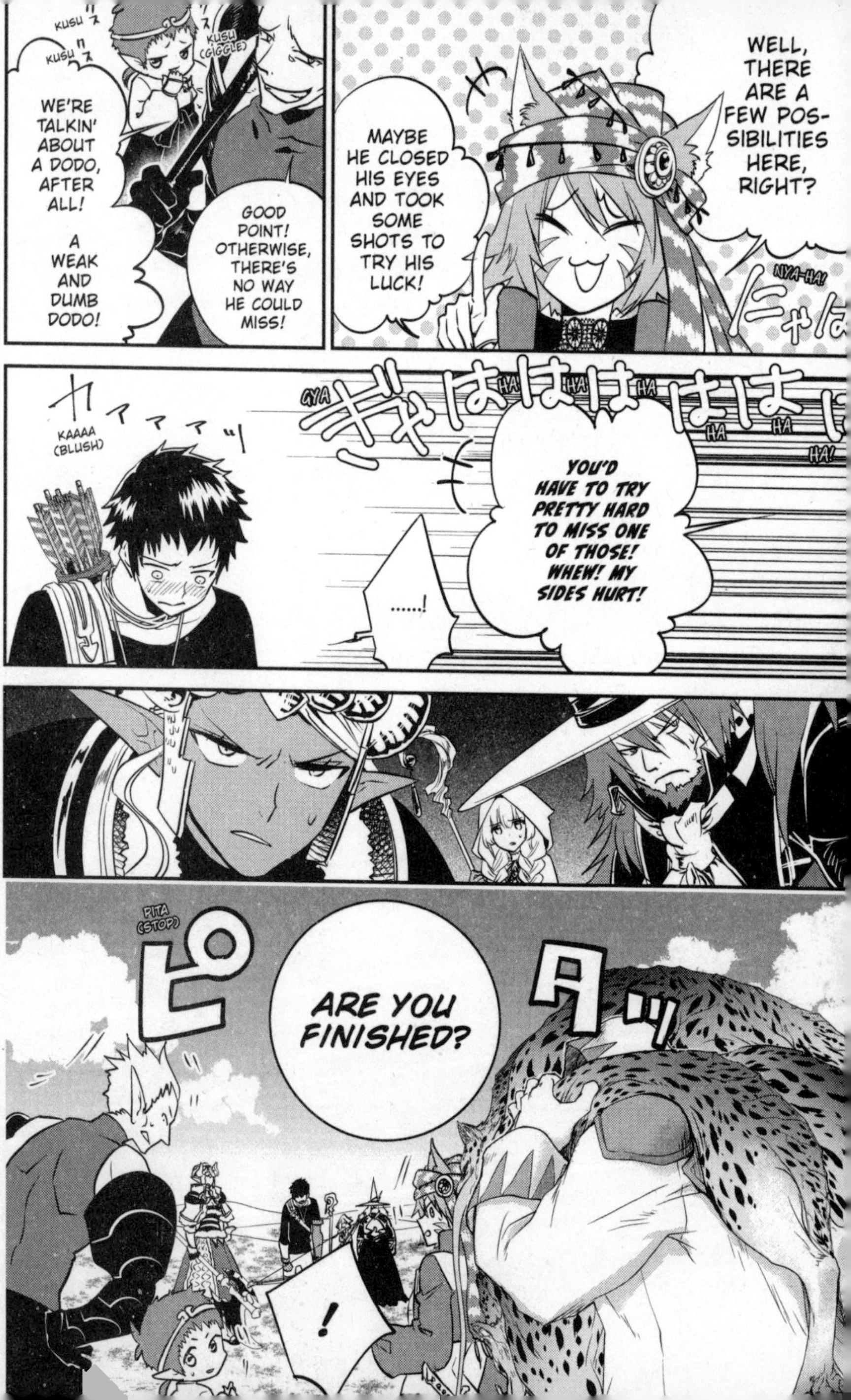
WELL, THERE ARE A FEW POSSIBILITIES HERE, RIGHT?
NYA-HA!
MAYBE HE CLOSED HIS EYES AND TOOK SOME SHOTS TO TRY HIS LUCK!
KUSU (GIGGLE)
GOOD POINT! OTHERWISE, THERE'S NO WAY HE COULD MISS!
KUSU
KUSU
WE'RE TALKIN' ABOUT A DODO, AFTER ALL!
A WEAK AND DUMB DODO!
GYA HA HA HA HA HA HA HA!
YOU'D HAVE TO TRY PRETTY HARD TO MISS ONE OF THOSE! WHEW! MY SIDES HURT!
......!
KAAAA (BLUSH)
ARE YOU FINISHED?
PITA (STOP)
!

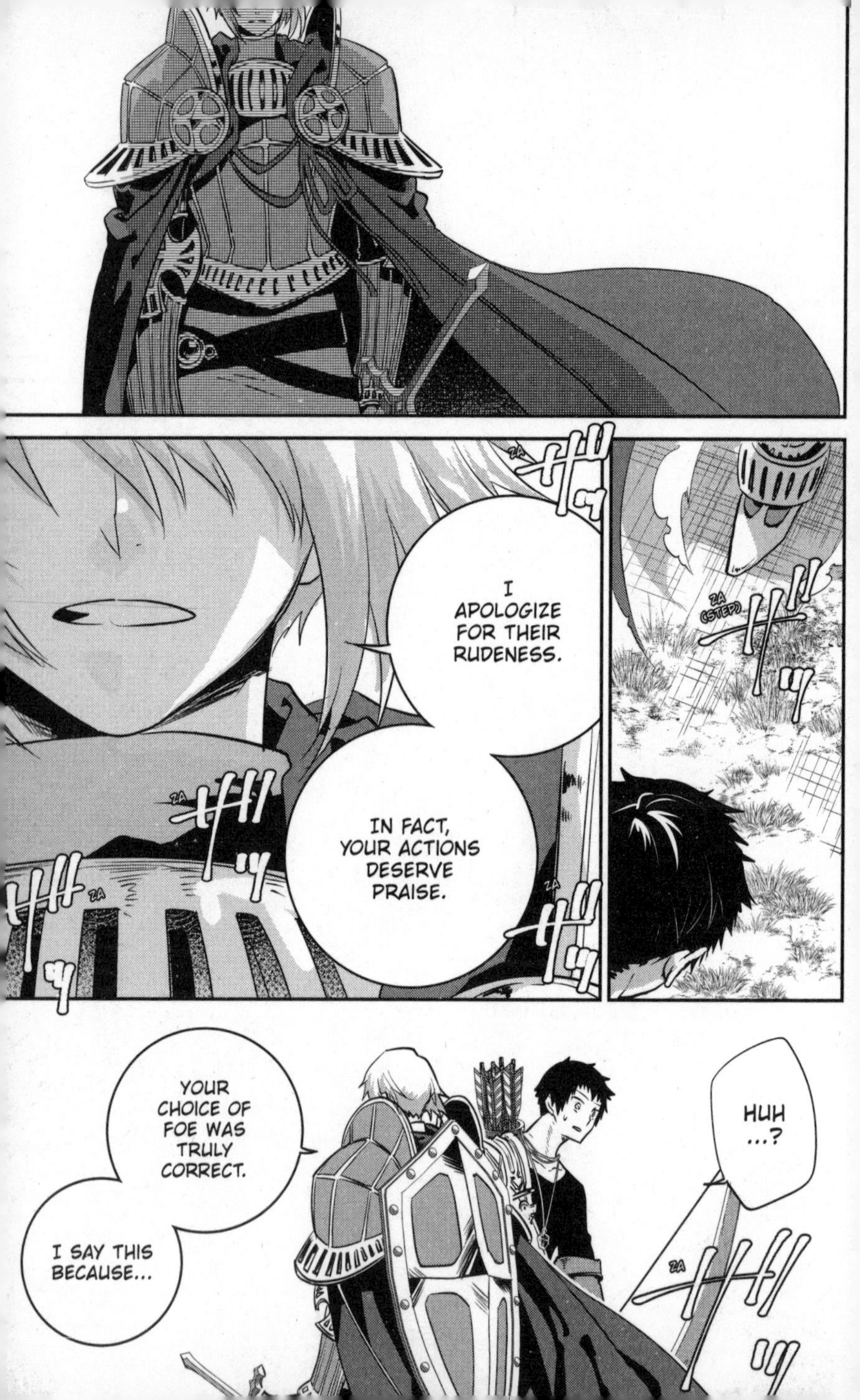
ZA (STEP)
ZA
I APOLOGIZE FOR THEIR RUDENESS.
IN FACT, YOUR ACTIONS DESERVE PRAISE.
ZA
ZA
ZA
HUH ...?
ZA
YOUR CHOICE OF FOE WAS TRULY CORRECT.
I SAY THIS BECAUSE...

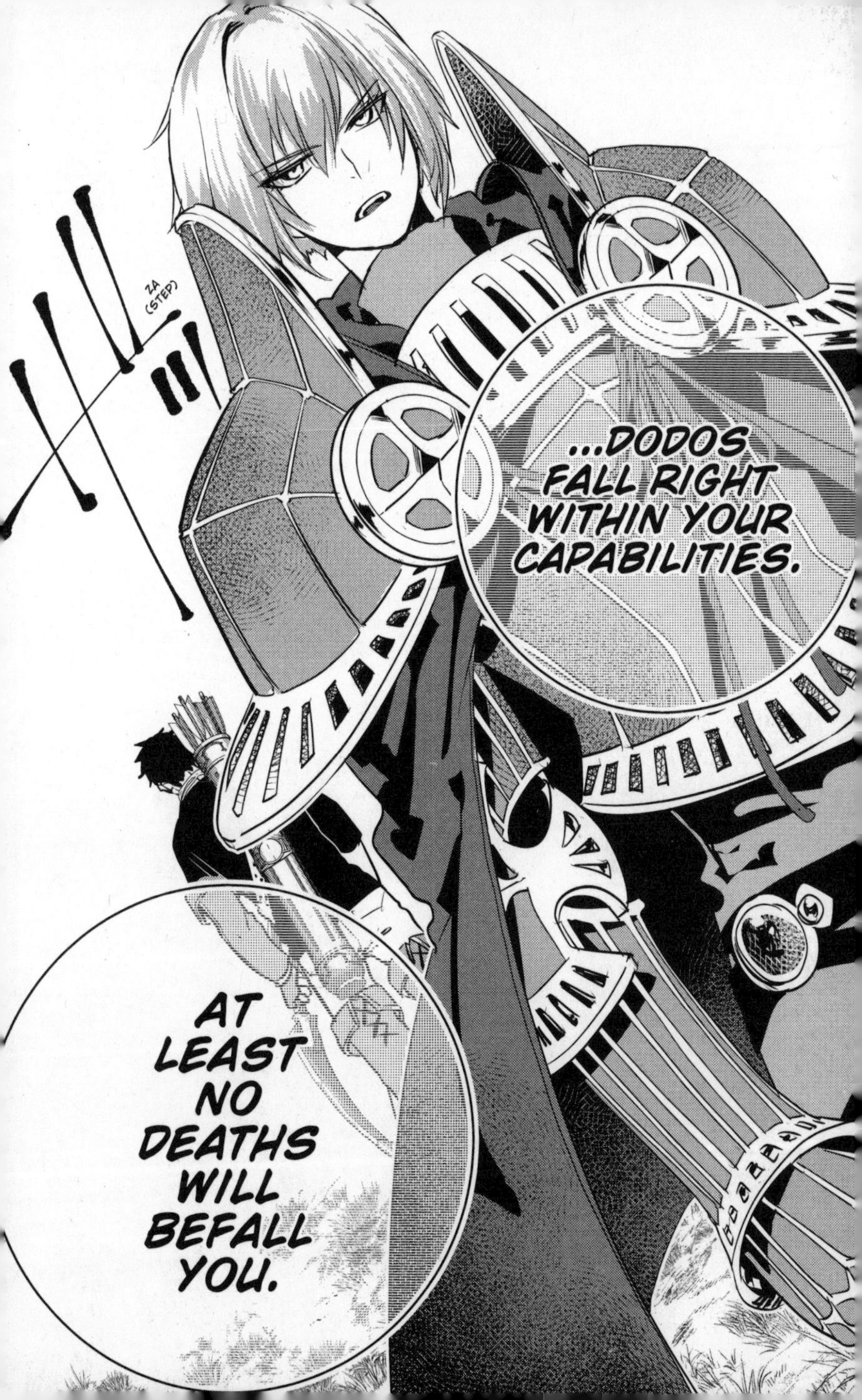
...DODOS FALL RIGHT WITHIN YOUR CAPABILITIES.
ZA (STEP)
AT LEAST NO DEATHS WILL BEFALL YOU.

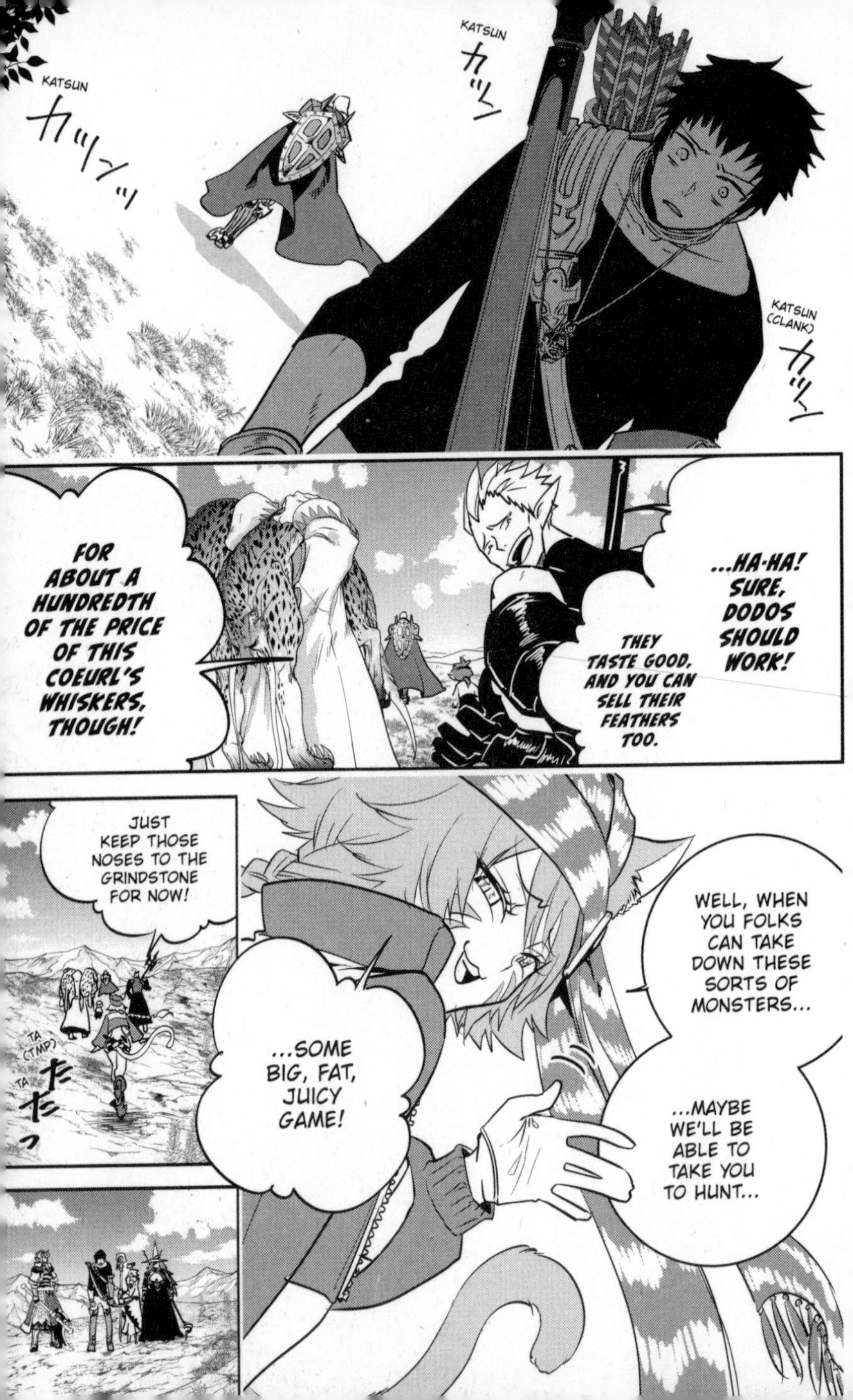

KATSUN (CLANK)
KATSUN
KATSUN
...HA-HA! SURE, DODOS SHOULD WORK!
THEY TASTE GOOD, AND YOU CAN SELL THEIR FEATHERS TOO.
FOR ABOUT A HUNDREDTH OF THE PRICE OF THIS COEURL'S WHISKERS, THOUGH!
WELL, WHEN YOU FOLKS CAN TAKE DOWN THESE SORTS OF MONSTERS...
...MAYBE WE'LL BE ABLE TO TAKE YOU TO HUNT...
...SOME BIG, FAT, JUICY GAME!
JUST KEEP THOSE NOSES TO THE GRINDSTONE FOR NOW!
TA (TMP) TA

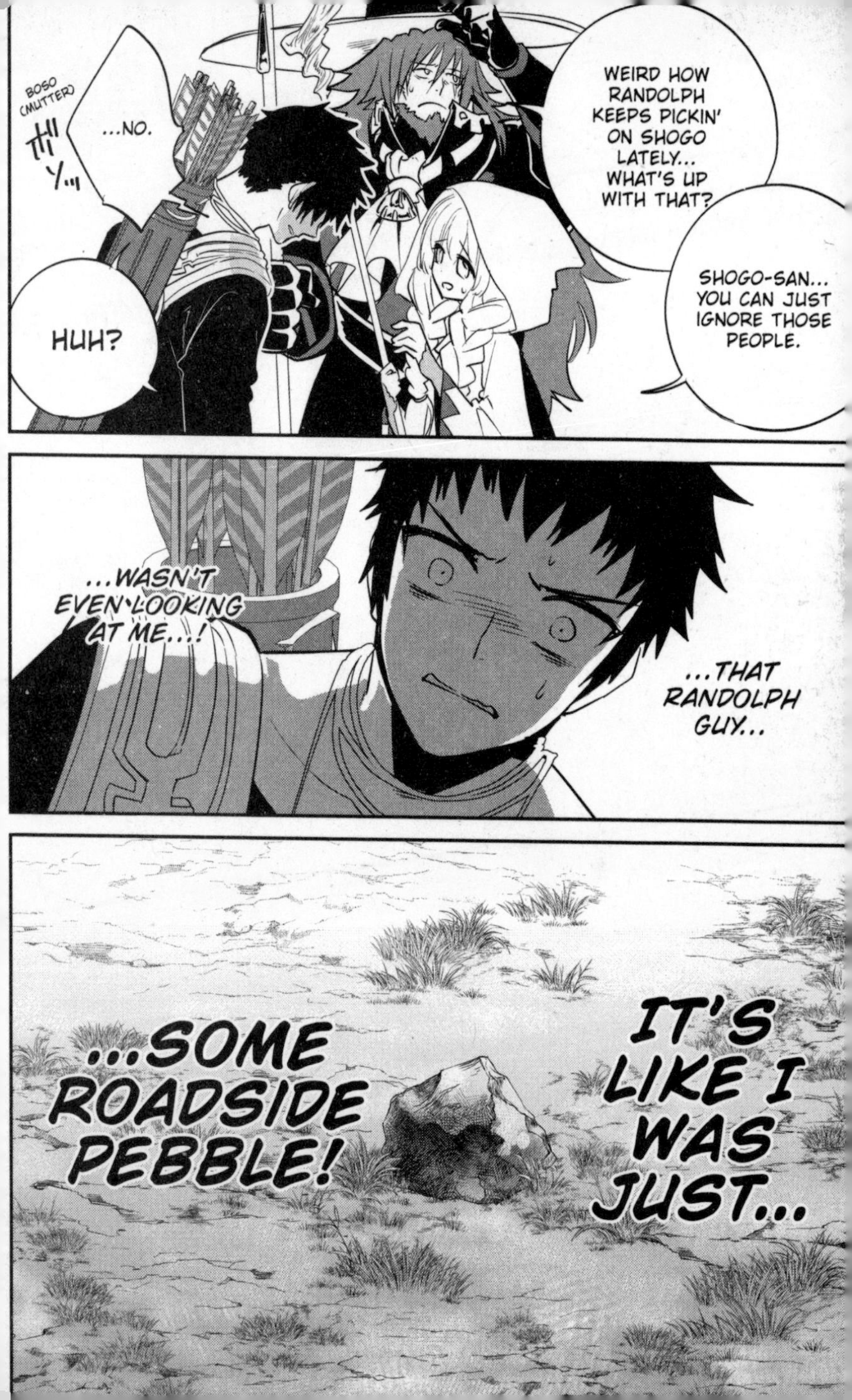
WEIRD HOW RANDOLPH KEEPS PICKIN' ON SHOGO LATELY... WHAT'S UP WITH THAT?
SHOGO-SAN... YOU CAN JUST IGNORE THOSE PEOPLE.
BOSO (MUTTER)
ボソッ
...NO.
HUH?
...THAT RANDOLPH GUY...
...WASN'T EVEN LOOKING AT ME...!
IT'S LIKE I WAS JUST...
...SOME ROADSIDE PEBBLE!

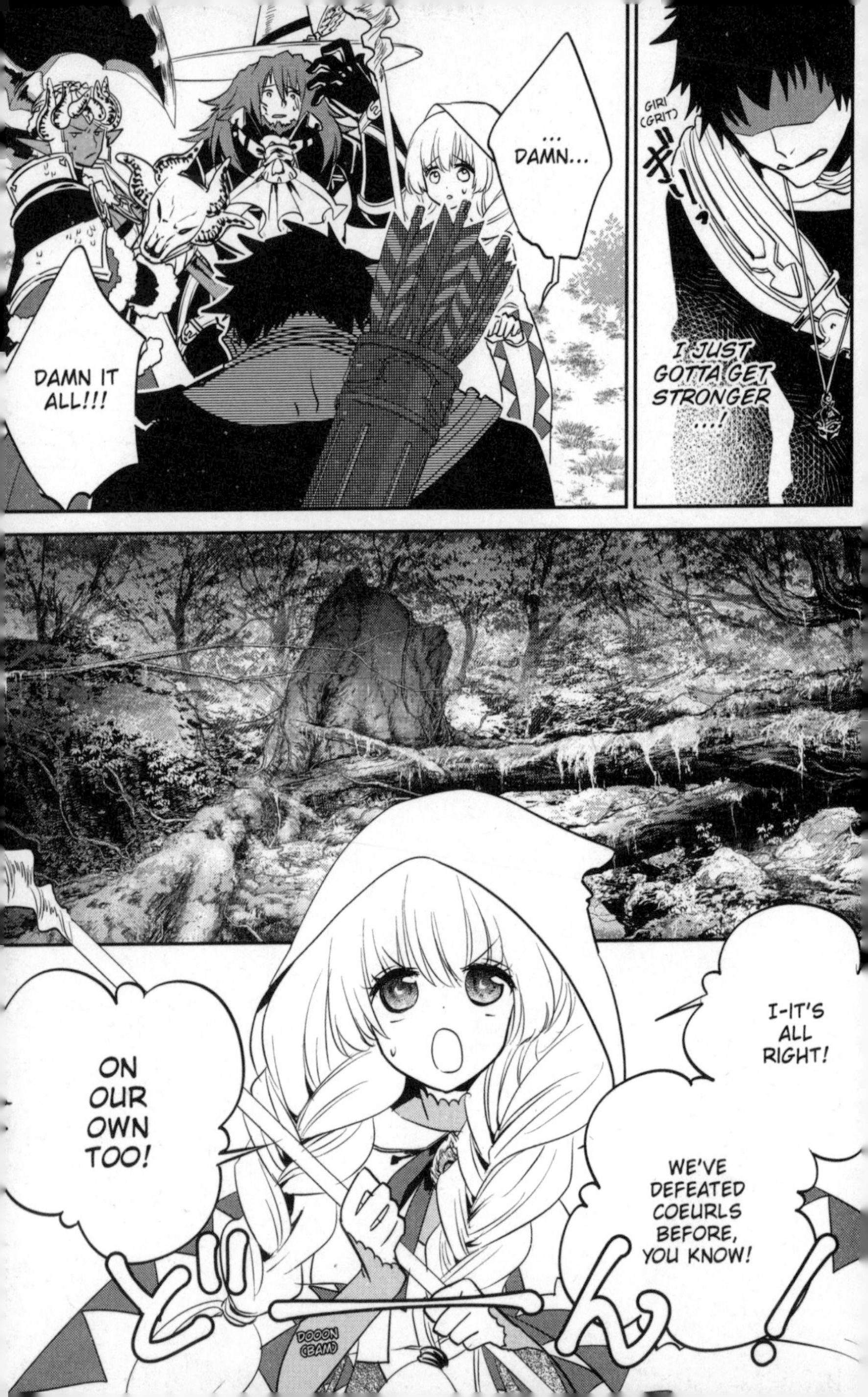
GIRI (GRIT)
I JUST GOTTA GET STRONGER ...!
... DAMN...
DAMN IT ALL!!!
I-IT'S ALL RIGHT!
WE'VE DEFEATED COEURLS BEFORE, YOU KNOW!
ON OUR OWN TOO!
DOOON (BAM)

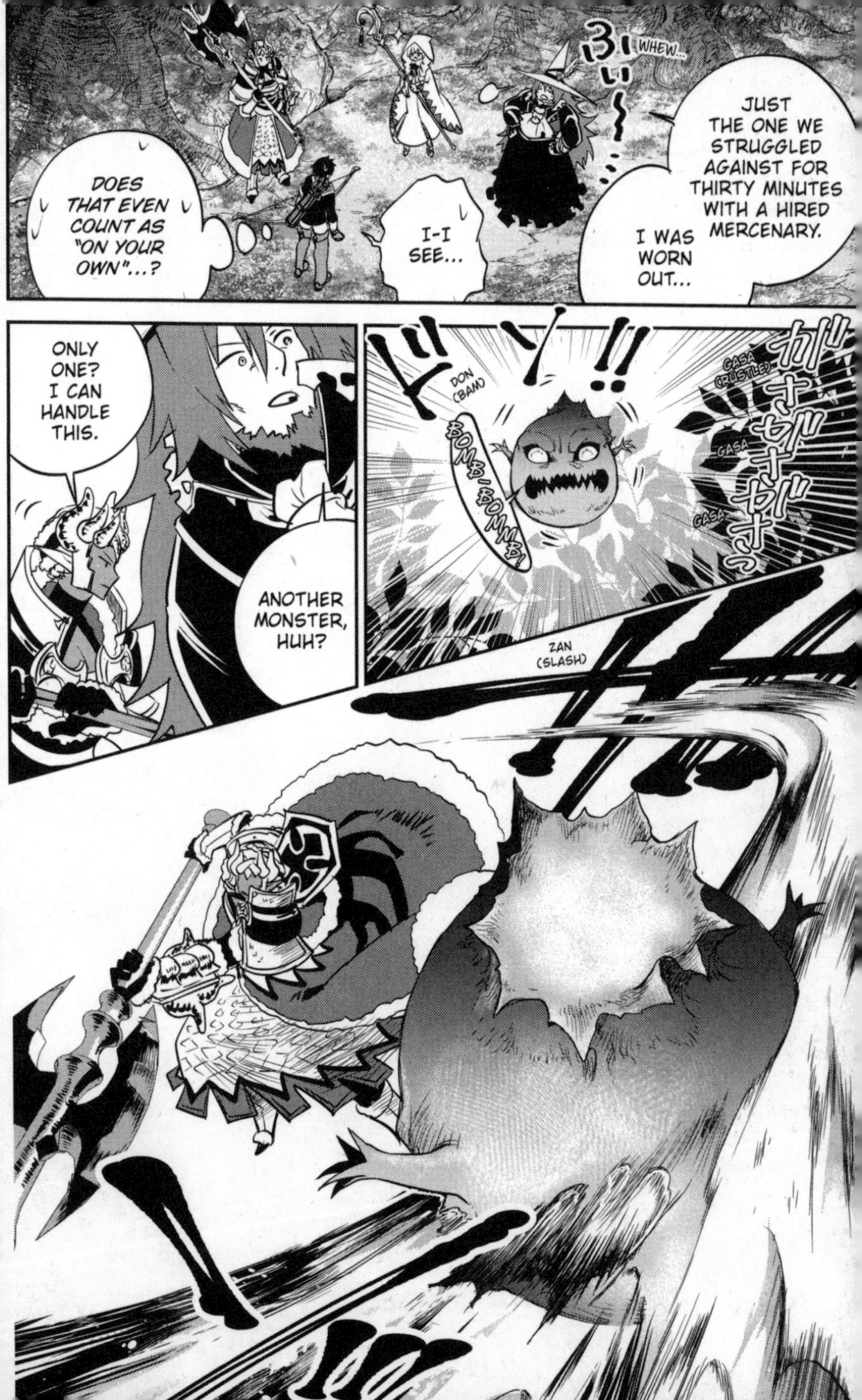
WHEW...
JUST THE ONE WE STRUGGLED AGAINST FOR THIRTY MINUTES WITH A HIRED MERCENARY.
I WAS WORN OUT...
I-I SEE...
DOES THAT EVEN COUNT AS "ON YOUR OWN"...?
GASA (RUSTLE)
GASA
GASA
DON (BAM)
BOMB-BOMMB!
ANOTHER MONSTER, HUH?
ONLY ONE? I CAN HANDLE THIS.
ZAN (SLASH)

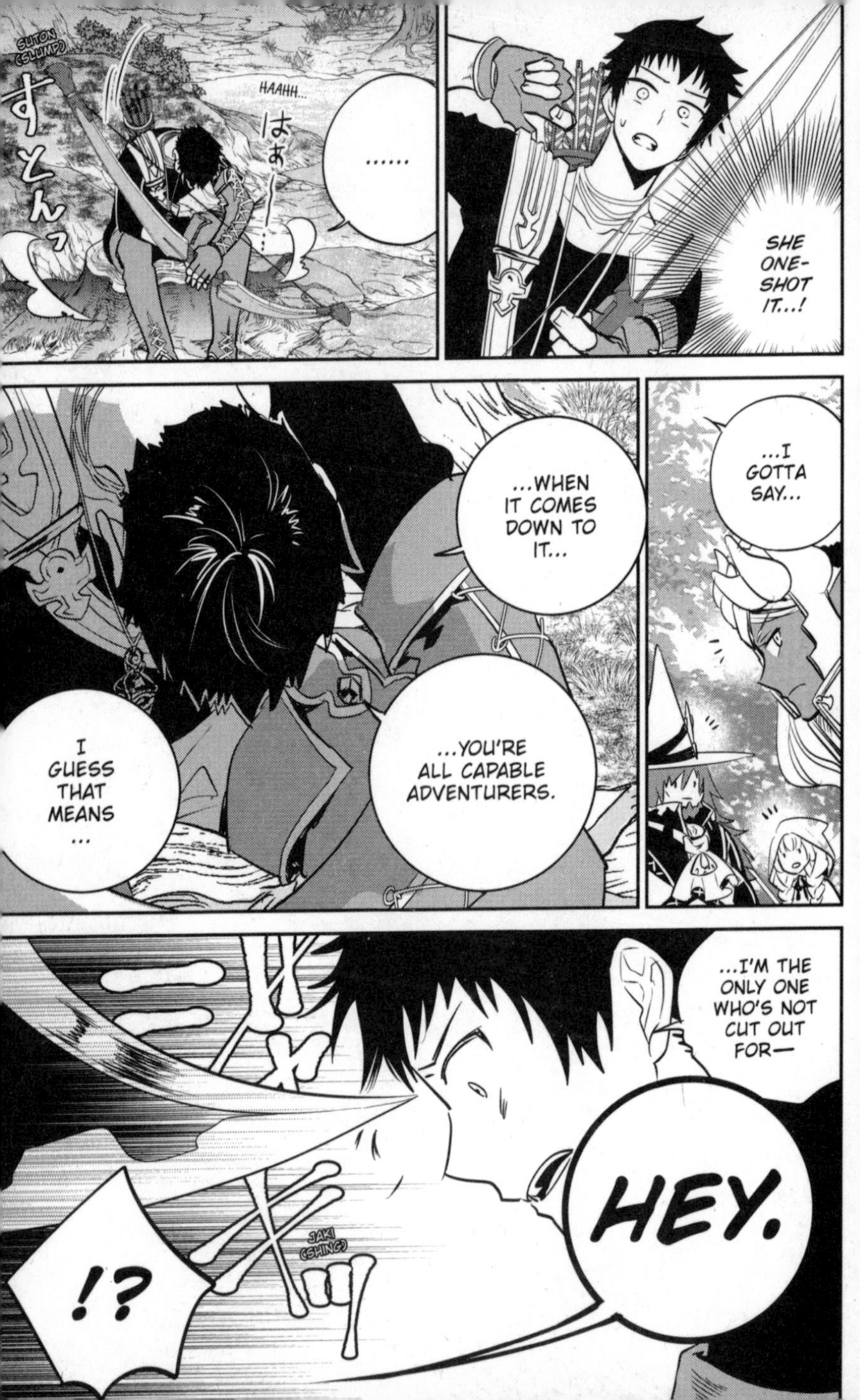
SHE ONE-SHOT IT...!
......
HAAHH...
はぁ～…
SUTON (SLUMP)
すとんっ
...I GOTTA SAY...
...WHEN IT COMES DOWN TO IT...
...YOU'RE ALL CAPABLE ADVENTURERS.
I GUESS THAT MEANS ...
...I'M THE ONLY ONE WHO'S NOT CUT OUT FOR—
HEY.
JAKI (SHING)
!?

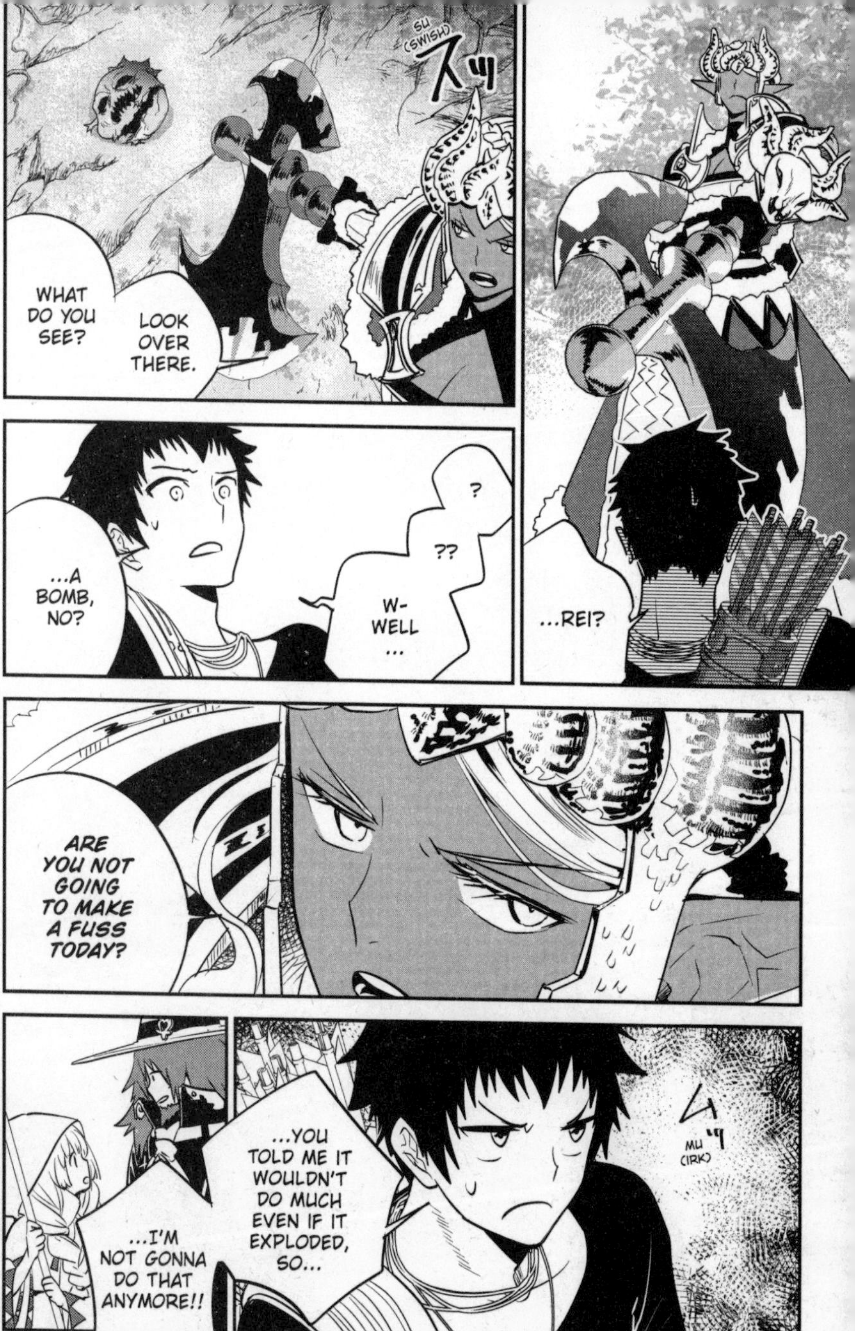
...REI?
スッ
SU (SWISH)
LOOK OVER THERE.
WHAT DO YOU SEE?
?
??
W-WELL ...
...A BOMB, NO?
ARE YOU NOT GOING TO MAKE A FUSS TODAY?
ム"
MU (IRK)
...YOU TOLD ME IT WOULDN'T DO MUCH EVEN IF IT EXPLODED, SO...
...I'M NOT GONNA DO THAT ANYMORE!!

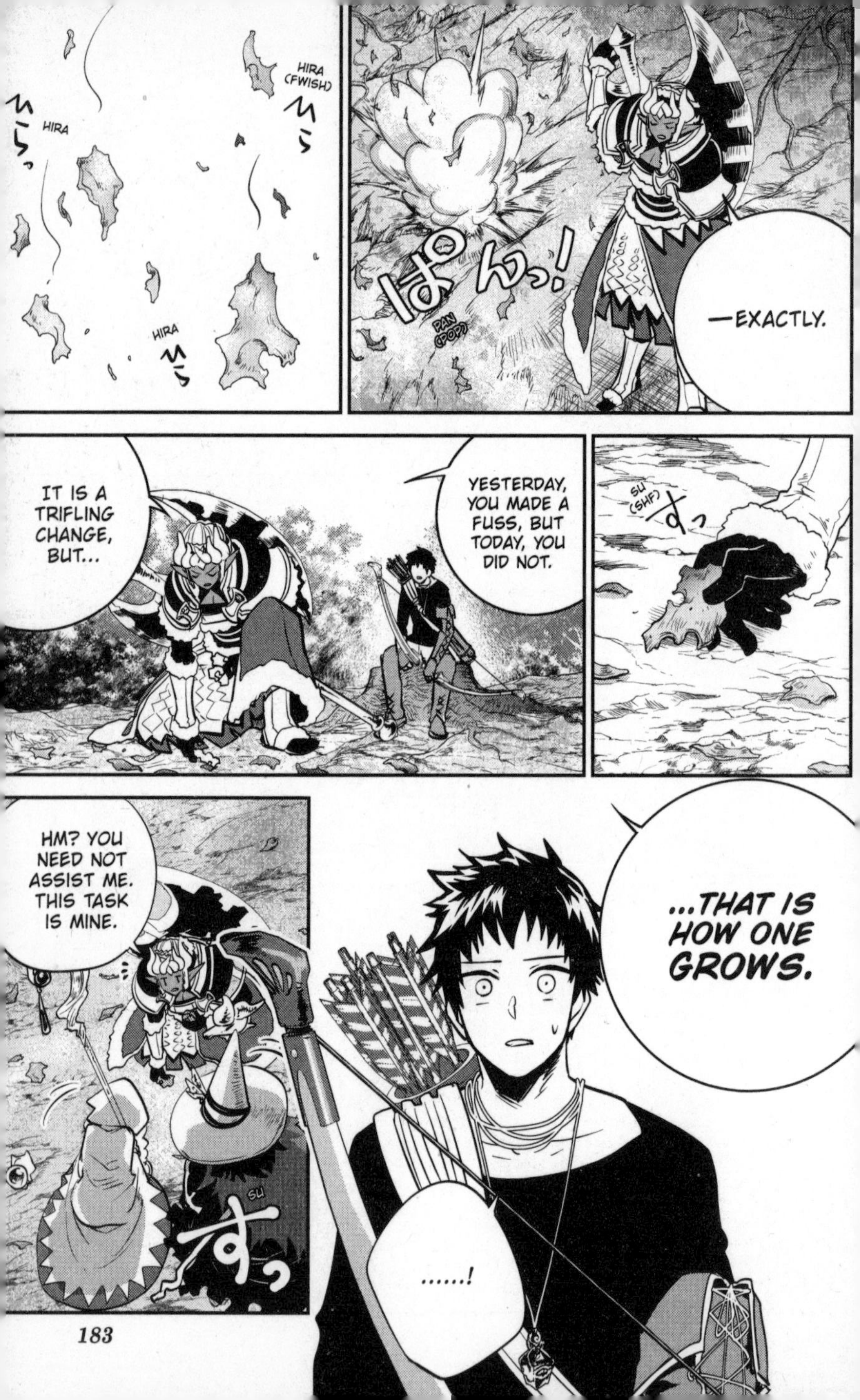
—EXACTLY.
ぱんっ!
PAN (POP)
ひらっ
HIRA
ひら
HIRA (FWISH)
ひら
HIRA
すっ
SU (SHF)
YESTERDAY, YOU MADE A FUSS, BUT TODAY, YOU DID NOT.
IT IS A TRIFLING CHANGE, BUT...
...THAT IS HOW ONE GROWS.
......!
HM? YOU NEED NOT ASSIST ME. THIS TASK IS MINE.
すっ
SU

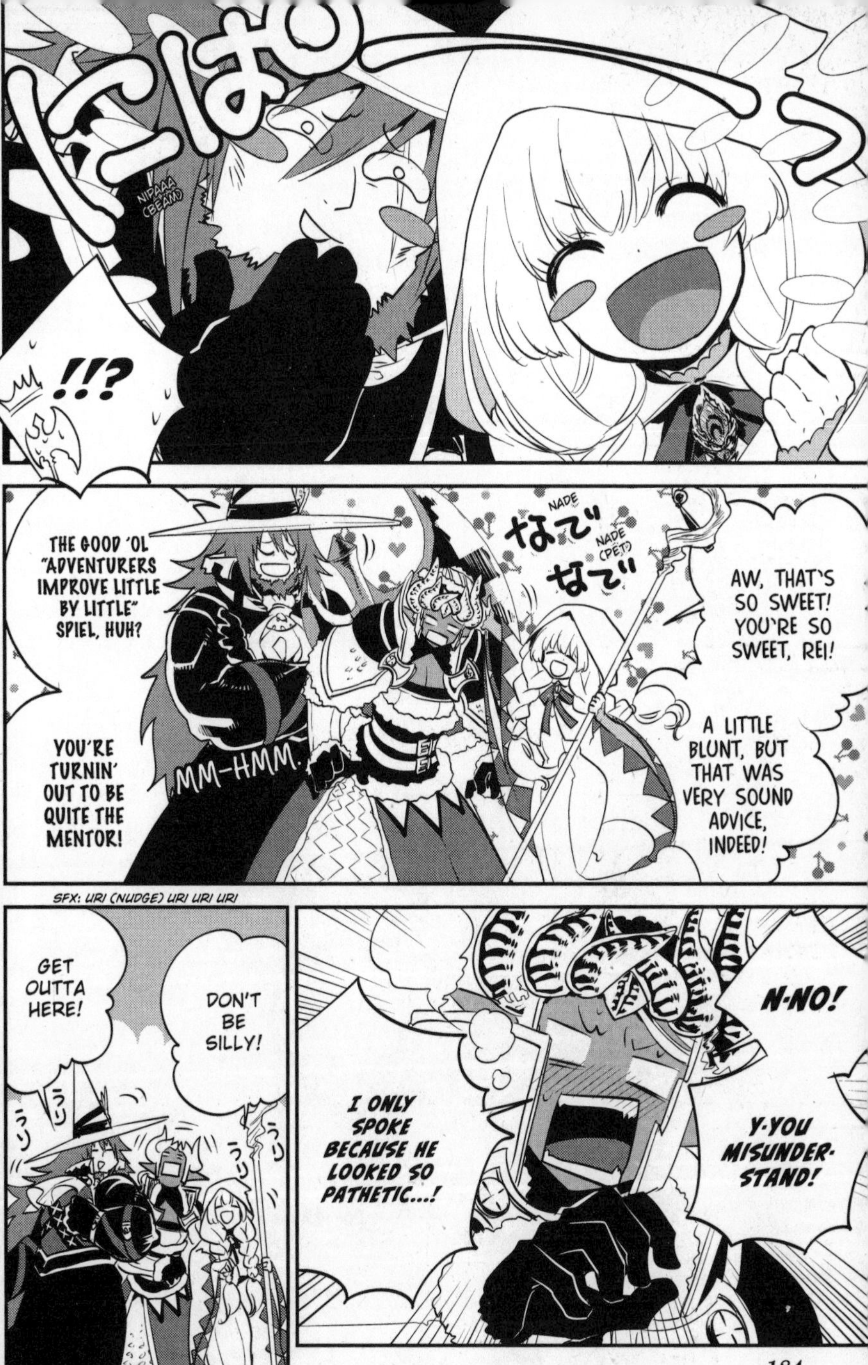
にぱ～っ
NIPAAA (BEAM)
!!?
AW, THAT'S SO SWEET! YOU'RE SO SWEET, REI!
A LITTLE BLUNT, BUT THAT WAS VERY SOUND ADVICE, INDEED!
なで NADE
なで NADE (PET)
THE GOOD 'OL "ADVENTURERS IMPROVE LITTLE BY LITTLE" SPIEL, HUH?
YOU'RE TURNIN' OUT TO BE QUITE THE MENTOR!
MM-HMM.
SFX: URI (NUDGE) URI URI URI
N-NO!
Y-YOU MISUNDER-STAND!
I ONLY SPOKE BECAUSE HE LOOKED SO PATHETIC...!
DON'T BE SILLY!
GET OUTTA HERE!
うり
うり

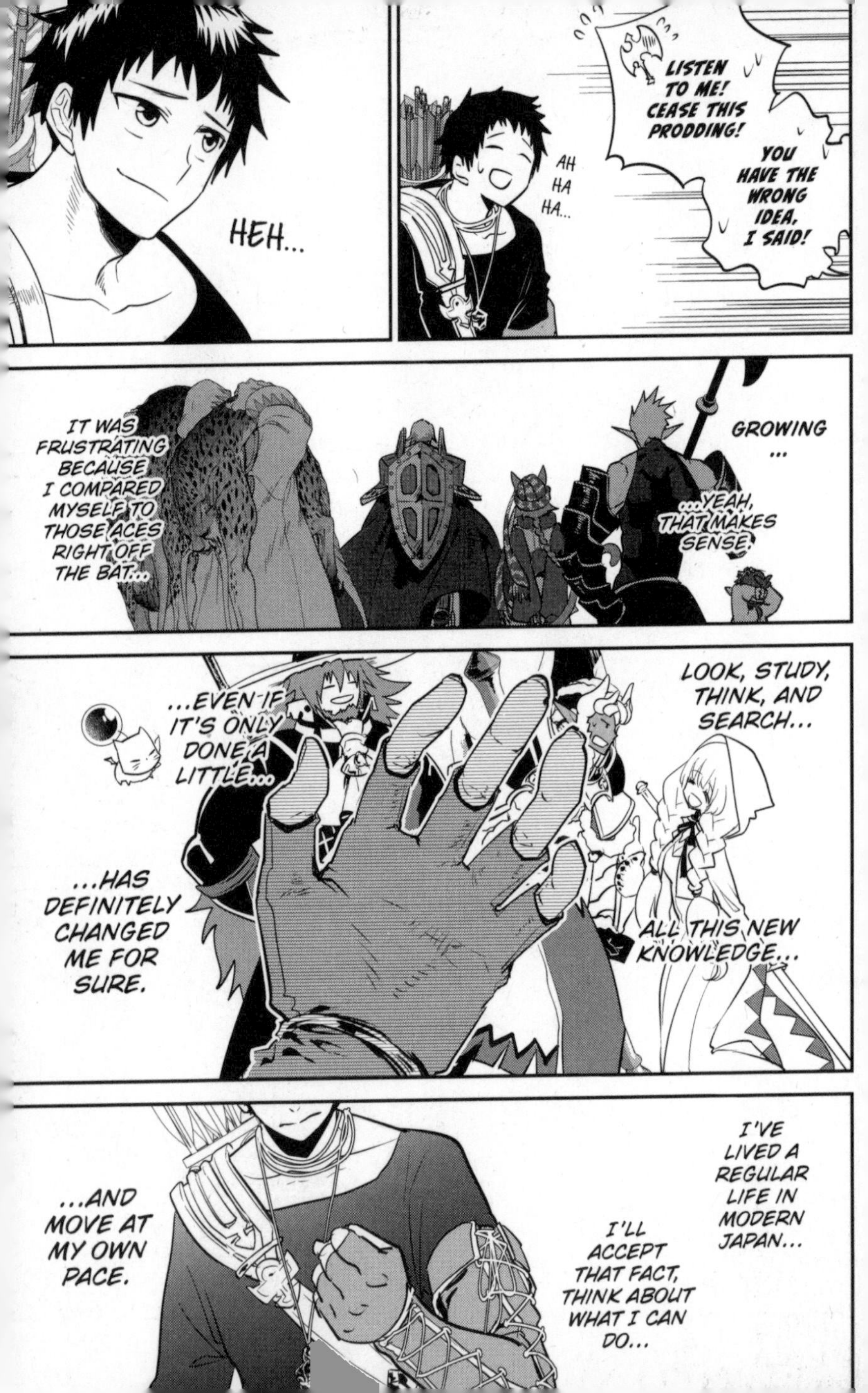
LISTEN TO ME! CEASE THIS PRODDING!
YOU HAVE THE WRONG IDEA, I SAID!
AH HA HA...
HEH...
GROWING...
...YEAH, THAT MAKES SENSE.
IT WAS FRUSTRATING BECAUSE I COMPARED MYSELF TO THOSE ACES RIGHT OFF THE BAT...
LOOK, STUDY, THINK, AND SEARCH...
ALL THIS NEW KNOWLEDGE...
...EVEN IF IT'S ONLY DONE A LITTLE...
...HAS DEFINITELY CHANGED ME FOR SURE.
I'VE LIVED A REGULAR LIFE IN MODERN JAPAN...
I'LL ACCEPT THAT FACT, THINK ABOUT WHAT I CAN DO...
...AND MOVE AT MY OWN PACE.

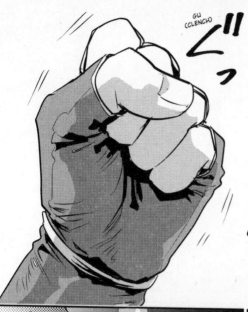

GU
(CLENCH)

I'LL START WITH WHAT'S RIGHT IN FRONT OF ME...

...AND WORK MY WAY UP!

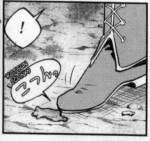

!

KOTSUN
(CLUNK)
こつん

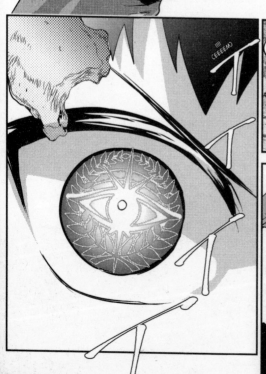

(EEEEM)

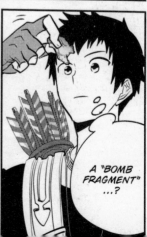

A "BOMB FRAGMENT" ...?

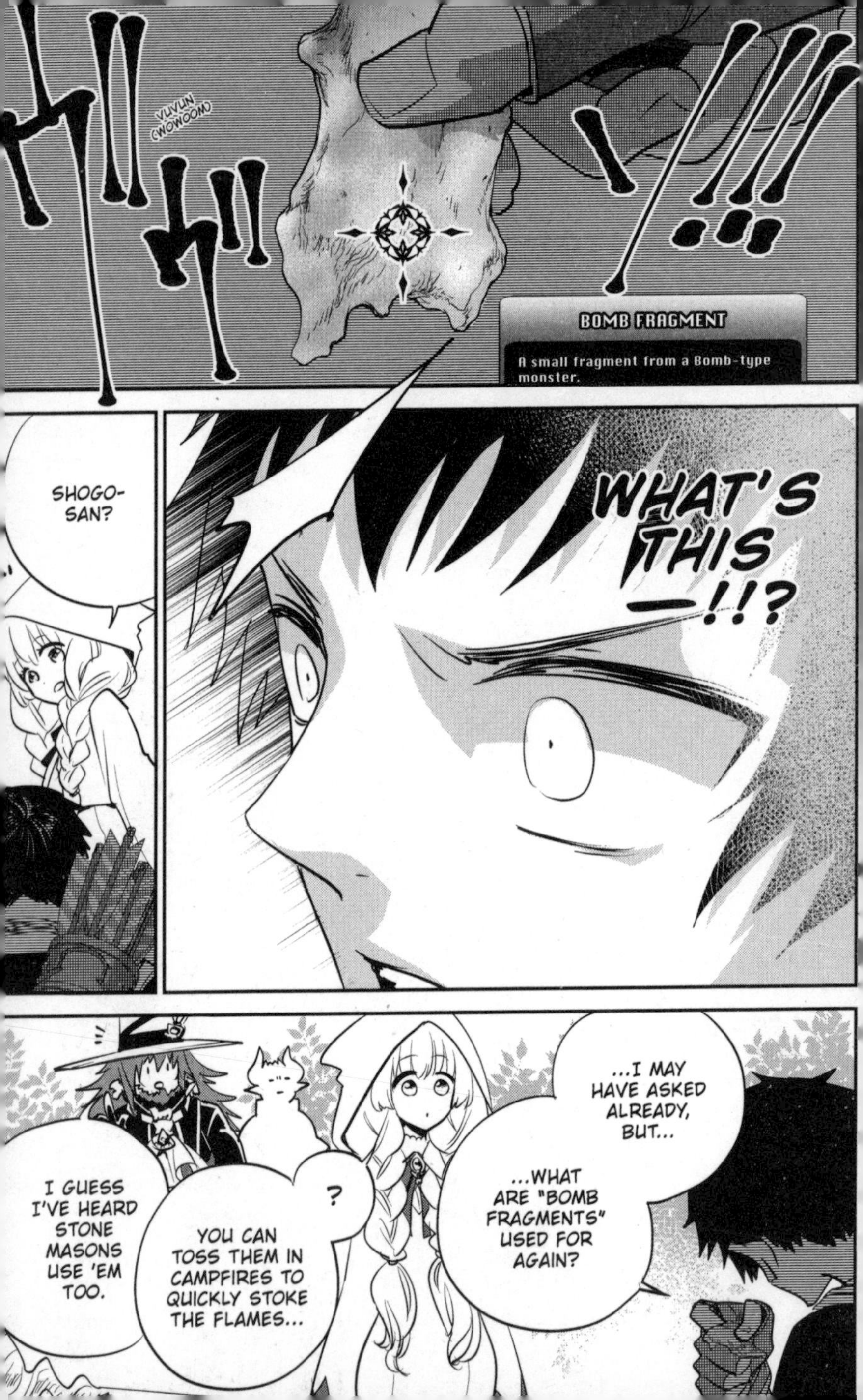
VUVUN (WOWOOM)
BOMB FRAGMENT
A small fragment from a Bomb-type monster.
WHAT'S THIS —!!?
SHOGO-SAN?
...I MAY HAVE ASKED ALREADY, BUT...
...WHAT ARE "BOMB FRAGMENTS" USED FOR AGAIN?
?
YOU CAN TOSS THEM IN CAMPFIRES TO QUICKLY STOKE THE FLAMES...
I GUESS I'VE HEARD STONE MASONS USE 'EM TOO.

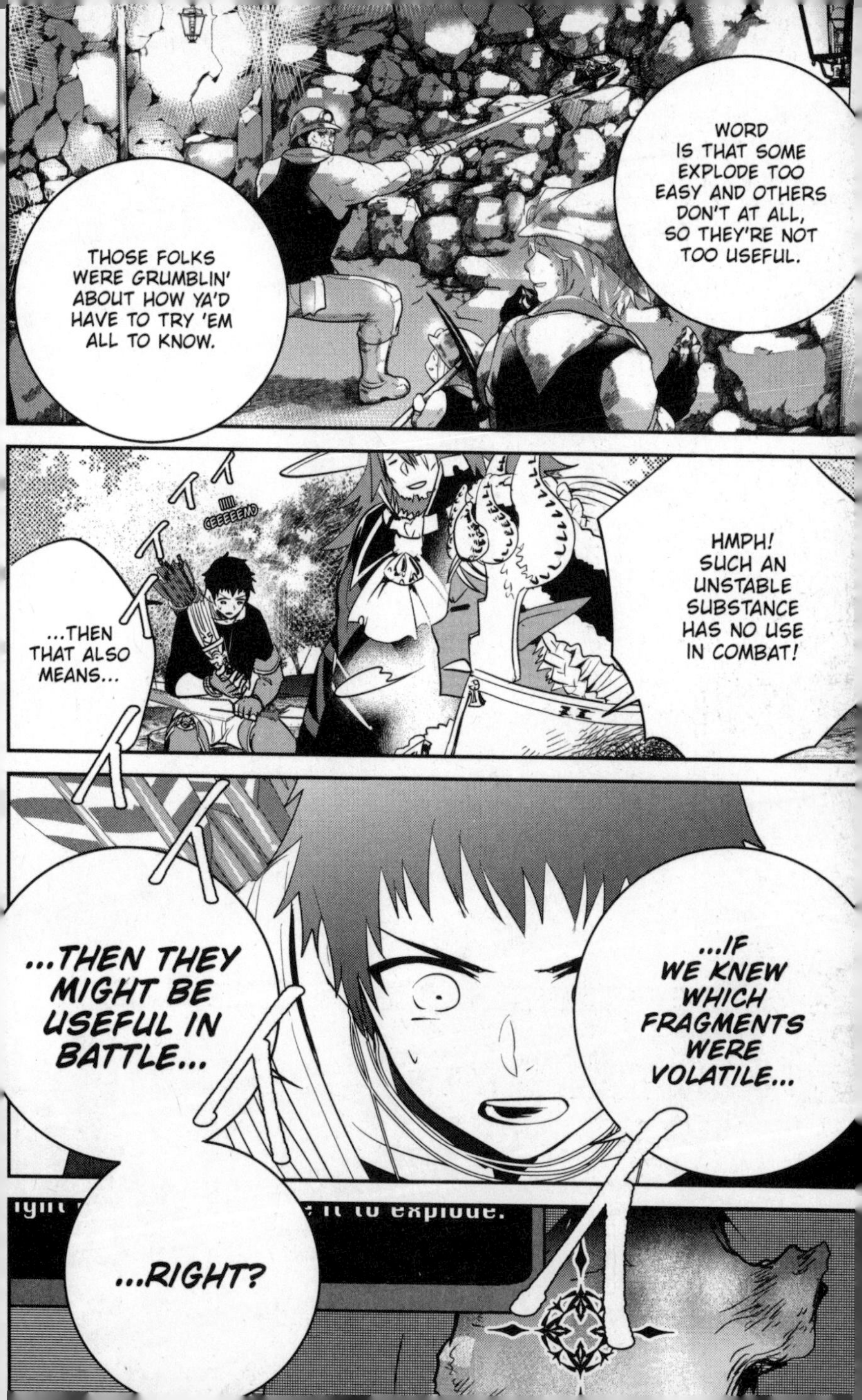
WORD IS THAT SOME EXPLODE TOO EASY AND OTHERS DON'T AT ALL, SO THEY'RE NOT TOO USEFUL.
THOSE FOLKS WERE GRUMBLIN' ABOUT HOW YA'D HAVE TO TRY 'EM ALL TO KNOW.
HMPH! SUCH AN UNSTABLE SUBSTANCE HAS NO USE IN COMBAT!
...THEN THAT ALSO MEANS...
...IF WE KNEW WHICH FRAGMENTS WERE VOLATILE...
...THEN THEY MIGHT BE USEFUL IN BATTLE...
...RIGHT?

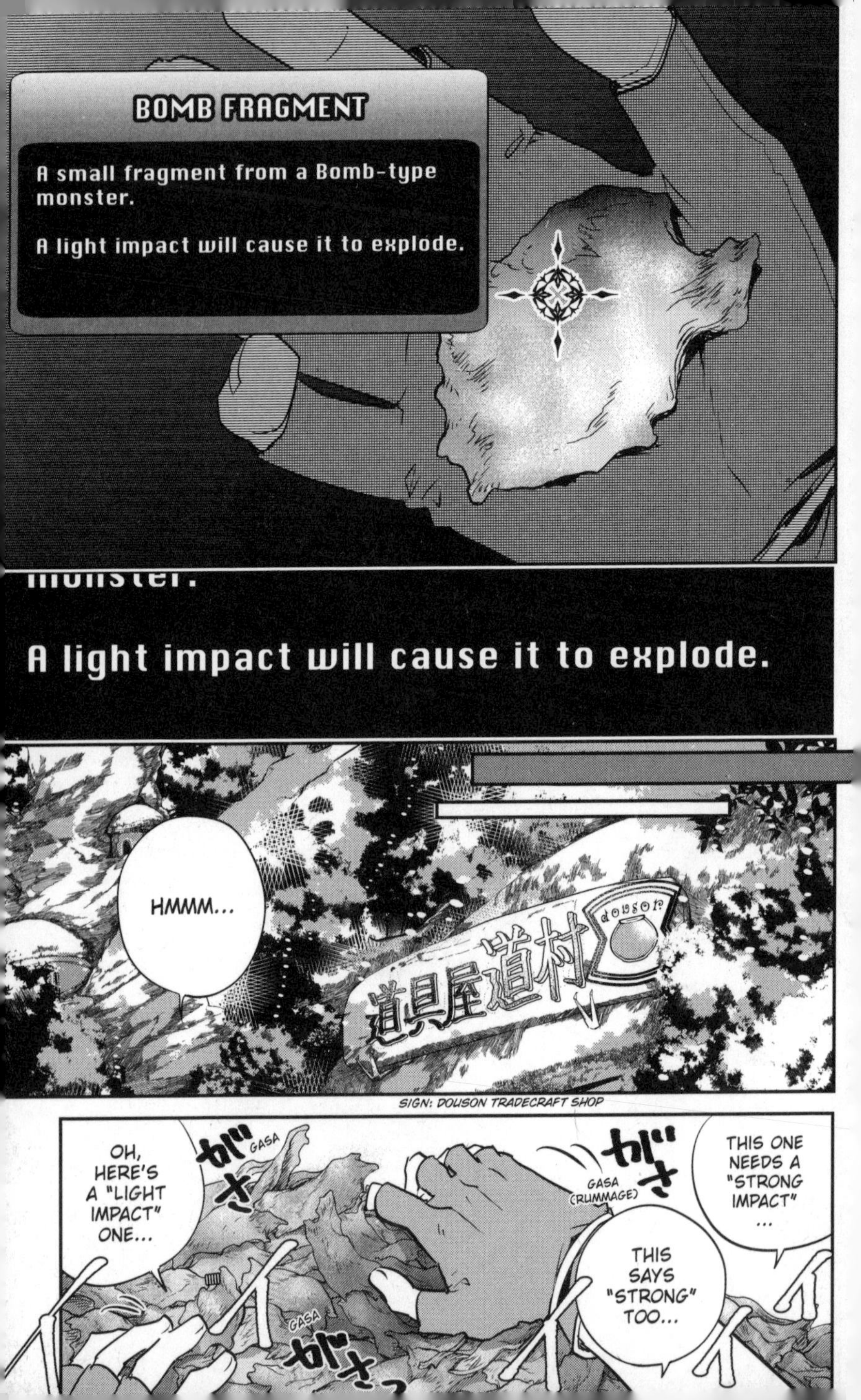
BOMB FRAGMENT
A small fragment from a Bomb-type monster.
A light impact will cause it to explode.
monster.
A light impact will cause it to explode.
HMMM...
道具屋道村
douson
SIGN: DOUSON TRADECRAFT SHOP
THIS ONE NEEDS A "STRONG IMPACT"...
がさ GASA (RUMMAGE)
THIS SAYS "STRONG" TOO...
がさ GASA
OH, HERE'S A "LIGHT IMPACT" ONE...
がさっ GASA

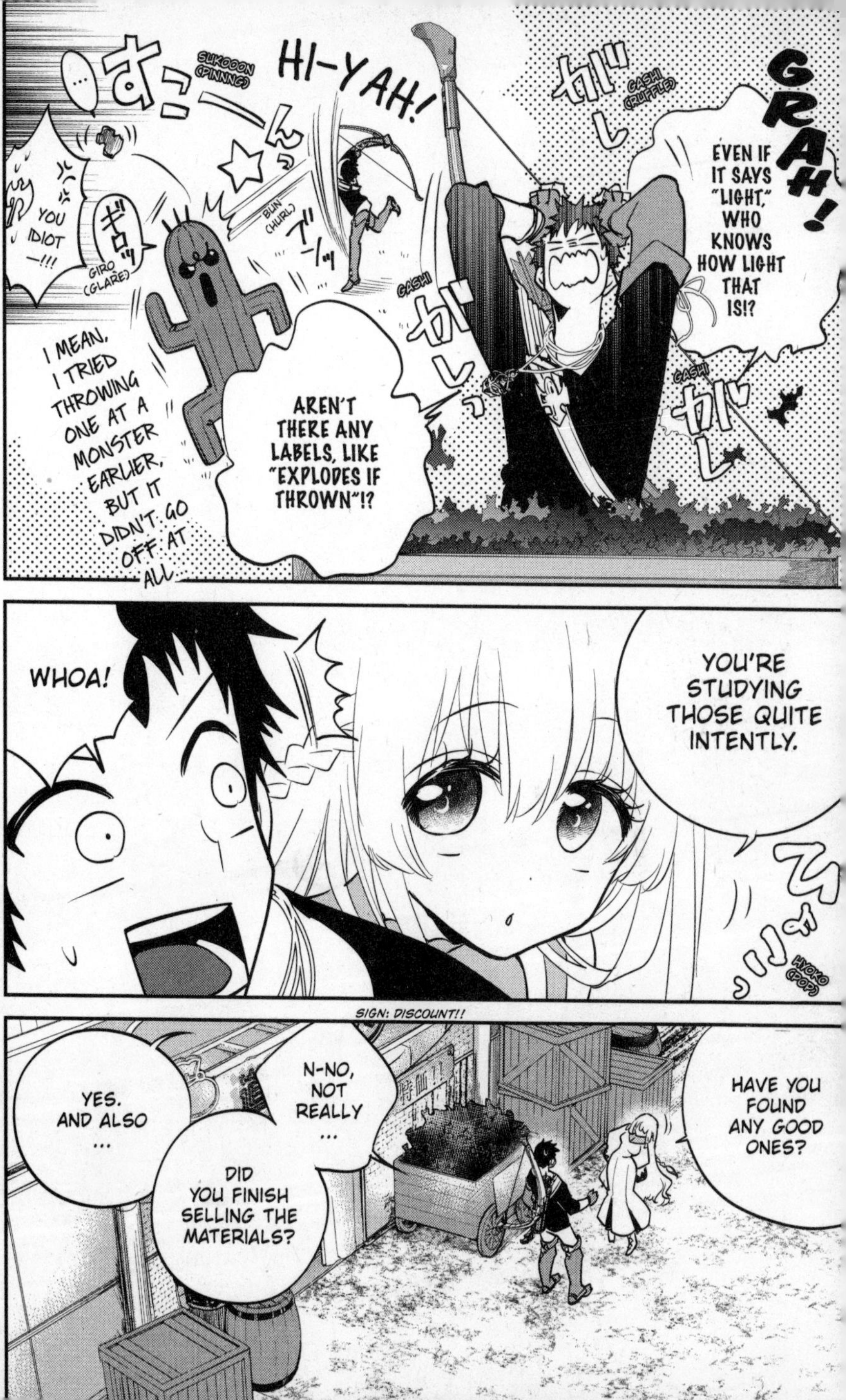
GRAH!
EVEN IF IT SAYS "LIGHT," WHO KNOWS HOW LIGHT THAT IS!?
GASHI (RUFFLE)
GASHI
GASHI
AREN'T THERE ANY LABELS, LIKE "EXPLODES IF THROWN"!?
HI-YAH!
BUN (HURL)
SUKOOON (PINNNG)
I MEAN, I TRIED THROWING ONE AT A MONSTER EARLIER, BUT IT DIDN'T GO OFF AT ALL.
GIRO (GLARE)
YOU IDIOT—!!!
...
YOU'RE STUDYING THOSE QUITE INTENTLY.
HYOKO (POP)
WHOA!
SIGN: DISCOUNT!!
HAVE YOU FOUND ANY GOOD ONES?
N-NO, NOT REALLY...
DID YOU FINISH SELLING THE MATERIALS?
YES. AND ALSO...

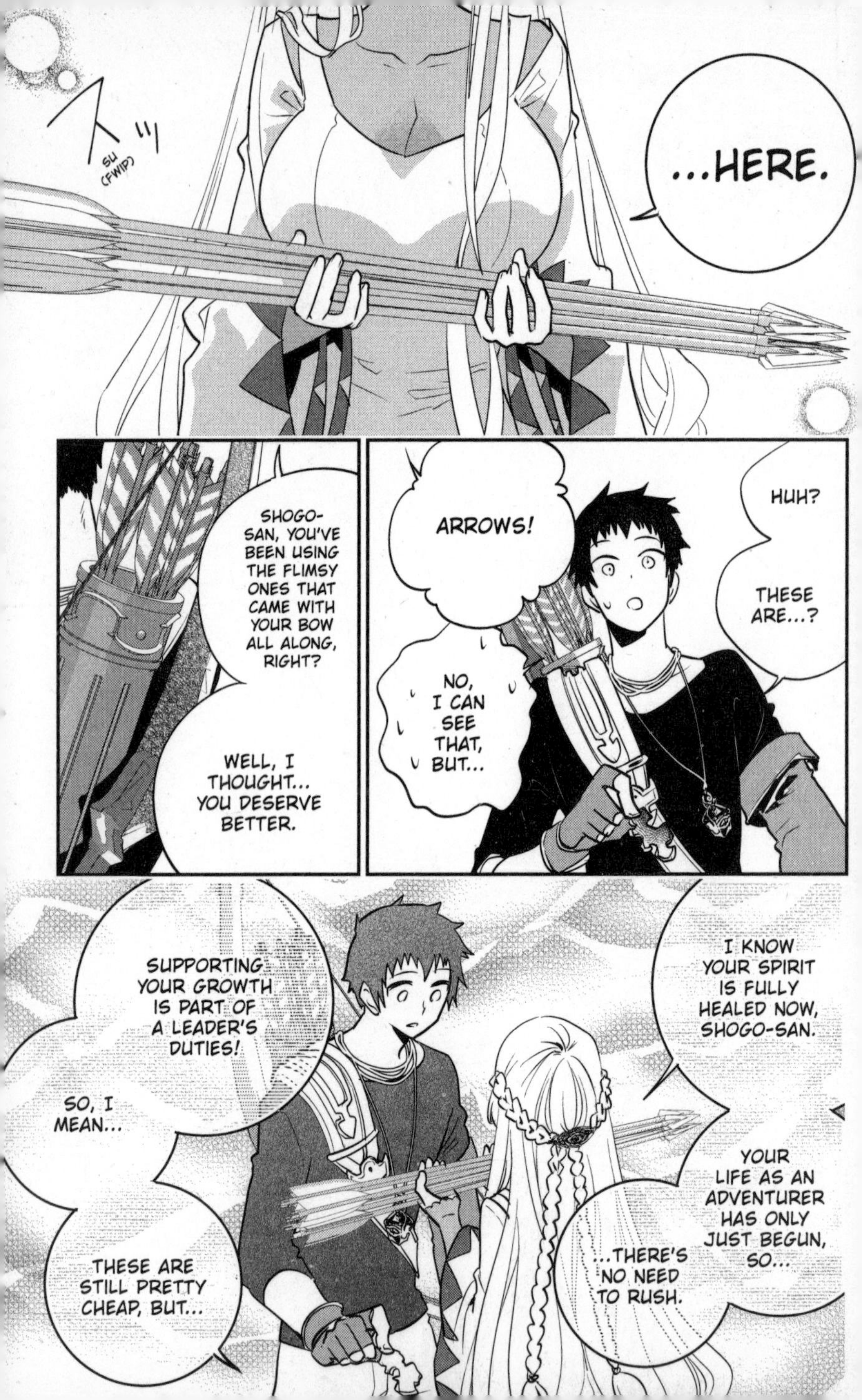
...HERE.
SU (FWIP)
HUH?
THESE ARE...?
ARROWS!
NO, I CAN SEE THAT, BUT...
SHOGO-SAN, YOU'VE BEEN USING THE FLIMSY ONES THAT CAME WITH YOUR BOW ALL ALONG, RIGHT?
WELL, I THOUGHT... YOU DESERVE BETTER.
I KNOW YOUR SPIRIT IS FULLY HEALED NOW, SHOGO-SAN.
YOUR LIFE AS AN ADVENTURER HAS ONLY JUST BEGUN, SO...
...THERE'S NO NEED TO RUSH.
SUPPORTING YOUR GROWTH IS PART OF A LEADER'S DUTIES!
SO, I MEAN...
THESE ARE STILL PRETTY CHEAP, BUT...

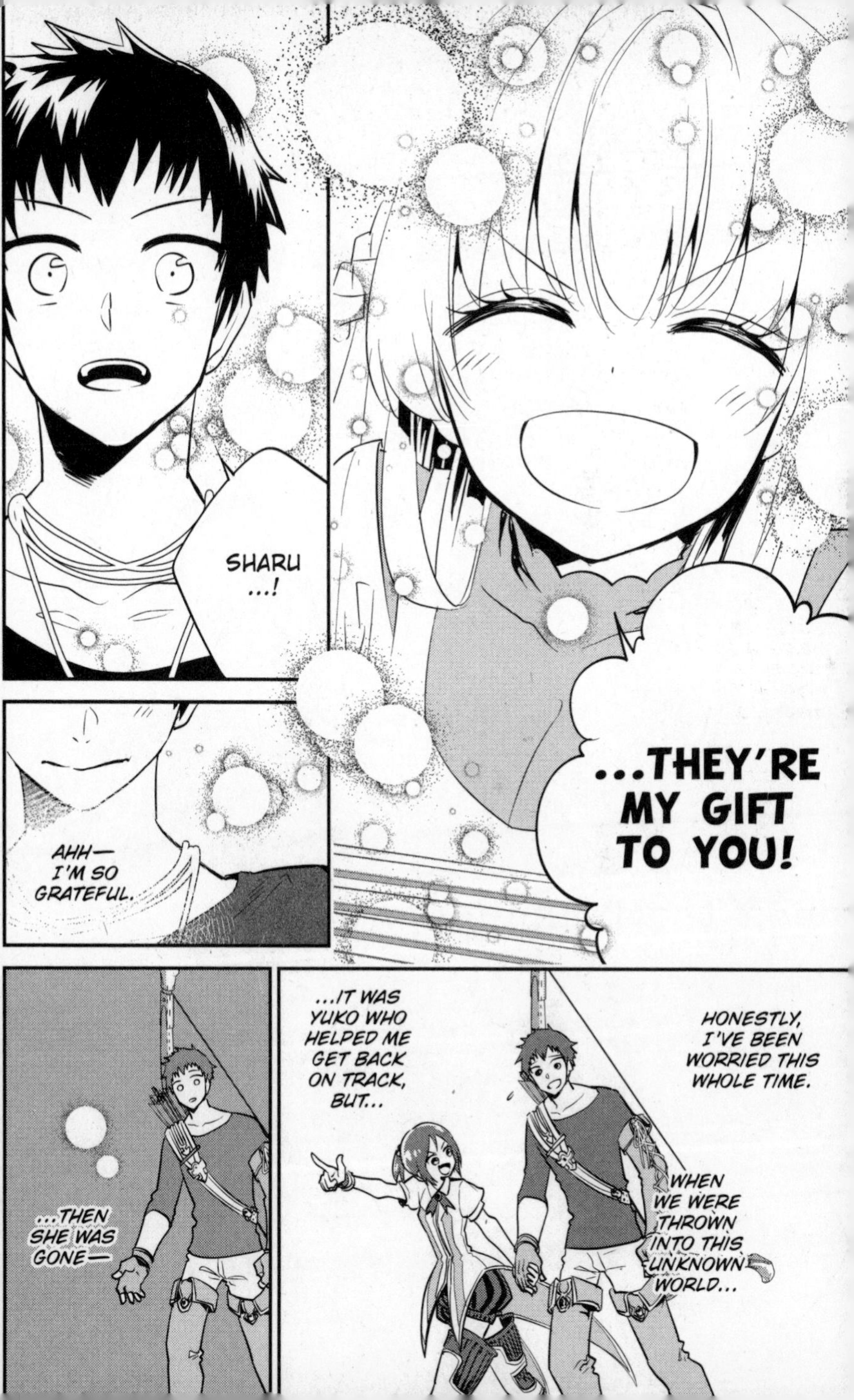
...THEY'RE MY GIFT TO YOU!
SHARU ...!
AHH— I'M SO GRATEFUL.
HONESTLY, I'VE BEEN WORRIED THIS WHOLE TIME.
WHEN WE WERE THROWN INTO THIS UNKNOWN WORLD...
...IT WAS YUKO WHO HELPED ME GET BACK ON TRACK, BUT...
...THEN SHE WAS GONE—

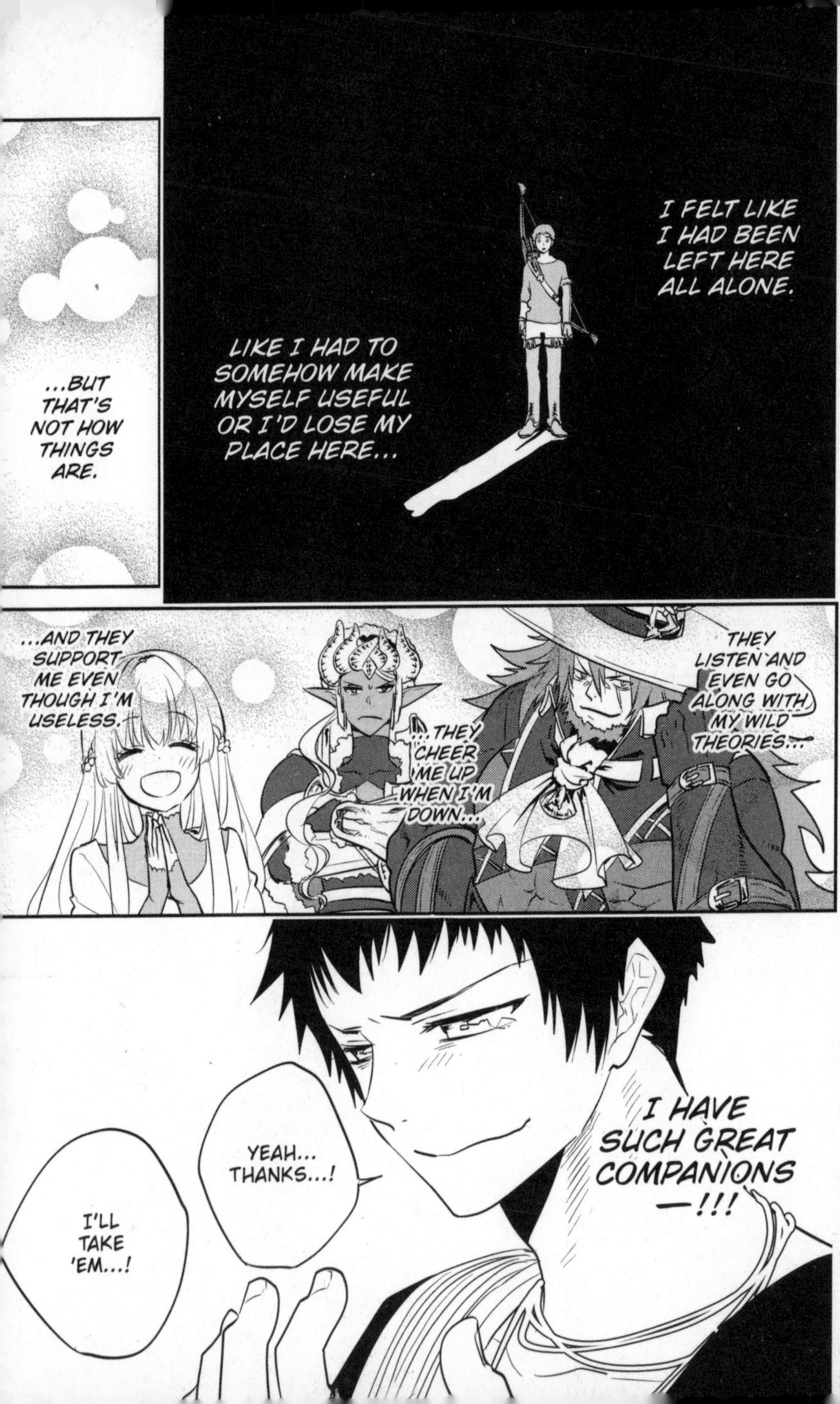
I FELT LIKE I HAD BEEN LEFT HERE ALL ALONE.
LIKE I HAD TO SOMEHOW MAKE MYSELF USEFUL OR I'D LOSE MY PLACE HERE...
...BUT THAT'S NOT HOW THINGS ARE.
THEY LISTEN AND EVEN GO ALONG WITH MY WILD THEORIES...
...THEY CHEER ME UP WHEN I'M DOWN...
...AND THEY SUPPORT ME EVEN THOUGH I'M USELESS.
I HAVE SUCH GREAT COMPANIONS—!!!
YEAH... THANKS...!
I'LL TAKE 'EM...!

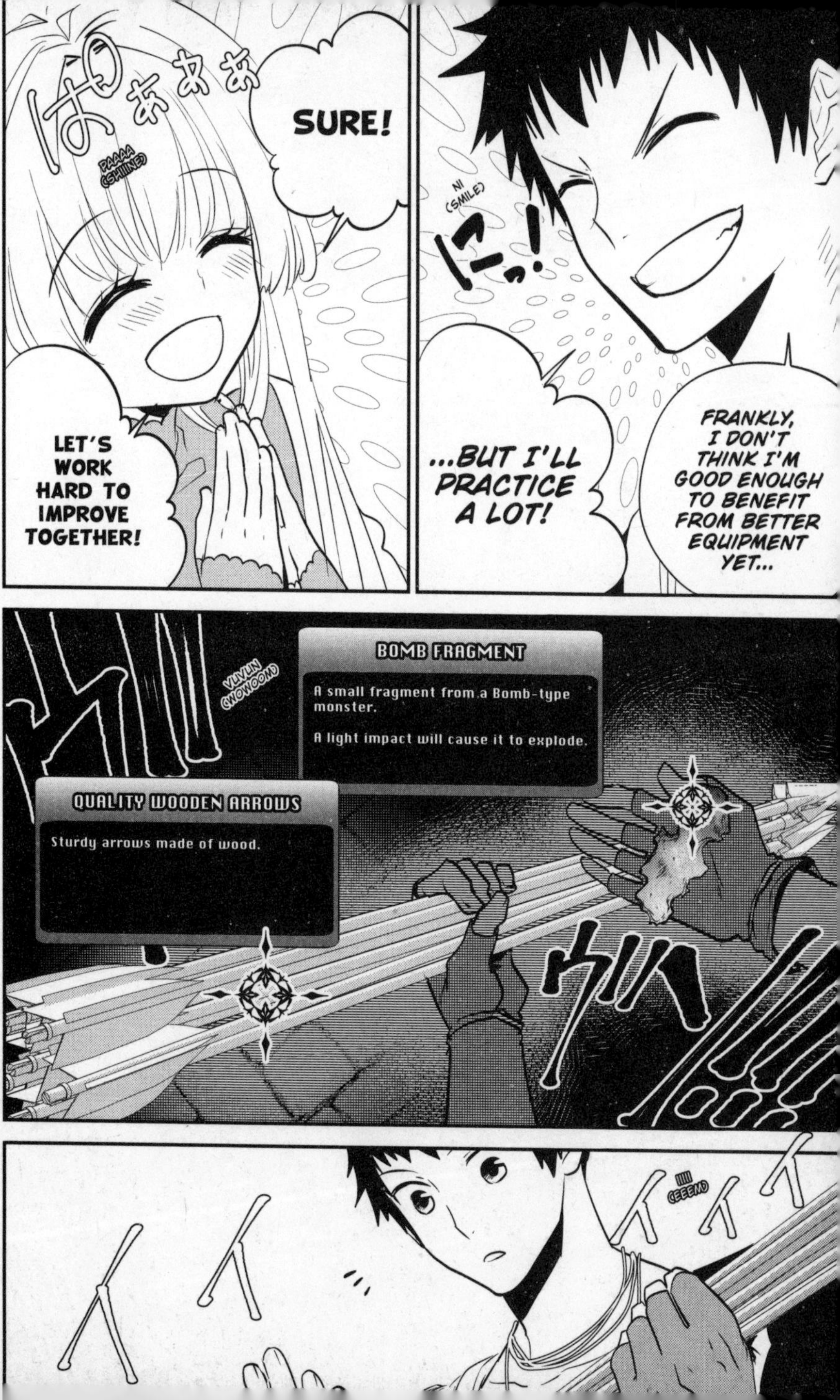
FRANKLY, I DON'T THINK I'M GOOD ENOUGH TO BENEFIT FROM BETTER EQUIPMENT YET...
...BUT I'LL PRACTICE A LOT!
NI (SMILE)
SURE!
PAAAA (SHIIINE)
LET'S WORK HARD TO IMPROVE TOGETHER!
BOMB FRAGMENT
A small fragment from a Bomb-type monster.
A light impact will cause it to explode.
VUVUN (WOWOOM)
QUALITY WOODEN ARROWS
Sturdy arrows made of wood.
IIIII (EEEM)

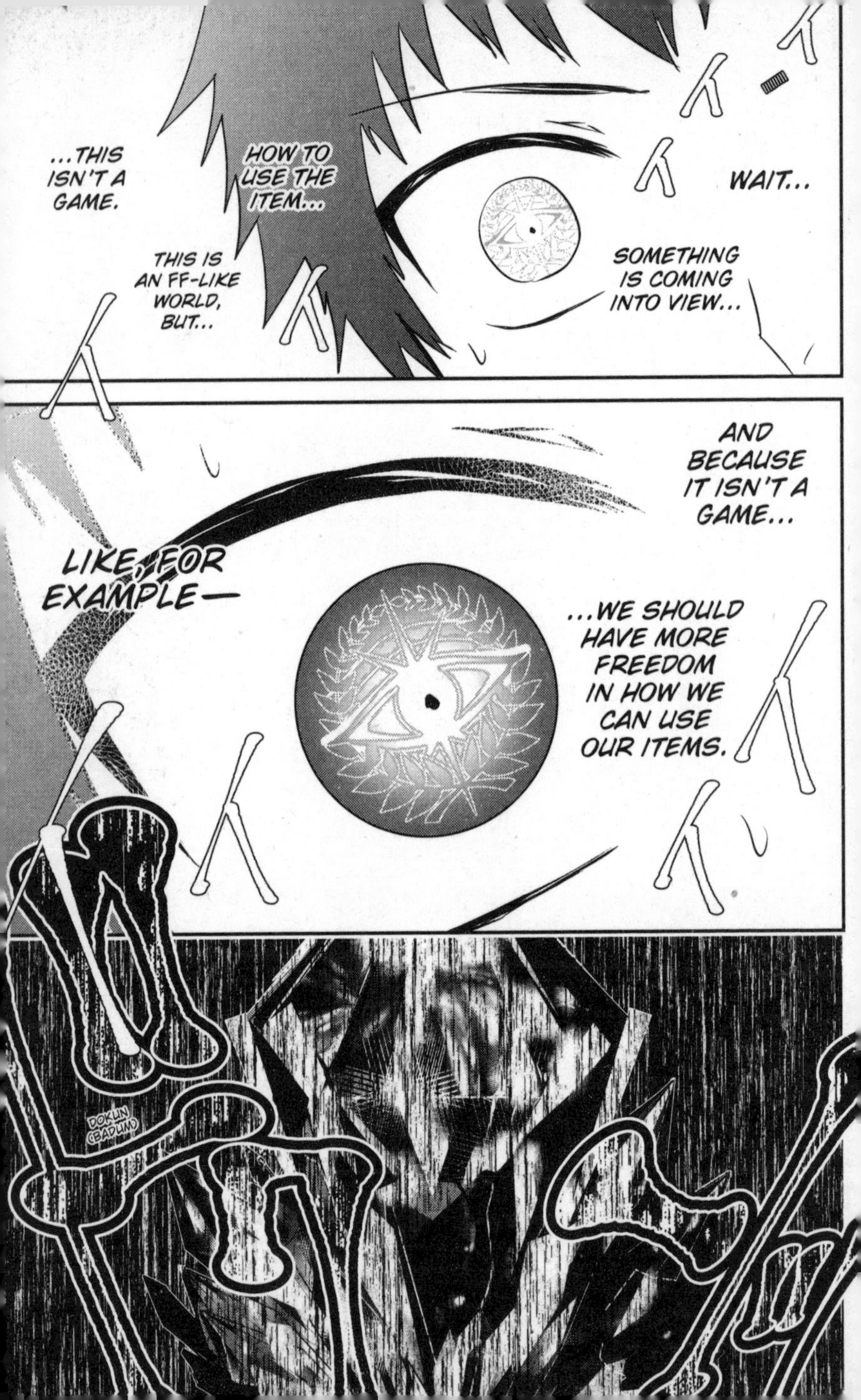
WAIT...
SOMETHING IS COMING INTO VIEW...
HOW TO USE THE ITEM...
THIS IS AN FF-LIKE WORLD, BUT...
...THIS ISN'T A GAME.
AND BECAUSE IT ISN'T A GAME...
...WE SHOULD HAVE MORE FREEDOM IN HOW WE CAN USE OUR ITEMS.
LIKE, FOR EXAMPLE—
DOKUN (BADUMP)

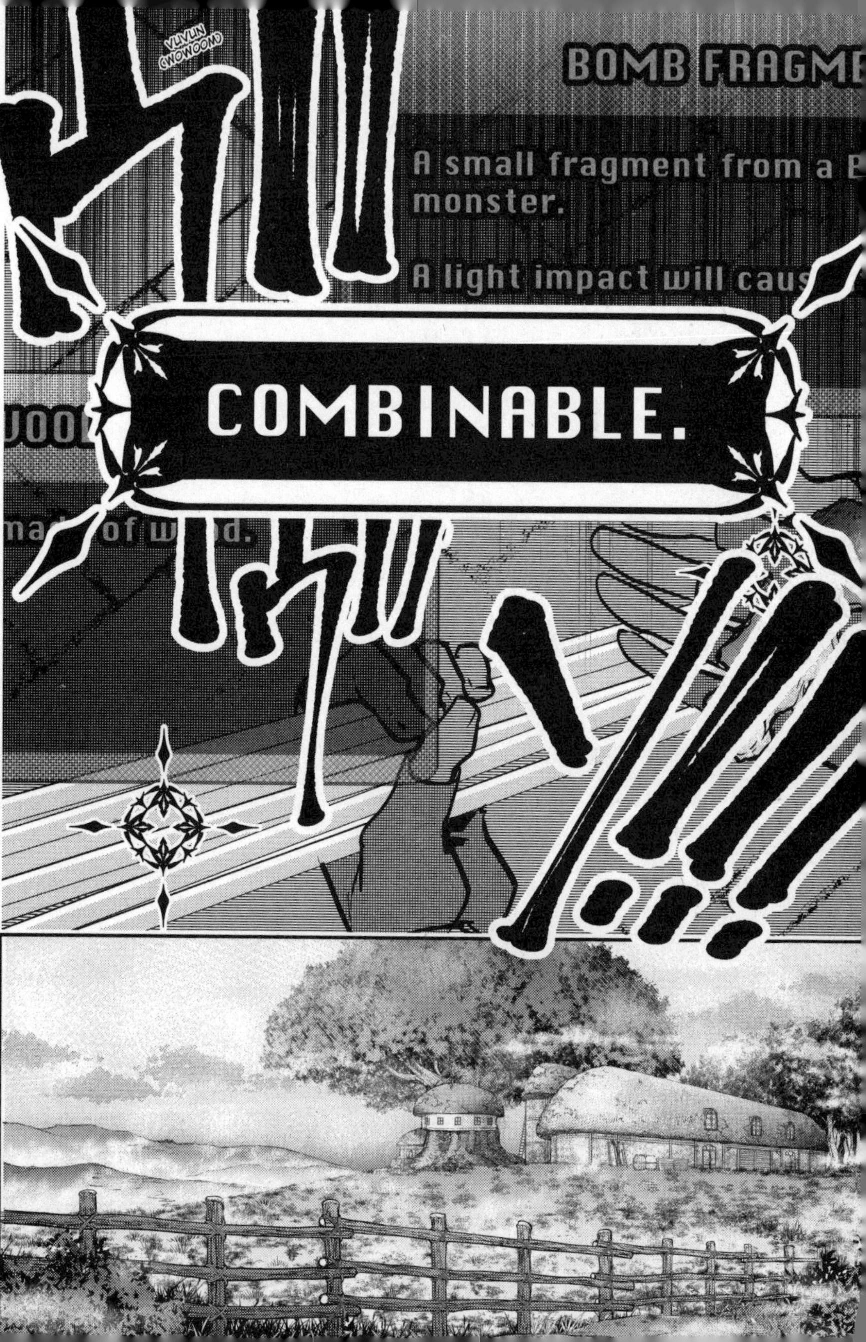
BOMB FRAGME
A small fragment from a B
monster.
A light impact will caus
VUVUN (WOWOOM)
WOOD
mad of w d.
COMBINABLE.

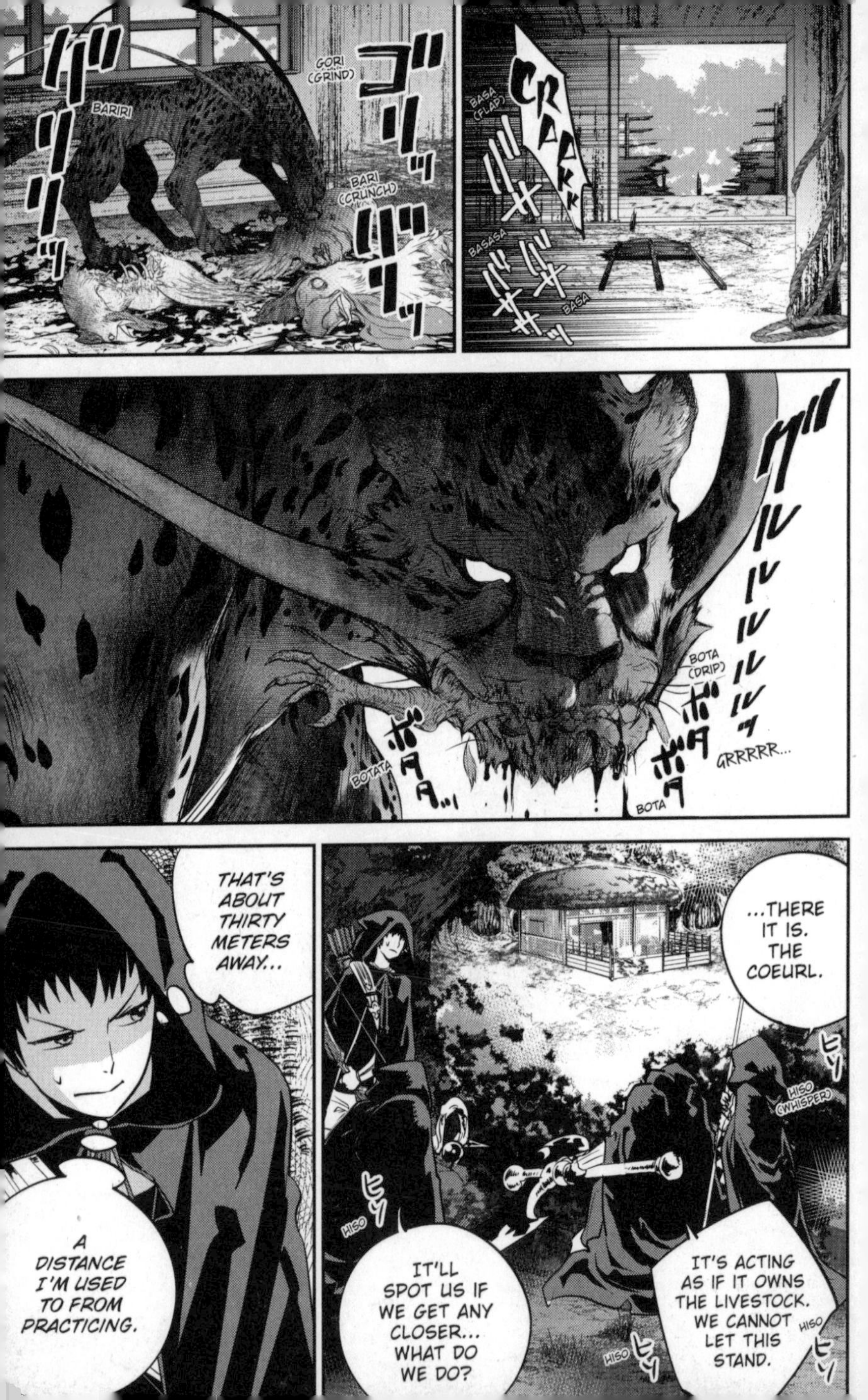
CRACK
BASA (FLAP)
BASASA
BASA
GORI (GRIND)
BARIRI
BARI (CRUNCH)
GRRRR...
BOTA (DRIP)
BOTA
BOTATA
...THERE IT IS. THE COEURL.
HISO (WHISPER)
IT'S ACTING AS IF IT OWNS THE LIVESTOCK. WE CANNOT LET THIS STAND.
HISO
IT'LL SPOT US IF WE GET ANY CLOSER... WHAT DO WE DO?
HISO
THAT'S ABOUT THIRTY METERS AWAY...
A DISTANCE I'M USED TO FROM PRACTICING.

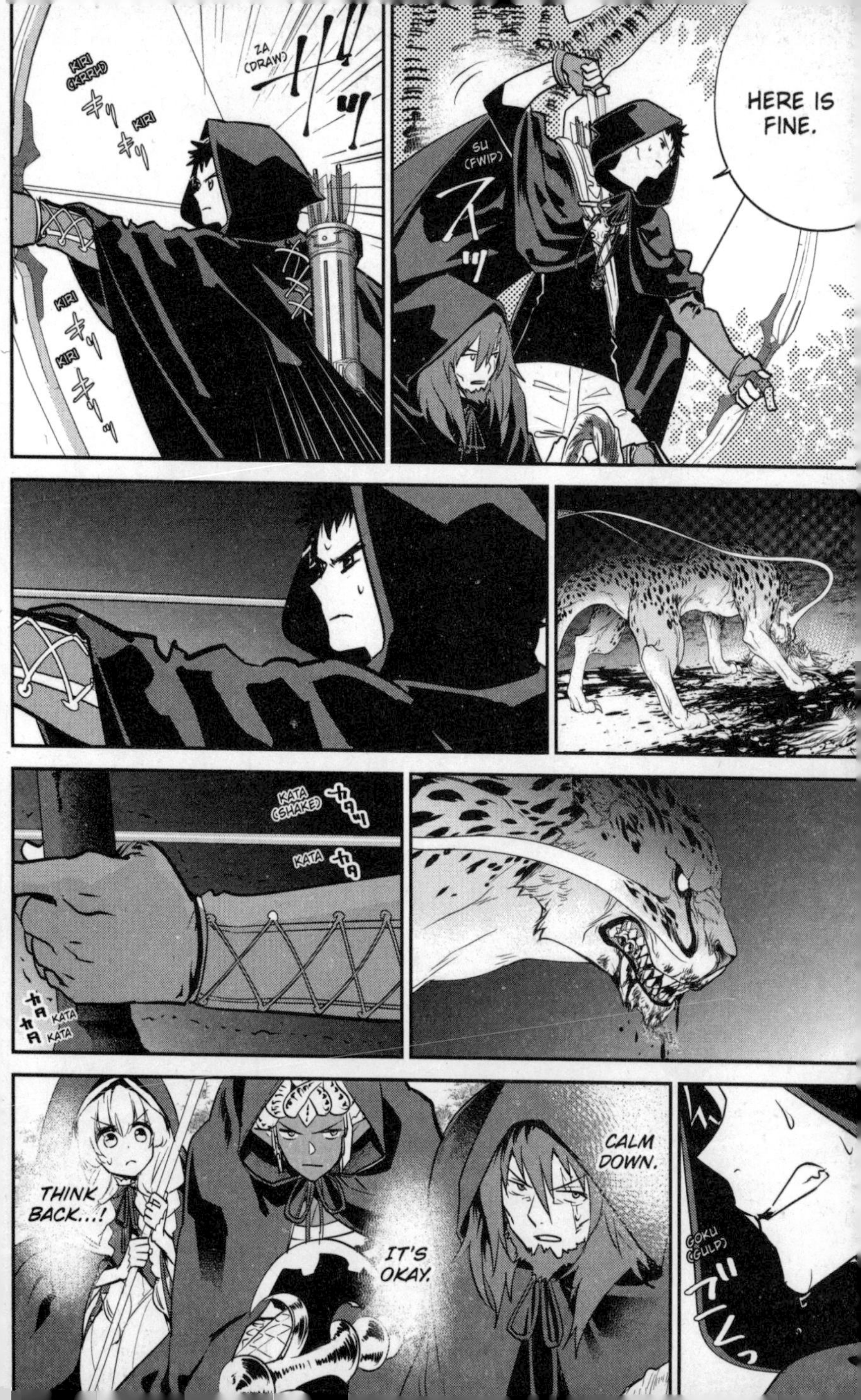

HERE IS FINE.
SU (FWIP)
ZA (DRAW)
KIRI (KRRH)
KIRI
KIRI
KIRI
KATA (SHAKE)
KATA
KATA
KATA
GOKU (GULP)
CALM DOWN.
IT'S OKAY.
THINK BACK...!

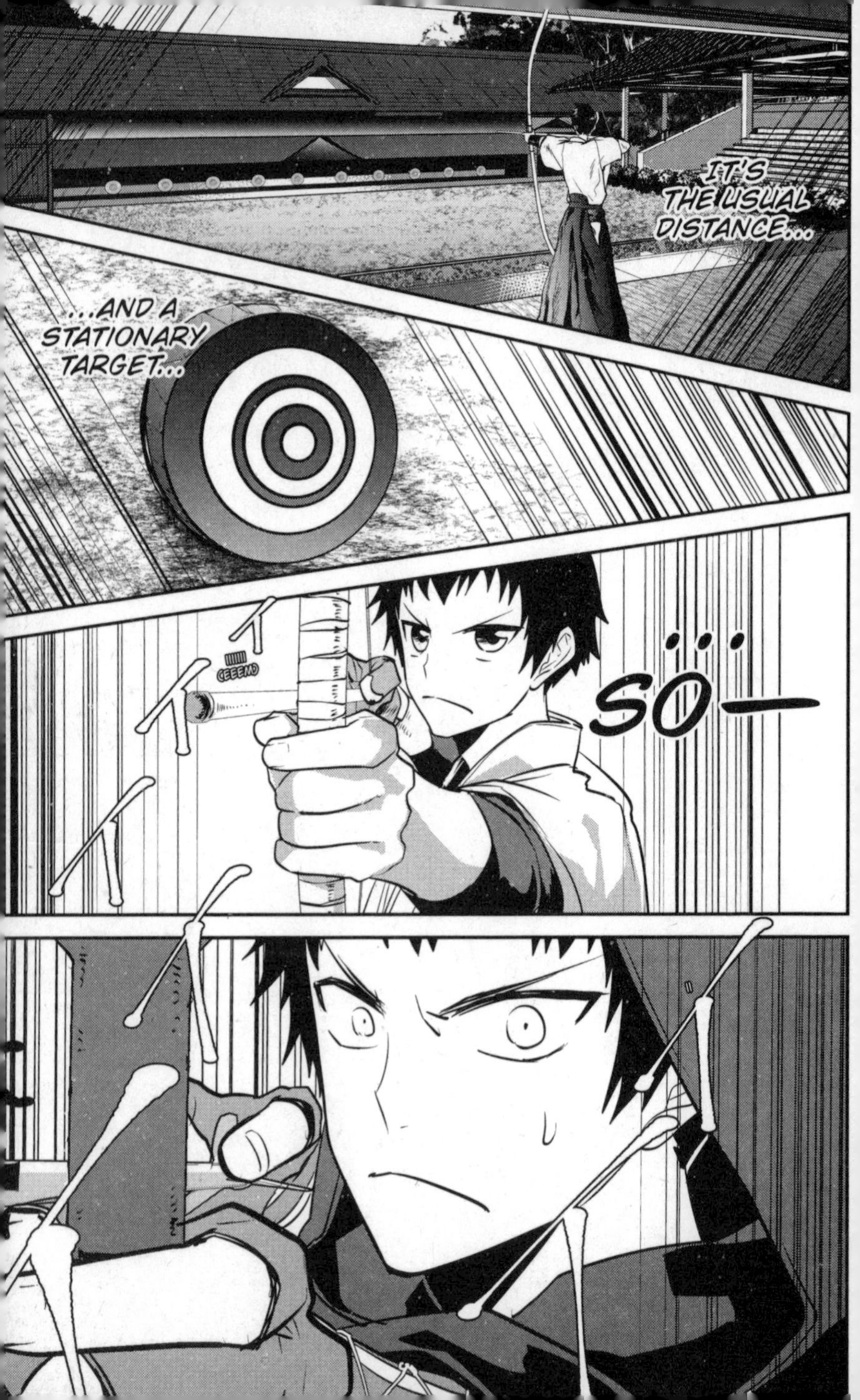
IT'S THE USUAL DISTANCE...
...AND A STATIONARY TARGET...
...SO—
(CEEEM)

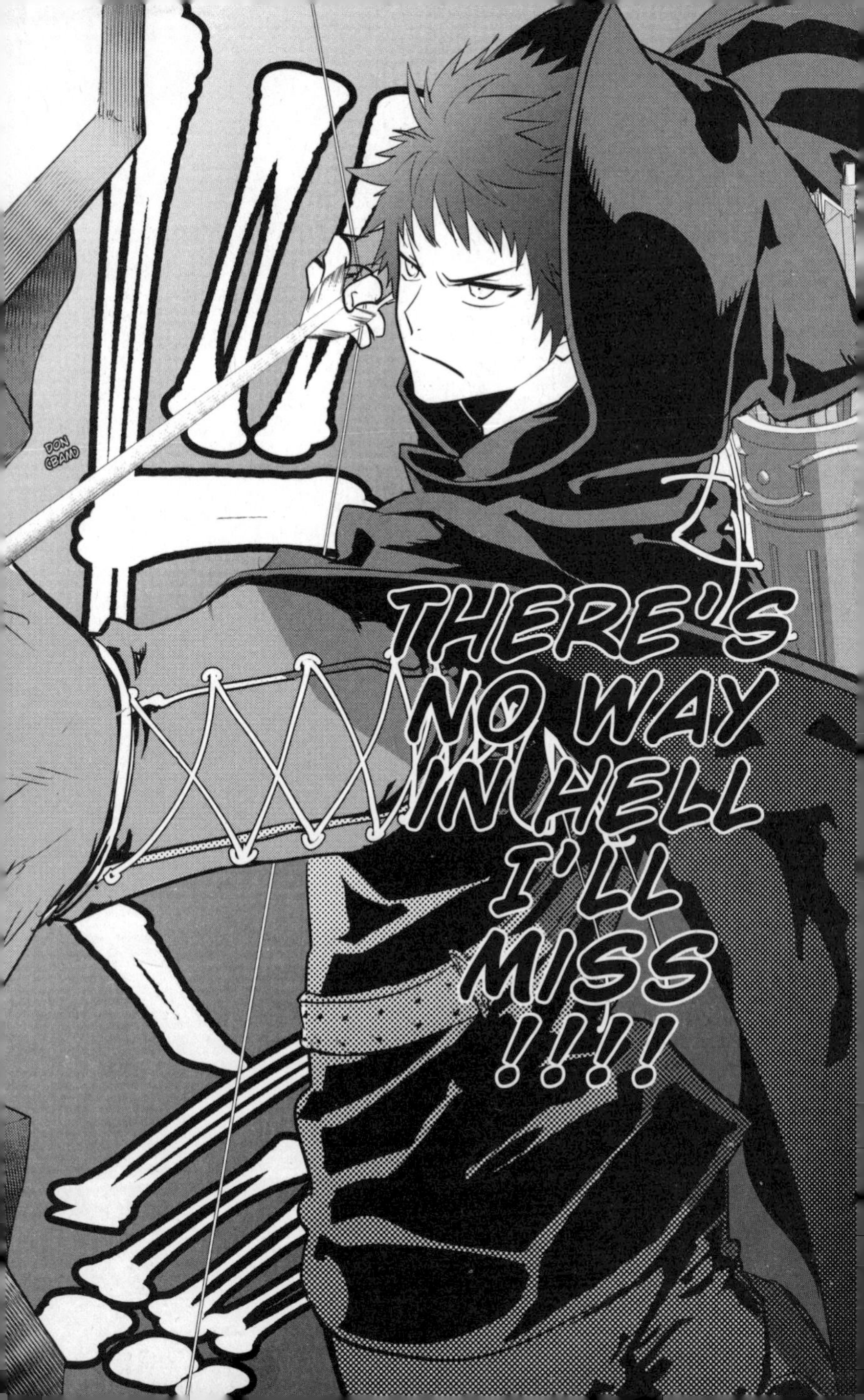
DON (BAM)
THERE'S NO WAY IN HELL I'LL MISS !!!!

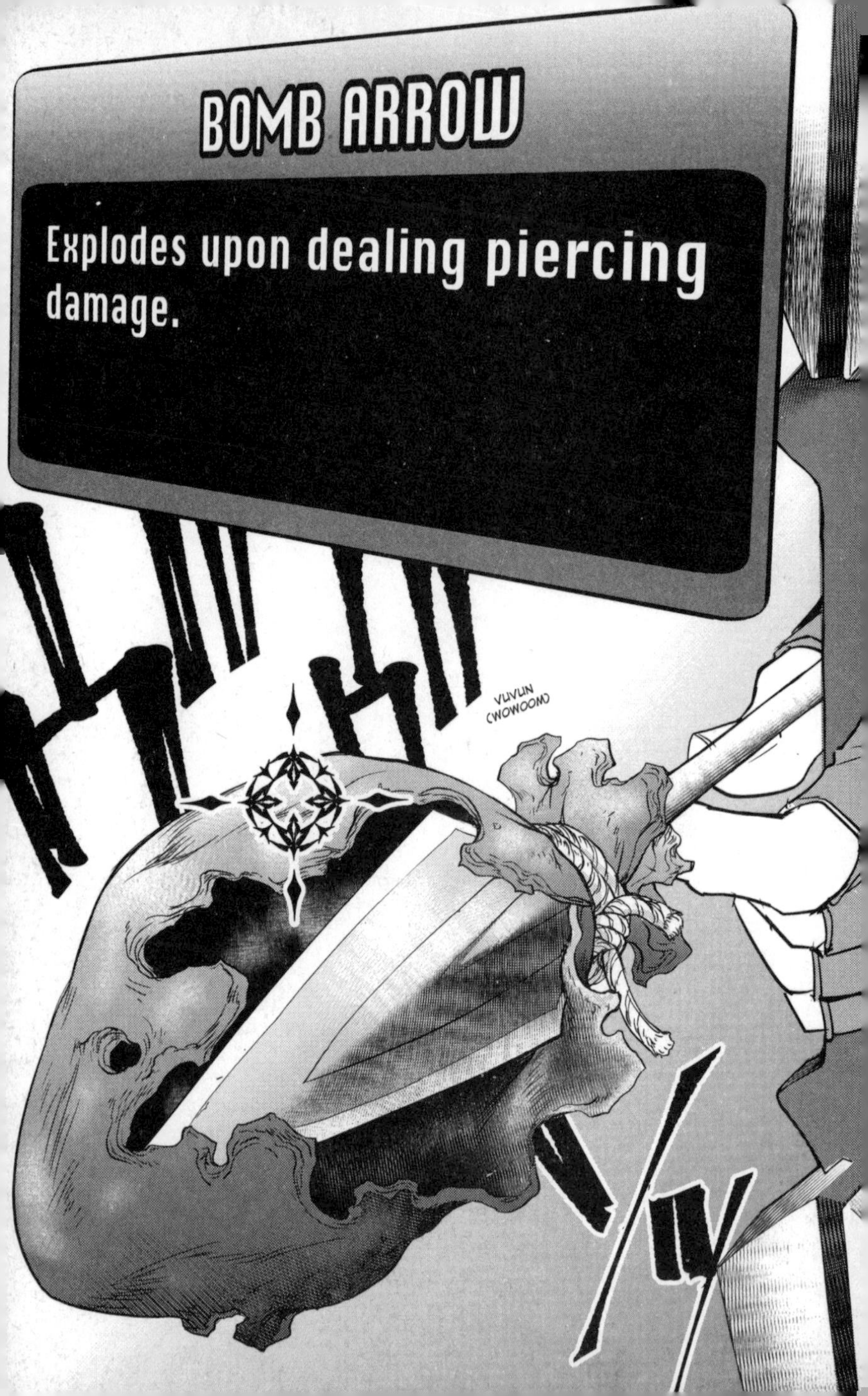
BOMB ARROW
Explodes upon dealing piercing damage.
VUVUN
(WOWOOM)

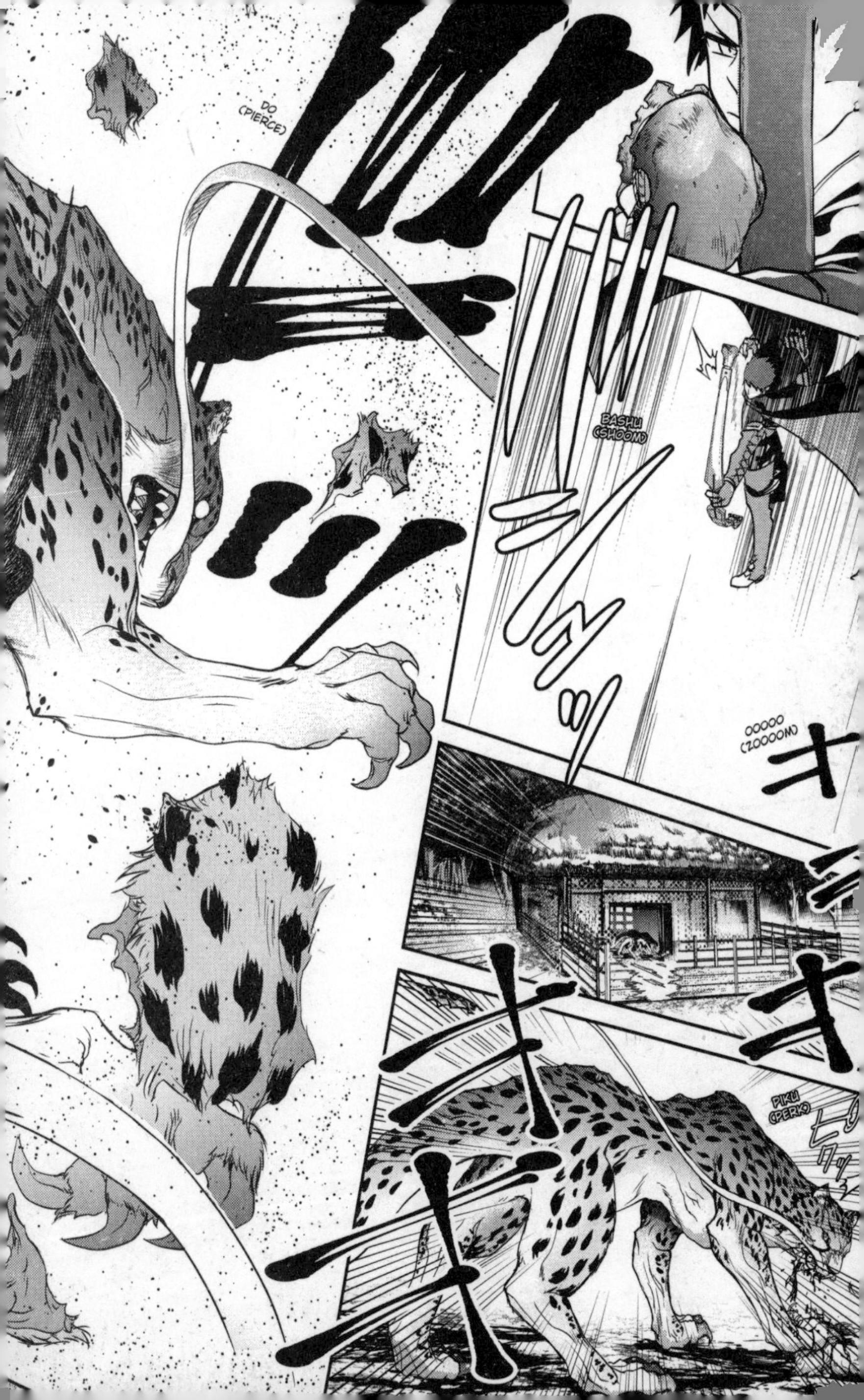
BASHU
(SHOOM)
OOOOO
(ZOOOOM)
PIKU
(PERK)
DO
(PIERCE)

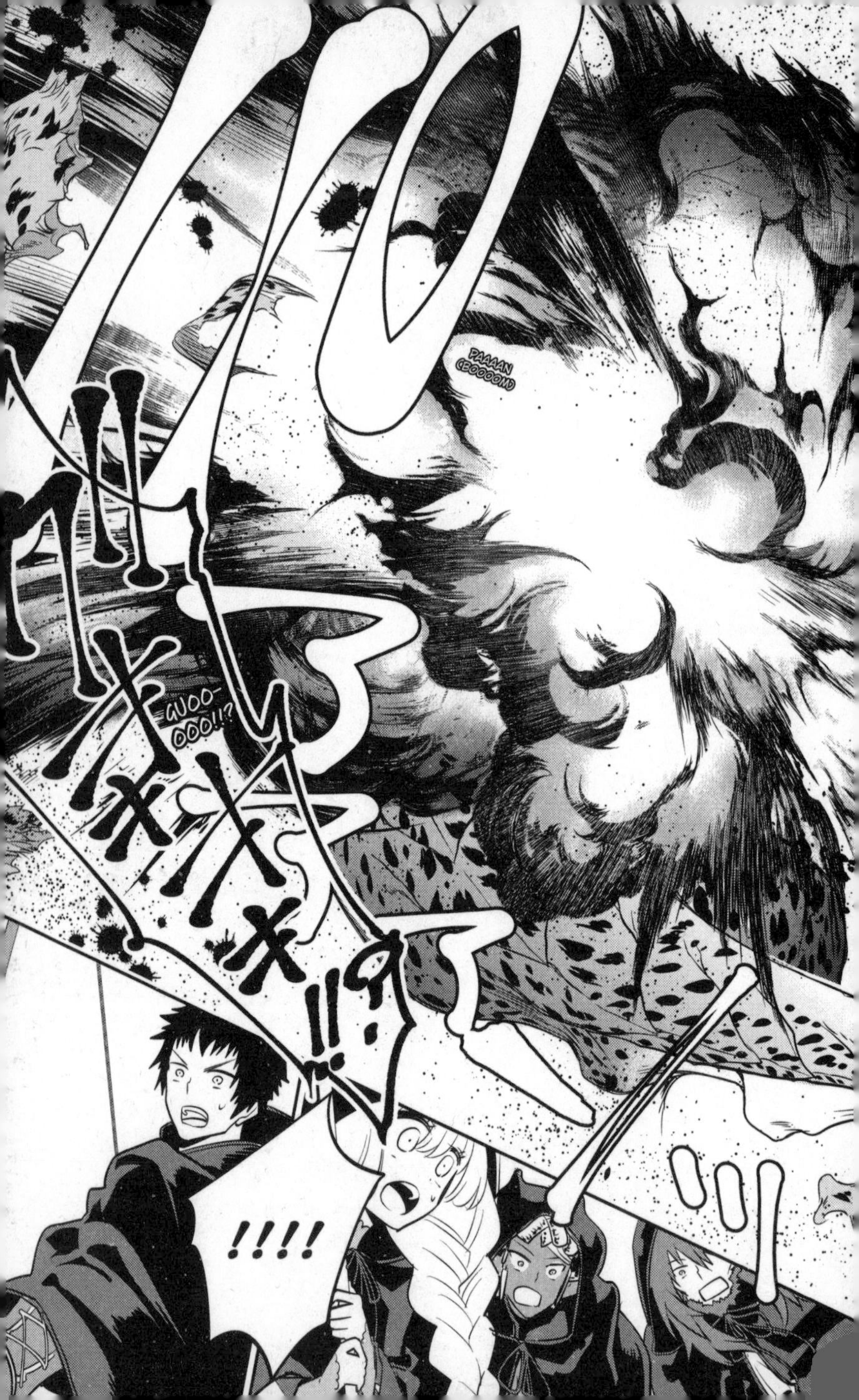
PAAAAN (BOOOOM)
GUOO-OOO!!?
!!!!

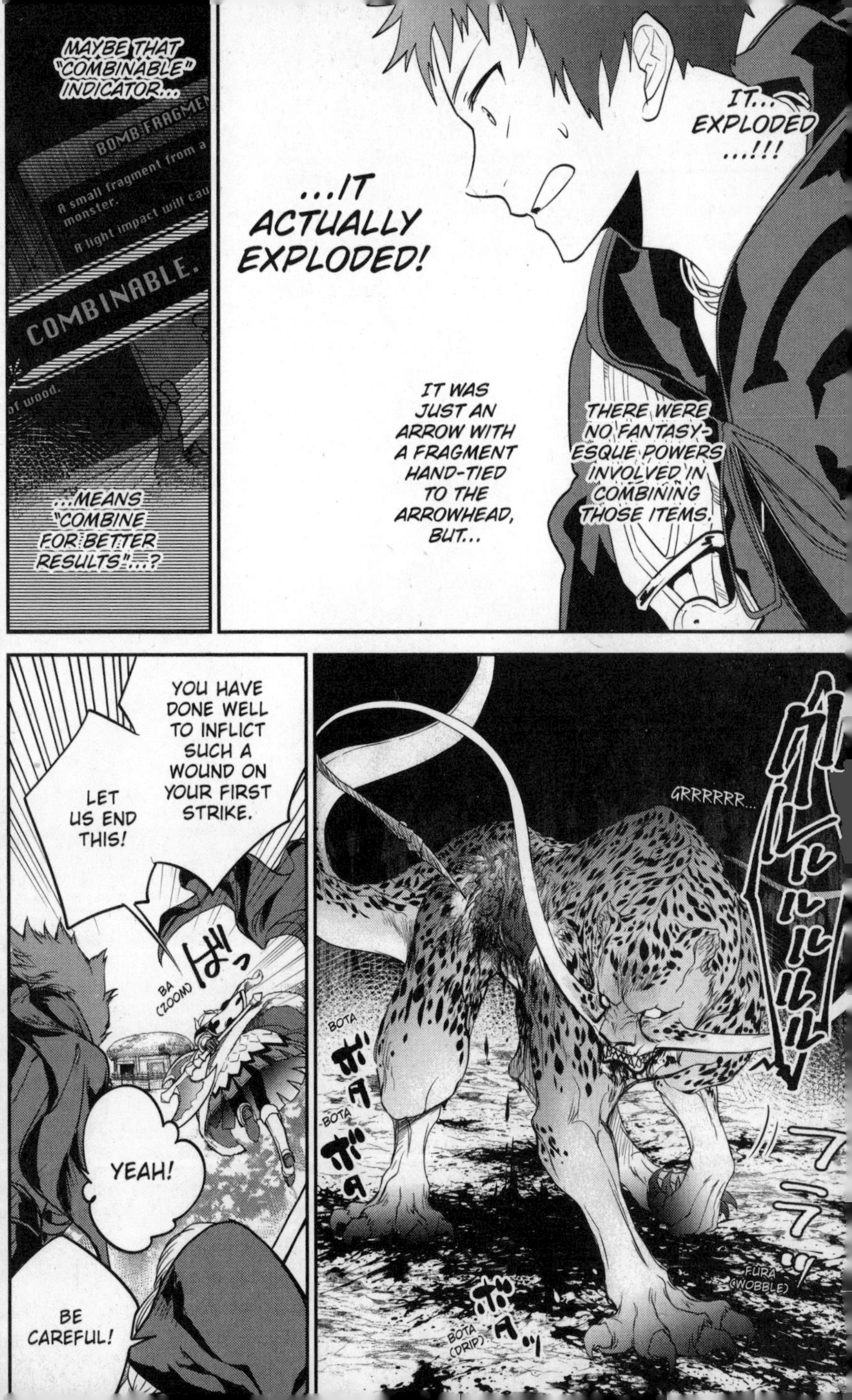
IT... EXPLODED ...!!!
...IT ACTUALLY EXPLODED!
THERE WERE NO FANTASY-ESQUE POWERS INVOLVED IN COMBINING THOSE ITEMS.
IT WAS JUST AN ARROW WITH A FRAGMENT HAND-TIED TO THE ARROWHEAD, BUT...
MAYBE THAT "COMBINABLE" INDICATOR...
BOMB FRAGMEN
A small fragment from a
monster.
A light impact will cau
COMBINABLE.
of wood.
...MEANS "COMBINE FOR BETTER RESULTS"...?
GRRRRRR...
FURA (WOBBLE)
BOTA
BOTA
BOTA (DRIP)
YOU HAVE DONE WELL TO INFLICT SUCH A WOUND ON YOUR FIRST STRIKE.
LET US END THIS!
BA (ZOOM)
YEAH!
BE CAREFUL!

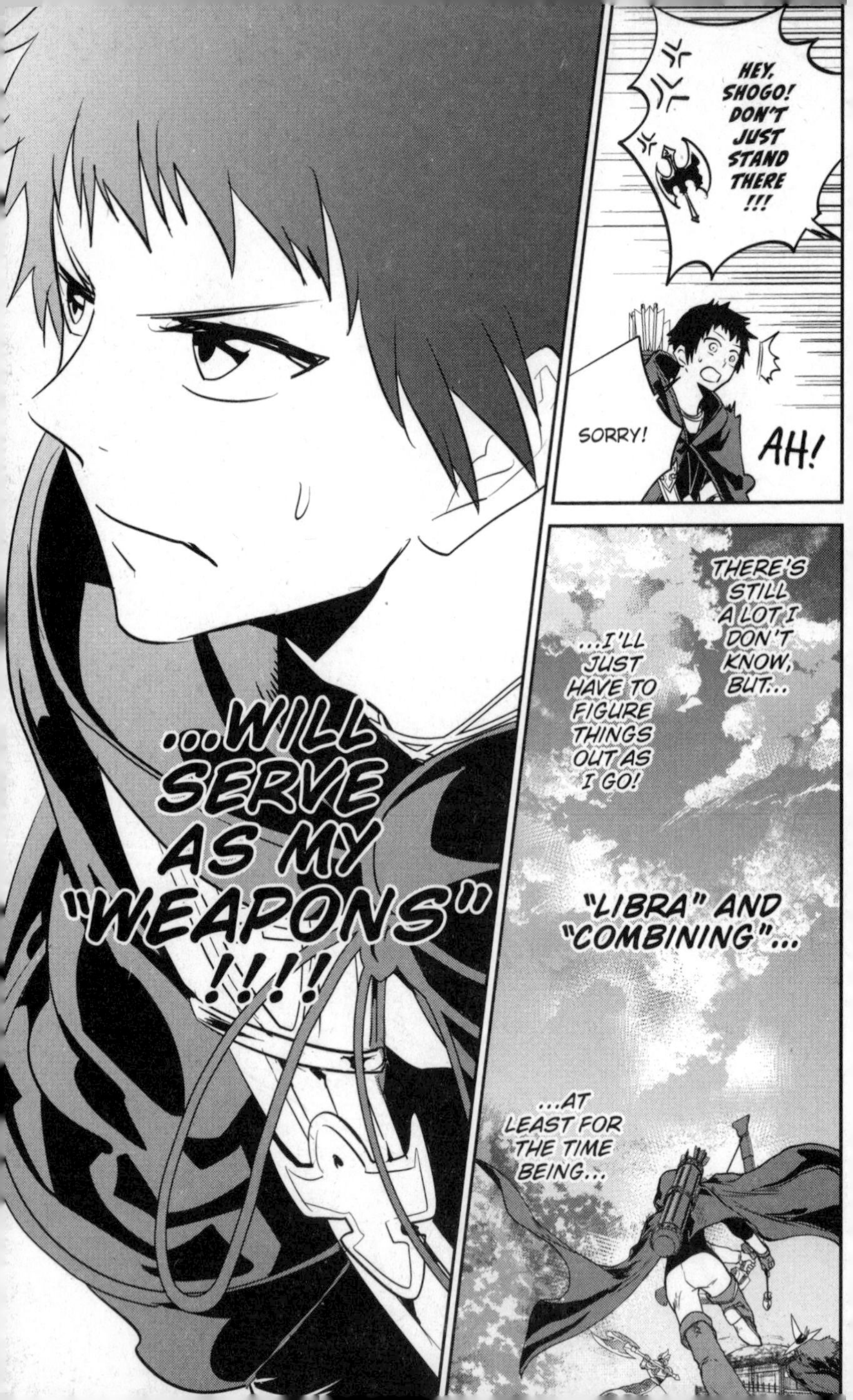
HEY, SHOGO! DON'T JUST STAND THERE !!!
AH!
SORRY!
THERE'S STILL A LOT I DON'T KNOW, BUT...
...I'LL JUST HAVE TO FIGURE THINGS OUT AS I GO!
"LIBRA" AND "COMBINING"...
...AT LEAST FOR THE TIME BEING...
...WILL SERVE AS MY "WEAPONS" !!!!

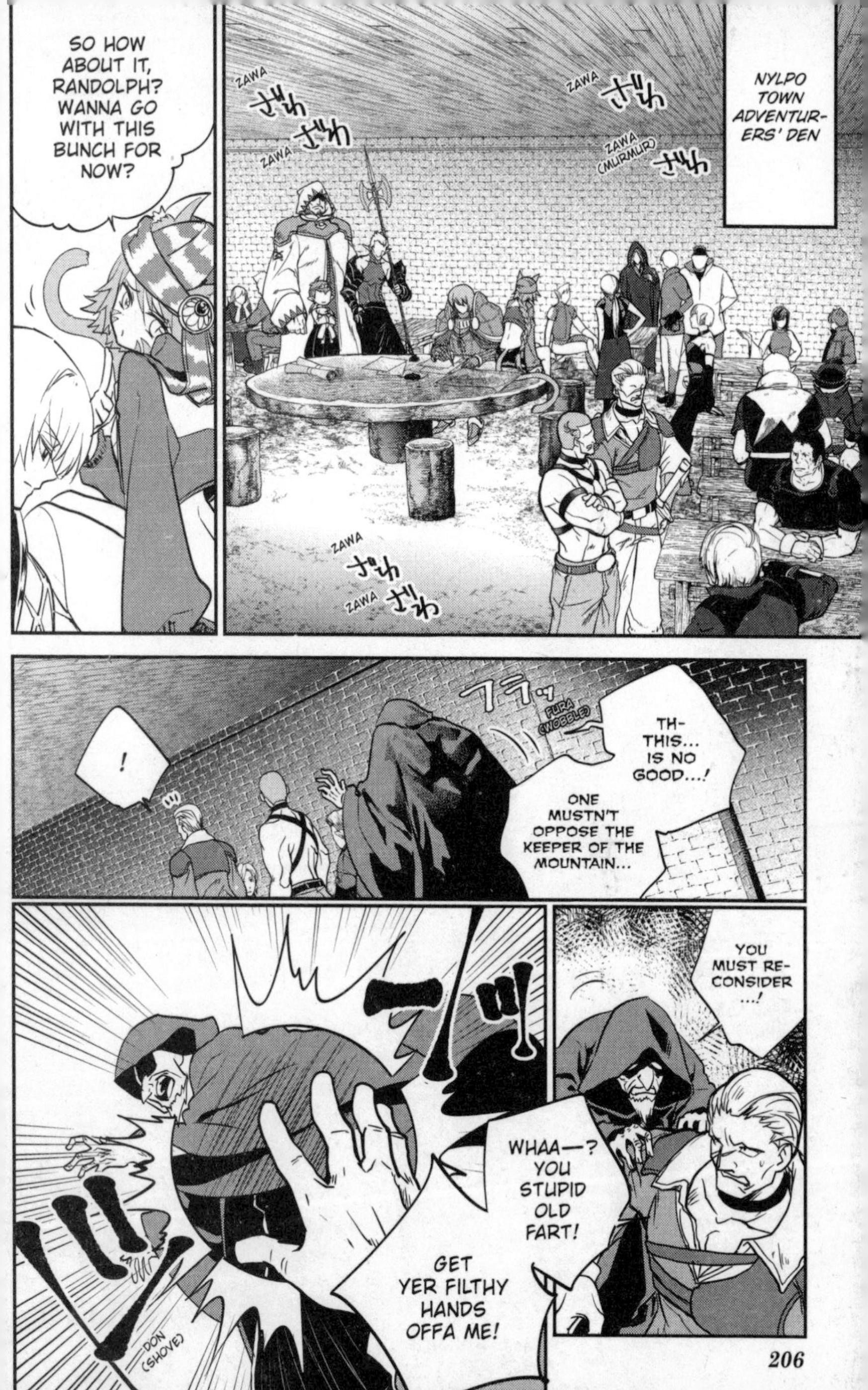

NYLPO TOWN ADVENTURERS' DEN
ZAWA ざわ
ZAWA (MURMUR) ざわ
ZAWA ざわ
ZAWA ざわ
ZAWA ざわ
ZAWA ざわ
SO HOW ABOUT IT, RANDOLPH? WANNA GO WITH THIS BUNCH FOR NOW?
TH-THIS... IS NO GOOD...!
ONE MUSTN'T OPPOSE THE KEEPER OF THE MOUNTAIN...
FURA (WOBBLE)
!
YOU MUST RE-CONSIDER ...!
WHAA—? YOU STUPID OLD FART!
GET YER FILTHY HANDS OFFA ME!
DON (SHOVE)

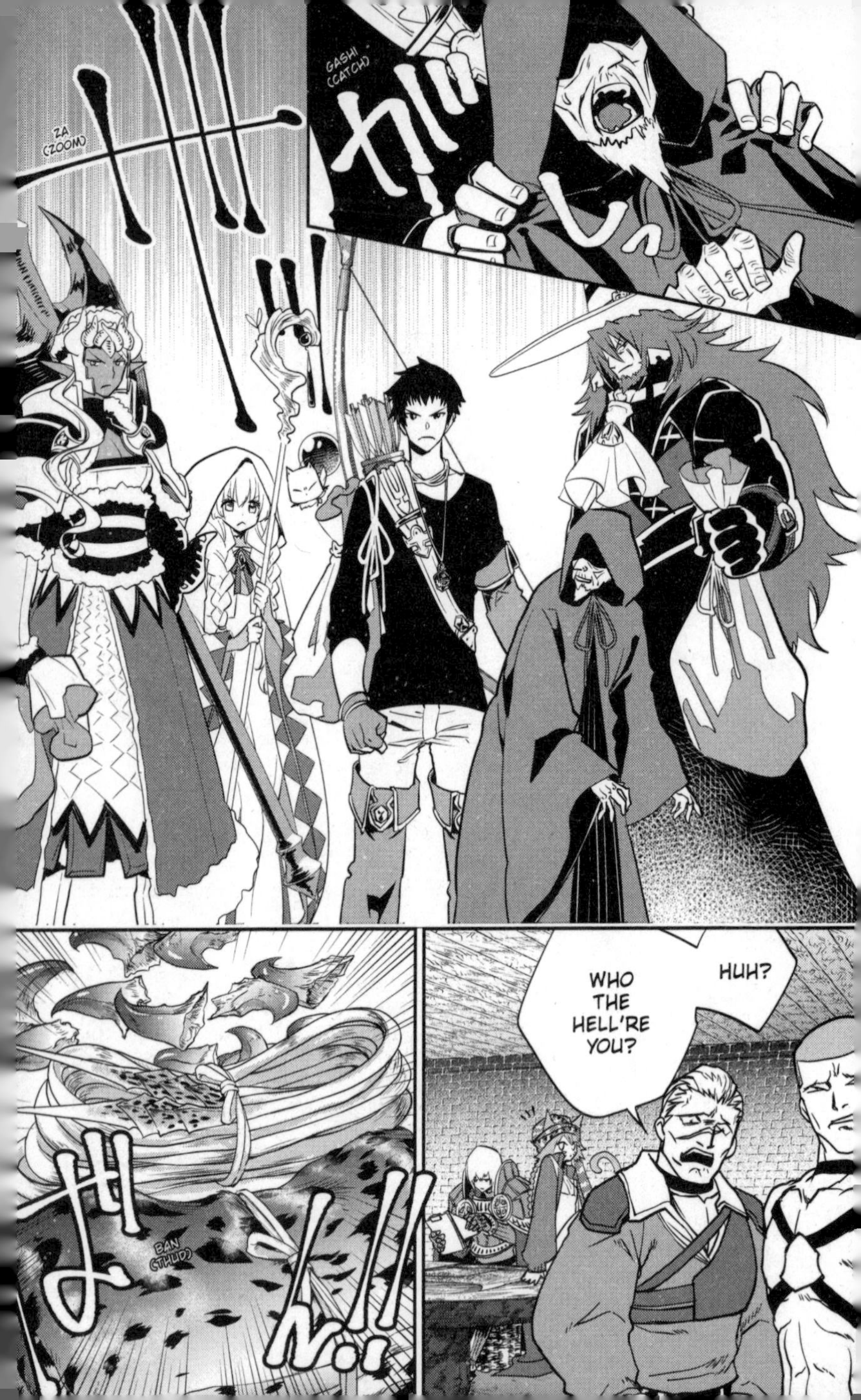
GASHI (CATCH)
ZA (ZOOM)
HUH?
WHO THE HELL'RE YOU?
BAN (THUD)

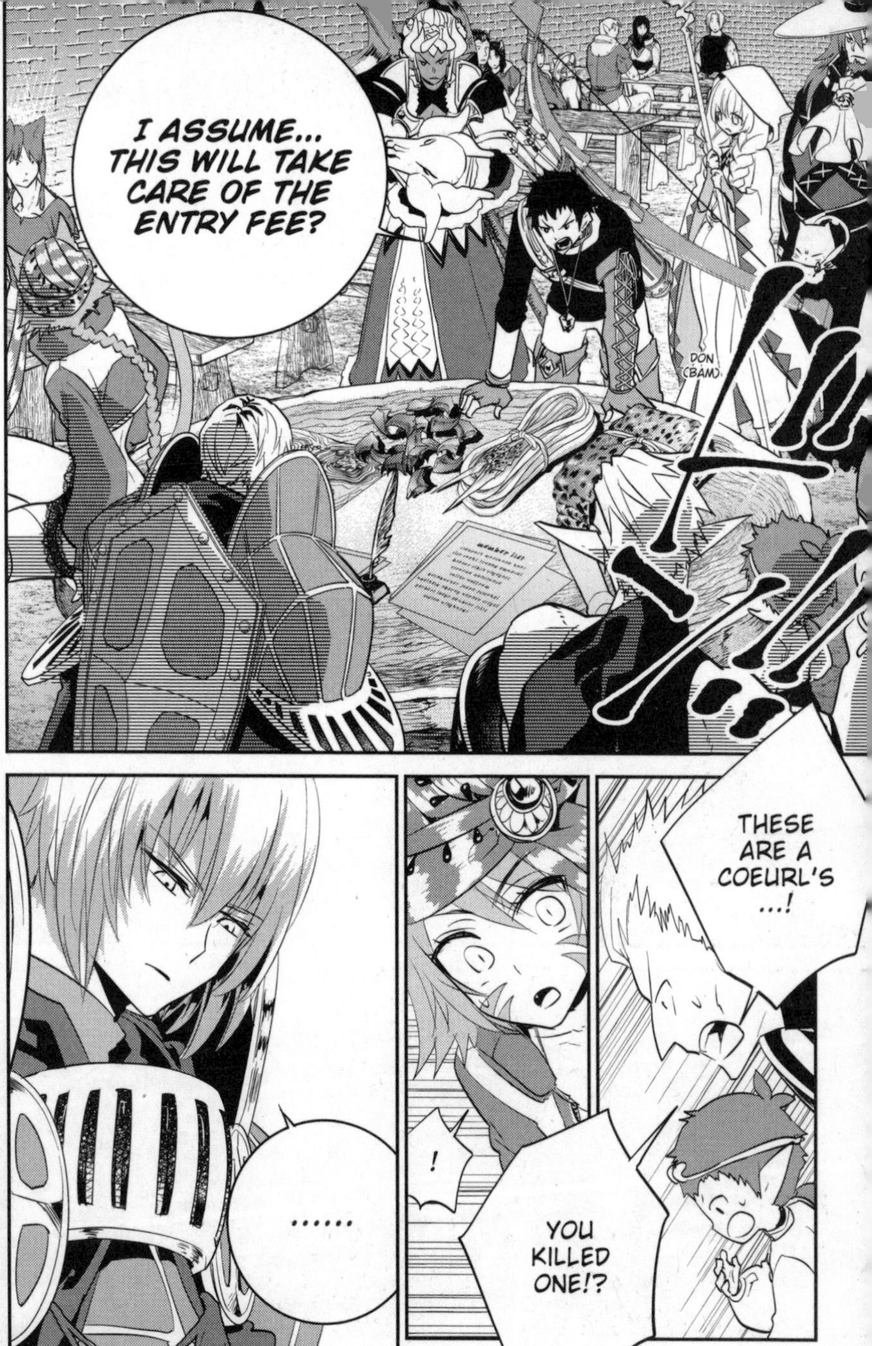
DON (BAM)
I ASSUME... THIS WILL TAKE CARE OF THE ENTRY FEE?
THESE ARE A COEURL'S ...!
YOU KILLED ONE!?
!
......

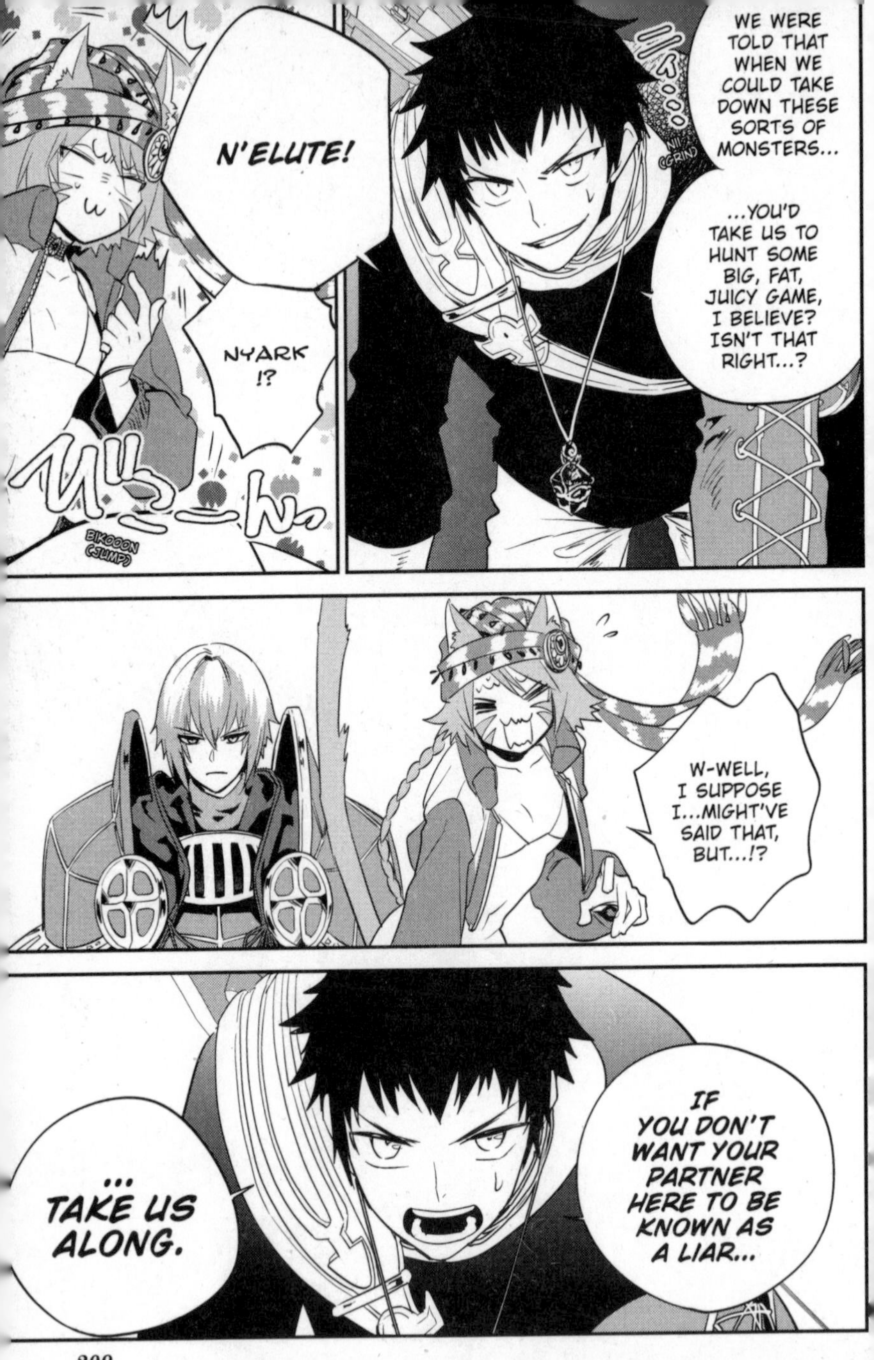
NII (GRIN)
WE WERE TOLD THAT WHEN WE COULD TAKE DOWN THESE SORTS OF MONSTERS...
...YOU'D TAKE US TO HUNT SOME BIG, FAT, JUICY GAME, I BELIEVE? ISN'T THAT RIGHT...?
N'ELUTE!
NYARK !?
BIKOOON (JUMP)
W-WELL, I SUPPOSE I...MIGHT'VE SAID THAT, BUT...!?
IF YOU DON'T WANT YOUR PARTNER HERE TO BE KNOWN AS A LIAR...
... TAKE US ALONG.

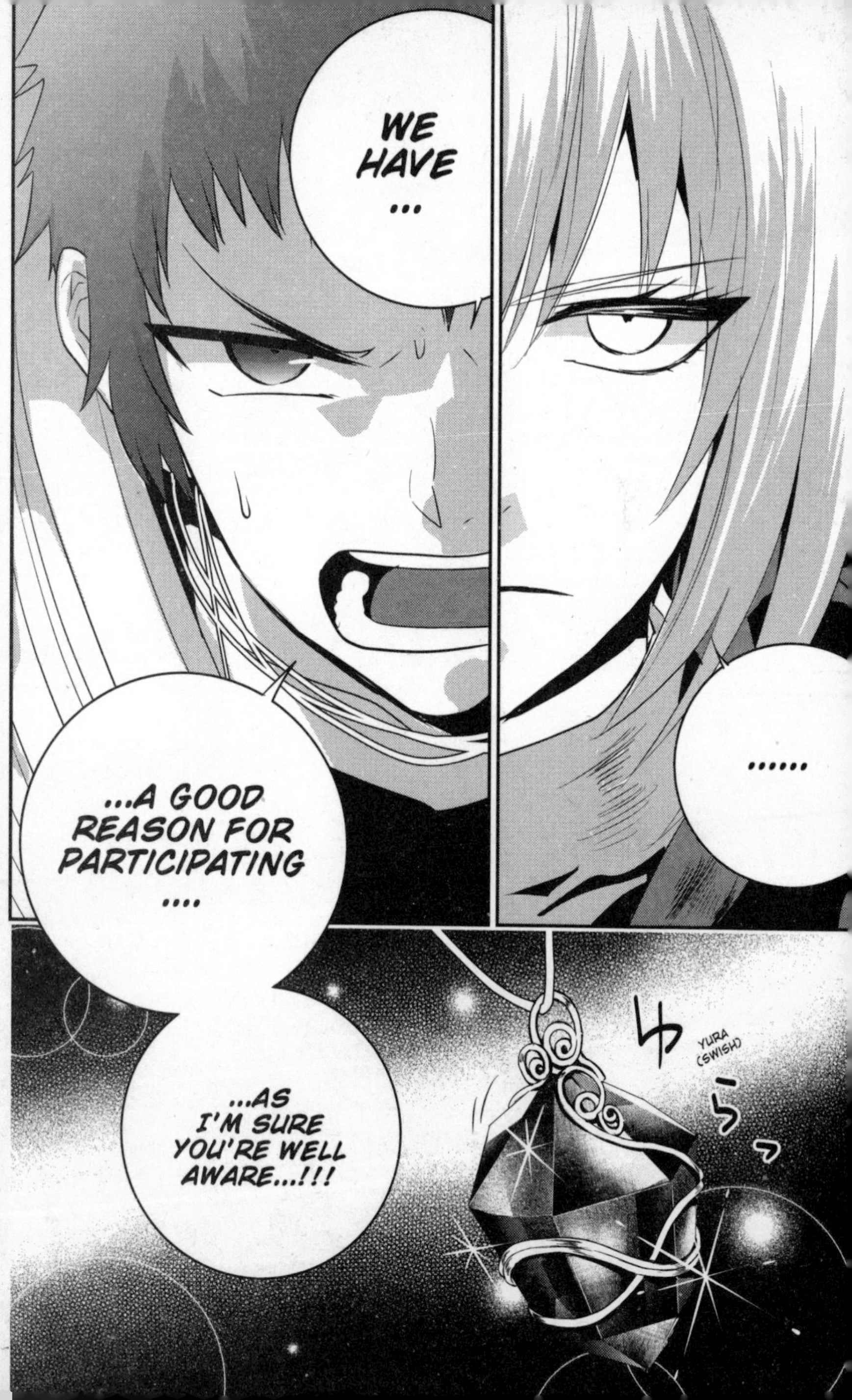
......
WE HAVE ...
...A GOOD REASON FOR PARTICIPATING ....
ゆらっ
YURA (SWISH)
...AS I'M SURE YOU'RE WELL AWARE...!!!

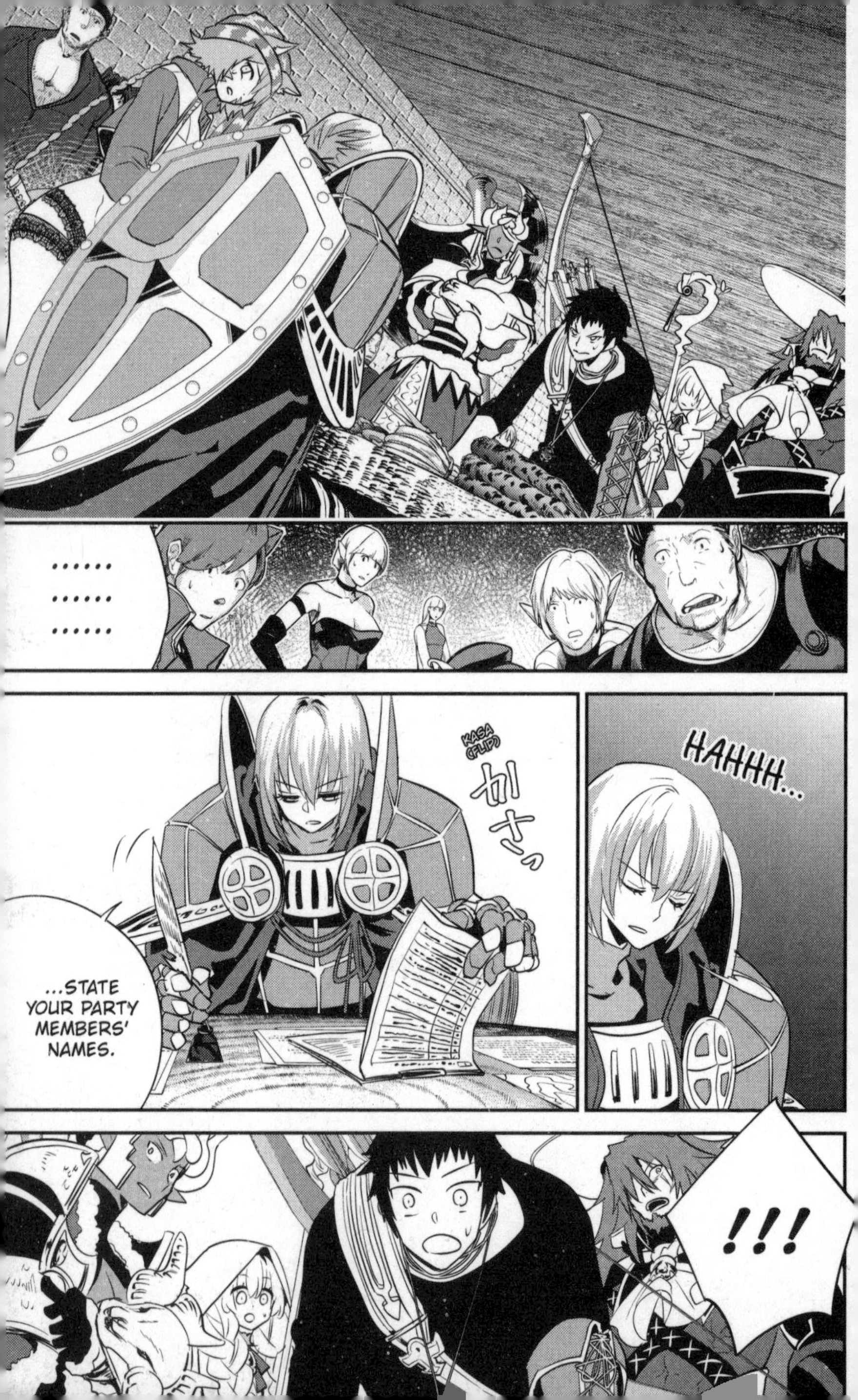
......
......
......
HAHHH...
KASA (FLIP)
カさっ
...STATE YOUR PARTY MEMBERS' NAMES.
!!!

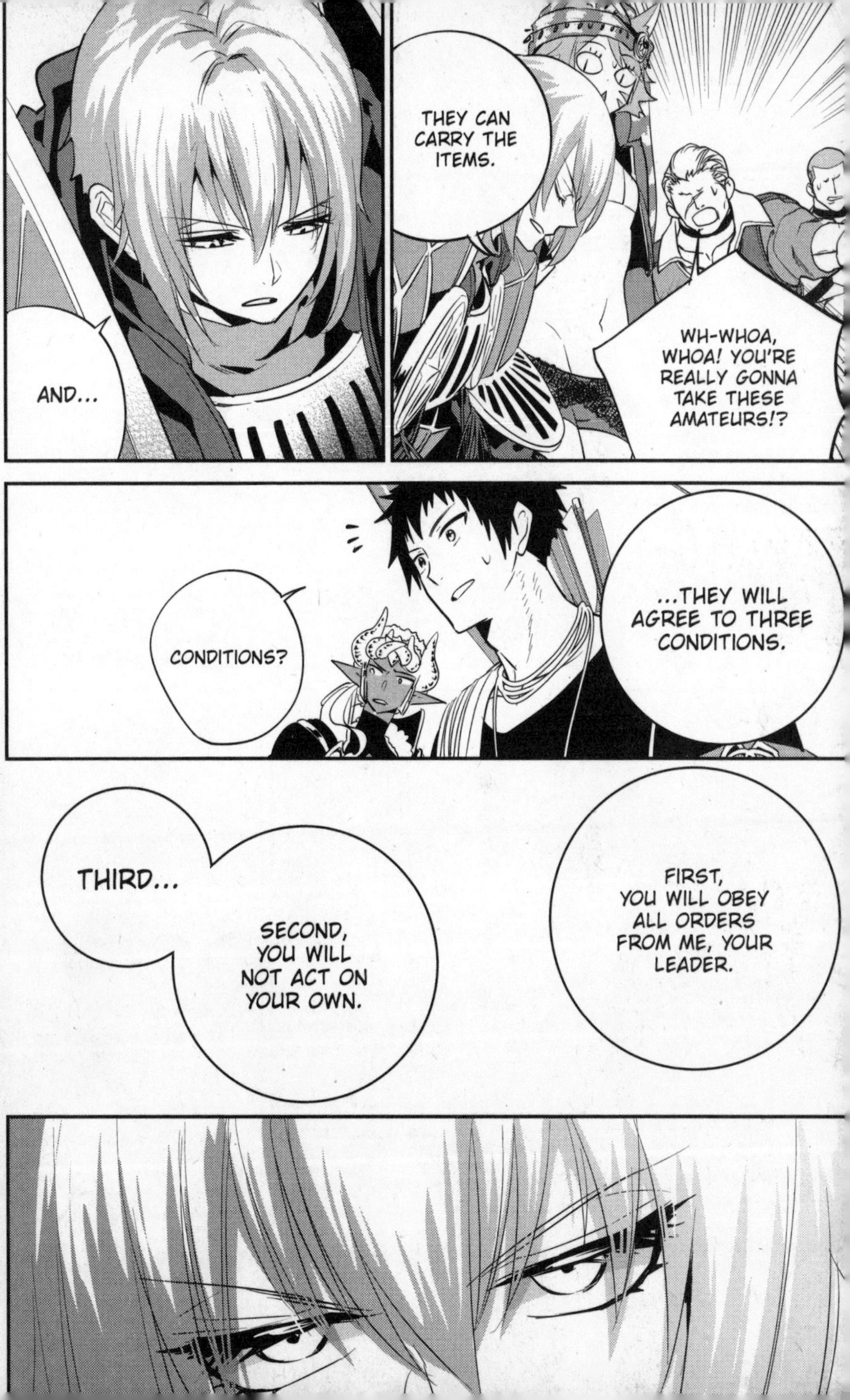
THEY CAN CARRY THE ITEMS.
WH-WHOA, WHOA! YOU'RE REALLY GONNA TAKE THESE AMATEURS!?
AND...
...THEY WILL AGREE TO THREE CONDITIONS.
CONDITIONS?
FIRST, YOU WILL OBEY ALL ORDERS FROM ME, YOUR LEADER.
SECOND, YOU WILL NOT ACT ON YOUR OWN.
THIRD...

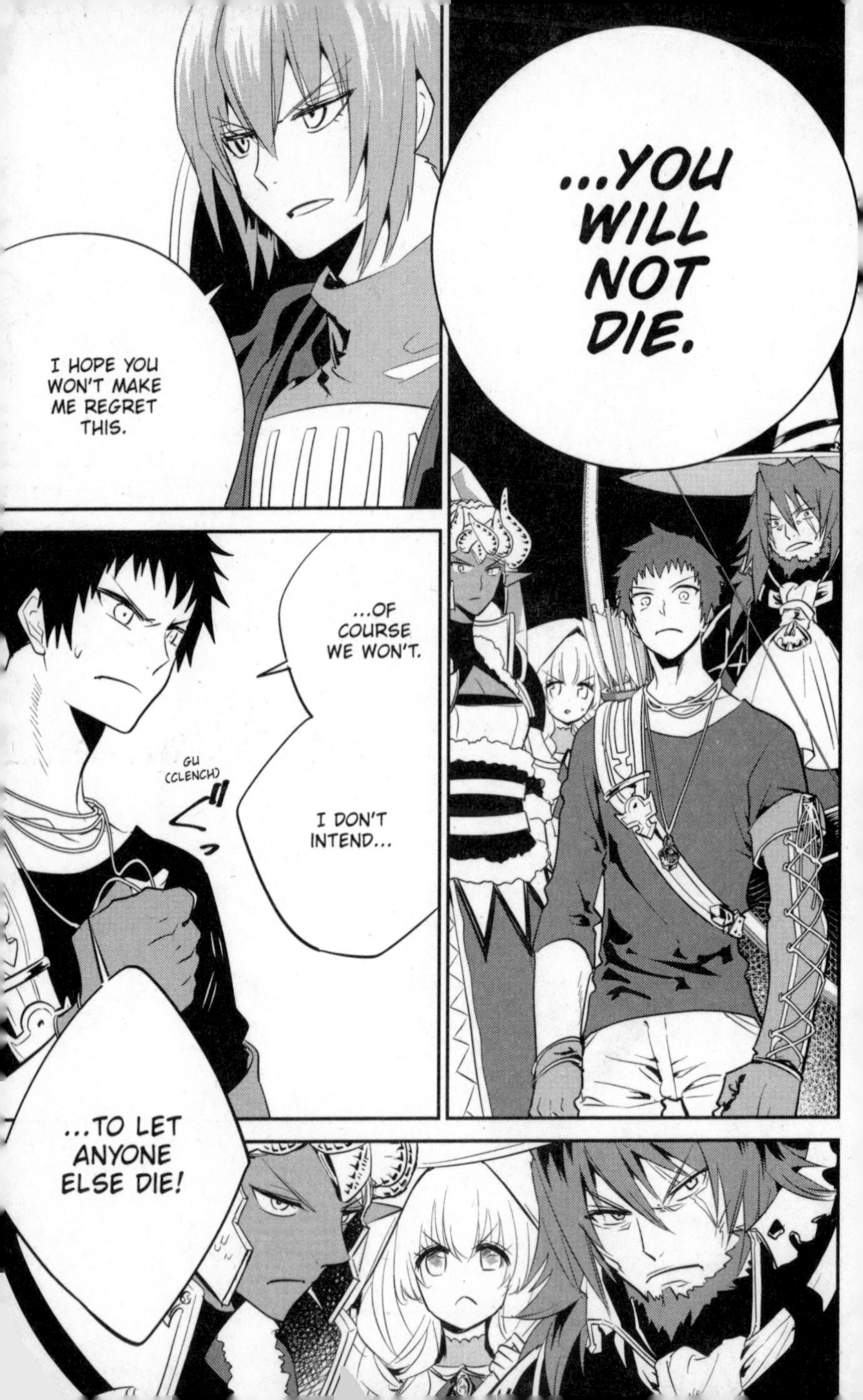
...YOU WILL NOT DIE.
I HOPE YOU WON'T MAKE ME REGRET THIS.
...OF COURSE WE WON'T.
GU (CLENCH)
I DON'T INTEND...
...TO LET ANYONE ELSE DIE!

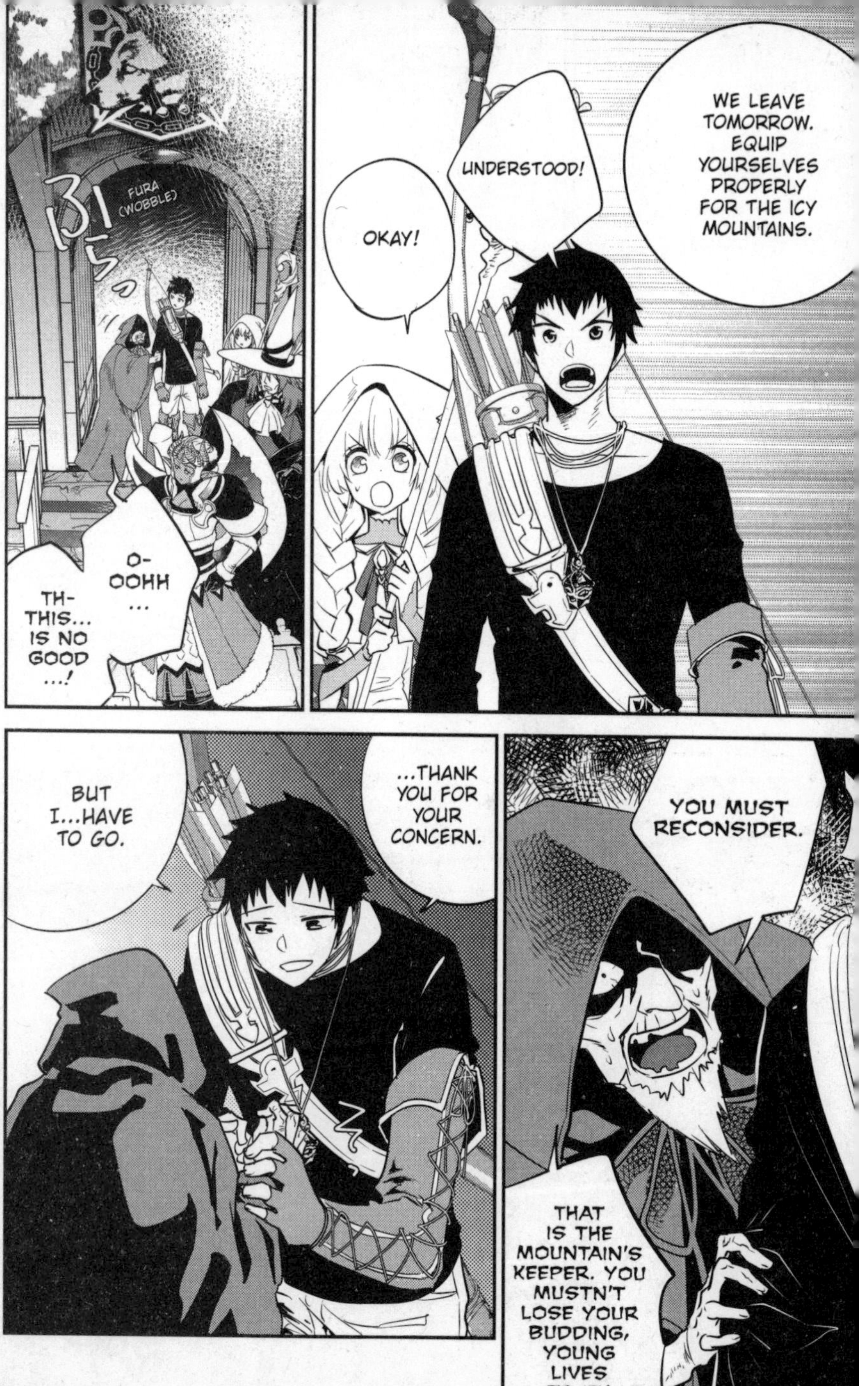
WE LEAVE TOMORROW. EQUIP YOURSELVES PROPERLY FOR THE ICY MOUNTAINS.
UNDERSTOOD!
OKAY!
FURA (WOBBLE)
O-OOHH...
TH-THIS... IS NO GOOD...!
YOU MUST RECONSIDER.
THAT IS THE MOUNTAIN'S KEEPER. YOU MUSTN'T LOSE YOUR BUDDING, YOUNG LIVES TO IT!
...THANK YOU FOR YOUR CONCERN.
BUT I...HAVE TO GO.

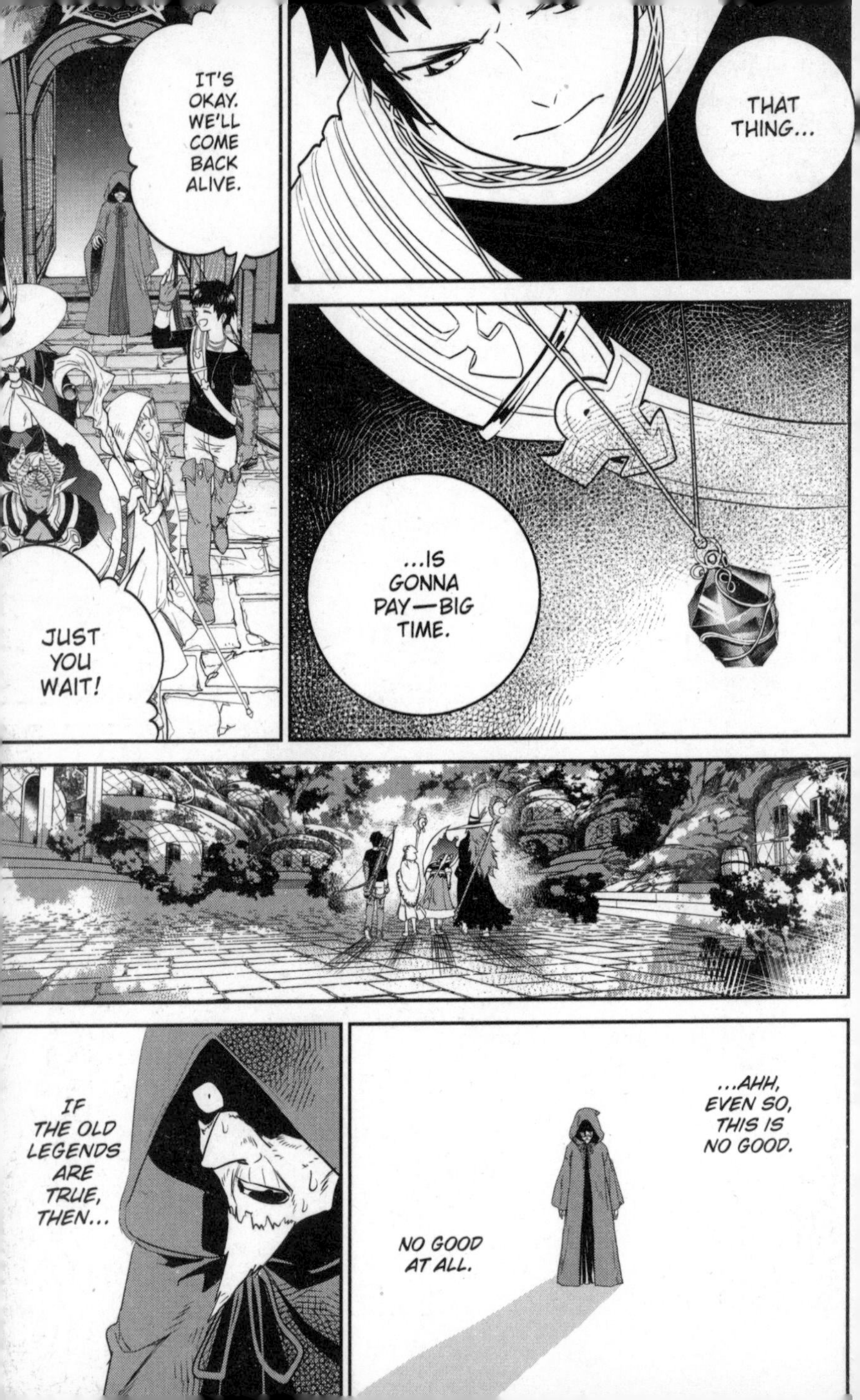
THAT THING...
...IS GONNA PAY—BIG TIME.
IT'S OKAY. WE'LL COME BACK ALIVE.
JUST YOU WAIT!
...AHH, EVEN SO, THIS IS NO GOOD.
NO GOOD AT ALL.
IF THE OLD LEGENDS ARE TRUE, THEN...

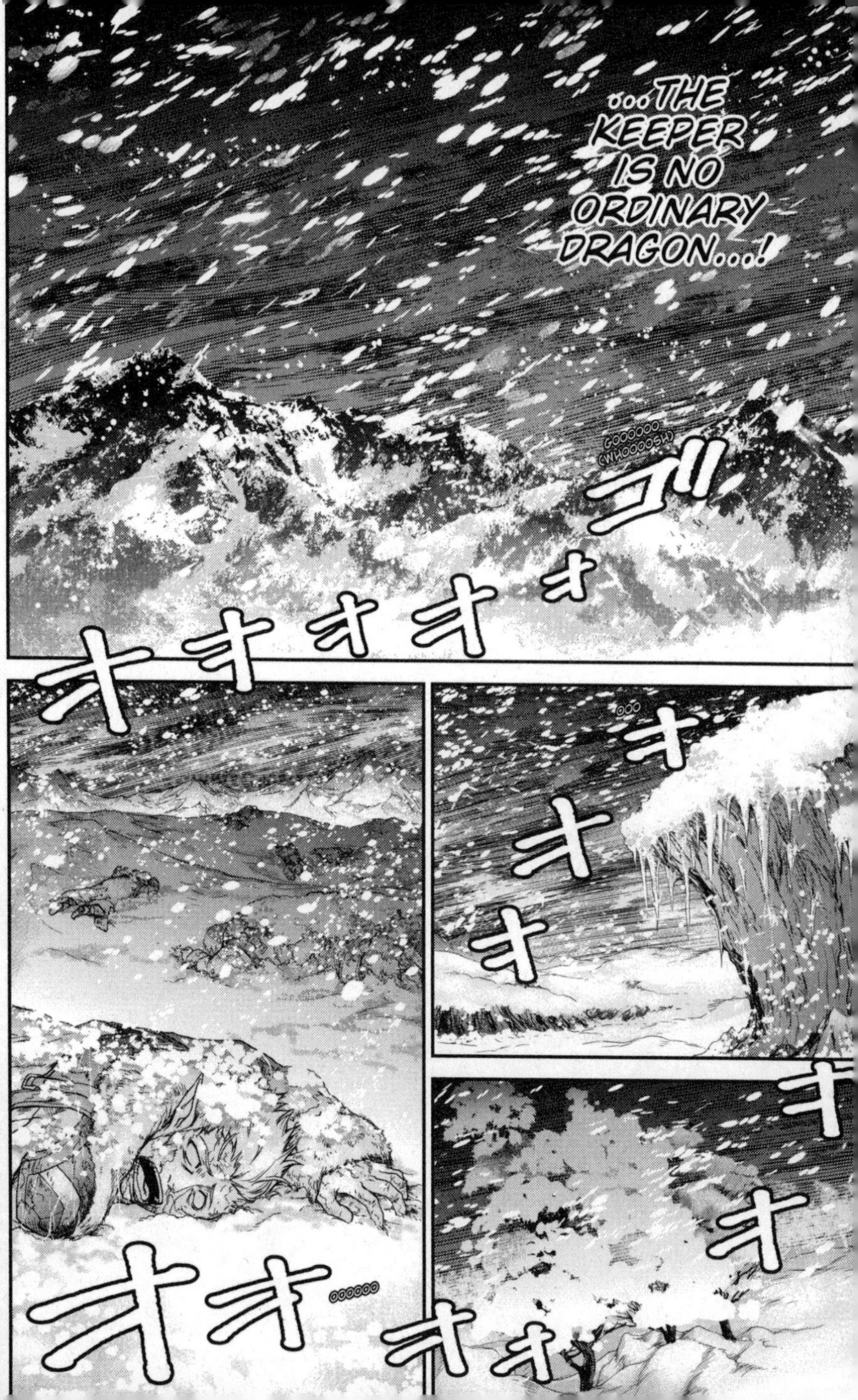
...THE KEEPER IS NO ORDINARY DRAGON...!
GOOOOOO (WHOOOOSH)
OOO
OOOOOO

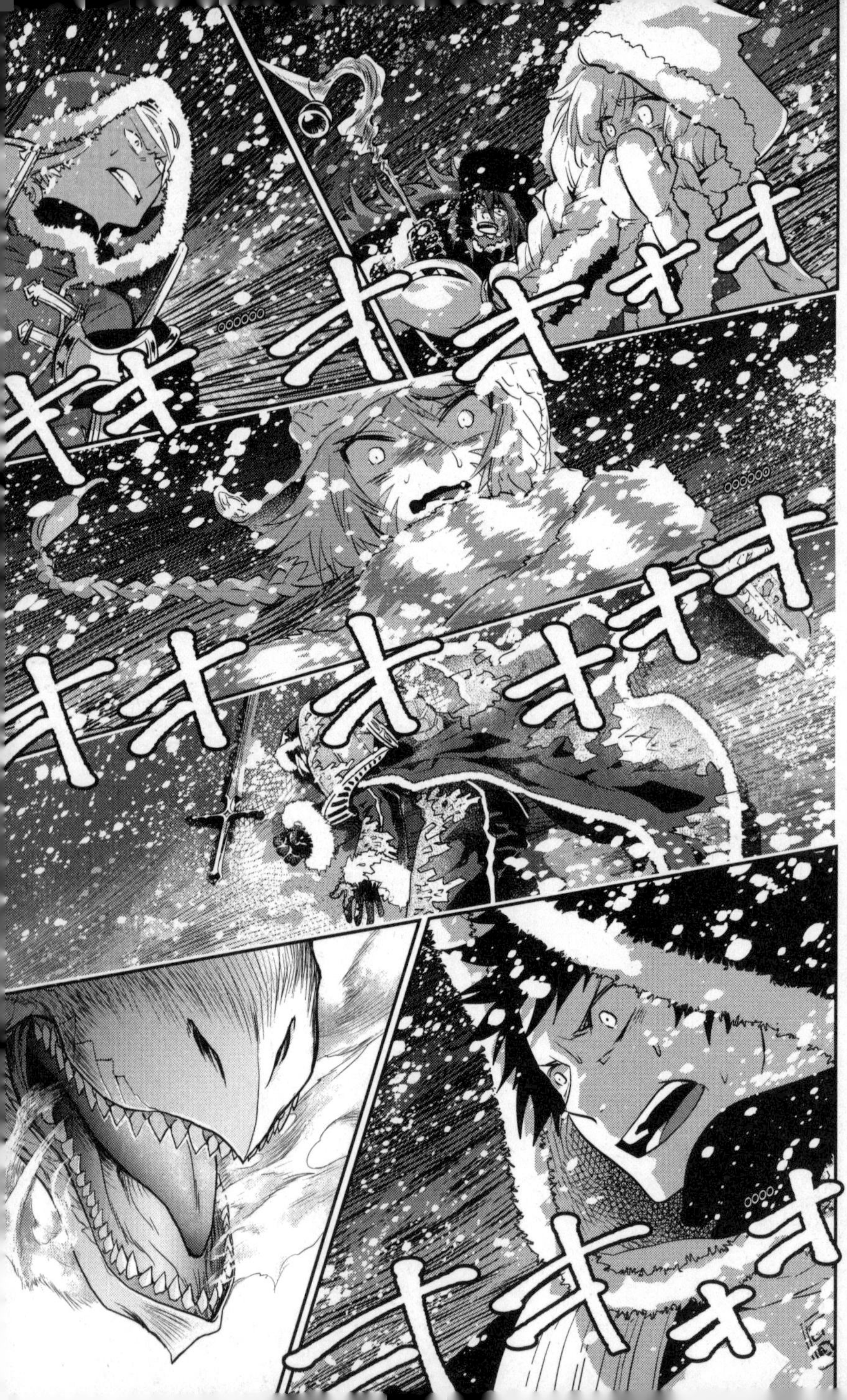

オオオオオ
OOOOOO
オオ
OOOOOO
オオオオオオオオ
OOOO
オオオオ

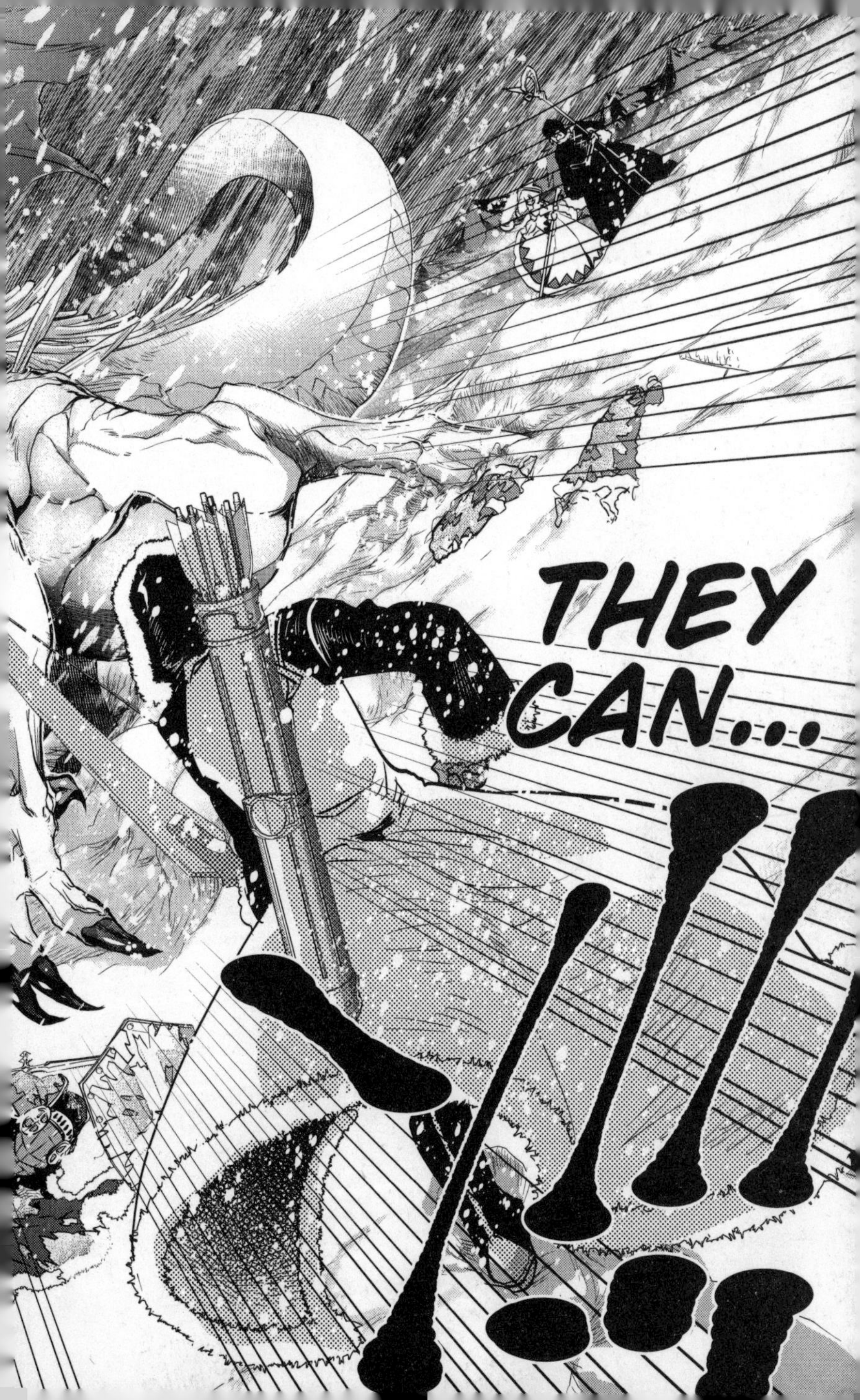
THEY CAN...
!!

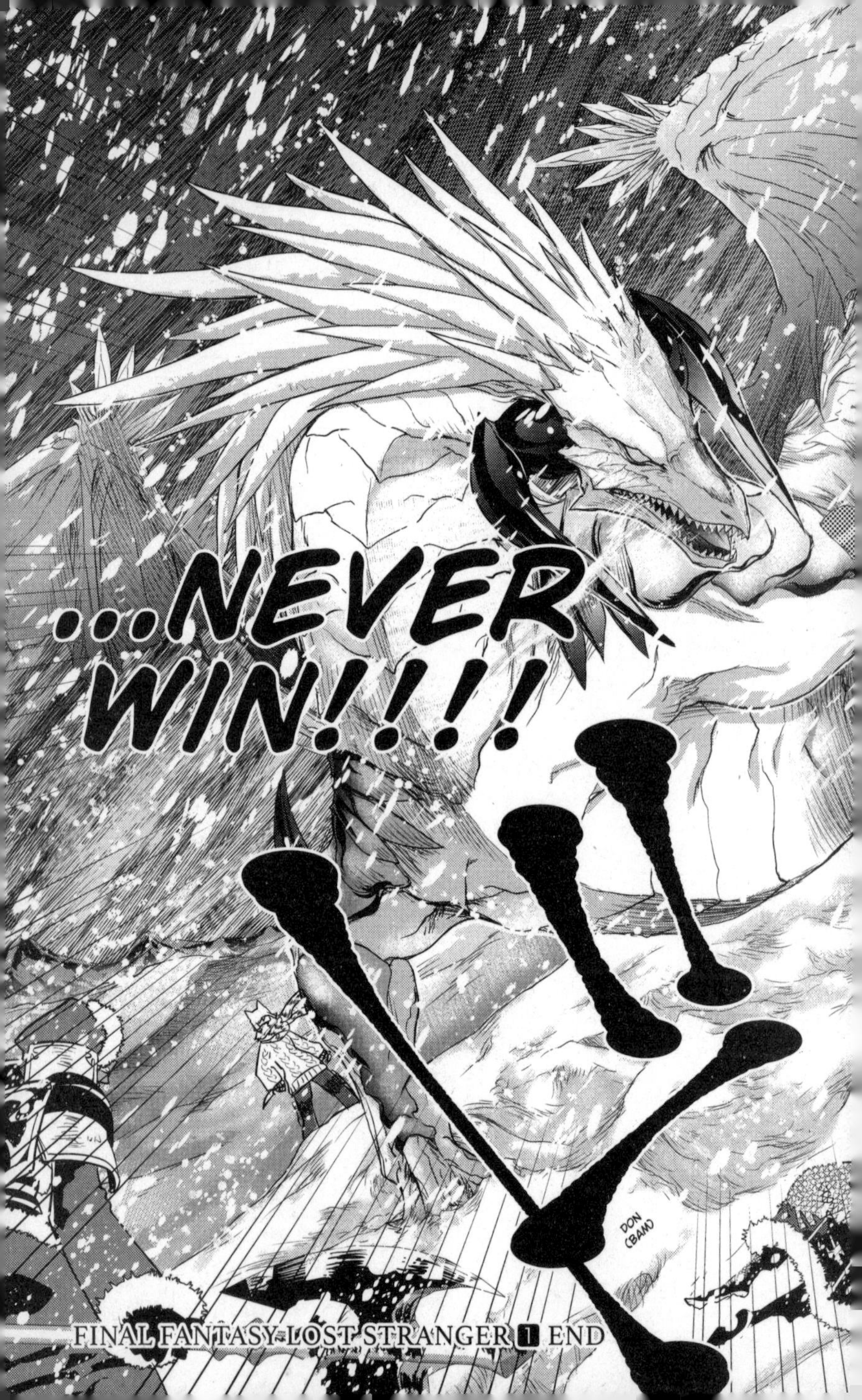
...NEVER WIN!!!!
DON (BAM)
FINAL FANTASY LOST STRANGER 1 END

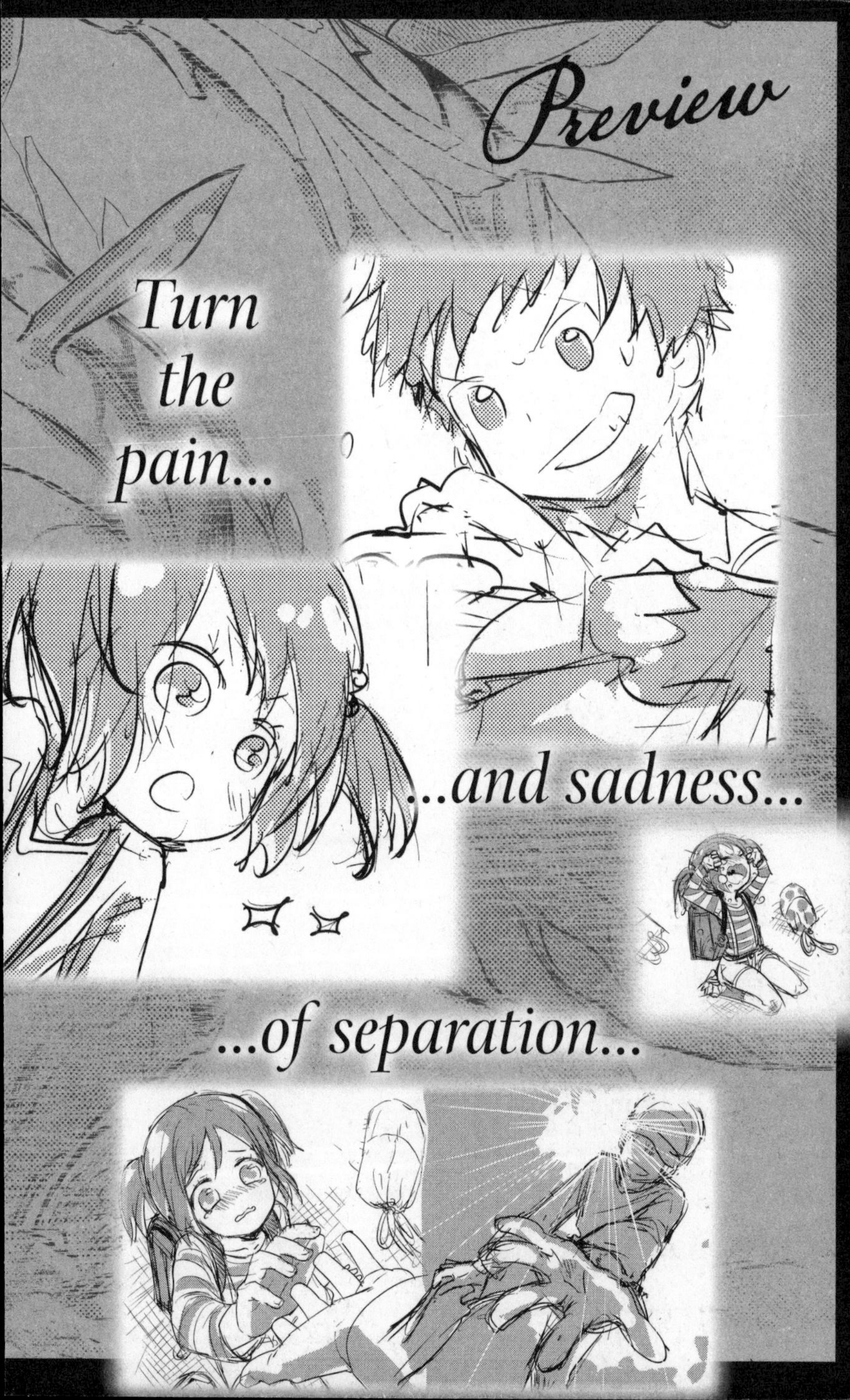
Preview
Turn the pain...
...and sadness...
...of separation...

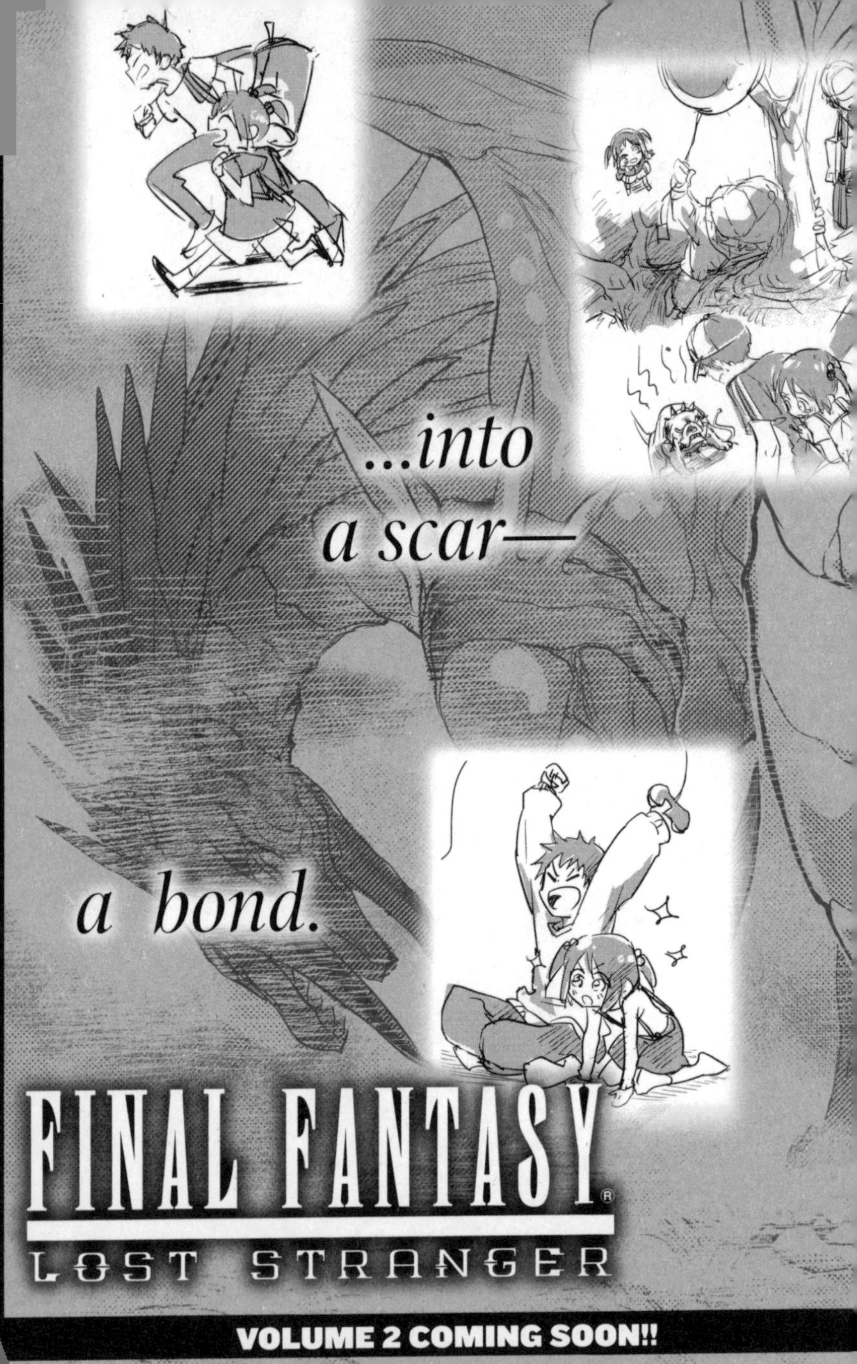
...into
a scar—
a bond.
FINAL FANTASY®
LOST STRANGER
VOLUME 2 COMING SOON!!

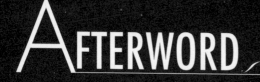AFTERWORD

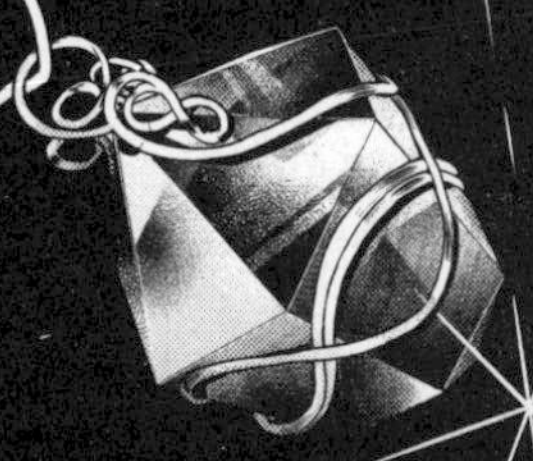

SPECIAL THANKS

◆ **Assistants**
Shinsai Kazusuke-san
R.F.-san
Ogiwara-san
Hidemasa Idemitsu-san

◆ **Managing Editors**
Iwata-san
Nesori-san
Hanada-san

◆ **Designer**
Yano-san
◆ Square Enix staff
◆ Everyone involved
◆ Our families

Supervisor: **NAOKI YOSHIDA**

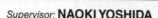

This is your *FFXIV* Producer / Director / *FFLS* Editorial Supervisor, Yoshida.
The *FF* franchise is a long-standing one that celebrates its thirtieth anniversary this year.

We face questions like "How far can we go with the setting?" and
"How authentic do we keep the magic and attacks?" among others...

As I get more involved in managing this project, it becomes more difficult to draw the line between fan
and supervisor. As supervisor, my role is to review things like names and illustrations ahead of time and
say, "Sure, you can go with what you'd like here," and spur our two creators onward...
That said, they too have endless amounts of love for the franchise and have created such a wonderful
manga in *FFLS* that it has undeniably carved out a place for itself in the *FF* series.

While on one hand, I am eager to see how Shogo levels up moving forward, personally, I have to make
sure that I remain diligent so that when Shogo returns to the real world (could he!?), he doesn't say to
me, "YOSHIDAAAA, I'm taking over!!!" (lol)

Please continue to enjoy this adventure that could only be told in the pages of *FFLS*.

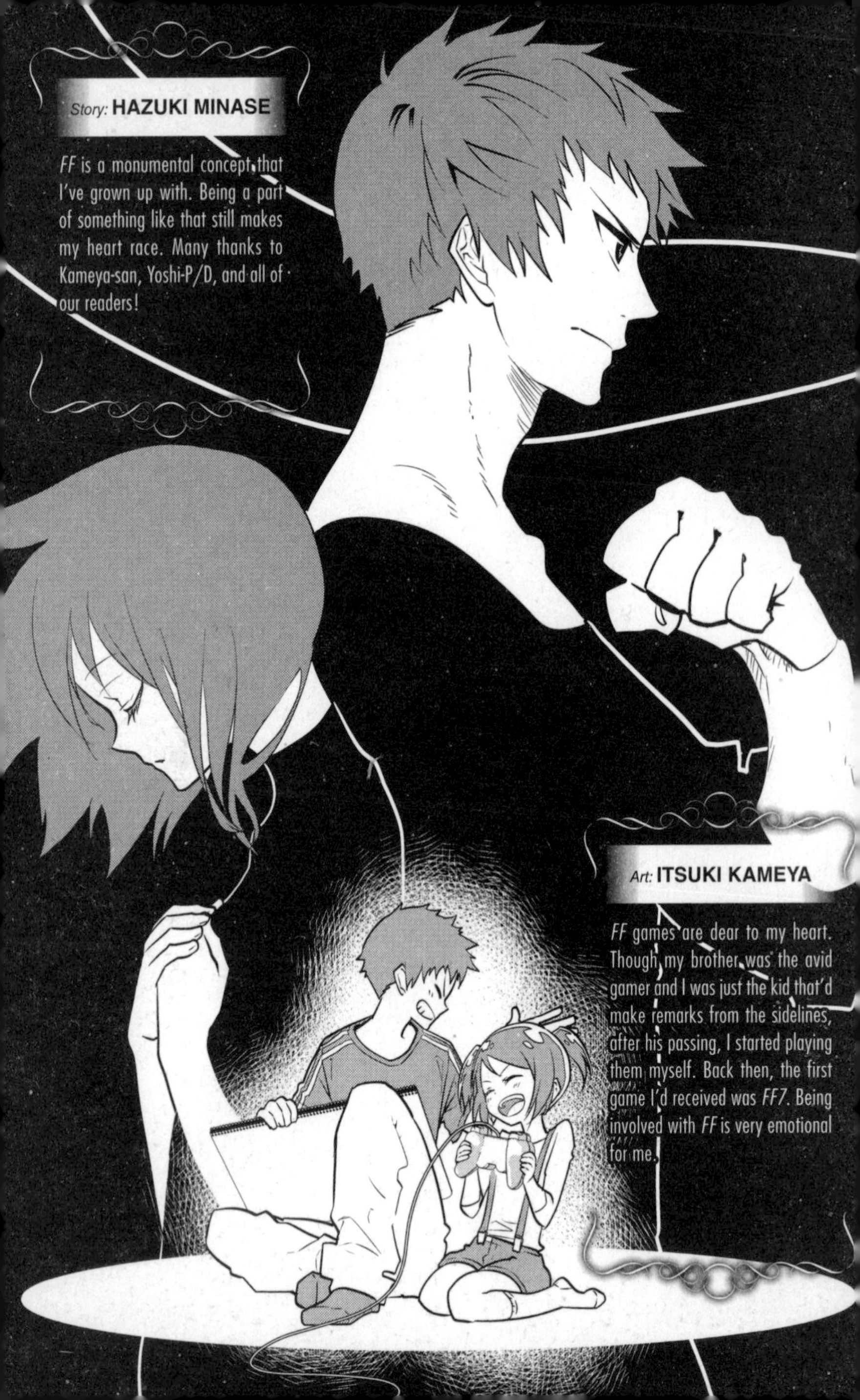
Story: HAZUKI MINASE
FF is a monumental concept that I've grown up with. Being a part of something like that still makes my heart race. Many thanks to Kameya-san, Yoshi-P/D, and all of our readers!
Art: ITSUKI KAMEYA
FF games are dear to my heart. Though my brother was the avid gamer and I was just the kid that'd make remarks from the sidelines, after his passing, I started playing them myself. Back then, the first game I'd received was *FF7*. Being involved with *FF* is very emotional for me.

TRANSLATION NOTES

COMMON HONORIFICS

no honorific: Indicates familiarity or closeness; if used without permission or reason, addressing someone in this manner would constitute an insult.

-*san*: The Japanese equivalent of Mr./Mrs./Miss. If a situation calls for politeness, this is the fail-safe honorific.

-*kun*: Used most often when referring to boys, this indicates affection or familiarity. Occasionally used by older men among their peers, but it may also be used by anyone referring to a person of lower standing.

-*chan*: An affectionate honorific indicating familiarity used mostly in reference to girls; also used in reference to cute persons or animals of either gender.

-*sensei*: A respectful term for teachers, artists, or high-level professionals.

Onii-chan: An affectionate term used for older brothers or brother figures.

PAGE 3

Prelude—Rebirth is the name of the first track of the *FFXIV: A Realm Reborn* soundtrack.

PAGE 6

A **planner** pitches ideas and guides all parts of the game development process.

PAGE 8

Houjicha is a type of roasted green tea.

PAGE 12

The books and video screencap in the background are all the guidebooks that Shogo wrote for the *FF* games he's played. They're all titled *My Ultimania. Ultimania* is the name of the official *FF* guidebooks published by Square Enix in Japan (none have been localized into English, but hard-core fans know them as *FF* bibles).

The video screencap is of *FF14*, and the comments scrolling across the screen are thanking Shogo for his helpful video—a guide to clearing what appears to be a four-man dungeon in the game.

PAGE 15

Raise is a spell used to revive fallen party members in the *Final Fantasy* series.

PAGE 27

Manjuu are steamed buns that often contain a red bean paste filling.

-◦- PAGE 31

Ronso and **Viera** are the names of races from *FF10* and *FF12*, respectively.

-◦- PAGE 35

Voidgates are dimensional rifts that connect the material world to the void in *FF14* lore—the player is tasked with closing one in the game's Black Mage questline.

The *Gran Grimoire* is a magic tome capable of transforming the world. It appears in several versions of *Final Fantasy Tactics*.

-◦- PAGE 84

Defiers of Fate is the name of the fourth track of the *FF13* soundtrack. A mix of it also plays during battle on the *Palamecia* airship in the game.

-◦- PAGE 121

The **Qu** are a race of gourmands from *FF9*.

-◦- PAGE 165

Hoohokekyo is the sound a Japanese nightingale makes, which could be likened to the sound of crickets chirping.

-◦- PAGE 189

Douson is a reference to the Lawson chain of convenience stores in Japan.

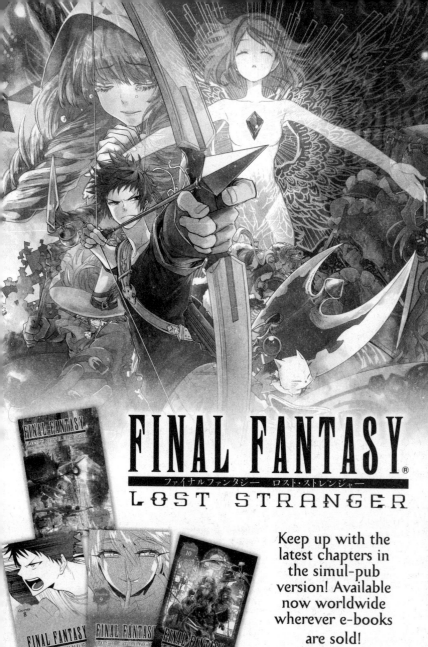

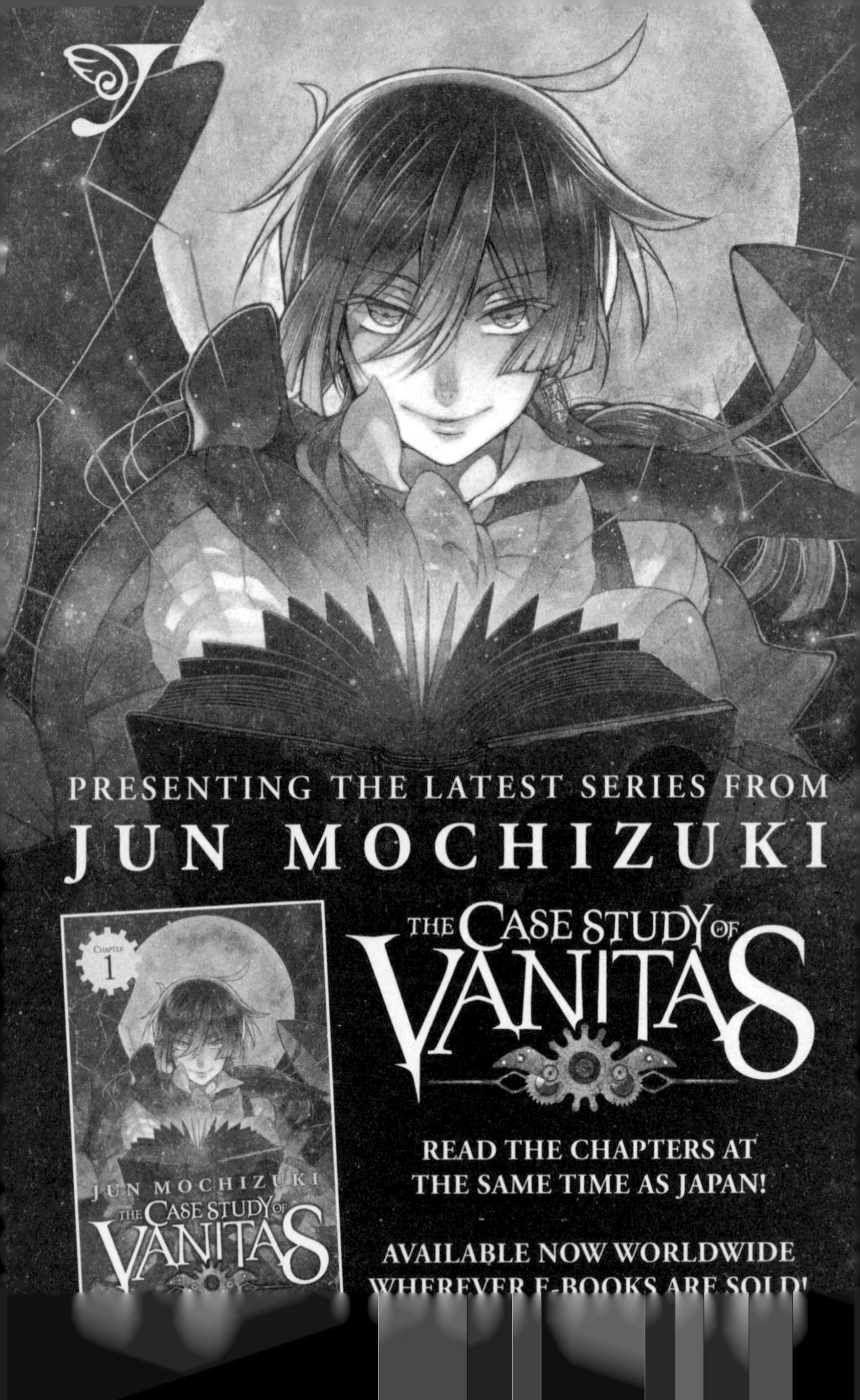
PRESENTING THE LATEST SERIES FROM
JUN MOCHIZUKI
CHAPTER 1
JUN MOCHIZUKI
THE CASE STUDY OF VANITAS
THE CASE STUDY OF VANITAS
READ THE CHAPTERS AT THE SAME TIME AS JAPAN!
AVAILABLE NOW WORLDWIDE WHEREVER E-BOOKS ARE SOLD!

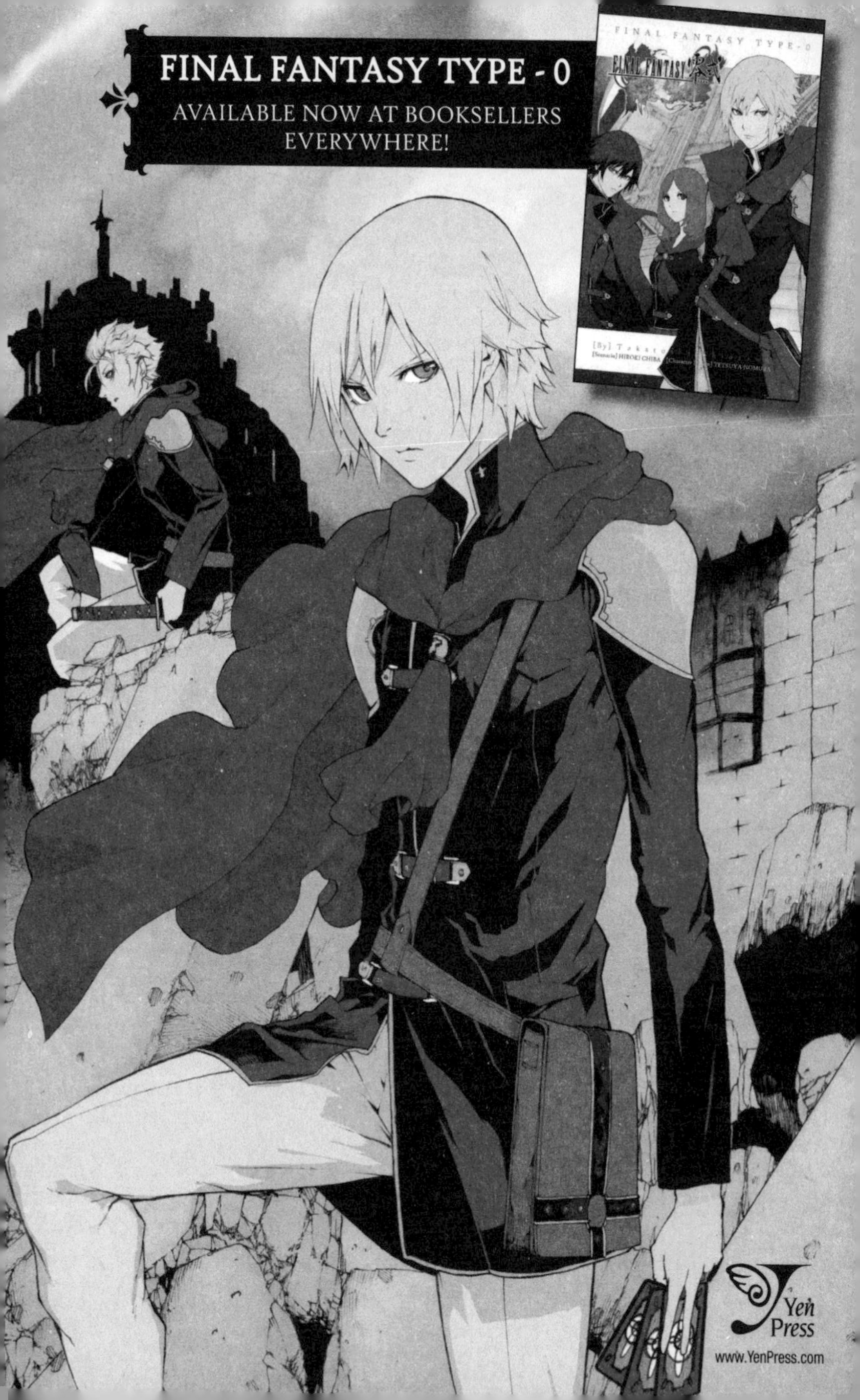
FINAL FANTASY TYPE - 0
AVAILABLE NOW AT BOOKSELLERS EVERYWHERE!
FINAL FANTASY TYPE-0
Yen Press
www.YenPress.com

FINAL FANTASY 零式 TYPE-0™

Art: TAKATOSHI SHIOZAWA
Character Design: TETSUYA NOMURA
Scenario: HIROKI CHIBA

The cadets of Akademeia's Class Zero are legends, with strength and magic unrivaled, and crimson capes symbolizing the great Vermilion Bird of the Dominion. But will their elite training be enough to keep them alive when a war breaks out and the Class Zero cadets find themselves at the front and center of a bloody political battlefield?!

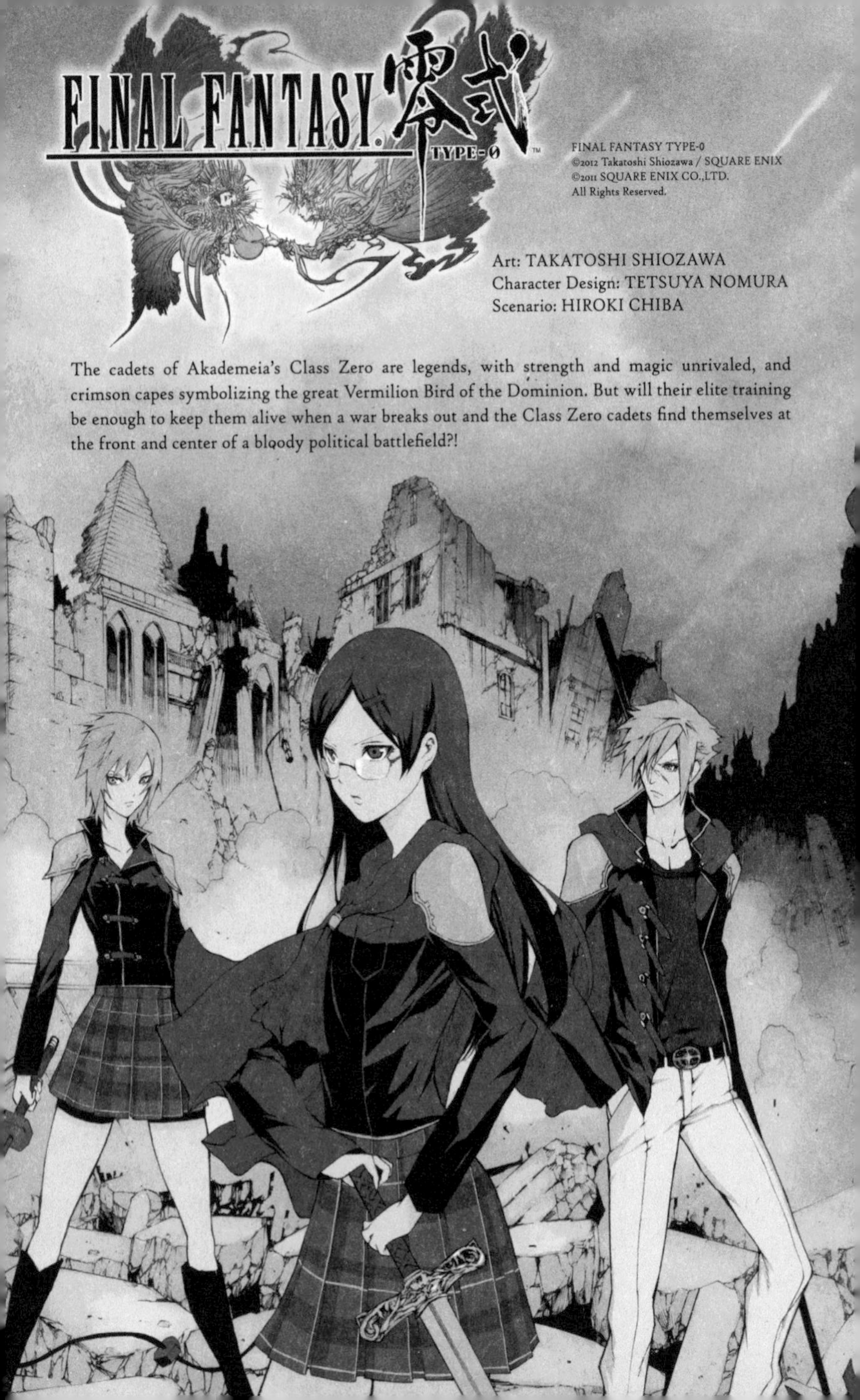

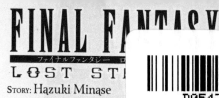

FINAL FANTASY

ファイナルファンタジー ロ

LOST STR

STORY: Hazuki Minase

D0547270

● — ● — ●

VOLUME 1

Translation: Melody Pan   Lettering: Bianca Pistillo

This book is a work of fiction. Names, characters, places, and incidents are the product of the author's imagination or are used fictitiously. Any resemblance to actual events, locales, or persons, living or dead, is coincidental.

FINAL FANTASY LOST STRANGER Volume 1 ©2017 Hazuki Minase, Itsuki Kameya/SQUARE ENIX CO., LTD. ©2017 SQUARE ENIX CO., LTD. All Rights Reserved. First published in Japan in 2017 by SQUARE ENIX CO., LTD. English translation rights arranged with SQUARE ENIX CO., LTD. and Yen Press, LLC through Tuttle-Mori Agency, Inc., Tokyo.

English translation © 2018 by SQUARE ENIX CO., LTD.

Yen Press
1290 Avenue of the Americas
New York, NY 10104

Visit us at yenpress.com
facebook.com/yenpress
twitter.com/yenpress
yenpress.tumblr.com
instagram.com/yenpress

First Yen Press Edition: August 2018
The chapters in this volume were originally published as ebooks by Yen Press.

Yen Press is an imprint of Yen Press, LLC.
The Yen Press name and logo are trademarks of Yen Press, LLC.

The publisher is not responsible for websites (or their content) that are not owned by the publisher.

Library of Congress Control Number: 2018948073

ISBNs: 978-1-9753-8090-8 (paperback)
978-1-9753-8092-2 (ebook)

10 9 8 7 6 5 4

WOR

Printed in the United States of America